# ASIAN ECONOMIC AND POLITICAL ISSUES

# VOLUME III

Asian Economic and Political Issues
A Series Edited by Frank Columbus


**Volume III ISBN 1-56072-733-X**

Volume II ISBN 1-56072-688-1
Volume I ISBN 1-56072-598-2

# ASIAN ECONOMIC AND POLITICAL ISSUES

# VOLUME III

## FRANK COLUMBUS
### EDITOR

**Nova Science Publishers, Inc.**
*Huntington, New York*

| | |
|---|---|
| **Editorial Production:** | Susan Boriotti |
| **Office Manager:** | Annette Hellinger |
| **Graphics:** | Frank Grucci and Jennifer Lucas |
| **Information Editor:** | Tatiana Shohov |
| **Book Production:** | Donna Dennis, Patrick Davin, Cathy DeGregory, and Lynette Van Helden |
| **Circulation:** | Latoya Clay, Anna Cruz, Lisa DeGangi and Michael Pazy Mino |

*Library of Congress Cataloging-in-Publication Data*

ISBN 1-56072-773-X

Copyright 2000 by Nova Science Publishers, Inc.
227 Main Street, Suite 100
Huntington, New York 11743
Tele. 631-424-6682Fax 631-424-4666
e-mail: Novascience@earthlink.net
e-mail: Novascil@aol.com
Web Site: http://www.nexusworld.com/nova

*Printed in the United States of America*

# CONTENTS

# PREFACE

This series is intended to provide a forum for substantial research contributions dealing with current political and economic developments in Asia. The papers have been selected for their quality, relevance and timeliness. The coherence of this book rests in its fit within the larger framework of the series and its goals. In this volume, the emphasis is on economic and trade developments as well as the China-Taiwan relationship.

# TRANSNATIONAL CAPITAL FLOWS AND EAST ASIA'S REVERSAL OF FORTUNES: IMPLICATIONS FOR STATE AUTONOMY

*Steven W. Hook*
Kent State University
P.O. Box 5190
Kent, Ohio 44242-0001

The economic crisis in East Asia has provoked numerous inquiries into the underlying causes of the fiscal and monetary turmoil that has afflicted the region in the late 1990s. Among the most common targets of criticism: permissive bank regulations, unstable currency values, rampant speculation in stock and bond markets, overvalued real estate prices and overbuilding, and government corruption and political repression.

Each of these factors is relevant to varying degrees within the most troubled economies of East Asia. Yet an additional factor must be incorporated into any systematic assessment: the volatile, unpredictable, and largely uncontrollable flow of foreign capital into the region during the 1990s. According to the Organization for Economic and Cooperation and Development (OECD), financial flows to all developing countries soared from US$130 billion in 1990 to $368 billion in 1996, then plummeted by nearly 25 percent in 1997 to $271 billion.[1] East Asia accounted for about 50 percent of all such flows during this period and an even greater share of the most recent cutbacks. Although the full extent of this reversal of fortunes is not yet known, it is clear that large-scale "capital flight" compounded the economic slump and diminished prospects for a prompt recovery.

As political leaders in East Asia openly acknowledge, the region's rapid economic growth of the 1980s and early 1990s was purposefully fueled by massive volumes of foreign capital. In shifting away from neo-mercantilistic growth strategies, governments opened their doors to foreign direct investments (mainly through multinational corporations), portfolio investments (in national stock and bond markets), and

---

[1] Organization for Economic Cooperation and Development, *OECD News Release: Aid and Private Flows Fell in 1997*, June 18, 1997.

concessional loans and grants from other states and international financial institutions. Their policies of export-led growth and openness to foreign capital served the regional economy well. While other developing regions suffered from zero or negative growth in the 1970s and 1980s, the gross domestic products (GDP) of East Asian countries grew by more than five percent annually. East Asian countries increased their share of global GDP from 5 to 20 percent while their share of manufacturing exports grew from 10 to 23 percent.[2] In assessing these trends, the World Bank declared in 1993 that *The East Asian Economic Miracle* was "largely due to superior accumulation of physical and human capital."[3]

Recent experience has demonstrated how reliant East Asia has become upon foreign capital and, consequently, how vulnerable the region is to abrupt disruptions of these capital flows. The sudden reduction of foreign investment was an important factor in prompting the International Monetary Fund (IMF) to provide more than $100 billion in emergency relief to Thailand, Korea, and Indonesia in 1997 and 1998, further revealing the vital role played by foreign capital, both private and public, in preserving economic stability and preventing "contagion" effects from enveloping the global economy. For a region whose economic development has long been based upon the principle of self-sufficiency, this dependency on foreign funds represents a historic departure for East Asia. More generally, it raises serious questions about the role of global economic resources in restricting the political autonomy of states.

This article confronts these questions by placing the East Asian economic crisis in the context of transnational capital flows, which have become a central feature of international economic relations throughout the world. The article seeks lessons from the East Asian experience that may be applicable elsewhere and instructive regarding the prospects for economic recovery in East Asia. Toward those ends, the phenomenon of transnational capital flows is first placed in the theoretical perspective of contending paradigms of international political economy. The key empirical patterns of capital flows between industrialized and developing states are then reviewed, with emphasis placed upon the experience of East Asia.[4] The article then examines the pivotal role played by Japan as a primary source of private investment and development aid whose own economic turmoil in the early 1990s precipitated the regional crisis. The next section considers the status of Korea, which turned to foreign capital to accelerate economic growth, promote regional and global economic integration, and hasten the country's

---

[2] The World Bank, *World Development Report 1991: The Challenge of Development* (Oxford: The World Bank, 1991), p. 21.

[3] The World Bank, *The East Asian Economic Miracle* (Oxford: The World Bank, 1993), p. 5.

[4] Comparative analysis of public and private flows has been rare in the scholarly literature. This may be due to the analytic segregation of the two types of capital flows. Development aid, directly involving state actors, has been thoroughly examined by political scientists, whereas research on private financial flows has been largely confined within the field of development economics. The result has been a lack of dialogue across the disciplines that has become more problematic as public and private capital flows have become densely intertwined in the 1990s.

"graduation" from a net recipient to donor of development aid. The final section summarizes the article's findings and explores their implications.

A central contention of this analysis is that the erratic nature of foreign capital flows is relevant to understanding East Asia's recent economic problems. A second and broader contention is that the phenomenon of transnational capital flows, on the massive scale witnessed in the past decade, represents a watershed in the evolution of national and international governance. In opening their markets to foreign investment, state leaders have surrendered a considerable degree of control over their economic development. And in adhering to explicit "conditionalities" as the price of development aid and emergency relief from foreign governments and international financial institutions, these leaders have further conceded their policy-making authority. In particular, non-state actors have exerted strong influence over developing countries' fiscal and monetary policy, vital pillars of national sovereignty. Growing economic interdependence has thus shifted the locus of governance from states to a diffuse array of actors--public and private; domestic, regional, and global--with profound implications for public policy.

## THEORETICAL CONSIDERATIONS AND POLICY DILEMMAS

The globalized network of transnational capital raises many long-standing and largely unresolved questions about international economic relations. At their core, these questions pertain to the ambiguous functional relationship between states and markets and to the tension between public policy at the state level and transnational economic forces that increasingly impinge upon the formulation of policy. Beginning in the 1960s, economic inequalities between North and South spurred the development aid regime as its members, organized institutionally within the OECD, established qualitative standards for aid flows and increased the volume of aid transfers directly and through multilateral channels.[5] More recently, the growing volume of private capital flows has overshadowed foreign aid as an engine of growth in the developing world, although the dispersion of these private flows has been far more concentrated than those of development aid. Additional questions of equity versus economic efficiency, therefore, have become central in the scholarly literature.

While this study does not aspire to settle these questions, it seeks to place them in clearer focus through a detailed examination of the empirical record. To better frame this analysis, three prominent paradigms of international economic relations--liberal,

---

[5] Previous applications of regime theory to development aid include David Halloran Lumsdaine, *Moral Vision in International Politics* (Princeton: Princeton University Press, 1993), and Robert E. Wood, *From Marshall Plan to Debt Crisis: Foreign Aid and Development Choices in the World Economy* (Berkeley: University of California Press, 1986).

nationalist, and neo-Marxist--are summarized below and considered in the context of transnational capital flows (see Table 1).[6]

The liberal paradigm envisions a world of integrating economic markets that are permitted to function with minimal government intervention. The globalization of capital flows is viewed as an inevitable and welcome outcome in the evolution of market economics--inevitable due to the growing interdependence of regional trade and capital markets, and welcome given the presumption that market-driven capital flows introduce efficiencies to the global economy and deliver the benefits of material and technological progress to previously isolated regions. Thus the ascendency of private capital flows *vis a vis* government-sponsored aid programs is consistent with the liberal paradigm, although aid projects effectively designed to facilitate long-term capital accumulation are consistent with this view.

**Table 1:** Contending Theoretical Perspectives

|  | Liberal | Nationalist | Neo-Marxist |
|---|---|---|---|
| Primary concern | Economic efficiency | National interests | Economic equality |
| Role of the state | Promote private enterprise, global economic integration | Promote domestic industries, enhance state power | Ensure equitable distribution of material resources |
| View of private capital flows | Crucial agent of global integration | Potential threat to national autonomy | Agent of economic imperialism |
| View of public capital flows | Support development of private enterprise | Promote self-interests of donor states | Support global distribution of wealth |

The nationalist paradigm, by contrast, emphasizes the impact of global economic pressures on the capacity of states to maintain domestic order and promote social welfare while ensuring protection from foreign threats. Economic assistance, from the perspective of donors, serves primarily as an instrument to facilitate these narrowly defined self-interests. Aid is viewed either as minimally related to recipient economic development or, if an effect is identified, as significant solely in terms of its effect on the donor's political influence, military security, trade relations, and foreign investments. Prescriptions range from the elimination of aid programs that are unrelated to donor interests to qualified support for aid based on demonstrable benefits to the donor. As for private capital flows, nationalists are wary about the integration of global economic markets that may deprive states of the necessary leverage to control their economic destinies. If foreign investments can be adequately secured over an extended period of

---

[6] For an elaboration of these paradigms, see Robert Gilpin, *The Political Economy of International Relations* (Princeton, NJ: Princeton University Press, 1987), pp. 25-64.

time, however, and if recipient governments are able to regulate the flow of foreign capital, such inflows are widely encouraged.[7]

Based upon critical assumptions about the role of economic wealth in enhancing the political power of elites in industrialized as well as developing countries, the neo-Marxist paradigm emphasizes the function of both foreign aid and private investment in preserving or widening economic disparities between rich and poor.[8] In this view, leaders of industrialized "core" states, through their control of both public and private sources of capital, are able to dictate the development strategies of "peripheral" states in the former Third World. Effects of this pattern include the reliance of developing countries on the monetary policies, consumption patterns, and export policies of core states and the effective subjugation of developing regions. Neo-Marxists are therefore critical of both public and private forms of overseas capital. Their primary concern, however, is with the lack of equity resulting from private investments, which have been concentrated among a small number of relatively prosperous developing economies.

While the economic policies of East Asian states varied considerably, nationalist strategies of import substitution and close coordination between public and private sectors prevailed in the early stages of the regional economic expansion, then gradually gave way to liberal strategies emphasizing the integration of global trade and capital markets.[9] During this transition, these governments accepted large volumes of development aid from other industrialized countries, particularly Japan and the United States, along with a rapidly growing influx of private capital. Neo-Marxist economic models previously adopted in China and Vietnam also gave way to market-driven growth strategies. These countries initially resisted the intrusion of foreign capital but more recently have openly appealed for development aid and private investment as a means to accelerate their economic growth.

While some consensus has emerged regarding these empirical trends, their normative implications remain the subject of contentious debate. As noted above, while liberals generally welcome the marketization of North-South capital flows on the grounds of economic liberty and efficiency, nationalists are most concerned with potential constraints on governmental autonomy, which is viewed as imperative. The failure of state socialism in the Soviet bloc and elsewhere has not dampened normative critiques by neo-Marxists regarding the subordination of developing countries to transnational capital interests. Indeed, the growing gaps in social welfare between rich and poor nations have only sharpened these critiques.

Central to this debate is the role of national governments and their functional relationship to major economic actors: financial institutions, manufacturers, shipping

---

[7] It is widely believed that the Japanese government pursued this strategy in its early phase of post-war development. See Chalmers Johnson, *MITI and the Japanese Miracle* (Palo Alto, CA: Stanford University Press, 1982).

[8] For elaborations of this view, see Ronald H. Chilcote, *Theories of Development and Underdevelopment* (Boulder, CO: Westview Press, 1984), pp. 49-78.

firms, retail outlets, and foreign economic ministries. As Table 2 demonstrates, national governments play multiple roles *vis a vis* transnational capital flows, both public and private, and these roles reflect a variety of cross-cutting national self-interests and global developmental concerns.

**Table 2:** Private and Public Capital Flows:
The Differing Roles of National Governments

| Private Flows | Public Flows |
|---|---|
| Administer trade-promotion bureaus | Administer agencies for providing and receiving foreign aid |
| Identify economic opportunities and joint ventures | "Tying" of aid to donor goods and services |
| Support regional economic integration | Support allies through security linkages and state-building funds |
| Promote economic liberalization and open markets | Advance state interests in multilateral aid organizations (e.g., OECD and IMF) |
| Promote favorable investment climate overseas | Promote transnational and humanitarian concerns |

With respect to private capital, state leaders have been primarily concerned with assisting domestic-based firms in expanding investment, manufacturing, and sales opportunities overseas. More generally, the major industrialized countries have worked together to integrate regional economies and to create a liberal international economic order (LIEO) that is hospitable toward open markets, foreign investment, and corporate expansion. This effort has resulted in ongoing friction with developing countries that have sought to protect their domestic markets while seeking concessions from industrialized states in such areas as commodity pricing and technology transfers.

By contrast, government involvement in public capital flows has been more complex and ambiguous. An array of strategic, political, and economic self-interests has mingled with concerns for "sustainable development," political reforms, and poverty relief. Differences among the industrialized countries have been significant in this regard. While the donors of the largest volumes of development aid have pursued transparent self-interests in providing aid to military allies, former colonies, and trading partners, smaller-scale aid donors have more closely adhered to the qualitative standards of aid provision adopted by the OECD and the United Nations.[10] Although private capital is considered the ultimate vehicle for promoting the LIEO, these industrialized states have

---

[9] See Kim Youn-Sik, "Korea and Developing Countries: Lessons from Korea's Industrialization," *The Journal of East Asian Affairs*, Vol. 11, No. 2 (Summer-Fall 1997), pp. 417-429.

[10] See Steven W. Hook, *National Interest and Foreign Aid* (Boulder, CO: Lynne Rienner Publishers, 1995).

freely turned to the Bretton Woods institutions--the IMF, World Bank, and the newly strengthened World Trade Organization--to facilitate market-driven economic integration. Thus even in the supposedly *laissez-faire* world of the LIEO, governments have played a substantial, and indeed essential, role.

## TRENDS IN TRANSNATIONAL CAPITAL FLOWS

The early 1990s witnessed a historic turning point in capital flows from rich to poor countries. While the volume of *public* resource transfers--mostly in the form of development assistance--declined during this period, *private* capital flows grew rapidly and exceeded public transfers by a growing margin. Thus, whereas in 1990 government transfers of $77 billion were nearly double those of private flows ($44 billion), by 1997 the volume of private capital flows ($206 billion) was nearly triple the $70 billion in public capital. Private investments, which accounted for about one-third of all capital flows to developing countries in 1990, represented 75 percent of these cash flows seven years later.[11] This marketization of North-South capital flows represents one of the most significant trends in the international political economy in the 1990s.

Leaders of industrialized states, international organizations, and private financial institutions have generally embraced the global integration of capital flows and, more specifically, the trend toward private investment. The critical views expressed within scholarly circles in the 1970s regarding the potential hazards of transnational capital networks have not been voiced in the 1990s.[12] To the contrary, the superiority of private capital flows *vis a vis* development aid has become axiomatic, and aid flows have increasingly been accorded a marginal role in global economic relations, with emergency relief from the IMF emerging as the major source of government-sponsored assistance. Many development experts envision a division of labor by which private and public capital flows serve distinctive, though complementary, roles within developing economies. As Chhibber observed, "It is now widely accepted that expansion of private investment should be the main impetus for economic growth, allowing public investment resources gradually to focus on social areas, including alleviation of poverty and the upgrading of social capital and resources."[13]

This section of the study briefly reviews the key trends in private and public transnational capital flows between industrialized and developing countries. Global trends are identified along with patterns relating to the primary East Asian economies. A common theme is the inherent turbulence that exists within global capital markets that undercuts the ability of political leaders to manage development policy or to adopt

---

[11] OECD, *Aid and Other Financial Flows in 1997*, Table 2 (Paris: OECD, 1998).

[12] See, for example, Richard J. Barnet and Ronald E. Muller, *Global Reach* (New York: Simon and Schuster, 1974).

[13] Ajay Chhibber, *Fiscal Policy and Private Investment in Developing Countries* (Washington, DC: The World Bank, 1990), p. 27.

credible long-term strategies in an environment that depends, ultimately, on sustained access to resources beyond their shores.

## The Growing Role of Private Investment

As noted above, private capital flows have become the primary form of capital transfer to developing countries. Between 1990 and 1996, the volume of private flows grew from $44 billion to $286 billion.[14] Among the many categories of private capital, bond lending increased from less than $1 billion in 1990 to more than $96 billion in 1996, direct investment increased from $27 billion to $64 billion, and international bank lending increased from $6 billion to $86 billion.

Just as dramatically, this surge in private investment reversed course in 1997, when the total volume of private flows fell from $286 billion to $206 billion. International bank lending plummeted from $86 to $12 billion while bond lending dropped more gradually, from $97 billion to $83 billion. Flows of direct investment, designed to facilitate long-term industrial development primarily through the expansion of multinational corporations (MNCs), continued to increase in 1997 to $75 billion. While figures for 1998 are not yet available, widespread withdrawals of portfolio investments, commercial bank loans, and, to a lesser extent, direct investment, have been reported. These withdrawals have, to a large extent, necessitated the large-scale transfers of emergency IMF relief.

East Asia served as the world's leading beneficiary of the private capital boom in the early 1990s. Private capital flows to East Asia soared from $13 billion in 1990 to $49 billion in 1996.[15] This latter figure represented 86 percent of all private capital invested throughout Asia during this period and 37 percent of global flows of private capital.[16] Of the top five developing recipients of private flows in the first half of the decade, four were located in East Asia: China, Hong Kong, Korea, and Singapore. East Asia's share of foreign direct investment (FDI), the most important form of long-term private capital, rose steadily from 14 percent in 1975 to 28 percent in 1985, to 45 percent in 1990, and to more than 55 percent in 1995. "As developing countries become more integrated into the international flow of goods, they are being pulled into international capital markets," the World Bank noted in 1996. "East Asia is at the forefront on both counts."[17]

Latin America served as the destination of the second largest share of private investment, with Eastern European states and former Soviet republics attracting the third largest share. Africa received the smallest share of private capital, less than 5 percent of

---

[14] OECD, Aid and Other Financial Flows in 1997 (Paris: OECD, 1998).

[15] OECD, Geographical Distribution of Financial Flows to Aid Recipients (Paris: OECD, 1997), p. 39.

[16] By comparison, the net flow of private capital to Africa was negative between 1990 and 1994, then increased to about $2 billion in 1995 and 1996.

[17] World Bank, *Managing Capital Flows in East Asia* (Washington, DC: The World Bank, 1996), p. 3.

the global total. A comparison between Latin America, which enjoyed accelerating economic growth during this period, and sub-Saharan Africa, which did not, is instructive in this regard: whereas Latin Americans received more FDI per capita ($62) than foreign aid ($13) in 1997, sub-Saharan Africa received much more per-capita aid ($27) than direct investment ($3). These numbers vividly illustrate a regional dimension in the division of labor between public and private capital flows. In both cases, however, the volumes of economic resources were much smaller than those directed toward East Asia.

Many factors account for the ascension of private capital as the primary form of resource transfers from industrialized to developing countries in the 1990s. These factors include the quickening pace of global economic integration, spurred by technological advances in transportation and communications that, in turn, enabled the globalization of finance, manufacturing, and distribution. In addition, economic integration encouraged and rewarded market-driven development strategies, in contrast to statist policies associated with the "new international economic order" (NIEO) of the 1970s and the neo-mercantilism practiced by newly industrialized countries in the 1970s and 1980s. Finally, the end of the Cold War removed many donor self-interests that previously drove foreign aid programs.[18] The "victory" of the West was widely viewed as a vindication of market-driven growth strategies and a defeat of command-economic models based on Marxism-Leninism, *dependencia,* or world-system theories.

The initial rise in private investment occurred in the 1980s as many developing countries sought alternatives to foreign aid, which was closely and transparently linked to the self-interests of donor states. While this inescapable aspect of the Cold War aid regime benefited strategic allies of the United States, former French colonies, and Japan's trading partners, other developing countries with comparable or greater social-welfare needs assumed a secondary role. These states, primarily in Latin America, turned to international banks that were flush with "petrodollars" deposited by members of the Organization of Petroleum Exporting Countries (OPEC) after the first oil shock of 1973-1974.[19]

Ironically, efforts by the leaders of Latin America to become self-sufficient by detaching themselves from foreign aid only led to greater dependency. This time, their dependence extended beyond the Northern governments and multilateral institutions with which they had become familiar. Now they were beholden to commercial banks, whose terms for repayment were even harder than those imposed by aid donors. As for the commercial banks, which agreed to forgive a large segment of the Latin American debt in exchange for the debtors' agreement to initiate economic reforms, this experience led to deep reductions in commercial loans to developing countries in all regions. The Latin

---

[18] For a review of cross-national patterns, see Steven W. Hook, ed., *Foreign Aid Toward the Millennium* (Boulder, CO: Lynne Rienner Publishers).

[19] Annual borrowing by developing countries in private financial markets grew from $6.5 billion in 1973 to $293 billion in 1981. See World Bank, *World Debt Tables: External Debt of Developing Countries* (Washington, DC: World Bank, 1983), p. iii.

American debt crisis demonstrated both the fragility of private capital markets and the extent to which industrialized states and financial institutions would work to protect them. For the IMF, the debt crisis served as a test of the institution's primary role under the Bretton Woods system: to inject short-term capital into hard-pressed economic regions, thus averting a cascade of regional economic crises.

East Asia quickly emerged as a primary destination of private investment in the 1990s. Not only were foreign-based MNCs granted access to East Asian manufacturing centers on hospitable terms, East Asia was viewed as a safe risk for international banks as well as for institutional and individual investors in regional stock and bond markets. The region's civil societies were valued for their emphases on education, discipline, family values, and domestic savings versus consumption. The large reservoir of domestic savings was paired with foreign capital to accelerate economic development throughout the region.

Among East Asian economies, Korea received the largest volume of private capital--more than $27 billion--during the five years before the onset of the regional economic crisis (see Table 3). Nearly $8 billion of the record $9.3 billion in foreign capital transferred to Korea in 1996 took the form of portfolio investment as the Korean economy become more open to overseas speculation in stock and bond markets. Foreign investors poured an additional $26 billion into the Chinese economy during this period, along with $23 billion into Thailand, $19 billion into Indonesia, and $8 billion into the Philippines. Among these economies, the primary forms of private investment varied: whereas China was most attractive to FDI, Thailand and Indonesia received most of their private capital in the form of portfolio investment. The sources of these FDI flows also varied widely, with the United States serving as the primary source of private capital to Korea and the Philippines while Japanese investors provided the greatest share of private capital to China, Thailand, and Indonesia.

**Table 3:** Net Private Capital Flows into Major East Asian Economies, 1992-1996

|             | 1992 | 1993  | 1994 | 1995 | 1996 | Total  |
|-------------|------|-------|------|------|------|--------|
| Korea       | 2503 | 3215  | 5012 | 7499 | 9287 | 27,516 |
| China       | 2046 | 3964  | 7515 | 5790 | 6192 | 25,507 |
| Thailand    | 2944 | 1528  | 6361 | 5813 | 6490 | 23,136 |
| Indonesia   | 1357 | 263   | 3780 | 5182 | 7901 | 18,483 |
| Philippines | 1056 | 1.027 | 1735 | 2649 | 3651 | 8,006  |

Figures in millions of current U.S. dollars
Source: OECD

The rapid increases in private flows were greeted approvingly within development circles. Foreign-based MNCs had long awaited a climate more receptive to FDI while institutional traders of stocks and bonds--representing individual investors along with managers of pension funds, mutual funds, and other pooled capital reserves--sought to diversify their portfolios through overseas investments. Meanwhile, leaders of industrialized countries and international development organizations embraced the trend toward private capital flows. To Cory Highland (1993: 22), an official in the OECD's Directorate for Financial, Fiscal, and Enterprise Affairs, "Private sector development and the promotion of foreign direct investment has moved from the margins to the center of economic development strategies in many developing countries."[20]

While the openness of East Asian economies to foreign capital is consistent with liberal economic theory, the strategy has exposed the region's governments to the periodic shocks and cyclical swings that characterize market behavior. Especially in the area of portfolio investments, which are traded on a massive scale daily and are especially prone to short-term speculation, private capital flows introduce a high level of uncertainty to the macroeconomic calculations of state leaders. As a result, policy is increasingly reactive rather than proactive as governments respond to the widely fluctuating inflows and outflows of capital. Of particular concern in East Asia, the free flow of private capital turns from a blessing to a curse when bank lending exceeds the ability of domestic markets to absorb new construction and industrial expansion, when investors retreat *en masse* toward safer harbors, and when national governments are forced to devalue currencies and impose import restrictions to remain competitive in global markets.

## Public Capital From Development Aid to IMF Relief

According to the World Bank, just 18 developing countries received more than 90 percent of all private flows during the first half of the 1990s. This concentration of private capital was directed toward developing countries that had already created basic economic infrastructure and established a sustained record of economic growth. Not surprisingly, newly industrialized countries in East Asia received a disproportionate share of private capital flows. Development assistance, by contrast, has been more evenly distributed among developing countries at various levels of economic development. According to the dominant liberal paradigm of international development, aid is viewed as a crucial instrument to build the foundations for long-term economic growth which then renders aid recipients attractive to private investment. It was in this spirit that flows of Official Development Assistance (ODA) increased steadily during the 1970s and 1980s.

This trend, however, was reversed in the early 1990s, well before the onset of the East Asian economic crisis. Global flows of ODA dropped annually in real terms to $47.5 billion in 1997, more than 20 percent below their peak levels of nearly $60 billion at the beginning of the decade.[21] As a percentage of donors' GNP, the volume of ODA

---

[20] Cory Highland, "How OECD Countries Promote Foreign Direct Investment to Developing Countries," pp. 21-26 in OECD, *Promoting Foreign Direct Investment in Developing Countries* (Paris: OECD, 1993).

[21] OECD, Aid and Other Financial Flows in 1997 (Paris: OECD, 1998).

disbursed by industrialized states fell from .33 in 1992 to .22 in 1997, its lowest level ever and less than one-half the rate of .70 percent/GNP previously established as a global standard. Most industrialized countries within the OECD--including the United States, Japan, France, and Germany--reduced their expenditures on development aid in the 1990s as "donor fatigue" set in and as flows of private capital began to soar.

Several factors account for the decline of development aid from industrialized countries since the Cold War. Domestic economic problems increasingly prevailed over transnational concerns, such as environmental decay, global population growth, and the need for sustainable development emphasized by the United Nations and a growing number of nongovernmental organizations (NGOs). Budget deficits within industrialized countries grew to an average level of 5 percent of GNP, a trend which provoked calls for cutbacks in government spending, particularly foreign aid. Among the primary donors, the United States reduced aid flows by more than one-third in the mid-1990s in response to concerns about the U.S. budget deficit.[22] In the European Union (EU), fiscal austerity became a prerequisite for monetary union, forcing EU members to reduce aid commitments. The Japanese government, faced with its own budget deficits, announced in 1997 that ODA commitments would be reduced by 30 percent between 1998 and 2000 as part of a cabinet-imposed fiscal reform effort. Throughout the industrialized world, consensus over domestic austerity, fiscal restraint, and market-driven economic growth translated into a preference for foreign investment over foreign aid.

At the same time, the remaining pool of development aid was increasingly attached to explicit donor conditionalities that required budget cuts, open markets, and other forms of "structural adjustment" by donors. Donor conditions steadily broadened in the mid-1990s, requiring aid recipients to institute democratic reforms, adopt environmental-preservation and population-control measures, and adhere to international conventions regarding nuclear proliferation and arms transfers. While these aid linkages often produced needed policy reforms, they allowed for the penetration of state economic governance to a considerable degree.[23]

Contrary to the general pattern of aid cutbacks during the 1990s, East Asian recipients continued to receive a steady flow of about $8 billion annually from foreign governments, especially Japan (see Table 4). This flow of aid represented about one-half the volume of aid provided to all countries in Asia. China received the largest volume of ODA, primarily from the Japanese government, which transferred an average of $1.2 billion in development aid annually to China.[24] Japan also served as the primary ODA donor to Indonesia, providing an average of $1 billion annually between 1992 and 1996, or nearly two-thirds of all bilateral aid received by the Indonesian government. The

---

[22] As a result, the U.S. dropped from first to third place among ODA donors, behind Japan and France. American development aid represented just .08 percent of U.S. GNP in 1997, the lowest level within the OECD's 21-member Development Assistance Committee.

[23] See Olav Stokke, "Aid and Political Conditionality: Core Issues and State of the Art," pp. 1-87 in Olav Stokke, ed., *Aid and Political Conditionality* (London: Frank Cass/EADI, 1995).

Philippines, meanwhile, averaged more than $1.2 billion in ODA receipts from all sources during this period, and the government of Thailand averaged more than $700 million annually in aid receipts. The Korean government, which used external transfers of development assistance to fuel its economic takeoff in the 1970s and 1980s, ceased to be a net recipient of ODA by the early 1990s. Indeed, Korea's primary activity during this period was repaying previous low-interest loans to Japan and the United States.

**Table 4:** Net Flows of Development Aid to Major East Asian Economies, 1992-1996

|             | 1992 | 1993 | 1994 | 1995 | 1996 | Total  |
|-------------|------|------|------|------|------|--------|
| China       | 3055 | 3271 | 3238 | 3534 | 2618 | 15,716 |
| Indonesia   | 2082 | 2018 | 1642 | 1390 | 1120 | 8252   |
| Philippines | 1716 | 1487 | 1058 | 886  | 883  | 6030   |
| Thailand    | 771  | 611  | 578  | 865  | 832  | 3657   |
| Korea       | -3   | -41  | -114 | 58   | -147 | -247   |

Figures in millions of current U.S. dollars
Source: OECD

While most industrialized countries reduced their aid budgets, their commitment of record volumes of IMF-sponsored emergency relief revealed the continuing importance of states in promoting global economic development. Taken together, the struggling economies of Indonesia, Korea, and Thailand received commitments for $112 billion in funding by the International Monetary Fund (IMF), the World Bank, the Asian Development Bank, and major industrialized countries, particularly the United States and Japan.[25] More than one-half of these funds--$58 billion--was directed toward Korea, including a $21-billion pledge by the IMF announced in December 1997. The government of Thailand, to which these funding sources committed $17 billion beginning in August 1997, was the first East Asian state to require large-scale economic relief. Within months, Indonesia succumbed both to economic and political upheaval, leading to the resignation of President Suharto, pledges of reform by his successor, and nearly $37 billion in relief commitments by foreign governments and international financial institutions.

In return for these commitments of short-term, low-interest loans, the East Asian governments made their own commitments: to reform domestic financial institutions, establish flexible exchange rates, dismantle national monopolies, reduce government spending, impose restrictive monetary policies, and provide "safety nets" for labor and other domestic groups victimized by the economic crisis. In addition, the East Asian

---

[24] Japanese aid dropped to $862 million in 1996, however, signaling a possible long-term decline in Japanese aid flows.

[25] These figures are derived from the International Monetary Fund, "The IMF's Response to the Asian Crisis" (April 16, 1998), p. 8. As of April 1998, $21 billion of the $35 billion in IMF commitments had been disbursed to these three countries, with an additional $1 billion provided to the government of the Philippines as part of an ongoing relief program.

governments also agreed to open their capital and manufacturing sectors to foreign interests. Taken together, these actions represented a profound concession of political autonomy by the East Asian governments. Their submission to transnational demands for structural adjustment, on a scale greater than that previously witnessed in Latin America, was unprecedented in the history of international economic relations. And as noted above, the surrender of autonomy by East Asian leaders contrasted sharply with their previous emphasis on self-sufficiency and political autonomy.

In East Asia, IMF funding commitments of $35 billion served as a catalyst for additional aid packages from other sources, including $53 billion from foreign governments and $25 billion from the World Bank and the Asian Development Bank. Support for the IMF became a contentious issue within several donors countries, including the United States, where the Republican-led Congress opposed adding more than $18 billion to the U.S. commitment to the IMF as part of the emergency relief effort. Adding to the uncertainty was the unstable political environment in Indonesia after President Suharto's resignation in May 1998, labor unrest in Korea, and the instability of the Thai *baht* in global currency markets. Russia's continuing economic plight remained a major concern to Western leaders, who faced the prospect of even greater demands on the IMF at a time when East Asia was fast depleting the fund's capacities. All of these problems, however, were overshadowed by the scale of Japan's banking crisis, with bad debts estimated at nearly $1 trillion late in 1998. It is to this question that we now turn our attention.

## JAPAN'S ROLE AS REGIONAL CATALYST

As noted above, much of the foreign capital which has flowed to developing countries in East Asia in the 1990s has originated in Japan. Since the inception of the Japanese aid program in the 1970s, East Asian countries have served as the primary destination of Japanese aid. In turn, Japanese-based MNCs and private investors have formed the nucleus of intra-regional capital networks in East Asia. Both patterns are consistent with Japan's post-war economic strategy of hastening domestic economic growth through the integration of regional economies. Given Japan's pivotal role as a catalyst of economic growth in East Asia, a more focused examination of Japanese-based capital flows is warranted. This section focuses on Japan's role as a leading donor of development assistance, a role which has been closely aligned with the government's effort to facilitate private investment throughout the region.

Japanese foreign aid first took the form of delayed reparation payments (*baisho*) to regional neighbors including the Philippines, Indonesia, Korea, Vietnam, and Thailand. The 1960s marked the graduation of Japan from net ODA recipient to donor. In 1963, Japan was a founding member of the OECD's Development Assistance Committee. In 1964, Japan joined the IMF and two years later helped establish the Asian Development Bank as a regional conduit for concessional funding. Japanese officials announced a series of aid-doubling plans for the periods 1977-1980, 1981-1985, and 1985-1992, identifying specific short- and medium-term targets that would collectively amount to $40 billion in ODA commitments. A fifth medium-term target was announced in 1993 for the period through 1997, during which Japan pledged to transfer more than $70 billion and to increase its share of GNP devoted to development aid.

Despite well-publicized efforts to satisfy critics, the Japanese government has been unable to avoid widespread charges that its aid programs are primarily designed to serve its own self-interests.[26] In contrast to most other ODA donors, the Japanese program has been characterized by loans at near-market interest rates and repayment terms, by aid concentrated among relatively affluent developing countries, and by aid packages "tied" explicitly or implicitly to the acquisition of Japanese products and services. Critics have also pointed to the concentration of Japan's trading and investment partners--largely in the East Asia --as evidence of this self-interested motivation.

In June 1992, the Japanese government adopted its first formal policy on development aid, *The ODA Charter,* which pledged that Japan would become a more responsible aid "citizen." The charter identified such factors as democratization, human rights, and restraint in military spending as preconditions for developing countries to receive Japanese aid. The Japanese government further pledged that "due consideration will be paid in particular to least-developed countries." Finally, the *ODA Charter* proclaimed that, beyond Asia, Japan would "extend cooperation, befitting its position in the world, to Africa, the Middle East, Central and South America, Eastern Europe, and Oceania."[27]

Japan's espoused new approach to foreign aid was well received within the aid regime. Members of the OECD welcomed the alignment of Japanese aid with the normative principles and qualitative standards established in the 1970s by OECD members. A consensus emerged in the scholarly literature that the long-held "geoeconomic" orientation of Japanese ODA was becoming less valid. The Japanese government, many analysts argued, had exchanged its self-interested aid strategy for a degree of leadership within the aid regime comparable to its economic contributions. Aid administrators, it was further argued, had switched from the "earning strategies" of linking aid with overseas trade and investment to the "spending strategies" of burden-sharing and regional security.[28]

Contrary to the Japanese government's claims, however, the record of Japan's aid flows in the mid-1990s reflected greater continuity than change. The geographical

---

[26] See David Arase, *Buying Power* (Boulder, CO: Lynne Rienner Publishers, 1995); Alan Rix, *Japan's Foreign Aid Challenge: Policy Reform and Aid Leadership* (New York: Routledge, 1994), and Margee Ensign *Doing Good or Doing Well? Japan's Foreign Aid Program* (New York: Columbia University Press, 1992).

[27] Japanese Government, Ministry of Foreign Affairs, *ODA Charter* (Tokyo: Government of Japan, 1992), pp. 193-194.

[28] See Fujisaki Tomoko, "Japan as Top Donor: The Challenge of Implementing Software Aid Policy," *Pacific Affairs,* Vol. 69, No. 4 (Winter 1996), pp. 519-39; and Ming Wan, "Spending Strategies in World Politics: How Japan has Used its Economic Power in the Past Decade," *International Studies Quarterly,* Vol. 39, Vol. 1 (March 1995), pp. 85-108.

distribution of Japanese ODA in East Asia remained virtually constant between 1986 and 1995 at about 30 percent, with states in South and Central Asia receiving the second-largest share (about 22 percent) of Japanese assistance. Eight of the ten largest Japanese ODA recipients in 1986 remained among the top ten in 1995, with China and Indonesia at the top of the aid rankings. As a percentage of total Japanese ODA, aid to the poorest developing countries fell from 24 percent in 1985 to 19 percent in 1995, a trend that was contrary to the government's pledges to extend its aid resources to the neediest populations.[29] The primary function of Japan's aid--the development of economic infrastructure--was also unchanged after the *ODA Charter* was implemented. Finally, the proportion of *yen* loans as opposed to grants increased to 60 percent by 1995, a trend that violated the aid regime's standards of aid "quality."

This latter trend is particularly important given a chain of circumstances that follows from the primary role of *yen* loans. In the Japanese ODA system, no country can be a major recipient of Japanese aid without receiving *yen* loans, and aid-supported projects have to be large enough to achieve economies of scale. Such economies are generally concentrated in East Asia: only a few African countries can afford to be the "customers" of *yen* loans. Because Japanese firms hold a comparative advantage in several of the infrastructure-related sectors of interest to Tokyo, and because these firms are familiar with Asian markets, the primacy of *yen* loans helps Japanese firms compete in the region. In this manner, the intimate relationship between Japan's industrial development and its aid program is clearly evident.

Japan's political and economic crisis in the mid-1990s, which coincided with the implementation of the *ODA Charter*, further threatened the government's announced aid reforms. The government's 1997 announcement that aid flows would be cut by 10 percent annually during the following three years confirmed that, in quantitative as well as qualitative terms, domestic economic problems would hinder Japan's ability to maintain a leadership role within the aid regime. The Japanese government, however, committed vast volumes of public capital to IMF-sponsored emergency relief efforts, along with additional bilateral assistance and support through the Asian Development Bank. In this manner Japan retained an important role in regional economic development, although its ability to promote economic growth on a global scale was significantly constrained by its own economic difficulties.

As for Japanese-based private investments to East Asia, which averaged about $60 billion annually in the mid-1990s, reductions in portfolio investments were partially offset by stability in longer-term foreign investments. Of greater concern, however, was the fate of Japan's heavily indebted banking system, its top-heavy industrial conglomerates, and its fractured political system. "The flow of funds is like the blood of society," newly elected Prime Minister Keizo Obuchi told the Japanese Diet in August 1998, "The financial institutions that are responsible for its circulation assume the role of

---

[29] These data were derived from the OECD's annual report entitled *Development Cooperation: Efforts and Policies of the Members of the Development Assistance Committee* (Paris: OECD, various years).

the heart."[30] As the self-appointed "heart" of East Asia's economy, Japanese leaders assumed a large measure of responsibility for regional industrial development, primarily through the circulation of public and private capital. Their strategy, however, also revealed the potential hazards of regional economic integration. Just as a thriving Japan stimulated rapid growth among its neighbors, a struggling Japan dragged down the regional economy, raising fears in capital markets and triggering widespread withdrawals of foreign investments. And when Japan's economy, twice the size of the rest of East Asia's combined, failed to absorb the growing volumes of exports from its neighbors, its own "Asian flu" became dangerously contagious.

## FINANCIAL FLOWS AND KOREA'S ECONOMIC TURMOIL

The Korean case further illustrates the central role played by transnational capital flows, public and private, in contributing to the onset and attempted resolution of the country's economic crisis. The slump was exacerbated by the steady flow of foreign investment capital, much of which was carefully controlled by the Korean government and recycled by Korean banks through loans to domestic firms. Korea's recovery, in turn, has been dependent upon the provision of emergency relief from international financial institutions and industrialized governments. These government-sponsored funds have come at the price of Korean openness to private foreign capital and to IMF-imposed demands for structural adjustments.

The IMF-led relief effort, coupling $21 billion in IMF funding with $37 billion from other sources, was accompanied by explicit demands that the Korean government undertake major reforms that struck at the core of the country's political economy. Among other measures, the IMF requirements included:

- developing a "privatization strategy" for Korean firms;
- strengthening bank supervision, accounting procedures, and financial disclosures;
- requiring large conglomerates to disclose liabilities;
- allowing for class-action suits against corporate executives and auditors;
- expanding a social safety net, particularly in the area of unemployment insurance;
- abolishing restrictions on foreign ownership of land and real estate properties; and

---

[30] Government of Japan, "Policy Speech by Prime Minister Keizo Obuchi to the 143rd Session of the Diet," August 7, 1998.

- permitting greater foreign ownership of Korea equities and industries in specified sectors, including the country's telephone service.[31]

Collectively, these measures sought to shatter the entrenched linkages between Korea's public and private sectors that figured prominently in the country's rapid economic expansion. Under the leadership of newly elected President Kim Dae-jung, the Korean government had little choice but to accept the imposed terms in order to prevent an even greater economic calamity. Surrendering a measure of state autonomy, strenuously resisted in the past, represented an acceptable price for economic relief.

Also important in the Korean case is the role of foreign aid in the country's economic development and in its emerging role as a regional economic power. Korean leaders pledged to become net aid donors by the mid-1990s and to become active members of the OECD's Development Assistance Committee (DAC). Inclusion in the 21-member DAC carried symbolic weight for Korea, signifying a leadership role in promoting economic growth beyond its shores and relieving distress in the most impoverished parts of the world.[32] By the mid-1990s, Korea had "graduated" from a net aid recipient to a net donor, providing more than $100 million annually to developing countries, largely in the form of bilateral aid.[33] Although the volume of Korean ODA reached a record level of $186 million in 1997, this sum represented just .04 percent of the country's GNP, far below the average level of OECD members and even further below the level of .70 percent/GNP established as a worldwide standard by the United Nations.

Although Korea's membership in the DAC was delayed by the economic crisis, the country officially joined the OECD in December 1996. Korean officials had pursued OECD membership for many years, seeking the prestige associated with the role of a supporter of global economic development. As the government declared, "Accession to the OECD means participation in a global and multilateral cooperation system, a reflection of Korea's growing role in the world community.... By becoming an OECD member, Korea assumes new responsibilities and rights in the international community and will strengthen its endeavors toward international peace, stability, and common prosperity, commensurate to its capabilities."[34] These statements were remarkably similar to those previously expressed by the Japanese government, which gained considerable stature by becoming the world's leading ODA donor in the early 1990s.

---

[31] Government of Korea, "Updated Memorandum on the Economic Program for the Second Quarterly Review, 1998," submitted to and released by the International Monetary Fund, May 2, 1998.

[32] Foreign assistance played an important part in Korea's own industrial expansion in the 1950s and 1960s. Western industrialized countries, led by the United States, transferred nearly $5 billion in ODA to Korea between 1953 and 1970.

[33] Korean ODA was geographically disbursed during this period, with major recipients including Nigeria and Indonesia (1987), Peru (1988), Fiji (1989), Sri Lanka (1990), Indonesia and Poland (1991), Kenya and Turkey (1992), and Bangladesh and Romania (1993).

[34] Government of Korea, "OECD Accession," Ministry of Foreign Affairs, 1998.

The lack of widespread domestic debate about the subordination of Korea's economic autonomy to transnational capital sources was revealing. Previously, government and business leaders steadfastly resisted external intrusion into their management of domestic and foreign economic policy. Indeed, it was the extensive public-private coordination of policy that played such a crucial role in propelling the country's economic takeoff. The depth of the economic crisis threatened this carefully nurtured relationship, forcing the transition of Korean policy toward a more liberal approach favored by foreign investors, MNCs, major industrialized countries, and international financial institutions. External demands that Korea guarantee a social safety net and protect the interests of organized labor appealed to influential segments of the Korean population that were recently empowered through democratic political reforms. The promise of immediate economic relief, meanwhile, was enough to subdue criticism of the effective takeover of government policy by transnational actors.

## CONCLUSION

This analysis has sought to promote understanding of the crucial role played by transnational capital flows both in promoting the economic development of East Asia and in abetting the region's economic crisis in the late 1990s. As noted above, Asian leaders looked to foreign capital to fuel the region's market-led economic expansion and openly competed for development aid as well as private capital in the form of FDI, portfolio investment, and commercial bank loans. This strategy reaped considerable economic benefits for the region, but it left East Asian states reliant upon continuing inflows of capital to maintain economic vitality. As the economic crisis set in, and as foreign governments curbed aid spending in response to their own economic pressures, the reliance of East Asia upon overseas capital markets proved to be perilous.

The East Asian experience reveals the uneasy coexistence of liberal and nationalist economic models in driving international development in the late 1990s. As noted above, the liberal paradigm envisions the formation of globally integrated financial networks such as those that emerged early in the post-war period and grew to unprecedented proportions in the 1990s. The expansion of Western- and Japanese-based MNCs into the newly industrialized countries of East Asia propelled their economic expansion, which was further assisted by the issuance of government bonds and the opening of national stock markets to international investors. Market-driven economic integration, despite its considerable benefits, rendered these economies vulnerable to the volatility of capital flows, particularly short-term portfolio investments that lacked the staying power and predictability of FDI. Risk-averse program traders, often drawing upon identical economic forecasts, raced to remove assets from marginal investments and sought safer outlets, often thousands of miles away. It was this herdlike behavior of institutional investors, who responded in tandem to the first hints of crisis by initiating capital flight, that produced East Asia's reversal of fortunes.

Ironically, the experience revealed that the top priority among East Asian leaders--economic self-sufficiency--could not be sustained in an era of rampant transnational capital flows. The massive injections of IMF-sponsored assistance vividly demonstrated how dependent these economies remained, not simply upon the maintenance of economic growth but also upon the economic insurance provided by international financial institutions. Conversely, the aggressive response by the IMF and the governments of major industrialized states revealed the extent to which their own economic fortunes were tied to those of the East Asian economies.

Given the fact that the acceleration in regional and global economic integration during the early 1990s was historically unprecedented, economic and political leaders entered an unexplored frontier of transnational economic relations. To a large extent, this explains the extent to which the regional economic crisis caught global financial markets, governments, and academic experts by surprise. As a result, the prospects for recovery in the region as the millennium approaches cannot be anticipated with certainty. While it is apparent that the East Asian contagion will likely impair economic growth in the United States and Europe in the years to come, the long-term consequences of the regional crisis are unclear.

More importantly, the lessons to be derived from the East Asian crisis are also open to conflicting interpretation. This study has focused on merely one of many compelling aspects of the crisis. Other factors--the role of government regulators and banks, the impact of currency fluctuations and bond markets, and the effect of restrictive government policies--are also significant and deserve the closer scrutiny they have received. From the limited perspective of this study, however, it appears that the unrestrained flow of private capital, primarily portfolio investment, virtually guarantees the cycle of boom and bust that has characterized the East Asian experience of the 1990s. If this is the case, measures must be adopted that provide for greater stability and predictability in transnational capital flows. Discouraging foreign investors, both individual and institutional, from seeking immediate gains at the expense of long-term returns is one obvious remedy. Although such a measure would undoubtedly steer such capital toward other regions and constrain economic growth in the short run, it would provide a stronger basis for long-term economic growth.

Taken together, the patterns reviewed in this study signify a new era in the conduct of "economic statecraft."[35] Global economic integration, the cherished objective of classical liberalism, has advanced to an unprecedented degree with the creation of overlapping trade, manufacturing, stock, and bond markets. Greater economic efficiency, however, has always entailed a high degree of risk and uncertainty. As we have seen, this risk includes the prospect of sudden disruptions of capital flows and their deleterious effects on national and regional economic stability. Uncertainty results when economic

---

[35] David Baldwin, *Economic Statecraft* (Princeton, NJ: Princeton University Press, 1985).

forecasting succumbs to these ever-shifting winds in global capital markets. The task of economic statecraft becomes ever more complex under such circumstances, eroding the capacity of state leaders to control their economic destinies. If such a trend continues, nationalist backlash and a reversion to widespread mercantilism is likely, leading to an even greater calamity for East Asia and the global economy.

# THE POETICS OF GRIEF AND THE PRICE OF HEMP IN SOUTHWEST CHINA

*Erik Mueggler*
University of Michigan
Department of Anthropology
1020 L.S.A. Building
Ann Arbor, Michigan 48109-1382

不續其麻

市也婆娑

Done splicing her hemp
She dances in the marketplace
Shi Ching (Book of Songs)[1]

One bright winter afternoon in 1992, in the mountains of Yunnan Province, China, Li Yong told me a story. Li Yong and I were crowded into a courtyard in his largely Yi (or Lòlop'ò) village, at a mortuary ritual for one of his affines. In the courtyard's center, where the corpse had lain in its coffin seven days before, a crude trough had been scratched into the earth, with a shallow hole at the end where the corpse's mouth had been. The dead woman's daughter, her husband's sisters and their daughters, and some of their female friends sat on benches on either side, singing formal poetic laments about labor and pain. To accompany her tears, the daughter ladled water from a bucket into the hole in front of

In memory of my brother Karl Mueggler, 1967-1997. I am indebted to Norma Diamond, Thomas Fricke, Stevan Harrell, Charles Mckhann, Sidney Mintz, P. Steven Sangren, Louisa Schein, G. William Skinner, and the participants in the University of Michigan Center for Chinese Studies Faculty Seminar for their comments and suggestions. The Committee for Scholarly Communications with China and the Wenner Gren Foundation for Anthropological Research funded the research for this chapter.

her. The water overflowed into the trough and gradually turned the lower surface of the courtyard to mud. Women from the dead woman's son's family moved about the courtyard pouring alcohol for the hundreds of guests, who drank while squatting, sitting or standing, their feet in the mud.

Li Yong called his story "the underworld ghost market" (*cími nè væje* in the Central dialect of Yi, his first language).[2] He intended it to illuminate the transactions between living and dead conveyed by the tears, water, alcohol and words that flooded the courtyard. This tale was widely known and often related; I had frequently heard encapsulated versions of it here and elsewhere in Yunnan, when people said, "When someone dies, it is said that he crosses a market street." Since that afternoon, I have come to consider it a kind of Plato's cave tale of highland Yunnan. Like that parable, it voices widespread assumptions about relations between visible and invisible, authentic and unauthentic, and true and apparent, as it describes an exchange between living and dead:[3]

> Long ago, the living [*ts'ɔ*] could see the dead [*nè*], and the dead could see the living. Living and dead both attended the market: on that side of the street the dead sold their things; on this side the living sold theirs, and the dead took the same form as the living. At that time they used copper money, not paper. The dead used paper to stamp out coins that looked just like the copper coins of the living, and with this money they bought things from the living. But the living were not to be trifled with. They put the coins in a pan of water: the real coins made of copper sank, and the paper coins made by the dead floated. They returned the false money to the dead, and gradually the dead could no longer buy from the living; they could buy only from other dead.

> If your father died, you could go to the market the next day and see him. But it was not permitted for living and dead to speak to each other. The dead were punished if they spoke to the living--their officials taxed and fined them--and the living were afraid to speak to the dead. So living and dead could only look at each other. Then as now, the dead sometimes harmed [*k'ə̀*, literally "bit"] the living, but the living could beat the dead in return, so the dead had no power over them. Disgusted with this situation, the dead asked for a sieve to be set up between them and the living. The living could see the dead only vaguely, but the dead [being closer to the sieve's holes] could see the living clearly. The living did not like this, for the sieve was too thick to beat the dead through. The living were stupid: some say they asked for a paper screen to be placed on their side of the street; they could beat the dead through the paper, but they could not see them at all.

Many people in Li Yong's village and the surrounding area had told me that the purpose of mortuary ritual was to disentangle the world of the dead (*nèmɪ*) from that of the living (*ts'ɔmi*). In this tale, coins, water, sieves and paper are manipulated selectively to cut off social intercourse between living and dead. Nevertheless, each rearrangement of boundaries is circumscribed by the marketplace and the political authorities imagined to govern it. These authorities' presence is always a given; living and dead both depend on them to regulate all their transactions with taxes and fines.

In this part of highland Yunnan, mourning the loss of a family member was a matter of weaving a screen between living and dead and conducting transactions that involved seeing, hearing, beating, biting, bribing, buying and giving through this screen--through, as it were, the openings in a bamboo sieve. In mortuary ritual another medium with similar weave took the place of the bamboo sieve: hempen cloth, used both as a shroud to separate the dead from the living and as a currency to enable their continuing transactions. Mourners explicitly associated the work of grieving with the labor of making hempen cloth (along with making offerings of cooked rice and buckwheat cakes) and with all the relationships this life-sustaining labor entailed--relationships with the market, with the political institutions that set its rules and regulated its prices, and with those who made claims on one's labor and its products on the basis of those rules. Female mourners worked hardest at these connections as they sat in the courtyard weeping, ladling water and singing laments. Their songs described in painstaking detail every step of the work of making the rice, buckwheat cakes, and hempen cloth they offered the dead, from crafting tools for plowing and sowing to cooking or weaving the finished product.

This chapter explores the nature of grief and mourning in this community by examining connections between the work of grief and work with hemp, the labor that historically had involved community members in the market most directly and massively. It investigates the values attached to hemp in this part of China, both its market values and the sensuous values entailed in its production and use, relating the verbal and material poetics of grief to the specific historical conditions under which hempen cloth was produced and marketed in the twentieth century, especially the latter half. To this end, it moves from (1) the history of hemp production and market values in the northern Yunnan highlands to (2) the uses of hemp to clothe the dead and bribe underworld officials during reinvigorated mortuary rituals in the early 1990s, and finally to (3) the poetics of ritual laments, particularly those which detailed the steps involved in growing, processing, spinning, and weaving hemp. The latter section focuses on a single such lament. As she grieved for her dead mother, I argue, the singer labored with those around her to fashion grief much as she had once worked with her mother to produce hempen cloth. The market conditions, under which the labor of making hempen cloth enriched or impoverished a household, were among the conditions of her grief. And under these conditions the transactions of mourning became, like market transactions, a matter of falling under or extricating oneself from the domination of others.

Though variations on these practices of grief take place throughout the mountainous northern part of Yunnan Province, my discussion centers on a single group of villages called Zhizuo,[4] where I conducted fieldwork in 1991-93.[5] Presently an "administrative village" (*cungongsuo*[M]), Zhizuo contains two large villages surrounded by about twenty small, scattered hamlets in the mountains of Yongren County (until 1962, Dayao County), Chuxiong Yi Autonomous Prefecture.[6] Throughout the 20th century, this group of villages maintained a strong corporate identity, centered, until the Socialist Education Campaign of 1962, on an ancestral trust and a set of ritual and political duties that rotated yearly among its wealthiest households (Mueggler 1998a). Based on claims of descent from an apical ancestor thought to have first settled this set of mountain valleys some 300 years before, about 95 percent of Zhizuo's inhabitants referred to themselves as Lòlop'ò, while the rest claimed to be Han. Lòlop'ò and Han alike spoke as their first language a variety of a dialect of a Tibeto-Burman language, currently considered to be the Central dialect of Yi. In the socialist government's massive ethnic identification project of the early 1950s, Lòlop'ò in Zhizuo were designated Yi, along with a diversity of mostly highland peoples in Yunnan, Sichuan, Guizhou, and Guangxi Provinces.[7] In the 1990s, however, most continued to insist on the self-ascription Lòlop'ò, to differentiate themselves from neighboring Central dialect speakers (whom they called Líp'ò or Mimp'ò) and from other Yi groups in general.

Recent work on the poetry of grief in China and elsewhere, inspired by a 'postmodern' politics of ironic resistance, has treated laments as rhetorical strategies in which mourners express grievances at social injustice, compete with other lamenters for social status, or subtly seek to improve their social position (Johnson 1988; Herzfeld 1993; Abu-Lughod and Lutz 1990; Kligman 1988). Though such analyses have received praise for honing our awareness of the role of poetic language in the micropolitics of social life, they have also been aptly criticized for missing the point of these poetic forms--the deeply felt grief, sadness and pain of which they speak. In response, some ethnographers have attempted to treat mortuary laments as outward expressions of profoundly personal and internal states of pain, grief, or loss (Desjarlais 1993; Maschino 1992). Neither avenue of approach is entirely adequate to the sense of mourning I wish to convey here. To treat ritual laments merely as strategic rhetorical positioning is to slip towards separating individuals into private, autonomous, competitive subjects. At its starkest, this is a vision of mourning in which the self "cannot experience truly transforming loss but plunders the world for the booty of its self-seeking interest" (Rose 1996, 37). Yet to understand laments as expressive of profoundly personal states of grief and loss is to rely implicitly on another version of this same vision, in which a subject's ultimate reality is a private, internal core or locus of self, where all affect takes place prior to being publicly expressed.

The connections Zhizuo residents establish between grief and labor lead towards an understanding of mourning as neither a rhetorical strategy nor an outward expression of a prior, inner state. They evoke a view of mourning as an ethical activity which, as Gillian Rose puts it, "acknowledges the creative involvement of action in the configuration of power and law" (1996, 12). This mourning is a collective, corporeal labor, which fashions a grief intended to sustain life rather than to debilitate it, as grief might easily do. Mourning engages with power not as private, micropolitical maneuvering, but as a collective ethics, meant to manage the ways the daily, creative activity of production is brought into relation with abstract economic forces and the political authority imagined to underlie them. This ethics acknowledges the laws of price, debt and repayment, along with the authorities that institute and enforce those laws, while it seeks actively to preserve the life-sustaining power of productive labor as much as possible from domination by others, living or dead.

The production of hempen cloth, marginal or nonexistent elsewhere in China, was central to domestic economy in Zhizuo and its surrounding mountains through most of the twentieth century. In this work, people experienced their vulnerabilities to power at both its most abstract and most immediate levels--both to the distant state institutions imagined to establish market prices, and to the local landlords or production-team leaders who claimed their labor. The effects of fluctuations in the price of hemp were immediate and intimate, while their cuases were distant and mysterious; they could only be imagined. As the first step in this exploration of work and mourning, I wish to show how Zhizuo residents conceptualized this indeterminacy in much the same way they understood the indeterminate relationship between living and dead: the dead had real and immediate effects on the lives of their descendants, but the forces that shaped these effects were as distant and abstract as those that shaped prices, causing them to fluctuate suddenly and mysteriously to bring disaster or wealth. This will require a brief exploration of the history of hemp production and prices in Yunnan, a history to which people in Zhizuo made repeated reference as they spoke of grief and mourning.

## CLOTHING THE LIVING: HEMP AND COTTON IN YUNNAN

"The Chinese readily mock people dressed in hemp,"[8] observed Alfred Liétard of the Société des Missions Etrangèrs de Paris around 1911, "so this cloth is disappearing gradually, especially in the plains, to make way for Chinese [cotton] cloth" (1913, 93). Liétard's parishioners, Lòlop'ò who inhabited a plain not far from Zhizuo,[9] were among a tiny minority of Chinese who still wore any hemp at all. In the Ming, cotton cloth, lighter than hemp, cooler in the summer and warmer in the winter, and taking as little as a tenth of the land to cultivate, had replaced hemp (*dama*[M]) and ramie (*zhuma*[M])[10] through most of China (Chao 1977, 33). By the Qing, cotton textile production had become the most important peasant industry, decisively shaping a unique, household-based production system (Elvin 1972). As Susan Mann has shown, cotton cloth production informed ideas about virtuous and productive peasant households: in the eyes of elite Qing men, cotton weaving was "an emblem of woman-as-wife-and-mother, the anchor of the household and the moral center of the family" (1997, 149). In their campaign to subdue and civilize the non-Han peoples of the Southwest, Qing officials sought to transplant these values to the high, rough soil of Yunnan, taking the cotton-weaving region of Jiangnan as a model for Yunnan's economic development, and drawing up plans to manufacture and distribute looms to peasant households there (Mann 1997, 148).

Despite such efforts, a native cotton-weaving industry did not develop in Yunnan until the late nineteenth century. Cotton plants could be cultivated in only a very few locations in the province, and raw cotton or yarn for household production had to be imported from elsewhere. Only during the 1890s did factory yarn begin to flow into the province from India, and some peasants begin to weave cotton cloth (Chao 1977, 181). The Lòlop'ò Liétard evangelized between 1896 and 1912 still clearly found hemp, grown, spun, and woven locally, to be competitive in price with cotton. He found the men dressed in wide, hemmed, hempen pants held up with a sash of white hemp or blue-black cotton, two shirts of hemp or cotton, and cotton turbans or cotton caps. The women wore unhemmed cotton pants and shirts and aprons of hemp or blue-black cotton and cotton turbans (1913, 94-98). Though the Lòlop'ò districts of this county exported over 500 mule loads of hemp a year to Kunming and beyond (Qiao 1996, 325), Liétard observed that many Lòlop'ò women found hempen cloth too tiresome to produce themselves. Preferring "to pass their time plaiting leather sandals, which they sell, eight cash a pair, to Chinese merchants" (Lietard 1913, 94), they bought most of their hemp from their neighbors in the mountains to the north, in Dayao county. Stretching from the salt wells of Baiyanjing to the Qinglin river,[11] these mountains were inhabited by "the numerous tribe of the *Li*," as Liétard called them,[12] who continued to produce hempen cloth well into the twentieth century. On the eastern slope of these mountains were the narrow valleys of Zhizuo, whose residents the Lòlop'ò of Liétard's mission called "*Métsè* ['cloth folk'], making allusion to the hemp that grows abundantly in their mountains and which they sell in great quantity to the Lòlop'ò" (1913, 43). The dun-colored hempen clothing of these mountain residents signaled their poverty and backwardness and made them objects of mockery to cotton-clad lowlanders, "Chinese" and Lòlop'ò alike.

Though residents of the plains snubbed hempen cloth as uncomfortable, aesthetically ridiculous, and onerous to manufacture, its production held decided advantages over cotton weaving for "the numerous tribe of the *Li*." In the late 1920s and early 1930s, cotton textile production expanded in Yunnan as improved transportation from the coast made cheaper foreign and domestic machine-spun cotton yarn available there (Chao 1975, 194). Nevertheless, by the 1930s and 1940s, households that engaged in handicraft cotton textile weaving found that it barely contributed to their subsistence. Pressed by competition from machine-woven cloth, both foreign and domestic, handwoven cloth merchants offered the lowest possible prices to producers (Walker 1993, 365). Capital outlay was significant: weavers had to buy paste, fuel, looms, and machine-spun yarn, which had replaced hand-spun yarn for most handicraft weaving in China in the late nineteenth century. By the late 1930s, in Yunnan's foremost textile-producing region only landed households or those with another reliable income source could weave; landless peasants could not afford to buy thread (Fei and Chang 1949, 240). In 1939, Fei and Chang calculated that in this area, a woman working all day weaving earned a wage of about 0.70 yuan, insufficient to buy her food, while women doing field work earned 1.70 to 2.00 yuan a day (1949, 243).[13] As in China's other handicraft cotton-weaving regions, the agricultural economy subsidized household cloth production, making it unnecessary for merchants to offer subsistence wages for this work, even as households grew dependant on this marginal sideline income (Walker 1993).

The crucial difference between hemp- and cotton-textile production lay in the cost of inputs. Most hemp-weaving households produced their own looms and other tools and few bought their thread: nearly all spun it from hemp they grew and processed themselves. In the mountains in and around Zhizuo, hemp was cultivated on land not suitable for grain production, in steep, high, shady ravines, where there was plenty of moisture and the stalks grew long and thin as they reached for the sun. Such land was cheap and abundant, and in some high-mountain hamlets people simply planted their hemp in unclaimed ravines. In 1950, a team of ethnographers sent to the nearby village of Yijichang under the new government's ethnic identification project found hempen cloth production to be a crucial sideline income-producing activity for nearly every household (*Yunnan Sheng bianjizu* 1986 [1950], 102). Grain land in these mountains was scarce: in 1948, farmers in Yijichang divided only 2.1 *mu*[M][14] per capita between irrigated paddy land for rice and winter wheat; unirrigated terraces for maize, wheat, and barley; and swidden land for oats, buckwheat, and potatoes. Only a few landlord households produced enough grain to feed their members for the entire year. To supplement grain income, women in all but one of the village's forty-six households, from the six classed as rich peasants to the twenty-two classed as poor peasants or agricultural laborers, produced hempen cloth for sale. All but a handful of households owned a few *fen* of hemp land; those that did not bought raw hemp in the market. Nearly every woman and girl spent most of her time processing and weaving hemp. The average household of about five people produced all the clothing worn by its members and sold an additional 767 *ke*[M] of cloth a year. This could buy 153 *sheng*[M] of husked rice, sufficient to feed one person well for over eight months. The most productive households sold 2,000 *ke* a year, enough to feed two people adequately for the entire year (101-2). Hempen cloth production was best suited to the most labor-rich and land-poor households, especially those with an abundance of women. A *mu* of hemp land took forty-eight days of labor for men and women and one ox day to cultivate; it produced an average of 400 catties of raw hemp. With hundreds of hours of additional labor, all performed by women, this could be made into 2400 to 4000 *ke* of hempen cloth, depending on the quality of raw hemp, and this cloth could be exchanged for between 480 and 800 *sheng* of husked rice. By contrast, a *mu* of the most productive rice land took only eighteen days of labor and three ox days to cultivate, but it produced an average of only 206 *sheng* of husked rice (102).

By 1950, most hempen cloth was made into gunnny bags to transport grain and other agricultural products: not even the Lòlop'ò of the plains where Liétard had once preached bought hempen textiles to wear. The demand for gunny bags created a strong, though fluctuating market for hemp through the early twentieth century. Zhizuo residents recall that after 1935, Líp'ò and Lòlop'ò from the surrounding mountains converged on Zhizuo's largest village every ten days for a periodic market where they sold their hemp to traders from a large hemp-buying corporation with branches all over northern and central Yunnan. In 1933, one catty of raw hemp at farm prices bought about 5.3 catties of rice, a ratio that was about the same in 1950 (Liu and Yeh 1965, 136; Zhang 1984, 17). Though one can only speculate about hemp prices in the intervening war years, it is very likely that throughout the 1930s and 1940s hempen cloth production remained economically crucial for most families in these mountains, as it had been from the time of Liétard's mission and before. Like cotton in the Yangze delta, hemp likely encouraged population growth and land subdivision, contributing to the scarcity of grain land in these mountains. These condions in place, hempen cloth production could not be dispensed with.

## Her Love Rests: the Price of Hemp

For people in Zhizuo, the phrase that best described Liberation in 1950 and Land Reform in 1952-53, was not "turning bodies" (*fanshen*[M])[15] but "changing clothes" (*chuanyi*[M]). Until Land Reform, nearly everyone in this community dressed in the undyed hempen clothing produced by their households. There was one cotton loom in the district, in the home of the hereditary chieftain, or *tusi*[M], 20 kilometers away, and within Zhizuo only the families of the two wealthiest landlords could afford cotton robes. Four decades later, in tones that recalled the "speak bitterness" meetings of the 1950s, Zhizuo residents spoke of hempen clothing as a reminder of past hardship. As Qi Shenlin, who was an adolescent at Liberation, recalled,

> It was ugly and rough. Women wore robes buttoned on the side--their clothes were all in the form of the clothes they wear to weddings and festivals today, but they were all hemp. . . . People wore straw shoes and hempen belts. Or they made shoes of hemp. Some people didn't have hemp and wore shoes of plaited banana leaves. . . . Not even landlords had the type of cotton quilts we use now. They made very thick blankets of hemp to cover themselves with. Imagine covering yourself with a mat of hemp! Cold! Some people made thick felt blankets out of wool, but this was very cold too, because it was stiff and couldn't be tucked around your body. When it rained, people wore thick, short, heavy cloaks of hemp or straw and bamboo hats. Some of those cloaks were as heavy as two or three kilos! Now you just stick a piece of plastic in your pocket and take it out when it rains.

By 1952, state procurement policies for hemp and hempen cloth allowed Zhizuo residents to change their dull hempen garb for blue or black cotton, as the Lòlop'ò of Liétard's mission had begun to do a half century before. Upon consolidating power in northern Yunnan, the revolutionary government created Supply and Marketing Cooperatives in prefectural centers and market towns. In order to attract mountain residents to these initially voluntary cooperatives, the state set the price they paid for hemp and hempen textiles well above market prices. Nationally, hemp procurement prices rose 33 percent between 1950 and 1952, far outstripping prices for grain and cotton (Zhang 1984, 10). In late 1953, the unified purchase and supply order (*tongguo tongxiao*[M]) eliminated private markets for hemp, grain, and cotton cloth altogether, allowing the state to sustain high hemp prices relative to grain and cotton prices for the next three decades. In 1952, one catty of raw hemp could purchase about 26 percent more rice than it could in 1950; by 1963, it could purchase up to 30 percent more than in 1950. More striking yet, one catty of hemp bought about 23 percent more cotton in 1952 than 1950 and around 73 percent more by 1963 (10; see Fig. 1).

Between 1953 and 1976, most peasants in China were subjected to a "scissors effect": the price of grain procurement prices was adjusted upward only periodically, while the price of inputs, especially chemical fertilizers, rose steadily (Oi 1989, 54). According to one calculation, by 1976 peasants growing grains could make a scanty profit only on rice; growing other grains required them to spend about 5.6 percent more on production than the procurement price yielded (Zhang 1984, 20). In dramatic contrast to grain, for raw hemp, procurement prices were about *86.6 percent higher* than production costs (21). And rendering the raw hemp into cloth added more value at a high cost in labor but little in other inputs. Moreover, grain-poor, hemp-producing brigades received free relief grain from richer brigades (from 1956 to 1962), then later bought relief grain at prices lower than the procurement price (from 1962 to 1976). In a period when real incomes for most peasants in China were stagnating or declining, this sideline nongrain cash crop, coupled with household craft production, enriched hemp-producing brigades.

Encouraged by these conditions, the residents of Yunnan's mountainous districts became prolific producers of hempen cloth: between 1949 and 1959, peasant handicraft hemp production in the province more than doubled (*Yunnan Sheng difangzhi bianzan weiyuanhui* 1992, 157).[16] In the mountians of Dayao County, where more hempen cloth was produced than in any but one of Yunnan's other 100 or so counties (158), cloth production replaced nearly all other peasant activities with which men in this area had once sought to generate cash for their households--such as working as porters along salt, sugar, and opium trading routes. At Land Reform, hemp-growing acreage was distributed evenly among each village's households. The families of the region's few former landlords had to learn to grow, process, spin, and weave hemp to survive, and formerly landless peasants grew hemp on their newly acquired land. In contrast to household cotton textile production, which the state quickly eliminated by controlling cotton yarn distribution to peasant households (Chao 1975, 199), hempen cloth production in this region remained almost entirely private. In 1956, as land and agricultural labor were collectivized throughout China, hemp cultivation was turned over to production teams, each of which assigned a few members to live in high-mountain seasonal houses (*tianfang*[M]), where they grew hemp and herded goats. The harvested stalks were divided among the team's households according to their number of able-bodied laborers, male and female. Households sold their hemp to the Supply and Marketing Cooperatives as raw hemp, thread, or cloth, depending on the price and their number of available female laborers. Cooperative officials divided the hemp into grades according to published national standards and priced it accordingly.[17] With the cash from hemp sales, women supplemented their households' rations of grain and bought clothing, salt, alcohol, utensils, and other necessaries.

Apart from the collective work of cultivating, harvesting and transporting hemp stalks, women performed every step of hempen cloth production. Men participated only by cooking meals and crafting tools. Making cloth went on all year, but it was busiest in the rainy season when agricultural work was only intermittent. It was exhausting, time consuming, and often painful labor. The raw hemp was soaked, peeled, washed, and pounded; the fibers were picked apart by hand, spliced with the fingers, soaked, dried, and spun; the thread was wrapped on a frame, dried, washed, boiled with ash, washed again, boiled with rice and beef fat, rinsed, boiled a third time with beeswax, and dried. The thread, now white, strong, flexible, and ready for weaving, was wound onto bamboo reels; a large, wooden, horizontal loom was set up in the courtyard, and the warp was strung onto the loom. Weaving was only the final step in this process, repeated as often as twice a month in the most productive households. As we shall see, women complained eloquently of the exhaustion and pain of this work in mortuary laments: washing hemp in winter streams turned feet into iron blocks, splicing wore away the thumbs and fingers; weaving strained the eyes and back. "When the old woman was weaving hemp," one man recalled, "she was always in a sour mood. You cooked her meals, left them out, and stayed out of her way." But however unpleasant, working hemp gave women the prestige of cash earners. As the husband of a woman who had worked hemp for thirty years put it, "One woman weaving hemp could earn as much as two or three schoolteachers." In most households, this prestige translated into authority over economic affairs, especially after Land Reform deprived men of significant opportunities to generate cash. Women handled most market transactions, kept the resulting money on their persons, and decided how it would be spent. This cash bought the crucial margin of grain to fill a granary, and in most households the senior woman kept the granary key with her money, using it to regulate her family's consumption of grain at each meal.

Women also clothed their families with the proceeds of hemp sales. In the 1950s, women began to use their more abundant cash to buy black or navy cotton cloth from the Supply and Marketing Cooperatives. Black clothing held a special appeal for Zhizuo residents. Before Liberation, wealthy landlords and officials had worn black cotton or silk robes. Ordinary people bred herds of all-black goats whose skin they made into glossy, black-haired capes, associated with youthful beauty, intimacy with one's ancestral origins, and a sense of warm connection to one's kin. Now women fashioned black cotton cloth into shirts, trousers, aprons, sashes, and carrying-cloths, ornamenting them with appliqué of colored cotton cloth. Those with extra cash bought embroidered shoes and caps or embroidered panels to sew onto their sleeves, collars and aprons. An ordinary women could now aspire to assemble an entire set of embroidered black or navy cotton clothing to wear at weddings and festivals, an elegance once restricted to the wealthiest. Women made wide-bottomed black or navy trousers and *zhongshan*[M] jackets for the men in their households. By the early 1960s, many women found it found it cheaper and easier to buy ready-made green army-style clothing, especially for men, but they kept black and navy clothing for festive occasions

Women were judged as wives, mothers, and daughters-in-law by their ability to clothe their families. "If I wear dirty or torn trousers, people don't laugh at me, they laugh at my wife for being unable to clothe me," a man in his early fifties told me. Young wives were expected to dress their entire households, which often included their husband's parents and unmarried brothers. For women, weaving hempen cloth to dress their families warmly or even sumptuously was an expression of love, care, and intimacy as much as of economic ability. Women spoke of the exhausting labor of making hempen cloth as the work of "raising" (*ho*) a family, an expenditure of love that could be recompensed only after death. In mortuary laments, a silent spinning wheel and loom were metaphors for a mother's death and the cessation of that life-giving love that fed and warmed her family:

| mother's hemp wheel rests | yè pó jo gə̀ ga |
| her hemp loom halts | yè jæ mǽ le ga |
| | |
| mother rests from love | su mo n ka̱ nò yi pe |
| her love rests | ka̱ nì nò tí pe |

The looms and spinning wheels of Zhizuo, steady generators of food, clothing, and love throughout the collective period, halted abruptly after the first wave of market reforms in 1978.

In the late 1970s China had begun to produce synthetic fibers at rapidly accelerating rates, and one of their earliest uses was to replace hemp in bags for grain and fertilizer (*Zhongguo fangzhi gongye nianjian* 1994, 122). At the same time, base-quota and above base-quota grain price were raised substantially: in Yunnan the median price rise in 1978 was about 23 percent (*Yunnan Sheng zhi jingji zonghe zhi* 1989-1995). In August 1980, unable to support procurement prices for hemp any longer, the the state instituted a floating price for hemp procurement and sales, causing prices to plunge over 12 percent over the next year (*Yunnan Sheng difangzhi bianzan weiyuanhui* 1992, 160; *Yunnan Sheng zhi jingji zonghe zhi* 1989-1995). By the end of 1981, a catty of raw hemp bought about 33 percent less grain than it had in 1978, less even than in 1950 (see Fig. 1). Throughout the 1980s, grain and cotton prices inflated as the state allowed increasing quantities of basic staples to be sold on the market. Hemp prices inflated apace for two years in the mid 1980s, but by 1987 they were again in free fall. By 1994, a catty of hemp (had anyone attempted to sell one) would have bought a quarter the grain and half the cotton it had bought in 1950 (see Fig. 1).

In 1980 and 1981, devastated by the first plunge in the price of hemp, families in Zhizuo abandoned cloth production almost entirely. For over thirty years, hempen cloth had formed the woven doorway through which mountain residents in northern Yunnan had entered the marketplace, cash in hand. Its loss decisively transformed many aspects of their relation to money and the marketplace, not least the gendered aspects. Searching for new means to generate cash, Zhizuo residents began to harvest timber illegally from the mountainsides, sawing it by hand into boards, which they hauled by mule to the lowlands for sale. As working hemp had been exclusively women's labor, working wood was entirely men's, and women saw their economic authority in their households disintegrate as they fought a losing struggle to control the cash wood generated. By the early 1990s, the best timber had all been cut, and most Zhizuo households depended heavily on free relief grain. Brigade and township cadres spent long hours and much money on schemes to recreate the magic of hemp in another form: Walnuts for shipment to Burma? Orchards of apples and pears? Workshops to make embroidered bags for tourists? The ground was said to be full of gold and silver, if only there were a way to find it.

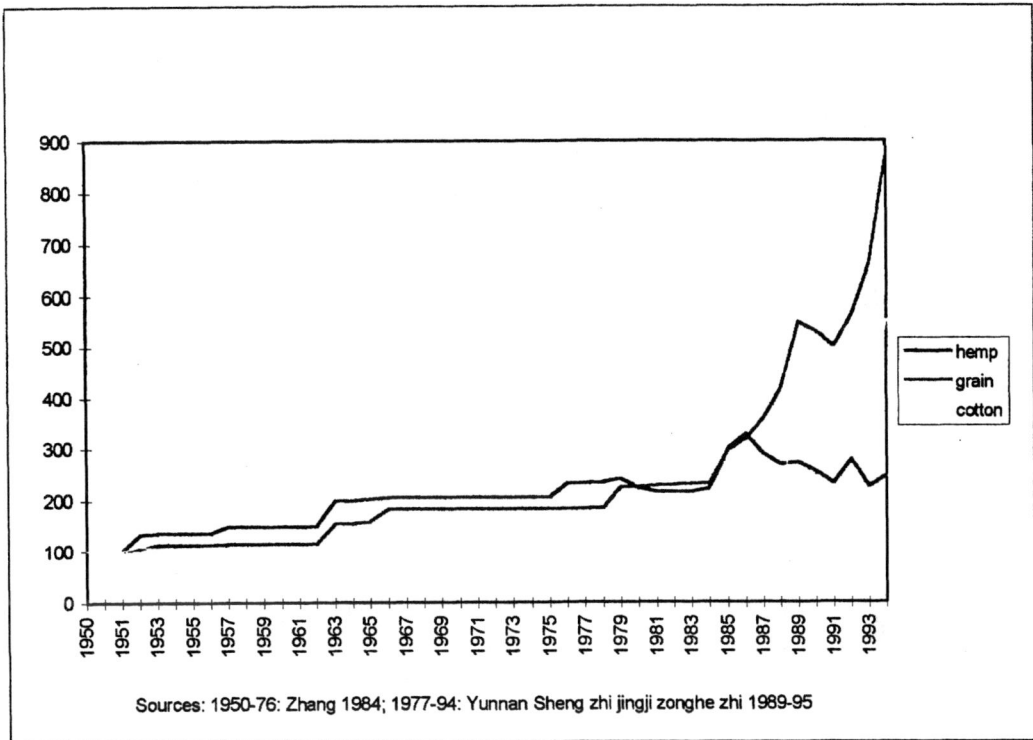

Figure 1. Procurement and market prices for hemp, grain and cotton, 1950-1994.
(All prices are indexed to 100 in 1950.)

**Figure 1**

People in Zhizuo traced for me many times in talk the trajectory I have retraced here with the help of national and provincial price statistics. They spoke of the price of hemp as a mysterious abstraction whose fate was decided as far away as Beijing by unnamed and unseen bureaucratic officials. At the same time, this price could not have had more concrete effects. It was as though the price of hemp connected two distinct realms: the mysterious and distant world of high officials and the immediate world of daily life. Woven hemp formed the porous screen or bamboo sieve between these realms, on whose surface distant officials cast signs, numbers and slogans that the knowing could read like omens. To talk of the price of hemp was to speak of an uncanny disjuncture between the immediacies of daily life and a mysterious place where decisions of officials created wealth and poverty, life and death in the immediate realm. And it was precisely this kind of disjuncture--the conditions for its existence, the procedures for generating or transcending it--that preoccupied people in Zhizuo as they mourned their dead.

Between 1964 and 1978, state sanctions against "superstitious practices" severely restricted the scope and complexity of mortuary ritual and highland Yunnan. Most families in Zhizuo held private, small-scale funerals for their dead, to which only a few of their closest kin were invited. But in the late 1970s, even as market reforms destroyed hemp's monetary value, Zhizuo residents took advantage of a political atmosphere more tolerant of large-scale ritual activities to invest mortuary rituals with new energy. Many families reinstituted a funeral process that included a night-long vigil three days after a death, a second, daytime vigil seven or nine days after the first, and yearly activities at the grave site.[18] By the mid 1980s, these activities often involved the participation of hundreds of the deceased's kin and friends. In mortuary rituals, where it formed both a screen or sieve between living and dead and a currency for their interaction, hempen cloth had lost none of its worth.

## CLOTHING THE DEAD: THE HEMP'S EYES

[In Chou times] the character pu [¥¬] denoted a certain type of spade-shaped money and
hemp cloth, both of which served as a commodity of exchange.
Dieter Kuhn (1988, 19)[19]

As people in Zhizuo were quick to point out, unlike most lowland rural residents they did not wear hempen cloth to mourn the dead (dai xiao[M]). Living mourners wore ordinary clothing; the dead wore hemp. Hempen shrouds separated dead from living and enabled the transactions of grief through their crossed threads. Clothing the dead took place during a vigil begun immediately after the moment of death and kept up for three days and nights as preparations for the funeral were made. A son or daughter[20] stripped the body, washed it with water boiled with a poisonous vine and combed its hair straight up from its head, to invert the hairstyle of the living. Around the corpse's waist lengths of hempen cloth, six ke each (about eight feet), were wrapped like sashes. Each of the deceased's brothers (if a woman) or wife's brothers (if a man) contributed one length of cloth. "They are belts, but they are also money. She has money under her shirt to use along the road," one funeral participant told me. A long hempen shirt, ideally spun, woven, and sewn by a daughter, was placed over these shrouds. "The shirt is one of the rules you must follow or be punished by the underworld officials. It is a tax you must pay so they allow you to pass." Each foot was clothed with two one-*ke* lengths of hempen cloth sewn into a pocket shape and tied at the ankles with strands of raw hemp, so that the dead could pay the entrance fee as it stepped over the threshold of the underworld gate. The corpse was given a hempen towel to wash its face and a cotton-lined hempen wallet to carry its silver or tobacco and wave away flies and wild bandit ghosts. "If he has no wallet to wave he will be terrified of the ghosts on the road to the underworld," a mourner commented. All these hempen offerings were to serve as currency to pay taxes or bribes to the many officials the corpse would encounter on its path. "It's like the paper scattered along the path when you carry the coffin to the grave; it's for the wild bandit ghosts and the ghost officials."

When Zhizuo residents began to sport dark cotton clothing in the 1950s, they clothed the dead with more elegance as well, adding layers of silk or cotton clothing to their hempen shrouds. In the 1990s, each son and daughter prepared at least one new, beautiful set of cotton or silk clothing for the corpse. Dead men were dressed in old-style black or blue robes, with buttons down the right side, women in black or blue embroidered shirts, aprons, and trousers. Men were given silken hats of the style once worn by local gentry; women were adorned with embroidered cotton hats, silver earrings, bracelets, and apron-clasps. Often sisters (of a deceased man or a deceased woman's husband) and their daughters also contributed sets of new clothing; some corpses were bundled in ten or twelve layers of cotton or silk. The coffin was lined with layers of cotton quilts, and more quilts were piled on top of the corpse. Nevertheless, as Li Huilin, one of those who explained the funeral process to me, succinctly put it, "The silk and cotton is just to look good; the hemp is to follow the rules." While the sartorial splendor of cotton and silk displayed a family's love and care, the drab hempen underclothing and accessories were the crucial woven sieve between living and dead, through which were borne gifts of rice, meat, wine, water, tears, work, and pain.

A red cloth veiled the corpse's eyes before it was carried to the coffin in the courtyard, hiding the preparations from it, "so it doesn't have unfulfilled expectations." The head was lain on a square pillow of hempen cloth stuffed with raw, unspliced hemp, the eyes closed, a piece of silver placed on the tongue, the mouth sealed, the arms aligned, and the clothing smoothed. Two six-*ke*-long hempen cloths were crossed diagonally over the corpse to form the last cloth layer beneath the coffin lid. Then the red veil was lifted, displaying to the corpse its elegant attire. "You lift the veil so it can see its good clothes and so it can see to walk the road." This veiling and unveiling was repeated with the coffin lid. Two men placed the lid on the coffin, lifted it off, and replaced it, seven times for a dead woman and nine for a man, before settling the lid into place. Benches were placed on either side of the encoffined corpse, and the dead's daughters with their mother's sisters and their daughters and other friends, placed their heads against the coffin and sang laments until daybreak.

The screens of cloth and coffin impeded and facilitated seeing, hearing, and speaking between living and dead. As the corpse was veiled and unveiled with cloth, covered and uncovered with the coffin lid, the mourners' sight of the dead was obstructed, but the dead's view of the living remained clear. Indeed, the work of grieving was intended to force the corpse to see and hear so it would understand the work and pain that went into making or buying its clothing and other gifts. As the lament we shall examine below belabors the dead with details of making its hempen shrouds, it repeatedly entreats the corpse to clear its mind and sharpen its ears as it walks the road to the underworld:

| | |
|---|---|
| mother, go with a clear heart/mind | su mo ni ní me t'e t'e pε yi |
| go with sharp ears | nó jù jù pε yi |
| | |
| mother, don't say you don't understand | so mo n sa t'à bε |
| don't say you don't see | m ma t'à bε |

The corpse was to see, hear, and understand so as to accept everything offered it, but it was not to speak. The command, "don't say you don't understand, don't say you don't see" participated in a more general injunction against speech by the dead, which was taken as a sign that the perilous segregation of living and dead had not been accomplished. People in Zhizuo frequently told stories of spirit possession, in which a dead parent or sibling spoke through one's mouth, bemoaning its hunger or tattered clothing and insisting on further gifts and mortuary rituals. This speech was the "biting" (k'ə) to which the story of the ghost market refers. Death from violence, hunger, suicide, or childbirth produced wild ghosts (chènè) who spoke with their descendants' voices or troubled their bodies, requiring additional, elaborate ritual action (chènèpi) to disentangle living from dead. According to the ritual specialists who treated them, possessions by dead parents or siblings increased dramatically after the Great Leap famine (1959-62) and remained a common source of chronic illness through the early 1990s. Those who had died in the famine and not been properly mourned because of restrictions on mortuary ritual between 1958 and 1978 still bit the flesh of their descendants.

As it sharpened the eyes and ears of the dead, grief dulled those of the living. Mortuary laments speak of a happy, noisy, cluttered house grown silent and empty: The orphaned sons and daughters listen for their parent's voice but hear only silence; they look for her form in her accustomed places but find them empty; they stumble about their daily tasks, eyes full of tears, seeing nothing:

| | |
|---|---|
| our happy shingled house | ŋǽ cí mo là he he chì he |
| our great tiled house | nǽ mo t'á he he chì se |
| | |
| like mushrooms around a pine | t'à dɔ mə lə chɨ̀ |
| this family of ours | ŋǽ he he chì he |
| a family of orphans | chɨ̀ zò chì he ko tí pe |
| | |
| mother, your bed grows cold | su mo buí dù je le tí pe ŋɔ |
| ears no longer hear you working | su mo mo nó n jò ga pe ŋɔ |
| your footfalls no longer sound | mo sæ n jò ga pe |
| | |
| and now | a pá he chì bo |
| your bed is silent as tangled vines | na shɨ̀ k'a yi tí pe ŋɔ |
| your orphaned son lifts his head without | |
| seeing the sky | zò chɨ̀ wú chǽ mùi m ma do ŋɔ |
| your orphaned daughter lifts her feet without | |
| seeing the earth | né chɨ̀ chì chǽ mi m ma lo shó do ŋɔ |
| | |
| mother, your embroidered clothing is hidden | su mo p'a p'o ni n ŋǽ lɔ |
| your body's clothing unseen | gə p'o lè n lè ga |

Even as it blunted their sight and hearing, grief facilitated mourners' speech. One of the tasks laments describe is making the warp--stringing hempen threads through the eyes of a bamboo warp frame to make hundreds of orderly parallel strands between posts set up in the courtyard. A chant sung by male ritual specialists in a mortuary ritual once performed in the tenth lunar month following a person's death (*ts'ɨhonèpi*) associates stringing an orderly warp with the abundant speech that bears the dead smoothly into the underworld.

| | |
|---|---|
| women string the warp for cloth | ǽ mǽ yè cæ mæ jɔ t'ù |
| threshed rice straw on drying frames | che dǽ bɔ̰ sə tsa |
| | |
| my speech is strong | bɛ kɔ̰ wò vǽ ga |
| my discussions are lengthy | t'ə kɔ̰ lo ci ga |
| | |
| I sit until my tongue wears out | tḭ a ló dò gə gɔ̀ |
| I discuss at great depth | t'ə lu nɛ̰ ga gɔ̀ |
| as you [the dead] go happily on | ni gə gə sa sa yi |

The even meter and parallel structures of mortuary laments form an orderly warp for the shroud of speech that divides and connects living and dead.

Hemp was woven in a simple tabby weave (*juan* ,h), in which each weft goes alternately over and under one warp end (Cheng 1992). Loosened a bit, this weave resembles that of the bamboo sieve through which the dead peered out at the living in the story of the ghost market. The warp and weft of simple tabby weaves frame orderly absences in the gaps between their threads. Weaving sieves of threads and gaps to dull the eyes and ears of the living unveiled as it veiled, making knowledge of the dead possible, as knowledge of absence. While in the best of circumstances the dead never spoke, they did communicate with their living descendants through mute signs cast onto the world's surface. In the early 1990s, most people in Zhizuo could list many omens which predicted disaster for oneself or members of one's household: masses of spider webs in a house's eaves, crows cawing from a rooftop, chickens laying double eggs, paired squashes or gourds, flattened circles in fields, mating snakes on the paths, rice stalks knotted in the paddies, to select only a few. People took such omens as messages from dead kin warning of the imminent death of a loved one. The dead, able to see clearly everything in this world, expressed their continued care for the living by watching out for future wealth or disaster that the living could not see. Upon an accumulation of omens people often went to diviners to seek more precise communications from the dead. In a technique used by the most powerful seers, the diviner laid a length of hempen cloth along his forearm. He examined the cloth and saw the messages of the dead spring out of the "hemp's eyes" (*yème*), the tiny square openings between the woven threads. Like the gaps in the weave of the bamboo sieve that divided the ghost market street, the hemp's eyes were apertures through which the dead, in their absence, could be known. As they watched for omens and consulted diviners, people in Zhizuo treated the entire world as a woven hempen shroud. The absent dead were everywhere, becoming known to the living wherever the world's weave loosened up to reveal another world through its gaps.

The hemp's eyes were also the unit of value of hempen currency. Weavers in Zhizuo were well aware that the more eyes in a length of hempen cloth (the closer its weave) the greater its market value. In mortuary laments mourners tell the dead that the silver and hempen currency they are offered will expand in value in the underworld: one silver coin will be worth ten, one hempen eye worth a hundred:

| | |
|---|---|
| go use one coin as ten | chì che ts'ɨ che tï zè yi |
| use one ounce as ten | chì lò ts'ɨ lò tï zè yi |
| | |
| wide woven eyed cloth | go exchange one eye for a hundred |
| go use one eye as ten | |

yè chæ yè me mò lo mæ
ni chì me ts'i me tì zè yi
chì me ho me jǝ zè yi

The absences that allowed the living to glimpse the dead through the weave of speech were the units that gave hemp its price--both in the underworld and the world of the living. The myriad empty spaces left in the world by the dead were windows through which fugitive messages from other worlds (the world of the dead, the world of distant market officials) could be sought. Whether omens of future death or speculations about future prices, these messages foretold prosperity or disaster for the living.

## HER PITIFUL EYES: THE POETICS OF RITUAL LAMENTS

I collaborated with two life-long residents of Zhizuo to record, transcribe and translate mortuary laments. Luo Lizhu, a widowed grandmother of five in her early seventies and the liveliest and most cheerful of friends and informants, was renowned as a master of multiple genres of poetic language, including laments. Li Qunhua, a married mother of three in her early forties, was a frequent presence on wailers' benches, though she claimed to be inept at the poetry of grief. Both women were well respected and extraordinarily well connected among their neighbors, and they seemed to have little trouble obtaining permission from kin and friends to sit beside them at mortuary rituals and record their songs. As we replayed these recordings, Luo repeated each line word for word so I could transcribe it accurately, and both women helped with translation by discussing the various metaphorical possibilities of each line and explaining difficult passages.

Luo and Qi divided mortuary laments into two genres. The first they called *chìmèkò*, "orphans' poetry." Female kin of the dead sang orphan's poetry in a vigil over the corpse from the moment of death until burial. These laments, usually in the form of antiphonal dialogues, described the orphan's life from her birth to her parents' deaths, elaborated each step of the funeral process, and detailed the labor required to make each of the gifts. The genre on which I will focus here was called *ɔchɔŋɔ*, "lamenting songs." Women sang these laments at *nihèpi*, "dawn-to-dusk offerings," the setting for this chapter's opening paragraphs, held seven days (for a woman) or nine days (for a man) after burial. At these events, people with ties of kinship or friendship to the dead's kin gathered in the courtyard where the corpse had been prepared for burial days before. The guests brought gifts for the dead, ranging from a small bag of unhusked grain to a chicken or a goat, depending on their relation to the dead and obligations incurred at earlier mortuary rituals. They distributed themselves through the courtyard with reference to the shallow hole and trough scratched in the dirt floor at the courtyard's center where the corpse had lain in its coffin. Those connected with the dead's brothers (if a woman) or wife's brothers (if a man) gathered at the "head" of this absent corpse, those associated with her sons (or uxorilocally married daughters) at its "foot," and those attached to her married-out daughters (or married-out sons) at the sides.

A row of benches was placed on either side of the trough, as though around a coffin. Near the absent corpse's head, a basket, a length of hempen cloth, some incense and a little bit of money sat on a small table. Female kin of the dead--her daughters, her husband's sisters and their daughters, and women with more distant connections--emptied small bamboo boxes packed with cooked rice and fatty meat into the basket and sat on the benches to sing *ɔchəŋə* laments. A married daughter sat near the shallow hole into which she ladled water from a bucket as she wept. The water flowed through the scuffed-out digestive tract and swamped the lower part of the courtyard. Grain alcohol flowed with the water and tears: the dead's daughters-in-law and their friends and daughters circulated through the courtyard pouring repeated libations for each guest, men and women alike, into jars or bowls they brought for this purpose. This drink changed hands rapidly: some women passed their share to their husbands; others confiscated their husbands' or sons' portions, which they delivered to other kin or friends or saved for later. Meat from the slaughtered goats and chickens circulated in large baskets; each guest took a handful and ate it, pocketed it, or passed it on to a child.

A skilled male mourner initiated the lamenting for a fee--the hempen cloth, the bottle of alcohol, and the money on the table by the absent corpse's head. He squatted at the foot of the mourners' benches and sang a lament called *shrtsiŋə*, "weeping for the dead." The same elderly man performed at most of the "dawn-to-dusk offerings" I attended. His melody was the same as that of the women, but his language was more formal, closer to ritual speech than the more ordinary language of female lamenters. He asserted that this was the correct day and hour for the offering, listed the gifts to the dead, and reported on the details of the surrounding scene--the table and benches, the buckets of water, the rice basket. He described the main task of the day for close male kin of the deceased: gathering the soul from a mountain slope where it had settled into a pine tree, "like a flying fox" and establishing it beneath the roof beam of the deceased's male descendants. And he sang of the flow of water and tears that began with the deceased's daughter ladling water into the absent corpse's shallow "mouth":

> oh your daughter's pitiful eyes        à mo me gè né de lɔ
> over there she ladles water          yi gɔ̀ nó ga bæ

| | |
|---|---|
| ladles over there for you | nó ga bæ gɔ̀ do |
| over here she ladles water | yi gɔ̀ he ga bæ |
| ladles over here for you | he ga bæ gɔ̀ do |
| | |
| oh, pails of water | à mo yi gɔ̀ yi bu bæ |
| clear clean water | yi lu cé lɔ bæ |
| | |
| oh, a river flows | à mo yi dɔ̀ gɔ̀ bu jɔ |
| clear water overflows | yi ji yi bu jɔ |
| flows to the underworld | cí mi jɔ dù yi |
| | |
| oh, the courtyard brims with tears | à mo kæ pe ŋɔ pi lɔ̀ |

The daughter, who began to sing and ladle immediately after the paid mourner, was quickly followed by the women sitting next to her on the mourners' benches. "Once you look at her weeping and ladling water, your own eyes begin to weep," Luo Lizhu explained. Women learned laments by sitting beside mothers, sisters, or friends and repeating their lines. With the exception of kinship terms for the dead, they inserted little biographical detail into their songs. Innovation consisted in elaborating the detail and metaphorical richness of the lament's standard subject--the labor of making the gifts for the dead--in ways that other women could admire and borrow. If the daughter's "pitiful eyes" moved her companions to tears, most of these were not tears for the newly deceased. With the exception of daughters and daughters-in-law, most lamenters mourned others who had died months or years before, begging the newly dead to deliver a portion of their gifts to these other, more remote dead. Here, for instance, a woman pleads with her newly deceased sister's husband's father to pass news and food on to her long-dead father's sister's son and his wife:

| | |
|---|---|
| red billed magpies in the hills | bæ bɔ̀ t'à chi zɔ̀ |
| their only orphaned daughter | né chɪ̀ né ti là |
| lonely and broken-hearted | chi ga go dú rò |
| tell them this | k'o nɪ̀ bɛ gɔ̀ lɔ |
| | |
| she doesn't know how to bear rice | chɪ̀ bùɪ bo kæ n sa ne lu bɛ |
| now you bear this rice on | chɪ̀ bùɪ æ mæ bo dú mà |
| | |
| no need to watch them chew it | su tsò dù me lɔ t'a hɔ nɔ |
| no need to watch them grab it | su dɔ́ dù le nɔ t'à hɔ nɔ |

| | |
|---|---|
| tell them all this | k'o nǐ bɛ le gə̀ lɔ ma |
| | |
| we brought extra meat | hò nà hò kǽ nà lɔ dụ |
| brought extra bowls for rice | chǐ k'ə̀ chǐ cị̆ kǽ lɔ dụ |
| sit on your golden bamboo mats | mo ca gə̀ tị̆ zò |
| | |
| elder sister's husband's father eat a mouthful | yǐ væ̀ su p'ò chǐ chè tsò |
| feed a mouthful to father's sister's son | dụ lè a lù chǐ chè jú lɔ mà |
| feed a mouthful to father's sister's son's wife | a lù lù mo chǐ chè jú lɔ mà |

In ɔchəŋə laments and in the context of their performance nothing--not food, wine, water, ords, tears, nor grief--remains an individual possession. Everything is put into motion, passed from hand to hand, mouth to mouth, and eye to eye. My first instinct as an ethnographer was to approach these laments as expressions of profoundly personal and internal states of grief and pain (Desjarlais 1993). This understanding of affect resonated with my own habits of experiencing grief. My grief is my singular possession; I may express it to others as I maneuver for their pity or respect, but none can truly share it with me. It isolates me even in the company of others who mourn the same person, for I know my relationship with him was unique. Sometimes it becomes a different kind of possession: a state of being. Then it might overwhelm me, take over my body, reduce me to tears or incoherence. But it is still my own state, still fundamentally inaccessible to others. By contrast, the grief these laments fashion is neither a possession nor an individual state of being; it is neither the property of a single grieving subject nor directed at a single object of grief. Mourners move each other and their audiences to tears, and their tears and gifts flow from one object of loss to another. Their sadness is made through shared labor, like the gifts they describe. It emerges from the pain and exhaustion of this labor to become the flows of tears, water, alcohol, and words that immerse those gathered in the courtyard. And it touches me as I wade through the mud it creates.

## GRIEF'S TRANSACTIONS

[Pain is] a medium of exchange, a currency, an equivalent.
Gilles Deleuze (1983, 134)

Of all the laments we collected, my two collaborators admired as most "complete" one sung for her dead mother by Su Ling, a mother of five in her mid-forties. In three lengthy sections, Su Ling detailed the processes of making the three gifts that laments discuss in greatest detail: cooked rice, buckwheat cakes, and hempen cloth. Here, I wish to quote at length from the final section, which describes the gifts of hempen cloth. (From this point on, all selections from this lament will be presented in consecutive order.) Unlike those who used her mother as a messenger to transfer their words, tears, and gifts to other dead, Su Ling addressed her directly. She began the final section as she began the previous two, by reflecting on a difference in the structures of value in the underworld and the world of the living:

| | |
|---|---|
| from today on | ǽ ni tsɜ̀ sɨ́ na |
| mother has passed away | su mo shr yi ga |
| mother has withered away | su mo hɜ̀ yi ga |
| | |
| it is said hemp is dear in the underworld | mó mi tsɨ̀ p'à k'a lo bɛ |
| it is said silver is dear in the underworld | mó mi p'u p'ɜ̀ k'a lo bɛ |
| | |
| mother don't say you don't understand | su mo n sa t'à bɛ |
| don't say you don't hear | m ma t'à bɛ |
| | |
| go use one coin as ten | chɨ̀ che ts'ɨ che tɨ zɛ̀ yi |
| use one ounce as ten | chɨ̀ lò ts'ɨ lò tɨ zɛ̀ yi |

People in Zhizuo agreed that the authorities that establish the value and authenticity of currency apply different standards of value in the underworld; a coin or length of hempen cloth that would insult a living official might successfully bribe a number of dead ones. In the story of the ghost market, the living use a pail of water to sort out these differences, separating coinage into silver and paper--true and false in this world. In mortuary ritual, a member of the deceased's household buys the water that will be ladled into the absent corpse's mouth by casting copper coins into the river. The coins increase in value ten to a hundredfold, and the water bought is a precious gift, for the dead pay dearly for water.

These diverging structures of value are not merely a convenient fantasy in which mourners imagine their gifts to the dead to escape market laws. Zhizuo residents had long experience with the differences in value created by geographical distance. In the first half of the twentieth century, Zhizuo was located on an important trading route, along which some of its inhabitants worked as porters, carrying salt cakes from the nearby salt wells to sale in the lowlands, sugar from the hot lowland plains to the mountains, opium from Sichuan to Yunnan towns, or manufactured goods from the provincial capital to the highlands. After market reforms in the late 1970s, many began again to carry cloth, thread, fruit, candy and patent medicine to sell in the mountains, or lumber from the mountains to sell in town. Mortuary laments take advantage of a similar geographical distance/difference to imagine a shift in the market value of gifts as they cross into the underworld. The flow of water, tears and words transports the gifts over this distance. Grief is transportation or, more accurately, *bearing*.

Laments are rich with images of bearing (*bùi*) on one's back and carrying (*ve*) in one's arms. In her lament, Su Ling repeatedly described how those gathered in the courtyard--her mother's residentially rooted agnatic kin (multiply branched ground-squash vines) and residentially dispersed affinal kin (fragrant but scattered *mə̀nə́* tree leaves)--come bearing and carrying gifts over the path to the underworld:

| | |
|---|---|
| fragrant *mə̀nə́* leaves | mə̀ nə́ p'è̜ jɔ |
| branched ground-squash vines | chì sæ̀ jo tɔ lu |
| | |
| three levels of grandchildren | sa jé̜ lí zò jɔ |
| three layers of great grandchildren | sa də̜ le zò jɔ |
| | |
| two generations of nephews | nì tsí zò tu jɔ |
| three generations of nieces | sa tsí né tu jɔ |
| | |
| come bearing grain on their backs | p'a ká chì̜ bùi k'ò lɔ pe̜ |
| come carrying grain in their arms | lè kò chì̜ te̜ k'ò lɔ pe̜ |
| grain to feed you, mother | chì̜ te̜ su mo jú gə̀ pe̜ |
| | |
| bearing grain on their backs to feed you, mother | p'a ká chì̜ bùi su mo jù gə̀ pe̜ |
| bearing wine to pour for you, mother | ji bùi su mo dɔ gə̀ pe̜ |

The flows of water, tears and words in *ɔchəŋə* laments are explicitly intended to bear gifts across the distance between worlds. Neither a possession nor a state of being, grief is a movement and an exchange. It is a conversion of value, working within the laws of the market while taking advantage of them by exploiting differences in value that pertain over geographical distances.

People in Zhizuo were acutely aware of the dangers of market participation in trade, especially when this involved borrowing capital. Su Ling's lament insisted repeatedly that the gifts for her mother were not borrowed or rented, but earned and saved.

| | |
|---|---|
| silver not rented from the village's head | che wú n jè p'u |
| not borrowed from the village's tail | che mæ n wo p'u |
| | |
| silver earned with your orphaned son's feet | su zò chì̜ chì k'a p'u |

| | |
|---|---|
| earned with your orphaned son's hands | su zò chɨ le k'a p'u |
| silver saved up by fathers and sons | su p'ò jo zò jo tsɔ́ lo p'u |
| gathered by grandsons and great grandsons | lí jo le jo tsɔ́ lo p'u |
| to give to you mother | su mo gɔ̀ yi ga |

Su Ling included similar sections for the gifts of cooked rice, buckwheat cakes, and hempen cloth. As she vouched for the origins of the latter, she implied that borrowing currency involved one in relations with fearsome and unknowable external forces, here figured as wild ghosts.

| | |
|---|---|
| cloth not from ghosts of gullies | sa ká mæ n ŋɔ |
| cloth not from ghosts of ridges | sa bɨ̀ mæ n ŋɔ |
| cloth from your orphaned daughters' hardship | né chɨ shó lo mæ |
| cloth from your orphaned son's pain | |
| | zò chɨ shó lo mæ |

In this mortuary ritual, transactions of gifts that stood for currency--money, paper, incense, and hempen cloth--were structured differently from transactions of other gifts. Grain, meat and wine were passed from hand to hand or mouth to mouth as mourners wept and were embedded in complex, deferred, reciprocal transactions among the participants, involving obligations incurred at numerous former events. But gifts that stood for currency were consumed directly by the dead--burned or buried in the coffin--and people insisted that the giver must either make them herself (in the case of hemp) or scrupulously pay for them with cash (in the cases of paper and incense). "All of these things you must pay for," said Li Hulin, one of those who took time to explain mortuary processes to me:

> Paper, incense, these things are not expensive. But even if you want to give them to me, I still must pay for them. I mustn't borrow a thing. If you don't agree to sell them to me, if you insist on giving them to me, I still must *speak* as though I am buying them.
> Underworld officials (*mómi tsɨ̀mà*) are *very careful about accounts*!

Discrepancies in these accounts can have serious consequences for the living. "For instance, if you steal incense for the dead," Li Huilin continued, "they will cause terrible trouble for you." This trouble might include chronic illness, possession by the dead, or sudden, accidental death. Both before Liberation and during the market reform era, poor mountain residents found that borrowing or stealing capital to participate in market trade was very likely to end in servitude or incarceration. In the 1930s and 1940s the hereditary chieftain, or *tusi*, who controlled the district where Zhizuo was located, lent money to Zhizuo residents at usurious rates. Many ended up working off their debts as laborers in his fields or as porters in his trading enterprises. Some still recall with horror a cell beneath his house where debtors were imprisoned up to their knees or waists in water until their families paid up (Wang and Liu 1989, 139-40). In the 1990s, after a decade of market reforms, those who borrowed substantially to set up tiny shops or engage in the mushroom trade sometimes spoke of their debts as a trap or a burial pit. Borrowing, renting or stealing the currency that guaranteed the dead's safe passage to the underworld had similar results: people described the feeling of being possessed or harmed by the dead as incarceration--being buried in a hole, trapped under an overturned back basket, or imprisoned beneath a tomb (Mueggler 1998b).

Anthropologists commonly interpret ritualized mourning as means to recovery and restoration of social structures or individual psyches breached or threatened by death (see for example Bloch and Parry 1982; Holmberg1989; Ahern 1973). In the poetry of ɔchəŋə laments, however, ritualized grief might as easily be debilitating as restorative; it might as easily incarcerate and punish one's soul as reassure or reconstitute it. Grief is a complex set of transactions that rearranges the boundaries of a living soul in the dead's absence. These transactions are regulated by the conventions of the market established by the state and its various, dispersed bureaucratic authorities: prices, interest, bribes for official services, punishment for unpaid debt. Historically, these conventions more often reduced mountain residents to poverty and servitude than enriched or liberated them, yet they nevertheless remained the conditions under which grief disabled or restored. The poetics of ɔchəŋə laments establish a practical ethics for these transactions, which allows mourners to work within the inevitable terms of power and the law while evading their most devastating effects. In this ethics, the proper currency for grief's transactions is not borrowed, rented, or stolen; it is made through the labor and pain of a family working together. The reason hempen cloth is so dear in the underworld, some in Zhizuo claimed, is that there it was accorded its *true value*--the value of the pain and sweat of its production. Why do underworld officials accept only hemp as bribes, not cotton? Li Hulin: "Because they know that hemp comes from an *extreme amount of work*. You have to grow it, peel it, soak it, boil it, wash it, splice it, spin it, weave it . . ."

The bulk of Su Ling's lament makes precisely this point, systematically describing all of this work, from preparing the mountain fields to weaving. Making the currency of grief, rather than borrowing or stealing it, the lament implies, also has its costs: pain, exhaustion, the gradual wearing away of one's living flesh. Yet it is only through such labor that the memory of the absent dead may be composed and decomposed in such a way as to evade its devastating effects. I will quote only a few brief sections of Su Ling's description of the work of making hempen cloth, beginning with the with the second and third months, when the family bears manure up the mountain:

| | |
|---|---|
| prepare leather carrying straps | hò ji bæ wú jù do go |
| prepare bamboo back baskets | mò cæ k'a má jù do go |
| prepare yellow wooden yokes | sí cæ ǽ pæ jù do go |
| | |
| the left hand takes a manure scoop | vǽ lè jin cho də do go |
| the right hand carries a hoe | rò lè tsɨ mò ve do go |
| to the yellow ox's barn | lò cæ lɔ pi he |
| the golden mare's stable | mò cæ ho pi he |
| the black pig's sty | vè ne t'ù pi he |
| the raven goats' corral | chì ne k'ə pi he |
| | |
| dig manure and fill a back basket | chì ka mò cæ k'a má jè do go |
| mothers and sons bear together | mo pɔ zò pɔ bùɨ do go |
| sons and daughters in law bear together | chì pɔ zò pɔ bùɨ do go |
| grandchildren and great grandchildren bear together | lí pɔ le pɔ bùɨ do go |
| spread manure on mountain fields | bùɨ yi wò mo mi ka hə̀ do go |

The manured fields must be plowed with "a harness of braided vines, a wooden yoke and plow frame, an iron tongued plow," Then, "within the pine-shingled barn, within the tile-roofed house," mothers and daughters winnow and sieve hemp seeds. They "shake and rattle to sieve, toss and circle to winnow." They "carve a yellow wood ladle, plait a golden bamboo urn, prepare a bamboo scoop" and scoop the seed into a little hempen bag. "Mothers and daughters-in-law, grandchildren and great-grandchildren bear hemp seed up the mountain, bear to the field's head, bear to the field's tail." Then,

| | |
|---|---|
| your orphaned son comes | zò chɨ zò te lɔ |
| uses a plow oxen in the field | mi ka lò mò zè do go |
| | |
| his left hand grasps the little hemp bag | vǽ lè tsɨ mæ lɔ́ zò jæ̀ |
| his right hand sows the hemp seeds | rò lè tsɨ shɨ́ shɨ́ do go |
| | |
| once the seeds are sown | tsɨ shɨ́ tsɨ wo le |
| where will the hemp grow? | tsɨ næ̀ dù m ma |

In the fourth and fifth months, when each hemp plant is but two slim leaves, mothers and daughters, fathers and sons, drive wild animals from the fields' head and livestock from the field's tail, only to find "all the earth's wild grasses, all the earths wild leaves" growing among the hemp seedlings.

| | |
|---|---|
| the right hand grasps an iron scythe | væ̀ lè hə la jæ̀ do go |
| the left hand takes the grass stems | rò lè cí la jæ̀ do go |
| | |
| cut down the grasses | cí chæ̀ p'i do go |
| pull up the weeds | cí mò p'i do go |
| cut grass from the field's borders | tí p'æ cí ji p'i do go |
| pull weeds from the field's center | mi ka cí mò p'i do go |

In the seventh and eight months, the hemp is harvested, separated into male and female, and stacked in round stacks in the fields to dry. Once dry, it is borne down the mountain, to "a house of mountain logs, a barn of stacked logs" and put away. Then, in the frosty eleventh and twelfth months, it is borne down to the river to soak. It is in speaking of soaking and peeling the stalks that Su Ling most eloquently evoked the pain and exhaustion hemp work entails:

| | |
|---|---|
| bear it to eleven gullies to soak | tsɨ̀ bùɨ ts'i tí kè chè tɨ́ do go |
| soak it in twelve stream mouths | ts'i nɨ̀ kə̀ lí tɨ́ do go |
| | |
| hands work like iron bars | lè və̀ hə̀ və̀ mo do go |
| fingers work like iron needles | lè ni hə̀ ka mo do go |
| | |
| labor in eleven gullies | ts'i tí kə̀ chè t'è̩ le |
| labor in twelves streams | ts'i nɨ̀ kə̀ lí t'è̩ le |
| | |
| press the stalks with huge rocks | lo ŋá tsɨ̀ mo p'æ t'è̩ zɨ do go |
| rocks are so hard to move! | lo ŋá shó do go |
| three sides of your thumb wear away | lè mo sa p'à kə |
| three knuckles of your fingers wear away | le ni sa tsɨ kə |
| clenching wet and cold | je chɨ̀r ni tə tə |
| | |
| such hard-won cloth | k'o nɨ̀ shò lə mæ̀ |
| to give to you mother | su mo gə̀ do go |
| | |
| painful thumbs grasp the stalks | tsɨ̀ tsa lè mo shó |
| painful fingers peel them | tsɨ̀ k'à lè ni shó |

peel all day                                          mùi ni k'a do go


The skins are washed "with painful toes" (hemp was washed in running streams with one's feet), borne back up to the house, and dried under its tiled eaves. Once dried, the skins are separated, "long from short, big from little" and then pounded into a tangled mass:

make a mortar from a split stone                     lo mo ts'ɛ k'ù pe̠
make a pounder's mouth from fir                      ŋə mo ts'ɛ mè pe̠
make a pounder's body from sæpɔ́ wood               sæ pɔ́ ts'ɛ me pe̠
make a peg from bætí wood                            bæ tí ts'ɛ lɔ pe̠
make a crosspiece from cedar                         tsæ̀ mo ts'ɛ cé pe

pound the hemp thus                                  k'o nǐ tsɨ k'u tí do go

once the hemp is pounded                             tsɨ k'u tí wo wo le
painful thumbs shred it                              tsɨ k'à lè mo shó do go
painful fingers splice it                            tsɨ je̠ lè ni shó do go

once the hemp is spliced                             tsɨ je̠ tsɨ wo le
where to spin it?                                    jè va dù m ma


The spliced strands are spun on a "yellow wood frame, a golden bamboo spinning wheel, a palm-leaf spindle." The thread is wound onto "golden wood spools," boiled in a pot on the stove, borne down to the river and washed "in eleven gullies, in twelve streams." It is then borne back to the house, dried out again under the tiled eves, unwound from the spools, pounded in the treadle pounder until it is soft, then wound onto bamboo reels. At last, the warp can be prepared:

once the thread is spooled                           p'i jo do go le
once the thread is reeled                            p'i jo p'i wo le
where to string the warp?                            yè cæ̠ dù m ma

prepare six posts of yellow wood                     sí cæ ŋɔ́ chè jù do go
plant six posts at the courtyard's head              kæ wú ŋɔ́ chè t'e̠ do go
plant six posts at the courtyard's tail              kæ mæ ŋɔ́ chè t'è̠ do go

prepare an eyed bamboo frame                         mò cæ cæ̠ me jù mæ̀ næ
string the warp thus                                 k'o nǐ cæ̠ do go
string it through the frame's eyes                   yè cæ̠ yè me mò do go

A loom is set up in the courtyard, its posts made of *bætí* wood, its beams made of pine, with hempen heddles and a bamboo comb to pound the weft. The thread is finally woven, "with painful laboring hands, with painful iron fingers."

These verbal reconstructions of sensuous bodily actions weave for the singer and those moved by her song a shroud that constitutes memory of her dead mother. This shroud wraps an absence: mother's absent corpse, her empty bed, her seat at the fire, her quiet loom, the courtyard where her footfalls are heard no longer. Like the woven gaps or "eyes" in her hempen shrouds, mother's absence is everywhere, in each of the pain-laden activities through which mothers and daughters together created gifts of hemp. Near the end of her lament, Su Ling sang of this absence as a loss of sensuous contact with her mother, of the mutual gaze of loving faces, the touch of elbows as mother and daughter sat together, and especially the breath of speech:

| | |
|---|---|
| unwilting flowers of the ghost world | nè mi tə hə̀ zò |
| mother has wilted away | su mo hə̀ yi ga |
| unripening persimmons of the underworld | cí mi tsæ̧ bæ zò |
| mother has ripened away | su mo bæ yi ga |
| | |
| her carrying strap has broken | bæ jò bæ mǽ ts'i |
| mother's breath has faltered [. . .] | mo cè ts'i yi ga [ . . .] |
| | |
| daughters tell mothers of their pain | ne shó mo t'ȩ̀ t'ə |
| they speak without resting [. . .] | t'ə ga t'ù n jɔ [. . .] |
| | |
| mother's breath has halted | à mo cè ts'i yi ga |
| our faces no longer gaze with love | p'à p'o ní n yæ̀ ga pȩ |
| our elbows no longer touch | tsɨ p'o lè n gə̀ ga pȩ |
| | |
| mother no longer tells her daughter of her pain | mo shó ne t'ȩ̀ n t'ə̀ ga |
| mother no longer pities her daughter | mo liñ t'ȩ̀ n tsa̧ ga |

The daughter's unending speech flows into this emptiness like water into the absent corpse's mouth. What is transported or *borne* by this flow is the shared bodily substance of a family working together--its pain, breath, tears, and flesh. The flow is a diminishment of living bodies to wrap and nourish the dead's memory, a wearing away of the fingers and thumbs that shred and splice hemp strands or grasp and peel stalks in icy water.

Yet even as it composes memory of the dead from the absences that texture the world, Su Ling's lament also decomposes that memory. It unravels the wraps that define the shape of the absent corpse into the labor of their production. It translates the empty shroud back into the bodily actions that created it, dispersing it in the long flow of words through walking and bearing to and from the mountain fields, washing and peeling in cold streams, shredding and splicing while tramping village and mountain paths. This balance between composing memory of absences and decomposing it into the presences of life and life-giving labor is the essence of the delicate transaction between living and dead cataloged in ɔchɔŋɔ laments. To negotiate this balance through grief is to extricate oneself from the domination of one's debts to the dead. At the end of her chant, Su Ling expressed the hope that the gifts her grief bore to her mother would forestall the possibility of her own future poverty and servitude. She asked her mother not to destroy the wealth of her family as she lived on forever in the memories of generations of descendants: "let herding go smoothly, let selling go well, let buying go smoothly . . . don't destroy our sea of wealth, don't destroy our overflowing granary."

Grief can nourish or destroy. If the absences left by the dead and woven together by grief become too palpable, assuming the vague flesh of ghosts, they might isolate and immobilize their descendants, trapping their souls as though under baskets or in holes, or weighing them down as though under tombstones. If those absences go unremarked, the unappeased dead may take out their wrath on their descendants' households, attacking the health and fertility of crops, animals and people alike. Su Ling picked out a precarious path between these possibilities as her flow of words and tears at once spun intimate threads of shared pain with her mother and gently unraveled those threads. The shroud with which she shut away her mother's absent corpse from sight and sound was intended to nullify at last the capacity of her debts to, and memory of, her mother to do her harm.

That the currency with which mourners escape domination by memory of the dead was hempen cloth was an irony of which Su Ling and her fellow mourners were acutely aware. Women in Zhizuo made hempen cloth the currency of their economic "liberation" between 1950 and 1978. In the early 1950s, work with hemp helped them extricate themselves and their households from the domination of landlords and trading enterprises; between 1956 and 1978, it helped them attain a measure of independence from the production teams that directly controlled their labor in all other significant economic activities. The hempen gifts in Su Ling's mother's coffin were probably made by mother and daughter together in the late seventies, and stored unsold after the precipitous fall in hemp prices left hempen cloth valueless. Su Ling's appeal to the differences in the structures of value in the realm of the living and that of the dead, implied that the officials of the underworld rendered hemp its "true" value, the value of the labor it embodied under the favorable price conditions of the collectivist era. Implicit in Su Ling's grief was a powerful complaint against the injustice of the current structure of prices and the distant socialist-bureaucratic edifice imagined to set prices. Yet, contrary to views of grief as ironic resistance, Su Ling did not sing to protest this injustice, nor to mourn the lost "sea of wealth" mother and daughter had once filled together. She sang to mourn her dead mother. Still, the forms of mourning subjected her grief to the bureaucratically established laws that regulated market transactions. The historical trajectory of these laws--including the liberating power of hemp work in the collectivist period and the recent and devastating loss of that power--were among the conditions of possibility for her grief. This history had powerfully shaped the shared pain of mothers and daughters of which lamenters sang. Now Su Ling and her companions fashioned it into the flow of words with which they moved each other to tears and transported their gifts across the screened market street that regulated their memories of the dead.

## CONCLUSIONS

In Li Yong's tale of the "underworld ghost market," distinctions between visible and invisible, and between authentic and unauthentic, were brought into being as living and dead negotiated transactions under the regulatory eye of underworld officials. Among the tasks of the living was to discriminate between authentic copper money--authentic because it was invested with value by the state--and unauthentic paper money. Before this distinction was made, living and dead transacted freely; afterwards, exchanges across the market street involving money gradually came to an end. It is the same with speaking, seeing, biting, and beating: in each case a discrimination is made and a porous barrier to exchanges created through the authority of underworld officials. In the poetics of mourning, to make the transition from an unregulated, potentially devastating state of grief was also to make discriminations that gradually subjected one's transactions with the dead to the abstract authority of the state. Mourning ritual engaged with state power as a distant, imagined unity rather than with the immediate, embodied authority of local officials. This abstract unity, essential to state legitimacy (Anagnost 1987; 1992), was made immediate and palpable to Zhizuo residents in the early 1950s as the socialist state raised hemp prices, decisively transforming the conditions under which people fed and clothed their families. When market reforms began in the late 1978, people in Zhizuo again found themselves directly affected by abstract market laws and the distant institutions imagined to control them, as hemp prices plunged, transforming every aspect of life and work at least as effectively as the periodic political campaigns to which they had been subject for thirty years. The poetics of mourning engaged people's imagination of this abstract and disembodied state authority through the use of hemp. Like work with hemp, the work of grief involved Zhizuo residents with invisible forces with the potential to bring them disaster or prosperity. As mourning wove a porous shroud to render the dead invisible, muffle their speech, and sharpen their hearing, it made their communications as mysterious and difficult to read as the messages emanating from distant state institutions, which the wise might also use to divine prosperity or disaster in the future. At the same time, mourning made hemp a currency for grief's transactions across this shroud, subjecting grief to the rules that governed market exchanges: price differences across spatial and temporal distances, punishment for unpaid debt, bribes for official services.

To submit grief to these laws was to make it social in a particular way. Mourning was not the expression of a prior internal state of grief and loss so much as a collective reorganization of boundaries. While pathological grief might be the singular possession of an individual--his trap, prison, or burial pit--ritualized mourning fashioned grief as a communal, corporeal labor, like the labor of making hempen cloth. In this way, mourning engaged with power and the law, not as a strategic competition for social status, but as a practical, collective ethics. Under this ethics, the work of grief, like the labor of making cloth, created an authentic currency for market transactions, not borrowed, stolen, nor rented, but created through shared labor and pain. Grief fashioned under these conditions evaded the pits and tombs of unpaid debt; it gradually raveled and unraveled a shroud for the absent dead, in the end rendering this absence powerless to do harm.

While in many ways the verbal and material poetics of grief I have touched on here were specific to one small mountainous corner of China's Southwest, in others they resonate with what we already know of ritualized mourning in China. Li Yong's tale of the "underworld ghost market," for instance, brings to mind a rich historical and ethnographic literature on detailed underworld "spirit realms" evoked by rituals and literature of mourning throughout China. In these realms, hierarchies of spirit officials oversee the dead, conducting tribunals, dispensing justice, ordering tortures, collecting taxes, circulating documents, engaging in corruption, and receiving honors and chastisements in ways that seem to mirror the activities of officials in the Imperial bureaucracy (see for example Teiser 1988; Kuhn 1990; Kleeman 1993; Ebrey and Gregory 1993; Johnson 1995). Scholarship on popular religions in China has inquired most frequently about the sociological function of transactions with these spirit realms: did they serve to legitimate state authority? Did they disguise the economic control that landholding elites exercised over all other classes? Did they enable ordinary people to mount resistance to this domination? Or did they teach people to understand and manipulate the real bureaucratic apparatus to which they were subject?[21] Though legitimate and interesting, these questions have tended to eclipse inquiries into the grief and loss which lies at the root of these transactions, and which must ultimately underlie any engagement of mourning with state or economic power. Like the "underworld ghost market," the spirit realms of Chinese popular religions were imagined arenas in which people worked out the discriminations between authentic and unauthentic, true and apparent, through which they gradually separated themselves from the dead. Imaginative transactions with the dead and the officials who oversaw them were very likely most often in the service of these discriminations--that is, ultimately in the service of the work of mourning, however distant or attenuated. That, in renderings of such spirit realms, each transaction was accomplished under the supervision of imagined officials should tell us as much about the topography of grief as it tells us about attitudes towards external bureaucratic authorities. Here I have attempted to show how in one corner of the Southwest a remembered history of market conventions and the imagined authority that backed them were among the conditions for grief's social existence. Further investigations into how the rituals and literatures of mourning in China fashion affect might sensitize us to the parts pain and loss play in the imaginative representations of political power still characteristic of popular religion everywhere in China.

## LIST OF REFERENCES

ABU-LUGHOD, LILA, and CATHERINE A. LUTZ. 1990. Introduction to *Language and the Politics of Emotion,* edited by Lila Abu-Lughod and Catherine A. Lutz, New York: Cambridge University Press.

AHERN, EMILY M. 1973. *Cult of the Dead in a Chinese Village.* Stanford: Stanford University Press.

_____. 1981. *Chinese Ritual and Politics.* Cambridge: Cambridge University Press.

ANAGNOST, ANN. 1987. "Politics and Magic in Contemporary China." *Modern China* 13:40-61.

_____. 1992. "Socialist Ethics and the Legal System." In *Popular Protest and Political Culture in Modern China: Learning From 1989,* edited by Jeffrey Wasserstrom and Elizabeth Perry. Boulder, Colo.: Westview Press.

BLOCH, MAURICE, and JONATHAN PERRY, eds. 1982. *Death and the Regeneration of Life.* Cambridge: Cambridge University Press.

BRADLEY, DAVID. 1979. *Proto Loloish.* London, Malmo: Curzon Press.

CHAO, KANG. 1975. "The Growth of a Modern Cotton Textile Industry and the Competition with Handicrafts." In *China's Modern Economy in Historical Perspective*, edited by Dwight Perkins. Stanford: Stanford University Press.

_____. 1977. *The Development of Cotton Textile Production in China.* Cambridge:

Harvard University Press.

CHEN SHILIN. 1963. "A Brief Description of the Yi Language." *Chinese Linguistics* 125:334-347.

CHEN SHILIN, et. al. 1984. *Yiyu jianzhi* [A brief description of the Yi language]. Chengdu: Sichuan minzu chubanshe.

CHENG WEIJI. 1992. *History of Textile Technology of Ancient China*. New York: Science Press.

CORNFORD, FRANCIS M., ed. and trans. 1951. *The Republic of Plato*. New York: Oxford University Press.

DELEUZE, GILLES. 1983. *Nietzsche and Philosophy,* translated by Hugh Tomlinson. London: Athlone.

DESJARLAIS, ROBERT R. 1993. *Body and Emotion: The Aesthetics of Illness and Healing in the Nepal Himalayas*. Philadelphia: University of Pennsylvania Press.

DUARA, PRASENJIT. 1988. Myth of Guandi: Chinese God of War. *Journal of Asian Studies* 47(4):778-95.

EBREY, PATRICIA BUCKLEY, and PETER N. GREGORY. 1993. "The Religious and Historical Landscape." In *Religion and Society in Tang and Sung China*, edited by Patricia Buckley Ebrey and Peter N. Gregory. Honolulu: University of Hawaii Press.

ELVIN, MARK. 1972. "The High-Level Equilibrium Trap: The Causes of the Decline of Invention in the Traditional Chinese Textile Industries." In *Economic Organization in Chinese Society,* edited by W. E. Willmott. Stanford: Stanford University Press.

FEI, HSIAO-TUNG and CHIH-I CHANG. 1949. *Earthbound China: A Study of Rural Economy in Yunnan*. London: Routledge.

FEUTCHTWANG, S. 1992. *The Imperial Metaphor: Popular Religion in China*. London: Routledge.

HARRELL, STEVAN. 1995. "Introduction: Civilizing Projects and the Reaction to Them. In *Cultural Encounters on China's Ethnic Fontiers*, edited by Stevan Harrell. Seattle: University of Washington Press.

Harvard Yenching Institute, eds. 1962. *A Concordance to Shih Ching.* Tokyo: Japan Council for East Asian Studies.

HERZFELD, MICHEAL. 1993. "In Defiance of Destiny: the Management of Time and Gender at a Cretan Funeral." *American Ethnologist* 20(2):241-55.

HINTON, WILLIAM. 1967. *Fanshen; a Documentary of Revolution in a Chinese Village*. New York: Monthly Review Press.

HOLMBERG, DAVID. 1989. *Order in Paradox: Myth, Ritual and Exchange among Nepal's Tamang*. Ithaca: Cornell University Press.

HSU, CHO-YUN. 1965. *Ancient China in Transition: An Analysis of Social Mobility, 722-222*

*B.C.* Stanford: Stanford University Press.

HSU, FRANCIS. 1967. *Under the Ancestors' Shadow: Kinship, Personality, and Social Mobility in Village China.* Garden City, N.Y.: Doubleday & Company, Inc.

JOHNSON, ELIZABETH L. 1988. "Grieving for the Dead, Grieving for the Living: Funeral Laments of Hakka Women." In *Death Ritual in Late Imperial and Modern China,* edited by J. L. Watson and E. S. Rawski. Berkeley: University of California Press.

KLEEMAN, TERRY F. 1993. "The Expansion of the Wen-Ch'ang Cult." In *Religion and Society in Tang and Sung China,* edited by Patricia Buckley Ebrey and Peter N. Gregory. Honolulu: University of Hawaii Press.

KLIGMAN, GAIL A.1988. *The Wedding of the Dead: Ritual, Poetics and Popular Culture in Transylvania.* Berkeley: University of California Press.

KUHN, DIETER. 1988. *Science and Civilization in China.* Edited by Joseph Needham. *Vol. 5, Chemistry and Chemical Technology. Pt. 9. Textile Technology: Spinning and Reeling.* Cambridge: Cambridge University Press.

KUHN, PHILIP A. 1990. *Soulstealers: The Chinese Sorcery Scare of 1786.* Cambridge: Harvard University Press.

LIÉTARD, ALFRED P. 1913. *Au Yun-Nan, Les Lolo p'o: Une tribu des aborigènes de la Chine meridionale.* Munster: Aschendorff.

LIN YUEH-HWA. 1961 [1947]. *The Lolo of Liang Shan.* Translated by Ju-shu Pan. New Haven: HRAF Press

LIU HONGCHU. 1957. *Wo guo di ma* [Our nation's hemp]. Beijing: Shizheng Jingji Chubanshe.

LIU, TA-CHUNG, and KUNG-CHIA YEH. 1965. *The Economy of the Chinese Mainland: National Income and Economic Development, 1933-1959.* Princeton: Princeton University Press.

MA XUELIANG. 1951. *A Study of Sani, an Yi Dialect.* Beijing: Academy of Sciences.

_____. 1992. *Minzu yanjiu wenji* [Collected works on nationalities research]. Beijing: Minzu chubanshe.

MANN, SUSAN. 1997. *Precious Records: Women in China's Long Eighteenth Century.* Stanford: Stanford University Press.

MASCHINO, THOMAS. 1992. "To Remember the Faces of the Dead: Mourning and the Full Sadness of Memory in Southwestern New Britain." *Ethos* 20(4):387-420.

MUEGGLER, ERIK. 1997. *Specters of Power: Ritual and Politics in an Yi Community.* Ph.D. diss. The Johns Hopkins University.

_____1998a. "Procreative Metaphor and Productive Unity in an Yi Headmanship." *Journal of the Royal Anthropological Institute (Incorporating Man)* 4(2):61-78.

_____1998b. "A Carceral Regime: Violence and Social Memory in Southwest China."

*Cultural Anthropology* 13(2).

OI, JEAN. 1989. *State and Peasant in Contemporary China, The Political Economy of Village Government.* Berkeley and Los Angeles: University of California Press.

QIAO FENG, ed. 1996. *Yaoan Xian zhi* [Yaoan County gazetteer]. Kunming: Yunnan remmin chubanshe.

ROSE, GILLIAN. 1996. *Mourning Becomes the Law: Philosophy and Representation.* Cambridge: Cambridge University Press.

TEISER, STEPHEN F. 1988. *The Ghost Festival in Medieval China.* Princeton: Princeton University Press.

WALKER, KATHY L. 1993. "Economic Growth, Peasant Marginalization, and the Sexual Division of Labor in Early Twentieth-Century China." *Modern China* 19(3):354-86.

WANG YUZHU and LIU ZEJIAN. 1989. "Dizhu Xia Hao de shuilao" [Landlord Xia Hao's water cell]. *Yongren lishi ziliao xuanji* [Selected materials on Yongren History] 1:139-40.

WATSON, JAMES L., ed. 1988. *Death Ritual in Late Imperial and Modern China.* Berkeley: University of California Press.

WELLER, ROBERT P. 1987 "The Politics of Ritual Disguise: Repression and Response in Taiwanese Popular Religion." *Modern China* 13(1):17-39.

Yunnan Sheng bianjizu, ed. 1986 [1950]. *Yunnan Yizu shehui lishi diaocha* [Investigations of Yunnan Yi society and history]. Vol. 162. Kunming: Yunnan renmin chubanshe.

Yunnan Sheng difangzhi bianzan weiyuanhui, ed. 1992. *Yunnan Sheng zhi. 17 juan. Gongxiao hezuoshe zhi.* [Gazetteer of Yunnan Province. Vol. 17. Supply and Marketing Cooperatives gazetteer.] Kunming: Yunnan renmin chubanshe.

Yunnan Sheng renkou tongji bangongshi, ed. 1990. *Yunnan Sheng disici renkou tongji shougong huizong ziliao* [Manual tabulation of major figures from the fourth population census of Yunnan Province]. Kunming: Yunnan renmin chubanshe.

*Yunnan Sheng zhi jingji zonghe zhi* [Economic statistics gazetteer of Yunnan Province]. 1989-1995. Kunming: Yunnan renmin chubanshe.

ZHANG, RUHAI. 1984. *Nongchan jige wenti yanjiu* [Research on some problems of agricultural prices]. Shanghai: Renmin chubanshe.

*Zhongguo fangzhi gongye nianjian* [Almanac of China's textile industry].1994. Beijing: Zhongguo fangzhi chubanshe.

## ENDNOTES

1. From song 137 in the Harvard Yenching Concordance (Harvard Yenching Institute 1962, 28); my translation.

2. Throughout this chapter, I use words, phrases, and chants from two different languages, in which nearly all Zhizuo residents were bilingual: Mandarin Chinese and Lòloŋo, which may be considered a subdialect of the Central dialect of Yi, a Loloish Tibeto-Burman language (Bradley 1979; Chen 1963). To distinguish these two languages, Lòloŋo terms and chants are left unmarked, while romanized Mandarin terms are followed in their first use by /[M]/. Chinese pronunciations in this region vary widely, from a local variation of Yunnan Mandarin to the standard Mandarin used in radio and television broadcasts. For the sake of clarity, however, I use the standard romanization system used in the People's Republic of China (*pinyin*[M]) to transcribe all Chinese words and phrases. My orthography of Lòloŋo emends in the following ways a version of the International Phonetic Alphabet employed by Ma Xueliang (1951, 1992) to record Yi languages: (1) Five aveopalatal consonants are represented as /ch/ (voiceless aspirated), /j/ (voiced), /c/ and /sh/ (voiceless fricative) and /r/ (voiced fricative). (2) Only three tones are distinguished: high level and mid-high rising tones are marked with an acute accent; low falling tones with a grave accent, and mid level and mid-high level tones are unmarked. (3) Underlining of vowels indicates laryngealization or a final glottal stop.

3. Commenting on Plato's cave parable, Cornford remarks, "The image was probably taken from mysteries held in caves or dark chambers representing the underworld, through which the candidates for initiation were led to the revelation of sacred objects in a blaze of light" (Cornford 1951, 227)

4. Zhizuo ( ᵃ½ -ˋ ) is the official, written name for this area, used on all maps and administrative documents. The second character means "hemp," hinting at outsiders' associations of that product with this area and its inhabitants. Zhizuo is a transliteration of the Lòloŋo name, Júzò, preferred by locals, and meaning "little valley."

5. Thirteen months of field research were conducted in Zhizuo between October 1991 and June 1993. Sponsoring units were the Yunnan Academy of Social Sciences in Kunming and the Yi Culture Research Institute in Chuxiong.

6. Zhizuo was part of Dayao county until 1962. In 1925, Yongren County was created out of the northernmost section (*fensi*[M]) of Dayao, but Zhizuo remained within Dayao's Zhonghe district (*qu*[M]), controlled by the Xia family of hereditary officials (*tusi*[M]). Chuxiong Yi Autonomous Prefecture was created in 1950, incorporating Dayao and Yongren as its northernmost counties. In 1958, when the political lines of China's rural areas were redrawn, most of Zhonghe district, including most of Zhizuo, was added to Yongren Commune. From 1958 to 1962, Yongren Commune was absorbed with four other former counties into Dayao County. It became an independent county in 1962, taking Zhizuo

with it. This redivision left a few outlying villages formerly included within Zhizuo in Dayao County (*Yunnan Sheng bianjizu* 1986 [1950], 109; *Yunnan Sheng renkou tongji bangongshi* 1990).

7. While many of these peoples had long been called Yi (彝 ) in historical and administrative texts, the Nationalities Commission adopted a different character with the same pronunciation (ÂU) to neutralize the derogatory connotations of the term as formerly written. Yi were one of the most complex and diverse of all the "nationalities" (*minzu*[M]) produced in this project: six major subgroups were identified, speaking six mutually mostly unintelligible dialects, and using at least four different varieties of written script (Chen et. al. 1984). Some of these subgroups exhibit very significant differences in social structure. Northern dialect groups, for instance, residing mostly in Sichuan, have neolocal marriage, highly developed patriclan systems, and a structure of strictly ranked and strictly endogamous social strata (Lin 1961 [1947]; Harrell 1995, 65), while the other dialect groups have mostly virilocal marriage, weak to non-existent clan organization and, in the case of the Lòlop'ò of this chapter, practices intended to level out some economic inequalities (Mueggler 1998a). The 1990 census put the number Yi at 6,572,173. Of these about 600,000 are members of the Central dialect group, which includes the people of Zhizuo. In Western writings, Yi groups most often appear as Lolo, from the derogatory Chinese term Luoluo, applied to many of these peoples by their neighbors and administrators for centuries. People in Zhizuo tend to find highly insulting the suggestion that the word Lòlop'ò (Lòlo people) might be derived from the former derogatory designation, insisting instead that it comes from the ancient Lòloŋo word for tiger or ox, *lò*.

8. Liétard found that Lòlop'ò often mixed their hempen yarn with yarn from a wild plant, *gerbera delavayi* (*huocao*[M]), which produced a boll resembling that of cotton (1913, 101-2).

9.The plain of Goudi, on the borders of Dayao and Yaoan counties.

10.*Cannabis sativa* and *boehmeria nivia*, respectively (Kuhn 1988, 27). Throughout this chapter, I use the word *hemp* to refer exclusively to the former plant and its products, rather than, as *hemp* is often used in English and *ma* in Chinese, to mean bast-fiber products in general.

11. Liétard's Pe-ien-tsin and Fleuve Bleu, respectively.

12. After the formal self-ascription used in many of these communities: "Lip'ò Limo," or "Li men and women."

13.Hsu made a similar calculation in 1943 for weavers in a village near Dali. There, according to Hsu, a woman weaving all day could earn about 60 percent of what she could earn in field labor (1967, 71).

14. Units of measure used here are as follows. A *mu* is about 1/15 hectare (or 1/6 acre), a *fen* a tenth of a *mu*. A *sheng* is about 1.08 liters (or 0.96 quarts). A catty *(jin)* is about ½ a kilogram (or 1.1 pounds); a *sheng* of husked rice weighs about 1.6 catties. A *ke,* the unit of measure used for hempen cloth, was about 17 centimeters wide by 50 long (or 6 by 18 inches). Zhizuo residents used these Mandarin terms (with local pronunciations) for marketing.

15. A phrase used throughout rural China to describe a person's personal, economic and ideological transformation during the land reform campaign (Hinton 1967).

16. In the 1960s and 1979s, hemp production in most of Yunnan declined in response to the state's renewed emphasis on grain production as the main peasant activity. Areas such as Yongren and Dayao counties, where hemp was planted land unsuitable for grain, became the province's largest hemp producers (*Yunnan Sheng difangzhi bianzan weiyuanhui* 1992, 158).

17. For examples of the tables Supply and Marketing Cooperative officials used to grade raw hemp, see Liu 1957, 8. The hemp grown in northern Yunnan was *huoma*[M], or Sichuan hemp, and was priced according to the standards for Sichuan, Hebei, Shanxi, Shandong.

18. *Kukædo* "courtyard dance," *nihèpi* "dawn-to-dusk offering," and *shangfen*[M] "ascending to the grave," respectively. This sequence was a truncated version of a much longer funeral process that Zhizuo residents once conducted after the death of every adult. Before 1953, two further large-scale mortuary rituals were performed for every adult: a "tenth-month sacrifice" (*ts'ïhonèpi*) held on the lunar calendar's tenth month following a death, and a "sleeping in the wilds" (*likádùhè*) ceremony held several years after a death. The latter ritual was prohibited during the Land Reform movement in 1953, the former discontinued during the Great Leap Forward in 1958 (see Mueggler 1997).

19. Kuhn's source is Hsu 1965, 123.

20. Here as in all mortuary responsibilities, parents, siblings or other kin could substitute for sons or daughters if the dead left no descendants.

21. For representative discussions of each of these positions, see Duara 1988; Feutchtwang 1992; Weller 1987; and Ahern 1981, respectively.

# POLITICAL STALEMATE AND ECONOMIC DYNAMISM: THE MAINLAND CHINA-TAIWAN RELATIONSHIP REVISITED

*Qi Luo*
East Asian Institute
National University of Singapore
AS5, Level 4
10 Kent Ridge Crescent
Singapore 119260
Tel: 65 – 874 4338; Fax: 65 – 774 1084
E-mail: eailuoq@nus.edu.sg

## ABSTRACT

This paper reviews the development of the mainland China-Taiwan relationship since 1979 by highlighting key features of and identifying major problems faced by political, economic, social and cultural relations between the two sides. In terms of political relations, the lack of channels through which Beijing and Taipei can regularly and meaningfully interact has characterized cross-Strait relations over the past two decades. As a result, both sides have been prone to misperception and miscalculation, as illustrated by the crises in 1995-96. Since then, with the second "Wang-Koo Meeting" in mainland China in October 1998, mutual understanding has significantly improved, stabilizing the bilateral relationship somewhat. However, deep disagreement and mutual suspicion remain over the terms of reunification.

With regard to economic interactions, the pursuit of commercial interests has often been caught in the tug-of-war between economic and political forces. On the ground of national security, Taipei has implemented a cautious and restrictive policy towards mainland-bound investments, but this has not stopped the Taiwan economy from becoming more reliant on the mainland market. Indeed, the strong desire to benefit from cross-Strait economic co-operation on the part of business communities on both sides has pushed such co-operation up to a more advanced level, despite frequent political bickering. There can be no doubt that growing economic, social and cultural exchanges have significantly narrowed the gaps between the two economies and societies.

The prospects for future cross-Strait relations are still far from certain. Washington's China policy could be deflected by strong pro-Taiwan sentiments in the U.S.; there are some on both sides of the Strait who advocate a quick resolution to the Taiwan issue through extremist actions. Furthermore, political democratization in Taiwan has made the future more unpredictable. Indeed, if Beijing and Taipei fail to agree upon mechanisms to stabilize their relationship, cross-Strait relations could easily fall back to the old pattern of oscillation between military confrontation and peaceful manoeuvring.

## INTRODUCTION

In the late 1970s, the People's Republic of China (PRC), having emerged from three decades of economic autarky and political upheavals of the Maoist era, launched the reform and open-door policy with a view to modernizing its economy by the end of the $20^{th}$ century. Following the abandonment of Mao's leftist ideology which favours political struggle over economic advancement, the post-Mao pragmatic leadership centred by Deng Xiaoping decided to make rapid economic growth as the top priority for the Chinese Communist Party (CCP) and the government over the next two decades or so. This fundamental change demanded a series of adjustments and changes in China's domestic and foreign policies in order to create what the new leadership called "favourable domestic and international conditions" for the country's modernization drive. Mainland China's policy toward Taiwan, as an integral part of its foreign policy, has thus come under review.

However, the key factor which eventually led Beijing to change its Taiwan policy was an important shift in Sino-US relations in the late 1970s. On 16 December 1978, the U.S. and the PRC governments signed a joint communiqué to officially recognize each other. From 1 January 1979, Washington would recognize the PRC as the sole legitimate government of China and sever its official ties with Taipei. No longer feeling the direct threat from the U.S. over the Taiwan issue, Beijing subsequently changed its Taiwan policy radically, with the objective shifted from "liberation" by force to "peaceful reunification." On 1 January 1979, the Standing Committee of mainland China's National People's Congress (NPC) issued a "Message to Compatriots on Taiwan," calling for the first time in the history of the PRC for the solution of all the disputes between the two sides through peaceful means, marking the beginning of PRC's new Taiwan policy. This paper is to review the development of the relationship between mainland China (hereafter shortened for "China" or "the mainland") and Taiwan since 1979. It will highlight major characteristics of cross-Strait political, economic, social and cultural interactions, and identify the main problems faced by the two sides and discuss prospects for the future bilateral relationship.

## POLITICAL RELATIONS

### The Oscillation between Military Confrontation and Peaceful Maneuvering

Since the establishment of the PRC on the mainland in 1949, Beijing had sought to "liberate" Taiwan by force. Such a policy led to a series of armed conflicts between the two sides of the Taiwan Strait, including an amphibious attack by the communist troops on the Nationalist-controlled island of Kinmen (or Quemoy, *Jingmen*) in October 1949, the occupation of the Tachen Islands (*Dachendao*) in January 1955, and the bombardment of Kinmen in August 1958. Indeed, the People's Liberation Army (PLA) continued to shell Kinmen from time to time until the late 1970s, reminding the Nationalist Party or Kuomintang (KMT) of the fact that its military ambition over Taiwan had not waned.

After establishing diplomatic relations with the U.S. in 1979, the post-Mao leadership decided to adopt a new approach toward Taiwan and consequently launched a peaceful offense on Taiwan. In its "Message" to the Taiwan people issued on 1 January 1979, the Standing Committee of the NPC expressed the hope that "Taiwan returns to the embrace of the motherland at an early date so that we can work together for the great cause of national development." This new approach was further elaborated by Ye Jianying, the Chairman of the Standing Committee of the 5th NPC, on 30 September 1981 in his nine-point proposal for peaceful reunification. Ye suggested talks be held between the CCP and the KMT and requested the resumption of *santong* (three direct links, i.e., direct transport, commercial and postal service links) and *siliu* (four exchanges, i.e., academic, cultural, economic and sport exchanges) as the first step to "gradually eliminate antagonism between the two sides and increase mutual understanding."[1] In 1984, Deng Xiaoping advanced the formula of "one country, two systems" *(yiguo liangzhi)* as the political settlement for Taiwan's eventual reunification with the mainland. Beijing's peaceful offense reached a climax when Jiang Zemin, the General-Secretary of the CCP and the President of the PRC, made an "eight-point proposal" on 30 January 1995, suggesting that Beijing and Taipei start negotiations on "officially ending the state of hostility between the two sides and accomplishing peaceful reunification step by step."[2]

Thus, Beijing's new policy toward Taiwan can be summarized as "peaceful reunification through the 'one country, two systems' formula." To make the formula more acceptable to Taipei, Beijing declared that under the prescription Taiwan would enjoy a high degree of autonomy, including administrative power, legislative power, independent judiciary power, the power to keep its armed forces, and certain powers in foreign relations, such as signing commercial and cultural treaties with foreign countries

---

[1] *Beijing Review*, vol. 24, no. 40, Oct. 5, 1981, p. 11.

[2] For the full text of Jiang's "eight-point proposal," see Appendix B.

although "only the PRC represents China in the international arena."[3] In short, the reunification under the "one country, two systems" formula will not be a take-over of Taiwan by the mainland, but peaceful co-existence between the two sides within one country, according to Beijing.

Taiwan, on the other hand, has experienced profound economic liberalization, social pluralization and political democratization since the 1980s. Taipei's decision to lift martial law in July 1987 and especially that to allow Taiwan private citizens to visit the mainland four months later have opened the floodgate for people-to-people exchanges between the two sides of the Taiwan Strait after almost four decades of estrangement. In March 1991, the Republic of China (ROC) government adopted the *Guidelines for National Unification* as the guiding principle of its mainland policy. The guidelines state that China's unification should be achieved in three phases: a short-term phase of exchanges and reciprocity, a mid-term phase of mutual trust and co-operation, and a long-term phase of consultation and reunification.[4] Thus, the present bilateral relationship is defined to be in the short-term phase, where Taipei hopes that Beijing will meet its three demands: 1) recognising its existence as a political entity, 2) renouncing the use of force against Taiwan, and 3) giving it enough international space for diplomatic manoeuvre. On political and national security grounds, Beijing's call for the resumption of the "three direct links" across the Taiwan Strait will not be considered at this stage. To respond to Jiang's "eight-point proposal," Lee Teng-hui, the President of the ROC, issued his "six-point proposal," insisting that the mainland and Taiwan are "two separate political entities" and hence negotiations between the two should be conducted "on an equal footing." In sum, Taipei's counter strategy toward Beijing's campaign for reunification is "one country, two equal political entities." To Taipei, unless Beijing concedes to the above demands any breakthrough in cross-Strait relations is out of the question.

The opposing political views, however, have not prevented the two sides from setting up semi-official organisations to handle civil and commercial disputes stemming from increasingly frequent social and commercial contacts across the Strait, i.e., the Strait Exchange Foundation (SEF) in Taiwan and the Association for Relations Across the Taiwan Strait (ARATS) in the mainland. In April 1993, Mr. Koo Chen-fu, chairman of SEF, and Mr. Wang Daohan, head of ARATS, met in Singapore and held talks in what was the first contact between the two rival governments since 1949. The two sides reached a preliminary consensus on regularizing and institutionalizing the Wang-Koo talks. Beijing hoped to move these talks gradually from the phase of discussing practical issues to that of political consultations and negotiations. However, the visit made by President Lee Teng-hui to the U.S. in June 1995 abruptly ended this short-lived but seemingly promising process. China angrily postponed the second "Wang-Koo Meeting" due to be held in Beijing in July 1995 in protest of the visit, and bilateral relations have

---

[3] The White Paper, "The Taiwan Issue and the Reunification of China," *China Daily*, September 1, 1993, pp. 4-5.

[4] For the full text of *the Guidelines for National Unification*, see Appendix C.

deteriorated rapidly since then. In order to warn what it called pro-independence forces in Taiwan, the PLA launched a series of surface-to-surface guided ballistic missile tests over the Taiwan Strait in July-August 1995 and March 1996. These missiles fell into the waters 30 to 50 nautical miles due west of Kaohsiung, Taiwan's largest port, and 20 to 40 nautical miles due east of Keelung, Taiwan's second largest port, bringing the two sides to the brink of a serious military conflict.

With political democratisation in Taiwan continuing to flourish, China's concern is growing over the burgeoning influence of pro-independence forces, notably the Democratic Progressive Party (DPP), in Taiwan's politics. Beijing has made it clear that no matter what happens in Taiwan's internal politics the fact that it is a part of China will never change.[5] Beijing is annoyed by the fact that Taipei claims itself as a "democratic government" and plays the "public opinions" (*minyi*) card in dealing with cross-Strait relations. China clearly fears the possibility that the DPP may one day come into power or a coalition government may have to be formed in Taiwan, which, it believes, will pave the way for Taiwan to become independent through a referendum.[6] In refuting Taipei's claim that Taiwan's sovereignty should be decided by its people (*zhuminzijue*) and not by the mainland, Beijing argues that "Taiwan belongs not only to the Taiwan people but also to the people of the whole of China." It also contends that "democratization" and "sovereignty" are two different concepts and hence that Taiwan's internal political changes should not infringe upon China's sovereignty over Taiwan.

The victory won by the DDP in Taiwan's local elections in November 1997 has further upset Beijing, prompting it to take a more flexible line on the "one China" principle in order to get the KMT-led Taiwan government back to the negotiating table. Wang Daohan has made informal comments to visitors from Taiwan that suggest the possibility of a new approach. He has said that "one China" does not mean the PRC or ROC, but a future unified China agreed upon by the people on the both sides of the Taiwan Strait --- a position close to Taiwan's. He has also said that sovereignty cannot be divided but it can be shared.[7] These informal remarks, although not publicly endorsed by authoritative policymakers in Beijing, has raised the hope that a compromise over the "one China" issue can be reached between the two sides, thus laying the foundation for political talks.

---

[5] Mr. Tang Guoqiang, the Chinese foreign ministry spokesman, made this comment when he was asked to comment on the local elections held in Taiwan in November 1997, see *Zhongguo Shibao* (China Times), Taipei, Dec. 4, 1997, p. 9.

[6] Beijing has already denounced the referendum held in Tainan City on 5 December 1998 over the issue of reunification and warned the organiser and supporters not to "play with fire," see *Lianhe Zaobao* (Singapore), 10 Dec. 1998, p. 20.

[7] Cited in Ralph N. Clough, "Cross-Strait Relations and U.S. Policy," paper presented at the Workshop on Cross-Strait Relations held at the University of British Columbia, Canada on 21-22 August 1998, p. 16.

## The Second "Wang-Koo Meeting"

The climax of cross-Strait relations in recent years has undoubtedly been the visit by Mr. Koo Chen-fu to mainland China in October 1998. The meeting between Koo and his mainland counterpart, Mr. Wang Daohan in Shanghai signaled the end of China's boycott on holding talks with Taiwan, imposed unilaterally three years ago in protest of Lee Teng-hui's visit to the US. Beijing feared that the legislative elections to be held in Taiwan in December 1998 could put the ruling KMT into a minority party in the parliament, which would make the prospect of a DPP candidate winning the presidential election in 2000 more likely. By resuming "Wang-Koo Meeting," Beijing believed that it could give KMT credit for improving cross-Strait relations and hence enhance KMT's electoral chances.[8]

Taipei, on the other hand, was never particularly keen on the meeting because it did not want to negotiate with Beijing at a time when the latter was seen as having gained an upper hand in the long-running diplomatic war between them.[9] The main reason for Taiwan to enter the talk seemed to be the pressure from the US, which has always been the invisible third party in cross-Strait relations. After military confrontations in 1995-96, which forced Washington to respond with the largest mobilization of US naval force in Asia since the Vietnam war, President Clinton was reported to have urged both sides to talk "sooner rather than later" in order to prevent similar incidents from happening again in the future.[10] But Taiwan felt that it was not ready to hold political talks with the mainland authorities on reunification. That's why it insisted that talks should focus on mundane matters, such as fishing disputes, the safety of Taiwan businessmen on the mainland, and compensation for mislaid mails.

Although the media described Koo's trip to the mainland as a "ice-melting tour" (*rongbing zhilu*), both Beijing and Taipei regarded that meeting as a preliminary discussion that will set the stage for more substantive talks in the future. After two days of discussions, the two sides issued an agreement on future ARATS-SEF interactions on 15 October, or the "Four Points of Consensus," which includes the following four points: 1) Wang Daohan is to visit Taiwan at an appropriate time; 2) the two sides will continue to hold meetings on matters of mutual interest in both political and economic areas; 3) more exchanges will be arranged between members at various levels of the two associations; and 4) there will be more co-operation from both sides in dealing with cases relating to the protection of property and the security of visitors.

---

[8] In the end, the KMT has won the elections, not only holding on to the majority in the parliament but also regaining the mayoralty of Taipei City.

[9] Apart from obtaining the "three no's" from Bill Clinton and "four no's" from President Yeltsin of Russia, China's recent diplomatic victories over Taiwan include forcing four countries, South Africa, the Republic of Central Africa, Guinea-Bissau and Tonga, to switch their official ties from Taipei to Beijing. Furthermore, its policy not to devalue the RMB in combating the Asian financial crisis has also won wide spread praise and support from the international community.

[10] Julian Baum and Susan Lawrence, "Breaking the Ice," *Far Eastern Economic Review*, Oct. 15, 98, p. 24.

**Table 1.** Main Political Differences between Beijing and Taipei

| | Beijing | Taipei |
|---|---|---|
| Basic Policy on Reunification | Peaceful reunification through the formula of "one country, two systems." | The reunification must be based on the principle of democracy, freedom and equitable prosperity. |
| The "One China" Principle | There is only one China in the world and Taiwan is a part of it. China is divided at present, both sides should seek the reunification through political negotiations on an equal footing. | Taiwan cannot accept the mainland's claim that it represents the whole of China. Taiwan is a part of China, and so is the mainland, i.e., "one country, two equal political entities." |
| The Right to Use Force against Taiwan | While making every effort to achieve a peaceful unification with Taiwan, China will not give up its legitimate right to use forces, if necessary, to safeguard its sovereignty and territorial integrity. | Beijing must renounce the use of military force against Taiwan. Only with sincerity and mutual respect can the ROC agree to the resumption of *santong* and hold political talks on reunification. |
| The Space for International Diplomacy | Based on the "one China" principle and international law, China can only represented by its central government, i.e. the government of the PRC. Taiwan, as a part of China, has no right to represent the whole of China in the international community. However, Beijing will not oppose Taipei's effort to develop non-governmental links with foreign countries. | The ROC was founded in 1912 and had exercised jurisdiction over the whole of China. After the PRC was founded on the mainland in 1949, China has been ruled separately. As a sovereign nation, the ROC government has the right to participate in international affairs. |
| Political Negotiations vs. Mundane Talks | The fundamental difference between the two sides is political, and the failure to solve this basic problem has seriously affected the settlement of many mundane matters. Hence, both sides should start to hold talks on the agenda and procedures of political negotiations as soon as possible. | The condition for both sides to hold political talks has not emerged yet. At present, both sides should endeavour to institutionalize consultations and talks with the focus placed on practical issues concerning the rights and interests of the people on both sides of the Taiwan Strait. |

Sources: based on the Taiwan Affairs Office, the State Council, PRC, *Taiwan wenti yu zhongguo de tongyi* (The Taiwan Issue and China's Unification) (Beijing: The State Council, August 93); the Mainland Affairs Council, the Executive Yuan, ROC, *The Mainland Policy of the Government of the Republic of China* (June 98) (http://www.mac.gov.tw); *MAC News Briefing*, Nos. 0097 (Oct. 19, 98), 0098 (Oct. 26, 98), 0099 (Nov. 2, 98); Su Changping, "On Cross-Strait Relations after the `Wang-Koo Meeting'," *Jingbao Yuekan* (The Mirror), Hong Kong, Nov. 98, pp. 78-79; Qi Lin, "Discarding Mutual Suspicion, Promoting Political Dialogue," *Guangjiaojing Yuekan* (Wide Angle), Hong Kong, Nov. 98, pp. 18-21; Jin Ziyang, "'One China' Has New Meaning," *Ming Bao* (Ming Pao Daily News), Hong Kong, Oct. 15, 98, p. A15.

Jiang Zemin's meeting with Koo in Beijing on 18 October marked the highest-level contact between mainland China and Taiwan since 1949. Both Beijing and Taipei hailed the visit as a milestone in the bilateral relationship. The mainland's *China Daily Commentary* called the agreement reached "a breakthrough" and "a new starting point", while Taiwan's Mainland Affairs Council believed that the visit had "opened a constructive dialogue between the two sides" and "generated the momentum for resuming institutionalized negotiations." [11]

It would of course be unrealistic to expect an early solution to the decades-old disputes between China and Taiwan, despite the signs of flexibility. In fact, the "four points of consensus" are nothing more than a commitment by both sides to continue to talk and expand the scope of contact in the future. Beijing and Taipei made no progress in persuading the other to accept its main political plank, namely the "one China" principle and the concept of "two equal political entities" (*liangge duideng zhengzhi shiti*) respectively. Wang's new definition of "one China" --- the future unified China, not the PRC or the ROC --- is applied only to cross-Strait relations, not to the PRC's relations with other countries. That is to say, Beijing still insists that in the international arena "one China" means the PRC. Equally, Taiwan is unlikely to change its position without being treated as an equal political entity in bilateral negotiations and allowed to join the international community as a sovereign state. Table 1 highlights the major differences between Beijing and Taipei emerging from the second "Wang-Koo Meeting."

Without doubt, Beijing's deep antipathy toward Lee Teng-hui has been the biggest stumbling block to the improvement of cross-Strait relations. Despite the improved atmosphere brought about by the second "Wang-Koo Meeting," both sides have remained poles apart in major issues, as shown in Table 1, and deeply suspicious of each other. Any hope for a political breakthrough in cross-Strait relations looks still a long way off.

## ECONOMIC INTERACTIONS

The economic interaction between mainland China and Taiwan has always been the cornerstone of cross-Strait relations since the late 1970s. Despite political stalemate between Beijing and Taipei, trade and investment activities across the Taiwan Strait have grown rapidly, bringing the two economies ever closer. Beijing believes that a close economic tie with Taiwan is not only beneficial to the mainland economy but also the best way to prevent Taiwan from going independent. As a result, it has repeatedly called for the resumption of direct transport, commercial and postal links between the two sides. Taiwan's policy toward the development of cross-Strait economic relations, however, has always been ambivalent and rather cautious. Central to Taipei's concern is

---

[11] . See *China Daily*, Beijing, Oct. 20, 98, p. 4; *MAC News Briefing*, Taipei, No. 0099 (Nov. 2, 98), pp. 4-5.

how to seek a balance between maximizing economic benefits (from developing economic links with the mainland) and safeguarding national security. Hence, it insists that all cross-Strait economic activities have to be conducted on an indirect basis (i.e., via a third place). Furthermore, to prevent Taiwan's economy from becoming too dependent on the mainland market, the policy of "restraining rush, exercising patience" (*jieji yongren*) has been instituted since 1996 to restrict investments made by large Taiwan companies in the mainland.

## Merchandise Trade

The trade between mainland China and Taiwan was dominated by indirect trade, i.e., re-exports via Hong Kong in the 1970s and 1980s.[12] By the 1990s, however, indirect trade was gradually replaced by direct trade. The direct trade includes 1) transhipment (*zhuanyun*) and 2) transit shipment (*guojin*) via Hong Kong and other intermediaries, 3) "minor trade" (*xiaoe maoyi*) conducted between mainland and Taiwan fishermen in the designated mainland ports, and 4) illegal direct shipment involving chartered ships flying flags of third countries.[13]

As can be seen from Figure 1, the total cross-Strait trade (including direct and indirect trade) has expanded steadily from US$76 million in 1979 to US$22,511 million in 1998, with a peak of US$24,433 million recorded in 1997. This represents an average growth rate of 30 percent per year, compared with 14.6 percent for China's total foreign trade and 12.1 percent for Taiwan's over the same period. Such high growth is very rare in the history of trade between any two territories. Today, mainland China and Taiwan are each other's fourth largest trading partner, indicating the importance of bilateral trade to the development of their respective economies.

Three important characteristics have emerged from cross-Strait trading activities. First, the investment-induced effect. About two-thirds of Taiwan's exports to mainland China were actually ordered by Taiwan-invested enterprises (TIEs) in the mainland, which have to import machinery and equipment, semi-products, parts and accessories,

---

[12]  Re-export in this context means that a consignment of cargo from China or Taiwan is sold to a third party in Hong Kong before it is re-sold to the buyer in Taiwan or China. As such consignments have to clear Hong Kong' customs, the Hong Kong authorities possess complete data on re-exports.

[13]  Transhipment, which is the dominant mode of the direct trade, is different from transit shipment in that the former involves the transfer of goods from one vessel to another in Hong Kong waters while in the latter case goods remain in the same vessel when passing through Hong Kong waters. As these goods do not clear Hong Kong customs, the Hong Kong authorities generally do not have any data on them, except the volume of transhipment by weight. This paper is to use the figures released by Taiwan's International Trade Board, Ministry of Economic Affairs to reflect cross-Strait trade. Taiwan has compiled the data consistently since the 1980s, taking into account Hong Kong's trade statistics.

and raw materials from Taiwan for their operations in the mainland.[14] However, it is predicted that with the gradual reduction in the number of Taiwan's export-processing/assembling projects in the mainland and the growing effort made by China to replace imported inputs with local ones, the investment-induced effect is likely to diminish gradually in the future.

Second, a growing trade surplus in Taiwan's favour. The cross-Strait trade has been dominated by Taiwan's exports to China. In 1980, Taiwan's surplus was only US$164 million, but by 1997 this figure had jumped to US$16,610 million, increasing by a staggering 100 times, compared with 76 times for the growth of total bilateral trade over the same period. Indeed, the surplus is so huge that if Taiwan had not traded with China, it would have incurred an overall trade deficit in recent years. For example, Taiwan would have suffered a deficit of US$8.97 billion in 1997, instead of a surplus of US$7.64 billion as actually registered, if the surplus from the cross-Strait trade (US$16.61 billion) were not included.[15]

And third, increasing trade dependence on each other. As can be seen from Table 2, in 1979 bilateral trade accounted for only 0.25 percent of Taiwan's total foreign trade and 0.27 percent of China's, but by 1997 the two corresponding ratios had jumped to 10.33 and 7.52 percent respectively. In particular, Taiwan relied on the mainland market for 16.81 percent of its total exports in 1997, far exceeding the warning line of 10 percent set up by Taiwan's Ministry of Economic Affairs.

In terms of the commodity composition (classified by upper tier 2-digit identifiers of HS codes),[16] Taiwan's exports to the mainland were dominated by electric machinery and parts (HS code 85), machinery and parts (84), plastics and related products (39), and manmade filaments (54), which accounted for 51 percent of Taiwan's total exports to the mainland in 1998, as shown in Table 3. Among the fastest growing exports were iron and steel (72) and electric machinery and parts (85), which expanded by 93 and 44 percent respectively from 1995 to 1998, compared with only 2.8 percent for total exports over the same period.

---

[14] Lin Changhua, "An Analysis of Deficits of the Cross-Strait Trade", *Taiwan yanjiu jikan* (Taiwan Research Quarterly) (Xiamen), No.1, 97, p. 20.

[15]. Board of International Trade, Ministry of Economic Affairs, ROC, *Guoji maoyi qingshi fenxi* (An Analysis of International Trade Situation), No. 12, 1997, p. 1.

[16] For detailed information of the Harmonized System Codes, see Technology Administration, United States Department of Commerce (1997), *HS-Codes: Harmonized System Codes* (http://mena-peacenet.nist.gov/Documents/HS-Code/hscode.htm).

# Figure 1. Merchandise Trade between Mainland China & Taiwan, 1979-1998

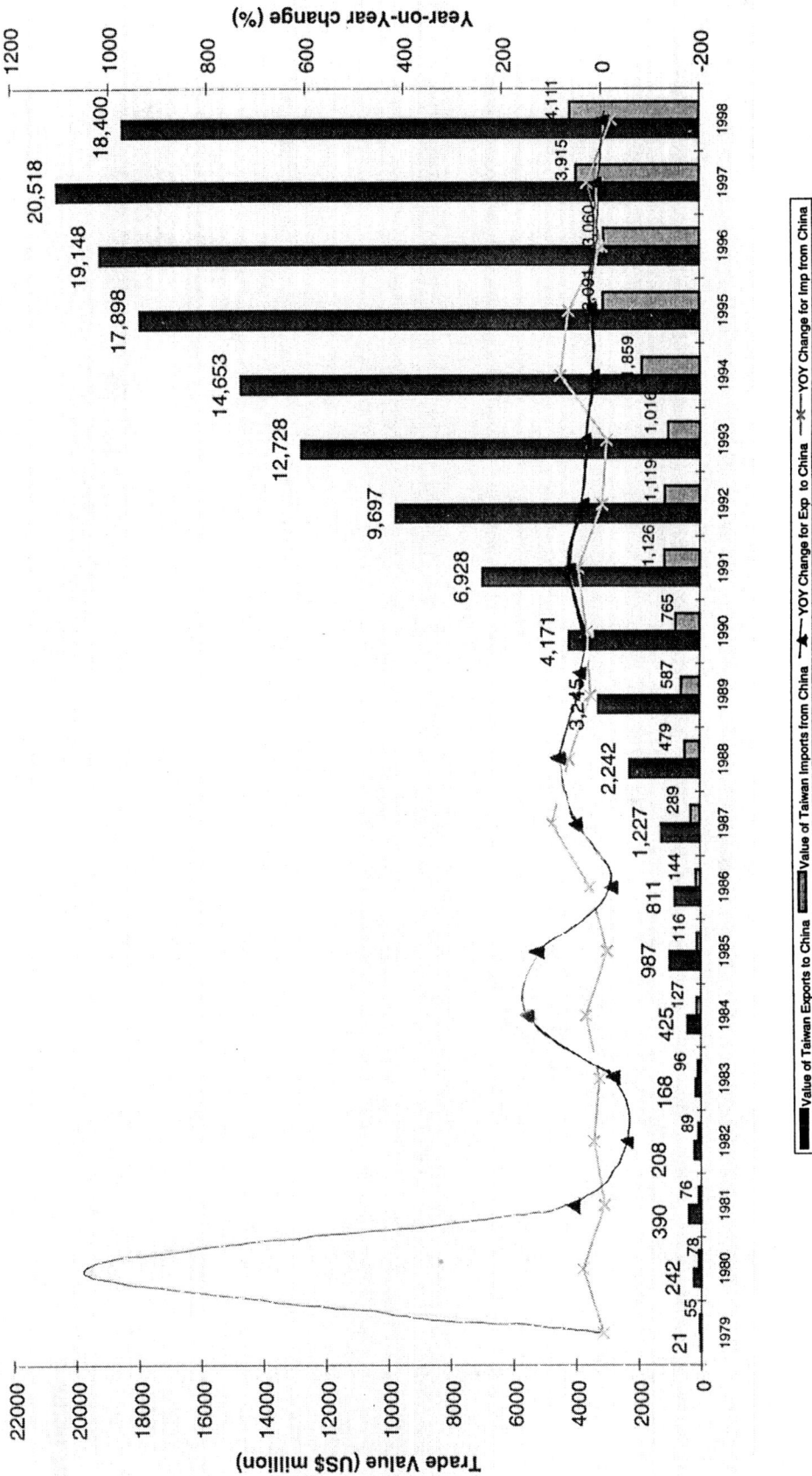

Legend: Value of Taiwan Exports to China | Value of Taiwan Imports from China | YOY Change for Imp from China | YOY Change for Exp to China | YOY Change for Imp from China

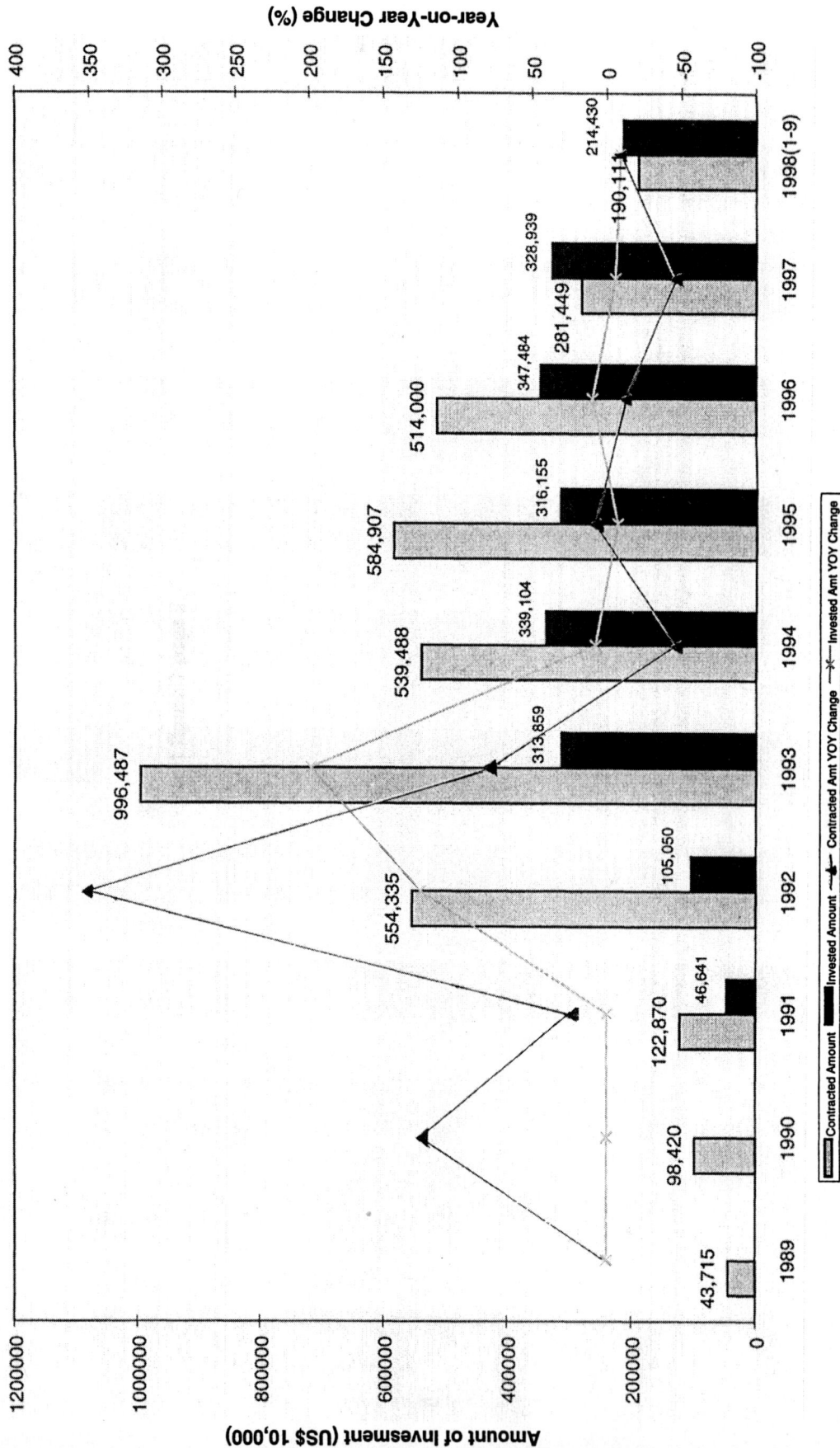

**Year-on-Year Change (%)**

400  350  300  250  200  150  100  50  0  -50  -100

**Amount of Invesment (US$ 10,000)**

1200000  1000000  800000  600000  400000  200000  0

1989  1990  1991  1992  1993  1994  1995  1996  1997  1998(1-9)

43,715
98,420
122,870  46,641
554,335  105,050
996,487  313,859
539,488  339,104
584,907  316,155
514,000  347,484
281,449  328,939
190,111  214,430

Contracted Amount ▬ Invested Amount ▬ Contracted Amt YOY Change ▬▲▬ Invested Amt YOY Change ▬✳▬

**Table 2. Trade Dependence between Taiwan and Mainland China, 1979-1997 (%)**

| | Taiwan on Mainland China | | | | | | Mainland China on Taiwan | | | | | |
|---|---|---|---|---|---|---|---|---|---|---|---|---|
| | Total Trade | | Exports | | Imports | | Total Trade | | Exports | | Imports | |
| | Re-exports via HK | Total | Re-exports via HK | Total | Re-exports via HK | Total | Re-exports via HK | Total | Re-exports via HK | Total | Re-exports via HK | Total |
| 1979 | 0.25 | ---- | 0.13 | ---- | 0.38 | ---- | 0.27 | ---- | 0.41 | ---- | 0.14 | ---- |
| 1980 | 0.79 | ---- | 1.19 | ---- | 0.39 | ---- | 0.82 | ---- | 0.42 | ---- | 1.17 | ---- |
| 1981 | 1.05 | ---- | 1.70 | ---- | 0.35 | ---- | 1.04 | ---- | 0.34 | ---- | 1.74 | ---- |
| 1982 | 0.68 | ---- | 0.88 | ---- | 0.44 | ---- | 0.67 | ---- | 0.38 | ---- | 1.01 | ---- |
| 1983 | 0.55 | ---- | 0.63 | ---- | 0.44 | ---- | 0.57 | ---- | 0.40 | ---- | 0.74 | ---- |
| 1984 | 1.06 | ---- | 1.40 | ---- | 0.58 | ---- | 1.03 | ---- | 0.49 | ---- | 1.55 | ---- |
| 1985 | 2.17 | ---- | 3.21 | ---- | 0.58 | ---- | 1.58 | ---- | 0.42 | ---- | 2.34 | ---- |
| 1986 | 1.49 | ---- | 2.04 | ---- | 0.60 | ---- | 1.29 | ---- | 0.46 | ---- | 1.89 | ---- |
| 1987 | 1.38 | ---- | 2.29 | ---- | 0.83 | ---- | 1.83 | ---- | 0.73 | ---- | 2.84 | ---- |
| 1988 | 2.47 | ---- | 3.70 | ---- | 0.96 | ---- | 2.65 | ---- | 1.01 | ---- | 4.06 | ---- |
| 1989 | 2.94 | 3.23 | 4.38 | 4.89 | 1.22 | ---- | 3.12 | 3.43 | 1.12 | ---- | 4.90 | 5.49 |
| 1990 | 3.32 | 4.05 | 4.88 | 6.21 | 1.40 | ---- | 3.50 | 4.28 | 1.23 | ---- | 6.14 | 7.82 |
| 1991 | 4.16 | 5.79 | 6.10 | 9.09 | 1.80 | ---- | 4.27 | 5.94 | 1.57 | ---- | 7.32 | 10.86 |
| 1992 | 4.83 | 7.05 | 7.72 | 11.90 | 1.55 | ---- | 4.47 | 6.53 | 1.32 | ---- | 7.80 | 12.03 |
| 1993 | 5.36 | 8.44 | 8.93 | 14.98 | 1.43 | 1.44 | 4.44 | 7.07 | 1.20 | 1.21 | 7.30 | 12.24 |
| 1994 | 5.50 | 9.26 | 9.15 | 15.74 | 1.51 | 2.17 | 4.14 | 7.00 | 1.07 | 1.54 | 7.36 | 12.67 |
| 1995 | 5.32 | 9.75 | 8.85 | 16.03 | 1.52 | 2.98 | 4.08 | 7.47 | 1.06 | 2.08 | 7.48 | 13.55 |
| 1996 | 5.19 | 10.20 | 8.37 | 16.49 | 1.55 | 3.00 | 3.90 | 7.66 | 1.05 | 2.03 | 7.00 | 13.80 |
| 1997 | 4.85 | 10.33 | 7.96 | 16.81 | 1.52 | 3.42 | 3.52 | 7.52 | 0.95 | 2.14 | 6.82 | 14.41 |
| 1998 | 4.67 | 10.45 | 7.55 | 16.63 | 1.57 | 3.92 | 3.09 | 6.95 | 0.91 | 2.24 | 5.97 | 13.12 |

Sources: Based on Board of International Trade, Ministry of Economic Affairs, ROC Government (http://www.moeaboft.gov.tw); China Economic Information Centre, PRC (http://www.cei.gov.cn).

**Table 3.** Main Commodity Groups Exported by
Taiwan to Mainland China, 1998 and 1995 (US$ million)

| Commodity Group | HS | 1998 | | 1995 | | Change over 1995 | |
| --- | --- | --- | --- | --- | --- | --- | --- |
| | | Amount | Share (%) | Amount | Share (%) | Amount | ± % |
| Taiwan's total exports to China | | 18,400.4 | 100.0 | 17,898.2 | 100.0 | 502.2 | 2.8 |
| Electric machinery etc.; parts thereof | 85 | 3,528.7 | 19.2 | 2,452.0 | 13.7 | 1,076.7 | 43.9 |
| Machinery etc.; parts thereof | 84 | 2,580.3 | 14.0 | 2,542.9 | 14.2 | 37.4 | 1.5 |
| Plastics and articles thereof | 39 | 2,065.6 | 11.2 | 2,150.1 | 12.0 | -84.5 | -3.9 |
| Manmade filaments | 54 | 1,245.9 | 6.8 | 1,551.0 | 8.7 | -305.1 | -19.7 |
| Iron and steel | 72 | 1,026.6 | 5.6 | 531.8 | 3.0 | 494.8 | 93.0 |
| Textile articles for industry | 59 | 972.0 | 5.3 | 1,272.4 | 7.1 | -300.4 | -23.6 |
| Manmade staple fibres | 55 | 686.4 | 3.7 | 855.8 | 4.8 | -169.4 | -19.8 |
| Raw skins and leather | 41 | 598.5 | 3.3 | 590.8 | 3.3 | 7.7 | 1.3 |
| Knitted or crocheted fabrics | 60 | 594.3 | 3.2 | 690.3 | 3.9 | -96 | -13.9 |
| Copper and articles thereof | 74 | 426.1 | 2.3 | ------ | ---- | ---- | ----- |

Notes: HS = Harmonized System; ---- = Data not available.
    Sources: The Board of Foreign Trade, Ministry of Economic Affairs, ROC Government: (http://www.moeaboft.gov.tw/boftnetx/D/d3329.htm), Table 3.1; *Zhonghua minguo jingji nianjian* 1997 (Economic Yearbook of the Republic of China 1997), p. 14.

At the same time, the mainland's exports to Taiwan were dominated by electric machinery and parts (85), Iron and steel (72), machinery and parts (84), and mineral fuel and oil (27), which formed 53 percent of the mainland's total exports to Taiwan in 1998, as revealed in Table 4. Notably, the first and third categories emerged as the fastest growing exports in 1998, jumping by 147 and 243 percent respectively over 1995, in sharp contrast to 33 percent for total exports over the same period.

**Table 4.** Main Commodity Groups Exported by
Mainland China to Taiwan, 1998 and 1995 (US$ million)

| Commodity Group | HS | 1998 | | 1995 | | Change over 1995 | |
|---|---|---|---|---|---|---|---|
| | | Amount | Share (%) | Amount | Share (%) | Amount | ± % |
| Taiwan's total imports from China | | 4,110.5 | 100.0 | 3,091.4 | 100.0 | 1,019.1 | 33.0 |
| Electric machinery etc.; parts thereof | 85 | 1,159.9 | 28.2 | 469.9 | 15.2 | 690 | 146.8 |
| Iron and steel | 72 | 435.1 | 10.6 | 742.7 | 24.0 | -307.6 | -41.4 |
| Machinery etc.; parts thereof | 84 | 379.0 | 9.2 | 110.4 | 3.6 | 268.6 | 243.3 |
| Mineral fuel and oil etc.; distilled products | 27 | 194.1 | 4.7 | 188.8 | 6.1 | 5.3 | 2.8 |
| Earth and stone; lime and cement plaster | 25 | 164.1 | 4.0 | 158.6 | 5.1 | 5.5 | 3.5 |
| Zinc and articles thereof | 79 | 116.8 | 2.8 | ------ | ---- | ---- | ---- |
| Organic chemicals | 29 | 112.8 | 2.7 | 114.4 | 3.6 | -1.6 | -1.4 |
| Footwear, gaiters etc. and parts thereof | 64 | 106.8 | 2.6 | 173.1 | 5.6 | -66.3 | -38.3 |
| Inorganic chemicals | 28 | 103.9 | 2.5 | ------ | ---- | ------ | ------ |
| Toys, games and sport equipment; parts and accessories thereof | 95 | 100.7 | 2.5 | ------ | ---- | ------ | ------ |

Notes: HS = Harmonized System; ---- = Data not available.
Sources: The Board of Foreign Trade, Ministry of Economic Affairs, ROC Government:
(http://www.moeaboft.gov.tw/boftnetx/D/d3329.htm), Table 6; *Zhonghua minguo jingji nianjian* 1997 (Economic Yearbook of the Republic of China 1997), p. 15.

The commodity structures shown by Tables 3 and 4 have exhibited a significant degree of intra-industry trade between Taiwan and the mainland. Among the top five exports from each of the two sides, three of them, electric machinery and parts (85), machinery and parts (84), and iron and steel (72) overlapped, with Taiwan's exports overwhelmingly outweighing those from the mainland. Thus, it would be very interesting to break the structures further down and find out exactly what kinds of goods were actually traded within each of the three categories.

Tables 5 and 6 list the top 20 exports classified by 6-digit of HS codes from Taiwan and the mainland respectively in 1997 and 1998. Within the division of electric machinery and parts (85), which was the single largest export for both sides in 1998, Taiwan appeared to concentrate on exporting the sub-division of 8542, namely, electronic integrated circuits, micro-assemblies, and parts thereof, which accounted for 43 percent of the total exports for Category 85. The mainland, on the other hand, seemed to focus on the sub-division of 8504, i.e. electric transformers, static converters and inductors, and parts thereof, which constituted 54 percent of the total.

**Table 5.** Main Commodities Exported by Taiwan
to Mainland China, 1997-98 (US$ million)

| Commodity | HS | 1998 | | 1997 | | Change over 97 | |
|---|---|---|---|---|---|---|---|
| | | Amount | Share (%) | Amount | Share (%) | Amount | ± % |
| Taiwan's total exports to China | | 18,400.4 | 100.0 | 20,518.0 | 100.0 | -2,117.6 | -10.3 |
| Parts & accessories for adp machines & units | 847330 | 551.0 | 3.0 | 510.4 | 2.5 | 40.6 | 8.0 |
| Textile fabrics, impregnated etc nesoi with pvc | 590310 | 444.4 | 2.4 | 577.8 | 2.8 | -133.4 | -23.1 |
| Monolithic integrated circuits, except digital | 854219 | 384.2 | 2.1 | 339.6 | 1.7 | 44.6 | 13.1 |
| Hybrid integrated circuits | 854240 | 360.1 | 2.0 | 158.1 | 0.8 | 202.0 | 127.8 |
| Acrylonitrile-butadiene-styrene (abs) copolymers | 390330 | 349.3 | 1.9 | 339.1 | 1.7 | 10.2 | 3.0 |
| Printed circuits | 853400 | 329.1 | 1.8 | 200.7 | 1.0 | 128.4 | 64.0 |
| Other integrated circuits | 854230 | 295.1 | 1.6 | 49.9 | 0.2 | 245.2 | 491.4 |
| Textile fabrics, impregn etc nesoi, polyurethane | 590320 | 270.5 | 1.5 | 361.0 | 1.8 | -90.5 | -25.1 |
| Other electrical parts of machinery nesoi in Code 85 | 854890 | 262.3 | 1.4 | 152.7 | 0.7 | 109.6 | 71.8 |
| Articles of plastics, nesoi | 392690 | 260.3 | 1.4 | 311.4 | 1.5 | -51.1 | -16.4 |
| Wov fab syn fil yn nesoi 85% nylon etc dyed | 540742 | 248.4 | 1.3 | 358.3 | 1.7 | -109.9 | -30.7 |

| Pts for elect transformers static converters indct | 850490 | 235.0 | 1.3 | 283.4 | 1.4 | -48.4 | -17.1 |
|---|---|---|---|---|---|---|---|
| Cathode-ray tv picture tubes, color inc monitor | 854011 | 228.2 | 1.2 | 143.0 | 0.7 | 85.2 | 59.6 |
| Syn stp fib nt crd, cmb or prsd spng: of polyester | 550320 | 219.6 | 1.2 | 234.5 | 1.1 | -14.9 | -6.4 |
| Oth knit/croch fabric nesoi, manmade fibers | 600293 | 196.5 | 1.1 | 272.3 | 1.3 | -75.8 | -27.8 |
| Pts, ex antenna, for trnsmssn, rdr, radio, tv, etc nesoi | 852990 | 186.3 | 1.0 | 158.7 | 0.8 | 27.6 | 17.4 |
| Flt-rld stnls stl 600mm om w cld-rld .5-1 mm thck | 721934 | 180.0 | 1.0 | 190.9 | 0.9 | -10.9 | -5.7 |
| Textile fabrics, impregn etc nesoi, plastics nesoi | 590390 | 178.8 | 1.0 | 246.6 | 1.2 | -67.8 | -27.5 |
| Other microwave tubes | 854040 | 165.6 | 0.9 | 107.9 | 0.5 | 57.7 | 53.5 |
| Bovine & equine leather nesoi, preprd aftr tanning | 410439 | 162.5 | 0.9 | 182.5 | 0.9 | -20.0 | -11.0 |

Notes: HS = Harmonized System.

Sources: The Based on Board of Foreign Trade, Ministry of Economic Affairs, ROC Government: (http://www.moeaboft.gov.tw/boftnetx/D/d3329.htm), Table 3.2.

**Table 6.** Main Commodities Exported by
Mainland China to Taiwan, 1997-98 (US$ million)

| Commodity | HS | 1998 | | 1997 | | Change over 97 | |
|---|---|---|---|---|---|---|---|
| | | Amount | Share (%) | Amount | Share (%) | Amount | ± % |
| Taiwan's total imports from China | | 4,110.5 | 100.0 | 3,915.3 | 100.0 | 195.2 | 5.0 |
| Static converters | 850440 | 197.7 | 4.8 | 184.2 | 4.7 | 13.5 | 7.3 |
| Bituminous coal, not agglomerated | 270112 | 176.8 | 4.3 | 198.4 | 5.1 | -21.6 | -10.9 |
| Smfd irn/nal stl lt .25 pct crb rect cs wid 2x thk | 720712 | 163.1 | 4.0 | 143.8 | 3.7 | 19.3 | 13.4 |
| Parts & accessories for adp machines & units | 847330 | 152.8 | 3.7 | 128.9 | 3.3 | 23.9 | 18.5 |
| Elect plugs & sockets f voltage not over 1000 v | 853669 | 124.2 | 3.0 | 43.1 | 1.1 | 81.1 | 188.2 |
| Zinc unwrt nt aly cnt wgt at lst 99.99 percnt zinc | 790111 | 100.5 | 2.4 | 111.3 | 2.8 | -10.8 | -9.7 |
| Footwear uppers and upper parts except stiffeners | 640610 | 64.5 | 1.6 | 69.9 | 1.8 | -5.4 | -7.7 |
| Smfd ios na u.25pct crbn rec/sq cs wdth un 2x thns | 720711 | 63.2 | 1.5 | 68.8 | 1.8 | -5.6 | -8.1 |
| Smfd irn or nonalloy stl, .25 pct or more carbon | 720720 | 62.4 | 1.5 | 78.2 | 2.0 | -15.8 | -20.2 |

| | | | | | | | |
|---|---|---|---|---|---|---|---|
| Transformers nesoi, power handling cap nov 1 kva | 850431 | 59.6 | 1.4 | 62.8 | 1.6 | -3.2 | -5.1 |
| Electrical inductors nesoi | 850450 | 54.9 | 1.3 | 69.2 | 1.8 | -14.3 | -20.7 |
| Diodes ex photosensitive or light-emitting diodes | 854110 | 53.4 | 1.3 | 36.7 | 0.9 | 16.7 | 45.5 |
| Nonalloy pig iron 0.5 prcnt or less phosphorus | 720110 | 47.0 | 1.1 | 83.1 | 2.1 | -36.1 | -43.4 |
| Down for stuffing cleaned/disinfect treat for pres | 050510 | 46.9 | 1.1 | 76.6 | 2.0 | -29.7 | -38.8 |
| Pts, ex antenna, for trnsmssn, rdr, radio, tv, etc nesoi | 852990 | 46.4 | 1.1 | 30.3 | 0.8 | 16.1 | 53.1 |
| Insulated electric conductors =< 80 v with cntrs | 854441 | 44.9 | 1.1 | 35.9 | 0.9 | 9.0 | 25.1 |
| Granite, crude or roughly trimmed | 251611 | 39.8 | 1.0 | 40.8 | 1.0 | -1.0 | -2.5 |
| Toys and parts and accessories, nesoi | 950390 | 37.7 | 0.7 | 33.4 | 0.9 | 4.3 | 12.9 |
| Portland cement except white portland cement | 252329 | 34.5 | 0.8 | 1.9 | 0.0 | 32.6 | 1,715.8 |
| Frames and forks, and prts for bicycles etc. | 871491 | 34.4 | 0.8 | 13.7 | 0.3 | 20.7 | 151.1 |

Notes: HS = Harmonized System.
Sources: The Based on Board of Foreign Trade, Ministry of Economic Affairs, ROC Government: (http://www.moeaboft.gov.tw/boftnetx/D/d3329.htm), Table 7.

Within the division of iron and steel (72), Taiwan mainly exported the sub-division of 7219, namely, flat-rolled stainless products (with the width of 600 mm or more) while the mainland primarily exported the sub-division of 7207, i.e. semi-finished products of iron and non-alloy steel.

Finally, in the division of machinery and parts (84), Taiwan and the mainland appeared to export the same commodity to each other, i.e. parts and accessories for automatic data processing machines and units (847330), although the mainland's export volume was under 30 percent of Taiwan's.

In fact, the above examination has to a large extent revealed the pattern of cross-Strait trade: the trade is on the whole complimentary to each other where Taiwan tends to export deeper-processed and/or higher value-added products compared to those from the mainland, as demonstrated in the first two cases above. However, it is undeniable that Taiwan investments in the mainland have over the years helped raise the competitiveness of some exporting industries there, which have gradually become a strong rival to Taiwan's own exporting sectors. The machinery industry (85), as shown above, is a case in point.

## Taiwan Investment in Mainland China

Cross-Strait investment activities have been characterized by one-way traffic, i.e., the capital flow from Taiwan to the mainland.[17] There are several motives for Taiwan businessmen to invest in the mainland, including making use of the cheap workforce, land, and other natural resources in the mainland; opening up the mainland market; diversifying investment risk; and fleeing from the deteriorating investment environment in Taiwan. Some Taiwan investors did not report their investments to the authorities because their investments might be illegal under Taiwan's laws and regulations and/or because they might try to avoid paying taxes. As a result, statistics released by Taiwan tend to be far smaller than those issued by the mainland.

By the end of October 1998 the mainland authorities had approved a total of 40,846 Taiwan investment projects, accounting for 14.4 percent of the total number of foreign-invested enterprises in the mainland. These projects involved more than US$40.16 billion of Taiwan capital, of which US$21.12 billion had actually been delivered.[18] Today, Taiwan is the third largest foreign investor in the mainland (after Hong Kong and the U.S.), contributing 7.2 percent of the total realized FDI in the mainland. About one-third of (or 143) Taiwan's listed companies have invested in the mainland.[19] Figure 2 records the dramatic growth of the inflow of Taiwan capital into the mainland since the late 1980s, revealing that the actual investment expanded by six times between 1991 and

---

[17] Recently, there have been some reports of investments from the mainland to Taiwan, but no concrete data have been produced. Nor is the magnitude of such investments expected to be large.

[18] *Wen Hui Po* (Wen Hui Daily) (Hong Kong), 12 Dec. 98, p. A3.

[19] Ibid.

1997. The average capitalization of Taiwan-invested projects topped US$1.6 million in 1996 but dropped to US$0.9 million only in the first half of 1998, due partially to Taipei's policy restricting large Taiwan companies from investing in the mainland and partially to the Asian financial crisis.

Taiwan investment in the early years was dominated by small, labour-intensive projects mainly manufacturing/processing light industrial products and consumer goods. However, this investment pattern was soon replaced by a new one where not only has the size of projects increased but also the investment structure been diversified and upgraded. Technology/capital-intensive manufacturing projects have now become the mainstay of investment activities, as demonstrated in Table 7. More and more Taiwan companies invest in the mainland together with their up-stream and/or down-stream operations, forming a complete and independent manufacturing system. At the same time, investments in the service industry, including catering, entertainment and real estate businesses, have been on the rise. Compared with other foreign investors, the Taiwanese prefer to set up wholly owned enterprises, instead of equity joint ventures or cooperative joint ventures.

**Table 7.** Composition of Taiwan Investment in Mainland China by Sector, by 1996

|  | Projects | | Contracted Amounts (US$1,000) | |
|---|---|---|---|---|
|  | No. | As % | Amounts | As % |
| Primary | 196 | 1.68 | 66,557 | 0.97 |
| Secondary | 10,548 | 90.64 | 6,378,894 | 92.80 |
| Of which: | | | | |
| Electronics & electrical appliances manufacturing | 1,564 | 13.39 | 1,159,800 | 16.53 |
| Rubber & plastic articles manufacturing | 1,453 | 12.50 | 892,062 | 13.12 |
| Foods & beverage manufacturing | 972 | 8.37 | 775,273 | 11.41 |
| Tertiary | 861 | 7.40 | 402,827 | 5.86 |
| Of which: | | | | |
| Services | 391 | 3.37 | 126,053 | 1.85 |
| Retail & wholesale | 111 | 0.95 | 123,284 | 1.78 |
| Others | 32 | 0.28 | 25,483 | 0.38 |
| Total | 11,637 | 100.00 | 6,873,724 | 100.00 |

Source: The Investment Commission, Ministry of Economic Affairs, ROC Government, *Zhonghua minguo dui dalu jianjie touzi tongji yuebao* (Monthly Statistics of ROC Investments in Chinese Mainland), cited in Xu Donghai (1997), p. 10.

Table 8 shows the regional distribution of Taiwan investment in the mainland. The Taiwanese appeared to favour the mainland's coastal provinces and municipalities, which had together absorbed 90 percent of the total contractual investment by the end of 1996, with Guangdong taking the lion's share (28.6%), followed by Jiangsu (16.7%), Shanghai (15.6%) and Fujian (12.9%).

**Table 8.** Composition of Taiwan Investment in Mainland China by Region, by 1996

|  | Projects | | Contracted Amounts (US$1,000) | |
|---|---|---|---|---|
|  | No. | As % | Amounts | As % |
| Guangdong | 3,733 | 32.07 | 1,969,665 | 28.56 |
| Guangzhou | 480 | 4.13 | 297,940 | 4.33 |
| Dongwan | 815 | 7.03 | 470,952 | 6.85 |
| Shenzhen | 934 | 8.04 | 414,669 | 6.03 |
| Fujian | 1,860 | 16.02 | 888,509 | 12.92 |
| Fuzhou | 393 | 3.39 | 208,040 | 3.02 |
| Xiamen | 622 | 5.35 | 334,968 | 4.87 |
| Jiangsu | 1,265 | 10.87 | 1,147,565 | 16.69 |
| Shanghai | 1,378 | 11.84 | 1,073,106 | 15.61 |
| Zhejiang | 608 | 5.22 | 294,773 | 4.29 |
| Hebei | 164 | 1.41 | 83,622 | 1.22 |
| Beijing | 382 | 3.29 | 151,687 | 2.20 |
| Tianjin | 260 | 2.23 | 261,647 | 3.80 |
| Shangdong | 366 | 3.14 | 190,892 | 2.77 |
| Liaoning | 231 | 1.99 | 134,006 | 1.95 |
| Others | 1,390 | 11.95 | 678,252 | 9.86 |
| Total | 11,637 | 100.00 | 6,873,724 | 100.00 |

Source: As Table 7.

## Major Problems

Although cross-Strait economic relations have, as shown above, been expanding at an extraordinarily fast pace in the last two decades, the development has not been plain sailing. Three major problems can be highlighted as follows:

First, Taiwan's ambivalent policy toward and the restrictions it imposed on cross-Strait economic activities. Taiwan is constantly torn between adopting a more liberal economic policy toward the mainland --- at the risk of national security --- to stimulate economic growth, and cooling down economic relations with the mainland --- with the consequence of economic slowdown --- to safeguard its national security. Like many of China's economic partners, Taiwan wants to have close trade and investment ties with the mainland and especially to develop southeastern China into its "economic hinterland," which is crucial to the success of its ambitious Asia Pacific Operation

Centre Plan.[20] On the other hand, Taiwan worries that too much capital outflow could lead to de-industrialization (*kongtonghua*) in the island itself and too much cross-Strait trading might cause the island's economy to become over-reliant on the mainland market, which would invariably undermine Taiwan's national security. As a result, the Taiwan authorities have, on the whole, been pursuing a cautious mainland economic policy, as reflected by the implementation of the "go south" (*nanxiang*) strategy and the policy of "restraining rush, exercising patience" (*jieji yongren*). This would inevitably handicap the development of cross-Strait economic exchanges and weaken Taiwan entrepreneurs' competitiveness vis-à-vis other foreign investors in the mainland market.

What makes the Taiwan authorities more worried is perhaps the mass exodus of Taiwan electronics firms - the pillars of Taiwan's economy and its best hopes for future growth - to the mainland in recent years.[21] According to Taiwan's National Federation of Industries, about one-third of some 30,000 firms approved by the Taiwan authorities to invest in the mainland are electronics firms. This has resulted in the doubling of the proportion of computer-related products manufactured by Taiwanese firms in the mainland, from 14 percent in 1995 to 29 percent 1998. This trend can also be detected in Table 5, where the electronics-related product group, i.e. electronic integrated circuits, micro-assemblies, and parts thereof (8542), was the fastest growing export from Taiwan, increasing on average by 90 percent within just one year (from 1997 to 1998).

Second, the lack of legal framework to regulate cross-Strait commercial activities in the mainland. For a long time, Taipei has accused Beijing of failing to provide proper legal protection to its businessmen and their legitimate rights and interests in the mainland. Indeed, there have been several cases in recent years in which Taiwan businessmen claimed that they had become the victims of "illegal acts" by the mainland authorities. Also, several Taiwan businessmen have been prosecuted by the mainland authorities for alleged economic crimes or espionage activities. Beijing has rejected Taipei's repeated requests to sign a mutual investment protection agreement on the ground that Taiwan is not a sovereign state.[22] Instead, it has unilaterally drafted the PRC Law on the Protection of Investments by Taiwan Compatriots recently to address the concerns of Taiwan investors. Whether or not it can reassure Taiwan investors still remains to be seen.

Third, Taiwan's continued restriction on the inflow of mainland capital. Taiwan used to ban any investment from the mainland on the grounds of national security. Since the retrocession of Hong Kong's sovereignty to the PRC, Taiwan has relaxed its restriction in this regard to reciprocate the decision by the Hong Kong Special Administrative Region to allow Taiwan's companies to continue to operate in Hong Kong after July

---

[20] The Plan, launched in 1995, envisages to build Taiwan into the manufacturing, financial, maritime transhipment, air transhipment, telecommunications, and media centres by early next century.

[21] For a detailed account of this development, see Julian Baum, "Dangerous Liaisons", *Far Eastern Economic Review*, March 25, 1999, pp. 10-15.

1998. At present, Taipei would permit investments from overseas companies with a mainland ownership less than 20 percent.[23] However, this position has already been challenged by Hong Kong. During the bilateral negotiations on Taiwan's admission to the World Trade Organisation, the Hong Kong trade representative was reported to have raised his concern over Taiwan's current restriction on investments from Hong Kong-based companies which may comprise more than 20 percent of mainland China ownership.[24] Indeed, Taiwan will soon find its position untenable. According to Article XIII of the Agreement Establishing the WTO, any member has the right to refuse to apply multilateral trade agreements, such as Most Favoured Nation status and National Treatments, to certain members at the time either becomes a member for some particular reason.[25] But this request must be approved by at least two-thirds of member states. China has already made it clear that it will not apply this clause to any party, and this has put Taiwan on the horns of a dilemma. There are signs that Taiwan seems to have softened its stance on this issue and is prepared to sign the treaty without applying the clause to China in order to increase its chance of being admitted into the Organisation.[26] However, how Taiwan is going to reconcile the conflict between the needs of its national security and the requirement of being a member of the WTO, which demands an open and unrestricted market access for all member states, remains to be seen.

## SOCIAL AND CULTURAL EXCHANGES

After four decades of estrangement, both mainland China and Taiwan have taken steps to facilitate social and cultural exchanges between the people on both sides of the Taiwan Strait. Efforts have so far been directed to assisting the reunion of families, relatives and friends between the two sides. As a result, the number of social visits made by private citizens from both sides has expanded rapidly since the lifting of the travel ban by the Taiwan authorities in the late 1980s. Between 1988 and 1998, the Taiwanese had made a total of 13 million visits to the mainland, involving more than three million individuals or one-seventh of Taiwan's total population. Over the same period, the

---

[22] That is certainly one of the important reasons why Taiwan entrepreneurs tended to invest via a third place which has signed the protection agreement with Beijing.

[23] Conversation with Dr. Chong-pin Lin, Vice Chairman of the Mainland Affairs Council, the ROC Government at the University of British Columbia on 21 August 1998.

[24] Cited in Yun-han Chu, "The Challenge of the 1997 Handover for Taiwan," paper presented at the international workshop on Cross-Strait Relations at the University of British Columbia on 20-22 August 1998.

[25] For more details of the Article XIII, see "Marrakech Agreement Establishing the World Trade Organisation," in Joseph F. Dennin (ed.), *Law & Practice of the World Trade Organisation: Marrakech Declaration Booklet* (New York: Oceana Publications. Inc., 1995), p. 17.

[26] Chen Gao-zhang, "Should We Apply the 'Non-Application' Clause to China?" *Taiwan jingji yanjiu yuekang* (Taiwan Economic Research Monthly) (Taipei), Vol. 21, No. 6 (June 1998), pp. 57-58.

mainlanders had made 240,000 visits to Taiwan.[27] That is to say, far more Taiwanese have been allowed to visit the mainland than mainlanders permitted to enter Taiwan, by a staggering ratio of 54 to 1 (13 vs. 0.24). This was due largely to the tight control imposed by Taipei in admitting mainland visitors. On the other hand, by July 1997 a total of 21,506 mainlanders, most of whom are spouses of Taiwanese or grandchildren of lonely elders in Taiwan, had been allowed to settle in Taiwan.[28]

To reduce animosity between each other and enhance mutual understanding, Beijing and Taipei also have placed a great emphasis on cultural exchanges between the two sides on a people-to-people basis. Large numbers of scholars, scientists, medical professionals, artists, journalists, sportsmen/women, and clergymen/women have been invited to make reciprocal visits. Taiwan, keen to spread the so-called "Taiwan experience" in the mainland, has targeted distinguished mainland scholars and celebrities, especially those residing overseas, for "study tours" or "research trips" to the island, and the record of such activities can also be found in Table 9. The highlight of such visits has been the one made by Ms. Zhu Linan, the mainland's Minister of Science and Technology in July 1998. She led a delegation of over 100 mainland scientists and researchers to attend a cross-Strait academic exchange conference organised by Taiwan's "Chinese Chambers of Industry" in Taipei, thus becoming the highest-ranking official from Beijing to visit Taiwan since 1949. Although she made the visit only in her academic capacity (a professor from Tsinghua University), the impact created by her visit has clearly gone beyond the academia.

**Table 9**. Social and Cultural Exchanges Across the Taiwan Strait, 1987-1998

| No. of mainland visitors to Taiwan on cultural exchange programmes (1988-Oct.98) | | | | | |
|---|---|---|---|---|---|
| Cultural & educational | 31,937 | Mass media | 3,424 | Scientific & technological research | 214 |
| Sports | 1,344 | Health care | 962 | Religious | 1,290 |
| Traditional and folk arts | 39 | Professional societies | 37 | Legal | 89 |
| No. of mainland publications and films allowed to enter Taiwan (1988-Oct.1998) | | | | | |
| Publications | 9,110,969 | | Films & TV/video programmes | 37,339 | |

Source: The Mainland Affairs Council, ROC Government (http://www.mac.gov.tw).

China, too, has been actively setting up links with prominent people in Taiwan in its bid to build a "united front" (*tongyi zhanxie*) with forces supporting the goal of reunification in Taiwan. Although detailed data on such activities are not available, it is believed that the size of cultural/academic visits made by the Taiwanese to the mainland is far bigger than that of the opposite flow, similar to the situation of the social visits.

---

[27] *Wen Hui Po*, Jan. 26, 1999, p. A5.

The opening of social and cultural visits between the two sides of the Taiwan Strait has led to some problems. The biggest one for Taiwan seems to be that quite a few mainland visitors have remained in Taiwan after their permission to stay expired. By the end of July 1997, for example, a total of 285 visitors had overstayed their terms and some of them were found to have worked illegally in Taiwan.[29] At the same time, the rapid increase in cross-Strait marriages have resulted in more and more applications by mainland spouses and children of Taiwan citizens to be allowed to settle in Taiwan, challenging Taiwan's tight immigration control imposed on mainlanders. On the other hand, the mainland authorities often complained that some Taiwan visitors had engaged in what they called "inappropriate activities" while travelling in China. For example, some Taiwan clergymen have been accused of carrying out "political infiltration" in mainland churches.[30] Furthermore, due to the loss of historical records and/or evidence and the different legal systems between the two sides, many cases involving inheritance disputes between mainland and Taiwan citizens could not be settled satisfactorily.

## PROSPECTS

The discussions in the preceding sections show that cross-Strait relations have gone through three different stages: a period of military confrontation (1949 – 1978); increasing economic and social exchanges (1979 – 1994); and continued economic interactions and political stalemate (1995 – present). While Beijing has alternated between military coercion and peaceful manoeuvring in different periods, Taipei has also shifted its position from the staunch "three no's" (no contact, no negotiation, no compromise) to "flexible and constructive engagement." Despite the fact that the political differences between the two sides remain deep, growing economic, social and cultural exchanges have considerably narrowed the gaps between the two economies and societies. Robert A. Scalapino describes today's East Asia as "a fascinating combination of economic dynamism and political fragility,"[31] and this description could, as we can see now, not be more accurate in the case of cross-Strait relations over the last two decades.

As far as economic relations are concerned, it is expected that future cross-Strait economic activities will continue to be caught in the tug-of-war between economic and political forces. So far, both Beijing and Taipei have been able to put their political differences aside in pursuing the common goal of economic development, provided that these differences are kept in check. Indeed, the strong desire to reap the benefits of

---

[28] Source as Table 9.

[29] The Mainland Affairs Council, ROC Government, *Kuayue lishi de honggou* (Bridging the Historic Gap), Taipei, October, 1997, p. 86.

[30] Ibid, p. 120.

[31] Scalapino, "Forward," in Jane Khanna (ed.), *Southern China, Hong Kong, and Taiwan: Evolution of a Subregional Economy* (Washington D. C.: The Centre for Strategic and International Studies, 1995), p. vii.

economic cooperation on both sides has prevailed in most cases despite frequent political bickering.

On the political front, the lack of channels through which Beijing and Taipei can regularly and meaningfully interact has characterized cross-Strait relations over the past two decades. As a result, both sides have been prone to misperception and miscalculation, as illustrated by the crises in 1995-96. It is in this sense that the second "Wang-Koo Meeting" has been significant in improving mutual understanding and stabilizing the bilateral relationship. However, deep disagreement and mutual suspicions remain over the terms of reunification.

Twenty years ago, the establishment of diplomatic relations between the PRC and the US played a decisive role in changing cross-Strait relations. Today, the Sino-US relationship still holds the key to the bilateral link. After the missile crises and subsequent military confrontation with the PRC in 1995-96, Washington realized that Taiwan's security could be best protected not by military means, but by building a constructive strategic partnership between the U.S. and the PRC, because "the more valuable the whole relationship becomes for PRC leaders the less likely that they would be inclined to jeopardize it by using force against Taiwan."[32] As a result, Washington clarified its China policy --- to oppose any use of force by Beijing against Taiwan and to oppose Taiwan's unilateral move toward independence. That is to say that the U.S. has to strike a balance between discouraging the PRC from resolving the Taiwan issue by force, and making it clear to Taiwan that they cannot rely on U.S. military intervention if it moves to declare independence. The best way for Washington to achieve this is to encourage Beijing and Taipei to negotiate and cooperate with each other but avoid pressing for early agreement on resolving the Taiwan issue. The "three no's" statement made by Clinton in Shanghai in June 1998 has undoubtedly served to improve the U.S.-China relationship and laid a foundation for subsequent talks held between Beijing and Taipei.

This does not mean, however, that the development of mainland-Taiwan relations will from now on be relatively harmonious. There is no guarantee that Washington's China policy will not be deflected by strong pro-Taiwan sentiments among the U.S. population and lobby forces in Capitol Hill. Despite numerous talks, Beijing and Taipei are still no nearer a solution to their political differences. There are still some on both sides who advocate a quick solution to the Taiwan issue through extremist action. Furthermore, the political democratization in Taiwan has made the future more unpredictable. All these indicate that the prospects for cross-Strait relations remain uncertain, potentially subject to reversal. Indeed, if Beijing and Taipei fail to agree upon the mechanisms to stabilize their relationship, cross-Strait relations could easily fall back to the old pattern of oscillation between military confrontation and peaceful maneuvering.

---

[32] Ralph N. Clough, *op. cit.*, p. 21.

# KOREA'S RELATIONS WITH THE UNITED STATES AND JAPAN

*Hee-Suk Shin*
Professor and Director-General, Division for Asia-Pacific Studies
the Institute of Foreign Affairs and National Security
Ministry of Foreign Affairs
Seoul, Korea

## 1. U.S., JAPAN AND KOREA IN THE CHANGING NORTHEAST ASIAN POLITICS

The end of the Cold War has brought about fundamental changes in world politics. The changing international environment embodies several tendencies. These include the multi-polarization of the international system, increasing political reconciliation among nation-states, the rising importance of economic relations and interdependence among nations.

Those changes require every nation to reassess its basic assumptions and priorities in making foreign and security policies. Korea faces such a situation. In particular, the United States and Japan, which have maintained very close relations with the Republic of Korea (South Korea) are currently in the process of restructuring their foreign policy objectives and behavior. Any resulting policy changes will have direct impact upon south Korea's international security environment and upon the stability of the Korean peninsula.

The United States has faced some difficult challenges in making and implementing foreign policy that will have a direct impact on Korea. Korean security interests and policies by and large have been affected by the direction of U.S. policy. The end of the Cold War and the American success in the Gulf War has made the United States the unique superpower in world politics. However, with America's relative economic decline and the multi-pluralization of the international system, there are divergent and contending views regarding the role that the United States should play in the post-Cold War world.

Japan undoubtedly has been one of Korea's most important countries before and after the end of World War II. Japan is reevaluating the basic premises of its post-war foreign and security policy characterized by dependence on the United States and low-posture diplomacy. In the past, it was primarily concerned with economic growth and regional stability for its export-driven economy to flourish. However, Japan is now beginning to articulate a stronger position in international politics, one commensurate with its position as an economic superpower. Japan's strong position in the international system is further strengthened by the reality that economic and technological power is gradually becoming more important than military capabilities.

Faced with the staggering budget deficit and the increasing pressure to trim defense expenditures, the Clinton administration should deal with calls for a significant reduction in the U.S. military presence abroad, particularly in the Asia-Pacific theater. Many people in the U.S. Congress feel that the time has come for the nations in the region to bear a greater defense burden.

This raises fears that the U.S. could prematurely disengage from the region, including the Korean peninsula, possibly prompting regional powers (Japan, Russia and China) to attempt to fill the resulting power vacuum.

It is widely held in Asia, including South Korea, that Japan is preparing to expand its political role and security influence in Asia. Japanese Diets' passage of the PKO bill and the emerging trend of new-conservatism have spurred its neighbor's suspicion and countervailing moves.

For many Asians and Americans, concerns about Japan's expansionism are gradually replacing those once held toward possible threat by the former Soviet Union which could have provided a strong ground for justifying a continuing U.S. military presence in the region. Their fear is that, in the event of U.S. military withdrawal, Japan might try to fill the power vacuum with its own power, prompted by either a sense of insecurity or a sense of its newly expanded responsibilities in the region.

## 2. DYNAMISM IN ASIA-PACIFIC AND KOREAN PENINSULA

Asia and the Pacific is a region where the interests of three nuclear powers (namely the United States, Russia, and China) and one economic superpower (Japan) intersect. In between these big powers, there are smaller states including the two Koreas. Over recent decades, the Asia-Pacific economy has grown more rapidly than any other places. As a result, the economy in the region has become the main source of dynamism in international trade and investment.

In view of this economic dynamism of the Asia-Pacific region, there are three general observations about the characteristics of the regional system.

To begin with, the strategic environment in the Asia-Pacific region is different from that in the Europe-Atlantic region. The former is characterized by greater diversity and regional disputes.

Secondly, in relative terms, the influences of the United States and Russia in the region seem to be on the decline, whereas those of Japan and China are on the rise, thus giving them more room for pursuing predominance over the region.

Thirdly, Japan and the Asian NICs, including Korea, have successfully pursued economic growth and technological development through a unique combination of the state role and market mechanisms. The Korean peninsula becomes geopolitically one of the important parts of this region.

The tension on the Korean peninsula is still high, particularly over North Korea's nuclear weapons program. Nevertheless, the Korean peninsula could not be immune to the dramatic changes in its international relations in the past few years.

Japanese efforts to normalize relations with North Korea stalled due to Pyongyang's reluctance to allow mutual and comprehensive inspections of its nuclear facilities by IAEA. The United States, Japan and South Korea have coordinated their efforts in persuading North Korea to abandon its suspected nuclear weapons project and to keep its commitments under the Nuclear Non-Proliferation Treaty (NPT), dropping the position with which North Korea announced its withdrawal in March 1993.

Since the Geneva Accord between the U.S. and North Korea in October, 1994, it can be believed that North Korea will eventually take the way of peaceful coexistence in its relations with South Korea in the future.

In such an event, a new era of genuine reconciliation and cooperation will emerge. Undoubtedly, settlement of the North Korean nuclear issue will lay a firm foundation for the establishment of peace on the Korean peninsula.

It will further contribute to making the Northeast Asian region a safer and more peaceful place. Recently, the diplomatic channels have been launched to move so fast to tackle this pressing issue. This nuclear issue has already become an international issue rather than local or regional one.

Since the Geneva Accord the United States, Japan and Korea have held official talks several times to finance U.S. $4 billion as part of the North Korea nuclear deal. The purpose of the talks was to establish an international consortium called the Korea Energy Development Organization (KEDO), which will eventually handle the matters including financing the project to shift from graphite nuclear reactors to light-water reactors in North Korea.

The three countries agreed that meaningful inter-Korean dialogues are also essential to secure a smooth implementation of the U.S.-North Korea nuclear agreement. It is our firm belief that South Korea should play a key role in the project proposed by KEDO and the light-water nuclear reactors to be supplied to North Korea should be South Korea's model.

## 3. NECESSITY FOR KOREA-JAPAN REGIONAL COOPERATION

South Korea's relations with the United States and Japan are the most important parts of its foreign policy. In general, Korea's relationship with the U.S. has been dominated by security commitments, and that with Japan by economic interests.

Despite the past colonial relationship between Korea and Japan, it is imperative to maintain the cooperative relationship that has been developing since the normalization of diplomatic ties in 1965, not only for both countries, but also for peace and stability in the Asia-Pacific region as a whole.

In such a context of Korea-Japan relations our immediate questions are: What kind of expanded role should and could Japan play in the context of Korea-Japan relations in the future, and will the twenty-first century be an age of the Asia-Pacific region with Japan at its center? Some people in Korea and the U.S. suspect that Japan could lead world politics.

In view of the fact that Northeast Asia is the principal area where Korean and Japanese interests intersect, the cooperation of the two economies in this area is a key test whether the Korea-Japan partnership could be possible or not. Korea-Japan diplomatic partnership is vital and prerequisite to bringing regional stability and economic dynamics. There have always been significant areas of cooperation and coordination between Korea and Japan.

As mentioned earlier, it is widely held in Korea that Japan is preparing to expand its role in the political and security affairs in Asia.

Recently, the Japanese government, expressing its regrets for Japanese military actions during World War II, has sought a permanent seat in the UN Security Council and has expressed its willingness to discharge its commitment as being "a nation of peace." Japanese Foreign Minister Kono has also reiterated the intention early this year. This requires an intimate diplomatic cooperation between Korea and Japan.

This year Korea and Japan will mark the 30th anniversary of the normalization of diplomatic relations in 1965. On the other hand, 1995 is the 50th anniversary of the end of World War II, and Korea will also mark the 50th anniversary of its liberation from the Japanese colonial occupation. Two decades of an unofficial relationship between the two neighboring countries until the normalization between Korea and Japan in 1965 could be characterized by the complicated nature of the Korea-Japan ties and the last three decades after normalization are also by different types of another complicated nature of relationship.

One of the characteristic aspects of the current Korea-Japan relations is that the competitive national sentiments (Kokuminkanjio) and the negative mutual image between the two peoples primarily formulated during the colonial period have been the major undermining factor of the relationship between the two countries.

Nobody can deny the necessity of mutual cooperation between Korea and Japan. In view of geographical proximity, historical and cultural ties and the existing security and economic interdependence, Korea-Japan friendly relations are mutually beneficial. In simple terms, the relationship has two different aspects. One is mutually competitive and the other is mutually complimentary.

Since last year, both Japan and Korea have undergone a similar process of political reform. The coalition government under Prime Minister Murayama also gave the final blow to the so-called "55 political system" under which the governing Liberal Democratic Party had enjoyed political dominance for nearly four decades. Political reforms attempted by the three different coalition governments of Murayama Cabinets, have been expected to usher in a more transparent and assertive Japan.

The relationship between Korea and Japan should develop into a future-oriented partnership after the 30th anniversary of the establishment of diplomatic ties and the 50th anniversary of Korea's liberation from the Japanese colonial rule. As the two countries need each other, the political and diplomatic leaders of both countries sometimes will agree on the necessity to strengthen the ties of friendship between the two countries. It is, indeed, in the context of such a shifting regional security environment that it requires more thorough analysis of the role of the U.S. and Japan in the Asia-Pacific in the years ahead.

## 4. ROLE OF THE U.S. AND JAPAN

### a) U.S. as a Regional Balancing Power

Since the end of World War II, the primary concerns of the United States in Northeast Asia have been focused on the matter of countering the perceived threat from the other superpower, the former Soviet Union. However, the U.S. regional priority has historically been given to Western Europe, because the United States has historically had its special interests in it, because Europe has been the most potentially dangerous theater of superpowers' rivals.

As U.S. relations with Asia-Pacific countries are becoming more extensive in recent years, firstly the growing importance of the entire region for the U.S. has begun to be recognized by U.S. policy-makers. The U.S. trade volume with the Asia-Pacific region is now even greater than any other part of the world, including Western Europe. As far as trade is concerned, no other region will be as important to the United States as the Asia-Pacific in the coming century.

Secondly, as long as there still exist a lot of uncertainties in the Asia-Pacific region, only the U.S. is regarded as being able to play a key role as a final guarantor of peace and security in the region. As was witnessed, the tensions which have politically and militarily existed for the past several decades in this region have been tremendously reduced with the sudden collapse of the old Soviet Union. Nevertheless, many Asian countries are nervous about the hidden intentions of some of their neighbors.

There has been no regional security system in the Asia-Pacific region. The United States, whose Pacific Coast shares the ocean with Asian powers, is in a unique position to help stabilize the region.

What would be the minimum role in this context that the United States should play in Northeast Asia? One view is that the United States should remain capable, even with its reduced military presence in the region, of projecting its troops into any troubled part of the Pacific. The U.S. role of acting as a balancing power in Asia and the Pacific would be essential to peace and prosperity in the region.

The U.S. policies, nevertheless, experienced with their trade frictions with the Asian countries and also influenced by costly domestic programs, may not be expected to support such a continuing U.S. role in Asia. Accordingly, the continued U.S. commitment to the region does not mean that the Asian nations will sit back and do nothing. It is the responsibility of Asian nations to create a peaceful and prosperous environment in which the United States would remain to play a constructive role engaged in the region in the next decades.

### b) Japan as a Non-Military Power

The emerging new world order requires new responses from Japan, a nation that has undergone a major transformation in international standing by virtue of its economic and technological capability. The watershed came in the middle of the 1980s when Japan became the largest creditor and investor in the world. This raised a new awareness of international responsibility among the Japanese people, and led to a surge of debates whether Japan's expanded role goes along with its economic strength.

Since the burst of the so-called "bubble economy" in the late 1980s, attention has momentarily focused on how to pull Japan out of the economic downturn and how to puts its economic and political house in order. As a result, the issue of Japan's new and larger international role has been put on hold while the nation is preoccupied with these domestic problems. But it is expected that Japan will come to tackle the issue again in order to prepare for the next century.

As mentioned earlier. The Asia-Pacific region has grown more rapidly over the past few decades than any other region in international political history. For the Asian nations, which are now on the threshold of dramatic transformation, an opportunity has come to establish long-term objectives for the future order of peace and security in this region. Three objectives for the region are economic prosperity, political development, and a new regional security arrangement.

Japan, as an economic superpower which possesses enormous investment capital, higher technology and well-established democratic system of government has the will and capacity with which it can achieve all three of these objectives.

First, in respect to its contribution to regional prosperity, as the "economic locomotive" for Asia and the Pacific, Japan could be an obvious leader for its economic success. In fact, Japan as a model state for economic development and as a source of investment capital and technology, has undoubtedly been an important factor in the recent dynamism of the Asia-Pacific economy.

The second role for Japan in the region is a political one. It is quite natural that Japan's economic dominance should accordingly transfer into political influence. Various initiatives by the Japanese Government have been taken to participate actively in such a U.N. peacekeeping operation as well as the Japanese foreign assistance programs. But Japan's political leadership in Asia and the Pacific should be taken into consideration by its foreign relations in recent history which was reflected on the darker parts of its foreign policy implementation, particularly before and after the Manchurian invasion. While taking an obvious economic role in Asia, Japan seems to suffer from its weakness derived from its past aggressive actions. From the Japan side, many approaches have been attempted to mitigate the uncomfortable feeling among Asian people.

Thirdly, Japan's role in the Asia-Pacific region also involves regional security. Many Asian countries have no serious objection to Japan's recent proposal for the establishment of a regional security framework and a multilateral dialogue among Asia-Pacific nations as mid- and long-term objectives. Needless to say, in view of Japan's colonial power in the prewar period, its security role has some limits. Therefore, Japan's involvement in world politics and economy in non-military areas is most recommendable.

Many Asian countries hope that Japan plays these three roles within the scope of the U.S.-Japan security framework, where the U.S. can play its role as a regional balancing power. Accordingly, Japan's security role also lies in supporting a continuing U.S. military engagement in the Asia-Pacific region, thereby constantly providing a collective good for regional stability. Japan's Asian neighbors, bearing an ever-standing fear of the revival of Japanese militarism, desire that Tokyo will not become a great military power again.

Thus, Japan could contribute to the peace and stability of Asia and the Pacific as a regional non-military power. In this context, the U.S.-Japan alliance system, primarily designed to deter the former Soviet threat in the past, is still a crucial factor even in the post-Cold War era.

From this perspective, however, what seems to be worrisome is a troubled partnership between the U.S. and Japan, mainly stemming from enormous trade imbalance, which might affect negatively otherwise to harm bilateral security relationship.

According to the Japanese Ministry of Finance, it is said that the United States and Japan have reached an agreement to allow foreign access to Japan's financial service market. The agreement would have great significance not only for U.S.-Japan bilateral relations, but also for international financial market liberalization. In the summit meeting between President Clinton and Prime Minister Murayama in Washington early this year, they have agreed on the need to cooperate on global security issues, trade disputes as well as North Korea's nuclear program. Since the U.S. and Japan are two of Korea's diplomatic partners, the continuing friendly ties between the two is desirable for Korea's foreign policy implementation in the future.

One of the best-sellers in Japan about U.S.-Japan relations for the last several years is, "The Coming War with Japan" written by George Friedman who is currently a professor of political science at Dickinson College in Pennsylvania. Though the author has envisaged some possibility of another Pacific War between Japan and the United States in his book, it is not conceivable to believe such a war will never occur again. People are confident that as long as they need each other, the international circumstance in Asia and the Pacific will never let them allow any type of war again.

Given the implications of the changing roles of the United States and Japan in the future, our last concern is how Korea will respond to this changing international environment.

## 5. CONCLUSION: HOW KOREA WILL RESPOND

As mentioned earlier, the international environment in the Asia-Pacific region is under an unprecedented transition.

To meet the upcoming Asia-Pacific era of the 21st century, Korea will not only actively participate in regional cooperation, but also pursue a constructive and diplomatic role which will contribute greatly to the regional goals.

There are some views in Korea about how to achieve the consolidation of peace and stability. One conceivable way is to form a multilateral forum in the region to chart its future course, which will seek comprehensive regional disarmament and security. The other way is to establish an Asia-Pacific multilateral security framework mainly consisting of the U.S., Japan, and Korea. Under this security framework, it could possibly include some regional forum like ASEAN for wider multilateral dialogue in that effect.

Korea's diplomacy for national reunification involves three related tasks: management of the division, achievement of reunification, and preparation for the post-unification era.

As mentioned previously, Korea's relationship with the U.S. has been dominated by security concerns, while that with Japan has been dominated by economic issues. But now, Korea's diplomatic normalization with China and Russia appears to have accelerated diversified processes to the reunification.

However, given the traditional and friendly ties between Korea and the United States, particularly since the end of the Korean War, the Korean people are very much thankful to the Americans for what they have contributed to Korea's nation-building and economic development process. The Korea-America alliance structure has been strengthened under the constant threat of North Korea during the Cold War period, since the threat from the North seemed to be considerably diminished and the economic securities of both nations are challenged.

In the coming years of the so-called "economic cold war," it is conceivable for the U.S. and Korea to become economic allies. As the U.S.-Korea security partnership has been successful, the U.S.-Korea economic partnership will also be possible. As the "comprehensive security" is more generally referred to as a new concept of the new world order, "comprehensive alliance" relationships may be desirable. The United States and Korea need to strengthen their bilateral relations in the spirit of comprehensive alliance.

And given the colonial relationship between Japan and Korea, it is imperative to maintain the cooperative relationship that has been developed since the normalization of diplomatic relations in 1965, not only for the benefit of the bilateral relationship, but also for the enhancement of peace and stability in the Asia-Pacific region.

Ever since the Korean War, South Korea has been preoccupied with the immediate possible threat from North Korea. As a result, security concerns were given the highest priority in domestic policy-making and budget allocation. As Korea's security environment is gradually becoming more complicated, Korea's perception to the external threat has also been changed.

These require Korea to look into the broader regional context and non-conventional defense issues such as the matters of nuclear safety, environment and economic security.

Korea-Japan relations are taking on a new shape in the midst of political reform. On the occasion of President Kim's visit to Tokyo last year, it was reported that the Japanese Prime Minister mentioned the need to diversity and internationalize the channels between the two countries in order to establish a future-oriented relationship. This also emphasizes the significance of building mutual trust between the two people by putting aside the uncomfortable past. Internationalization means to expand the scope of bilateral ties to the regional and global ones. In constructing new Korea-Japan ties, there is a real need for cooperation in areas with regional or global implications.

In order to overcome the historical animosity, both Korea and Japan are urged to take a forward-looking stance and future-oriented diplomatic posture toward each other. These would be possible ways to implement regional cooperation in the security and economic fields. For this purpose, the Japanese should be more sincere for what they did during the wartime period. By doing so, we can expect a much more cooperative and future-oriented Korea-Japan regional partnership in the years to come.

# DOES EXCHANGE VALUE OF THE YEN PLAY ANY ROLE IN THE JAPANESE TRADE?

*Mohsen Bahmani-Oskooee*
Professor, Department of Economics
The University of Wisconsin-Milwaukee
Milwaukee, WI 53201

## I. INTRODUCTION

Since the advent of current floating exchange rates, the yen has appreciated in nominal terms against different currencies at different rates. Over the same period, Japan's trade balance has improved substantially against her trading partners. This pattern of movement in the trade balance and the value of the Yen contradicts our theoretical expectation that a strong currency should hurt external position of a country. Is there any relation between exchange value of the Yen and the Japanese trade balance? If yes, why Japan's trade balance has improved despite appreciation of the Yen?

The purpose of this paper is to investigate the relation between exchange value of the Yen and the trade balance of Japan. In doing so, in section II, we consider several different concepts related to the exchange value of the Yen and the trade balance. We then introduce a trade model and report estimation results in section III. In section IV we provide a summary.

## II. DEFINITION AND CONCEPTS

The statistics reported in international publications such as International Financial Statistics (IFS) by the International Monetary Fund (IMF) shows that the value of one dollar in terms of the Yen was about 360 Yen per dollar in early 1971. That rate stands at 124 Yen per dollar as of writing of this paper. Such rate that is also reported by news media every day and is used in exchanging currencies for the purpose of traveling or financing the trade between Japan and the United States, is referred to as **nominal bilateral exchange rate.** Thus, using the numbers cited above, we conclude that while the U.S. dollar has depreciated nominally against the Yen from 360 Yen to 124 Yen, the Japanese Yen has appreciated from 1/360 = 0.0028 dollar to 1/124 = 0.0081 dollar per yen. When the yen appreciates against the dollar or it becomes expensive in terms of the dollar, all Japanese exports become expensive in dollar, leading to a decline in Japanese exports. On the other hand, depreciation of the dollar against the Yen or cheaper dollars makes Japanese imports from the U.S. cheaper resulting in an increase in Japanese imports from the U.S. The decrease in exports and increase in imports is expected to cause a deterioration in the Japanese trade balance. However, cheaper imports from the U.S. can spread through the Japansese economy resulting in a general deflation in overall price level including those of exportables. Thus, increase in the price of Japanese exports due to strong Yen could partially be offset by a general deflation. Thus, in investigating the effects of a change in nominal exchange rate on trade flows we need to adjust the nominal exchange rate by price levels in both, the United States and Japan. The resulting rate is known as **real bilateral exchange rate.** If we denote the nominal bilateral exchange rate between country i and Japan by $R_{ji}$ (number of i's currency per Yen), the price level in Japan by $P_j$ and the price level in country i by $P_i$, the real bilateral rate is then calculated as $(P_j.R_{ji})/P_i$. By construction, an increase in this measure will reflect a real appreciation of the Yen and a decrease, a real depreciation. Note that real appreciation which makes Japanese exports relatively expensive could be due to an increase in $R_{ji}$, i.e., nominal appreciation; inflation in Japan, i.e., an increase in $P_j$, and a deflation in trading partner i, i.e., a decrease in $P_i$.

However, the real value of a country's currency may rise against one currency and decline against another. What happens to the overal real value of a currency like the yen? A measure that reflects overal movements of the real value of a currency is known as **multilateral real exchange rate** or **real effective exchange rate.** Since in this paper our concern is the relation between Japan's total trade and its relation with the value of the yen, we need to use a more comprehensive measure of the real value of the Yen throughout our analysis, i.e., real effective rate. How do we construct it? This measure using data from 25 major trading partners is already constructed for the yen by Bahmani-Oskooee and Shabsigh (1996) using a simple method and needs no repeat here. We only extend the sample to include more recent available data.[1] What has happened to the real effective value of the Yen over time. The quarterly data are plotted in Figure 1.

---

[1]. For more details of how to construct real and nominal effective exchange rates see Bahmani-Oskooee (1995).

**Figure 1. The Real Effective Value of the Yen**

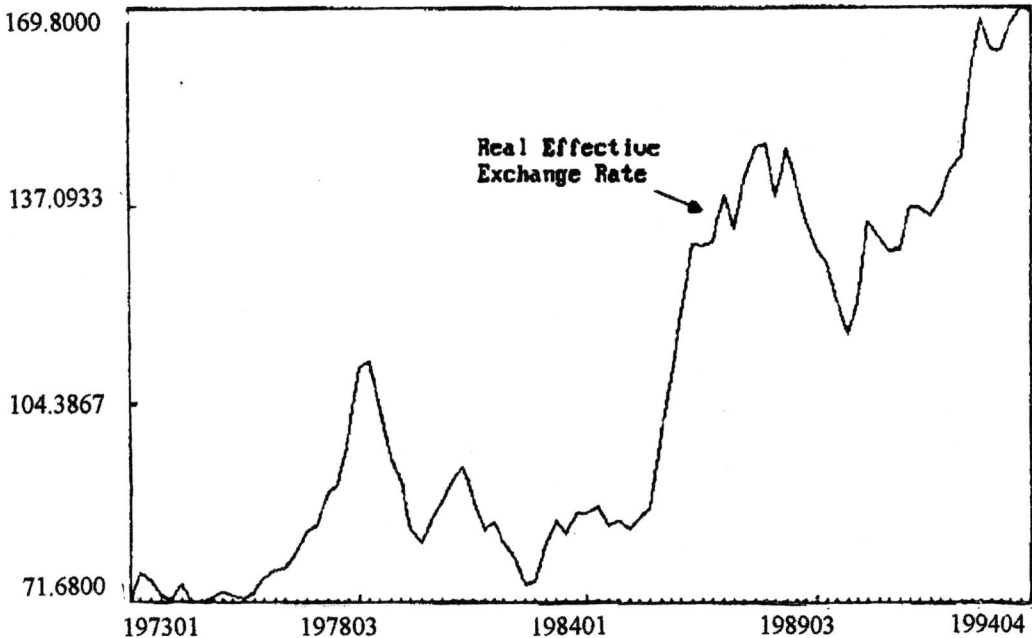

As can be seen from Figure 1, the trend of the real value of the Yen is on the rise. Overall, between 1973 and 1994, it has appreciated. What has happened to the trade flows of Japan over the same period? A country not only exports goods and services, but it also imports. A measure that summarizes performances of imports and exports in one concept is know as the **trade balance**. The trade balance is usually defined as the difference between domestic or foreign currency values of imports and exports. However, in trying to establish the empirical relation between the trade balance and the exchange rate (as well as other determinants of the trade balance), previous studies has shown that the results could be sensitive to the units of measurements of the trade balance.[2] Should the trade balance be meassured in domestic currency or foreign currency? Due to conflicting results from the previous research, we follow Haynes and Stone (1982) and Bahmani-Oskooee (1991) and rely upon the ratio of imports over exports, say M/X. Bahmani-Oskooee has argued that this measure is not only unit free, but it also reflects the the performance of the trade balance in real or nominal terms. After all, the numerator and the denominator in M/X must be deflated by the same price

---

[2]. For conflicting results see Miles (1979) versus Himarios (1985).

index to arrive at real values. What has then happened to the Japanese imports/exports ratio over 1973-1994 period? The ratio is depicted in Figure 2.

**Figure 2. The Ratio of Imports over Exports of Japan**

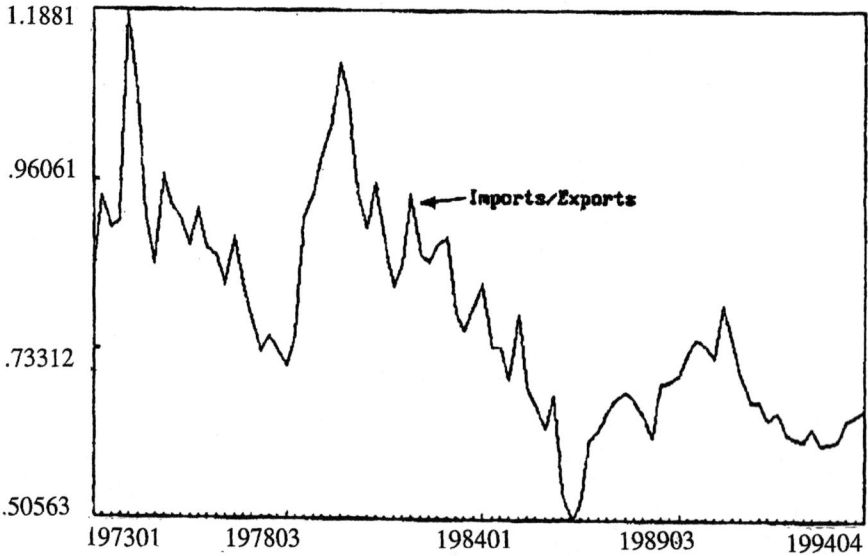

As can be seen from the figure, although there are ups and downs, the trend of the ratio has been on the decline, implying that Japan's trade balance has improved, either due to less imports or increaed exports. To get an insight into the relative importance of imports and exports as contributing factors to the favorable trade performance of Japan, we plot them separately in Figure 3.

**Figure 3. Japan's Imports and Exports in Billions of Yen**

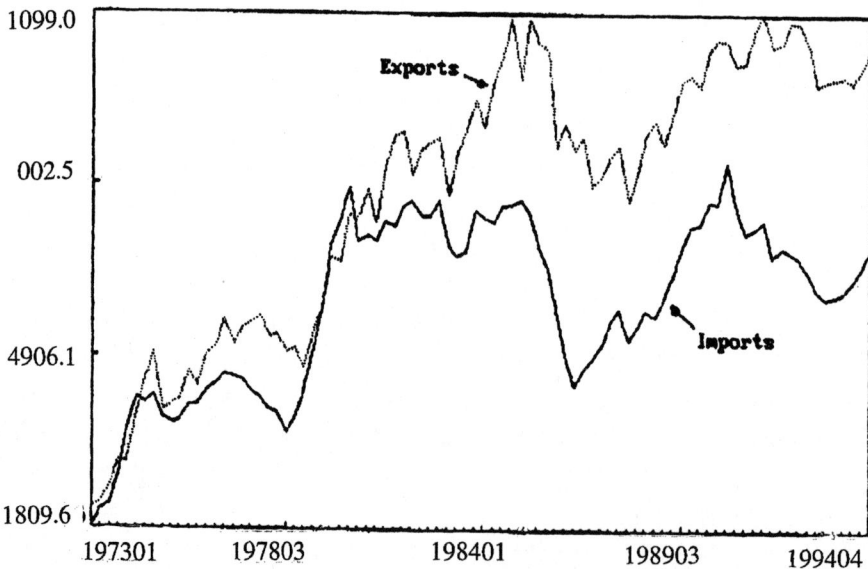

It is evident from Figure 3 that although exports and imports have moved in a parellel phashion, exports have always exceeded imports resulting in a trade surplus. The trade surplus is specially noticable since early 1980s. Why Japan has enjoyed trade surplus despite real appreciation of the yen as we evidenced in Figure 1? Does real exchange value of the yen have anything to do with the Japanese trade? The answer to such questions are provided in the next section.

## III. THE TRADE MODEL AND THE RESULTS

As we indicated in the previous section, we intend to use the ratio of imports over exports, i.e., M/X as a measure of the trade balance. Haynes and Stone (1982) used this measure in order to express their model in log form so that they can estimate elasticities. Bahmani-Oskooee (1991, p.404) also used the ratio and provided two additional justifications, that the ratio is not sensitive to units of measurement and that the ratio could be interpreted as nominal or real trade balance.

By glancing through Figures 1 and 2 one forms an opinion that either the real exchange value of the yen and Japan's trade balance are not related or if they are, the relation is in contrast with our theoretical expectation that it should be a positive one. However, this type of approach to infer the relation between just two variables is inaccurate, mainly due to the fact that we are ignoring other factors. For example, if economic growth in Japan has contributed to her increased exports over time, we need to incorporate this factor into our analysis and determine whether real appreciation of the Yen exerts its expected effect after allowance is made to economic growth in Japan. For this reason, we employ the ratio definition of the trade balance coupled with its determinants from Rose and Yellen (1989) as in equation (1):

$$\text{Log } (M/X)_t = a + b \text{ Log } Y_t + c \text{ Log } YW_t + d \text{ Log } EX_t + \varepsilon_t \tag{1}$$

where
M = Japan's nominal imports,
X = Japan's nominal exports,
Y = index of real domestic income,
YW = index of real world income,
EX = index of real effective value of the Yen.

What are the expected signs of coefficients in equation (1)? Following the literature, if a growing economy is to import more, estimate of b should be positive. However, if increase in production in Japan is due to an increase in the production of import-substitute goods, Japan could actually import less. Thus, it is expected that estimates of b could also be negative. Furthermore, as indicated above if economic growth in Japan contributes to export growth, again we could expect b to be negative. If an increase in world income is to stimulate Japan's exports, estimate of c should be negative. Finally, if a real appreciation, i.e., an increase in EX is to increase Japan's imports and reduce her exports, estimate of d should be positive.[3]

How are we going to estimate equation (1). With the existing evidnece on the non-stationarity of the time series data, we apply Johansen-Juselius (1990) cointegration analysis. In applying the cointegration technique, we first must determine whether each variable in the model is stationary or has a unit root. To that end, we apply the ADF test (with trend) to the level of each variable as well as to the first differenced variables and report the results in Table 1.

**Table 1.** The ADF Test Results for the
Level and for the First Differenced Variables.

| Variable | Level | First Differences |
|----------|-------|-------------------|
| Ln (M/X) | $-3.23[4]^{a,b}$ | -4.85[4] |
| Ln Y | -2.20[4] | -4.82[1] |
| Ln YW | -0.45[2] | -4.44[4] |
| Ln EX | -0.60[1] | -4.66[4] |

Notes:   a. Number inside the bracket is the number of lags in the ADF test.
b. Mackinnon (1991) critical value of the ADF statistic (with a trend term in the procedure) is -3.46 at the 5% level of significance.

From Table 1 we gather that our calculated ADF statistic is less than its critical value only for the first differenced variables. This indicates that all variables have one unit root.

Next we try to eatablish the long-run equilibrium relation among all four variables of equation (1) using Johansen-Juselius (1990) cointegration technique. The attractiveness of this method is that it allows feedback effects among the variables in the model. Johansen and Juselius (1990) introduce two test statistics known as $\lambda$-max and trace tests. These two tests are used to identify the number of cointegrating vectors among the variables in the model. It has been shown that the results produced by the Johansen-Juselius technique could be sensitive to the choice of the order of VAR. Since the data are quarterly over 1973-1994 period, we first impose four lags on the VAR. We carry out the procedure with and without a trend term and report the results in Table 2.

---

[3]. All data come from different issues of International Financial Statistics except the world income (YW) which proxied by the index of industrial production in OECD countries and is collectd from OECD Main Economic Indiators.

**Table 2.** Johansen's Maximum Likelihood Procedure
Results with Four Lags ( r = number of cointegrating vectors).

Panel A: The Results of $\lambda$-Max and Trace Tests

Case 1: No Trend in the Procedure

| Null | Alternative | $\lambda$-max Statistic | 95% Critical Value | Trace Statistic | 95% Critical Value |
|------|-------------|------------|-----------|-----------|-----------|
| r = 0 | r = 1 | 28.71* | 28.14 | 71.71* | 53.11 |
| r<= 1 | r = 2 | 23.14* | 22.00 | 43.00* | 34.91 |
| r<= 2 | r = 3 | 12.04 | 15.67 | 19.87 | 19.96 |
| r<= 3 | r = 4 | 7.82 | 9.24 | 7.82 | 9.24 |

Case 2: Trend Term in the Procedure

| Null | Alternative | $\lambda$-max Statistic | 95% Critical Value | Trace Statistic | 95% Critical Value |
|------|-------------|------------|-----------|-----------|-----------|
| r = 0 | r = 1 | 23.92 | 27.14 | 57.54* | 48.28 |
| r<= 1 | r = 2 | 23.00* | 21.07 | 33.62* | 31.53 |
| r<= 2 | r = 3 | 9.16 | 14.90 | 10.61 | 17.95 |
| r<= 3 | r = 4 | 1.44 | 8.18 | 1.44 | 8.18 |

Panel B: Estimates of Cointegrating Vectors

| Cases | Ln M/X | Ln Y | Ln YW | Ln EX |
|-------|--------|------|-------|-------|
| Case 1 | -1.00 | -5.01 | 9.72 | -0.86 |
| | -1.00 | -9.56 | -1.26 | 0.82 |
| | [6.17] | [13.4] | [12.9] | [5.37] |
| Case 2 | -1.00 | -3.78 | 6.39 | -0.17 |
| | -1.00 | 0.77 | -4.42 | 1.21 |
| | [5.59] | [14.5] | [13.4] | [4.61] |

Note: In panel B the degrees of freedom of $\chi^2$ statistic is the same as number of cointegrating vectors in each case. The critical value of $\chi^2_{(2)} = 4.61$, at the 10% level of significance.

Panel A in Table 2 reports the calculated $\lambda$-max and trace tests. It is clear that the null hypothesis of no cointegration (i.e., r = 0 ) is rejected by both tests in case 1 and by trace test in case 2, mainly due to the fact that our calculated statistics are larger than their critical values. This notion of a significant statistic is identified in the table by an * next to the statistic. Therefore, we know that there exists at least one cointegrating vector in each case. The null of at most one vector is also rejected in favor of r = 2. However, the null of at most two cointegrating vectors cannot be rejected in favor of r = 3. Thus, in each case there are two cointegrating vectors. In order to infer about the expected sign of each variable in the model, we report the two cointegrating vectors for each case in Panel B of Table 2. Note that we normalize the vectors on Ln (M/X) by setting its coefficient at -1.00. Additionally, we also report in Panel B, inside the bracket beneath estimated coefficients, the likelihood ratio (LR) test for the exclusion of each variable from the cointegrating space. It has been shown by Johansen and Juselius (1990, p. 194) that the LR test of restrictions is based on the estimates of eigenvalues of unrestricted and restricted cointegrating space according to

$$2Ln(Q)= T\Sigma^r_{i=1}ln\{(1-\lambda^*_i)/(1-\lambda_i)\} \hspace{2cm} (2)$$

where r is the number of cointegrating vectors, $\lambda^*$ is the eigenvalue of the ith vector from the restricted space and $\lambda$ is the eigenvalue of the ith vector from unrestricted cointegrating space. They show that quantity (2) is distributed as $\chi^2$ with degrees of freedom that is equal to number of cointegrating vectors in each case.[4] It is clear that the LR test is significant for all estimated coefficients, implying that all variables belong to the cointegrating space. The income variable carries a negative coefficient in three out of four vectors indicating that in Japan an increase in domestic production increases exports more than it increases imports leading to an improvement in Japan's trade balance. The remaining two variables carry positive coefficients in two vectors and negative coefficients in the other two. Specifficaly, as far as the effects of exchange rate is concerened, we are not sure whether real appreciation of the yen has hurt Japan's trade balance. Further analysis is necessary. We thus, do some sensitivity analysis by increasing the order of VAR to five. The results are reported in Table 3.

**Table 3.** Johansen's Maximum Likelihood Procedure Results
with Five Lags ( r = number of cointegrating vectors).

**Panel A:** The Results of λ-Max and Trace Tests

Case 1: No Trend in the Procedure

| Null | Alternative | λ-max Statistic | 95% Critical Value | Trace Statistic | 95% Critical Value |
|------|-------------|-----------------|--------------------|-----------------|--------------------|
| r = 0 | r = 1 | 36.45* | 28.14 | 88.11* | 53.11 |
| r<= 1 | r = 2 | 30.20* | 22.00 | 51.65* | 34.91 |
| r<= 2 | r = 3 | 15.26 | 15.67 | 21.45* | 19.96 |
| r<= 3 | r = 4 | 6.18 | 9.24 | 6.18 | 9.24 |

---

[4]. For more details of this test and its application, see Bahmani-Oskooee (1996).

Case 2: Trend Term in the Procedure

| Null | Alternative | λ-max Statistic | 95% Critical Value | Trace Statistic | 95% Critical Value |
|---|---|---|---|---|---|
| r = 0 | r = 1 | 34.58* | 27.14 | 75.94* | 48.28 |
| r<= 1 | r = 2 | 23.81* | 21.07 | 41.36* | 31.53 |
| r<= 2 | r = 3 | 13.22 | 14.90 | 17.55 | 17.95 |
| r<= 3 | r = 4 | 4.32 | 8.18 | 4.33 | 8.18 |

**Panel B:** Estimates of Cointegrating Vectors

| Cases | Ln M/X | Ln Y | Ln YW | Ln EX |
|---|---|---|---|---|
| Case 1 | -1.00 | 1.22 | -5.02 | 1.17 |
| | -1.00 | -1.21 | 2.08 | -0.47 |
| | -1.00 | -18.5 | 35.5 | 1.24 |
| | [23.4] | [16.0] | [19.2] | [13.9] |
| Case 2 | -1.00 | 0.08 | -1.66 | 0.38 |
| | -1.00 | -2.24 | 4.82 | -0.94 |
| | [15.6] | [8.43] | [10.9] | [8.33] |

Note: In panel B the degrees of freedom of $\chi^2$ statistic is the same as number of cointegrating vectors in each case. The critical value of $\chi^2_{(2)} = 4.61$, and $\chi^2_{(3)} = 6.25$, at the 10% level of significance.

From Table 3 we gather that at least by the trace test, there are three cointegrating vectors in case 1 and two vectors in case 2. Again Panel B shows that all variables are highly significant, therefore, they all belong to cointegrating vectors. Now, the real effective exchange rate carries theoretically expected positive sign in three out of five vectors, indicating that most likely the real appreciation of the yen has had unfavorable effect on Japan's trade balance.

It should be noted that this unfavorable effect of real appreciation of the yen is only revealed after taking into account the economic growth of Japan which is said to boost her exports substantially, more than offsetting any decline due to real appreciation.

## IV. SUMMARY AND CONLUSION

Since the advent of current flexible exchange rate system, the Japanese yen has continued to appreciate in real term. At the same time, Japan has enjoyed a trade surplus. Has the economic relation between an exchange rate and a trade balance broken down in the case of Japan or could strong yen have hurt Japan's trade balance if there was no economic growth in Japan?

In this paper we investigated the response of Japan's trade balance to the real value of the yen by specifying a trade balance model which included a measure of domestic and world income in addition to exchange rate. Using quarterly data over 1973-1994 period, coefficient estimates of the model using Johansen-Juselius cointegration technique revealed that in most instances, real appreciation of the Yen had unfavorable effect on Japan's trade balance.

## REFERENCES

Bahmani-Oskooee, Mohsen, "Is There a Long-Run Relation Between the Trade Balance and the Real Effective Exchange Rate of LDCs? *Economics Letters*, Vol. 36, August 1991, 403-407.

Bahmani-Oskooee, Mohsen, "Real and Nominal Effective Exchange Rates for 22 LDCs: 1971I-1990IV," *Applied Economics*, Vol. 27, 1995, 591-604.

Bahmani-Oskooee, Mohsen, "The Black Market Exchange Rate and Demand for Money in Iran", *Journal of Macroeconomics*, Vol. 18 (winter 1996), pp. 171-176.

Bahmani-Oskooee, M. and Ghiath Shabsigh, "The Demand for Money in Japan: Evidence from Cointegration Analysis", *Japan and the World Economy*, Vol. 8 (1996), pp. pp. 1-10.

Haynes, Stephen E., and Joe A. Stone, "Impact of the Terms of Trade on the U.S. Trade Balance: A Reexamination," *The Review of Economics and Statistics*, Vol. 64, November 1982, pp. 702-706.

Himarios, Daniel, "The Effects of Devaluation on the Trade Balance: A Critical View and Reexamination of Mile's New Results." *Journal of International Money and Finance*, Vol. 4, December 1985, pp. 553-563.

Johansen, Søren and Katarina Juselius, "Maximum Likelihood Estimation and Inference on Cointegration-With Application to the Demand for Money," *Oxford Bulletin of Economics and Statistics*, Vol. 52, May 1990, 169-210.

MacKinnon, James J., "Critical Values for Cointegration Tests," in Long-Run Economic Relationships: Readings in Cointegration, ed. R. F. Engle and C. W. Granger, Oxford, Oxford University Press, 1991, 267-276.

Miles, Marc A., "The Effects of Devaluation on the Trade Balance and the Balance of Payments: Some New Results," *Journal of Political Economy*, Vol. 87, June 1979, pp. 600-620.

Rose, Andrew K. and Janet L. Yellen, "Is There a J-Curve?" *Journal of Monetary Economics*, Vol. 24, July 1989, pp. 53-68.

**Table 4.** Johansen's Maximum Likelihood Procedure Results with Six Lags ( r = number of cointegrating vectors).

**Panel A:** The Results of λ-Max and Trace Tests

Case 1: No Trend in the Procedure

| Null | Alternative | λ-max Statistic | 95% Critical Value | Trace Statistic | 95% Critical Value |
|------|-------------|-----------------|--------------------|-----------------|--------------------|
| r = 0 | r = 1 | 39.38* | 28.14 | 89.22* | 53.11 |
| r<= 1 | r = 2 | 24.86* | 22.00 | 49.84* | 34.91 |
| r<= 2 | r = 3 | 16.50* | 15.67 | 24.98* | 19.96 |
| r<= 3 | r = 4 | 8.48 | 9.24 | 8.48 | 9.24 |

Case 2: Trend Term in the Procedure

| Null | Alternative | λ-max Statistic | 95% Critical Value | Trace Statistic | 95% Critical Value |
|------|-------------|-----------------|--------------------|-----------------|--------------------|
| r = 0 | r = 1 | 28.40* | 27.14 | 74.83* | 48.28 |
| r<= 1 | r = 2 | 24.61* | 21.07 | 46.44* | 31.53 |
| r<= 2 | r = 3 | 14.77 | 14.90 | 21.81* | 17.95 |
| r<= 3 | r = 4 | 7.04 | 8.18 | 7.04 | 8.18 |

**Panel B:** Estimates of Cointegrating Vectors

| Cases | Ln M/X | Ln Y | Ln YW | Ln EX |
|-------|--------|------|-------|-------|
| Case 1 | -1.00 | -1.94 | 4.17 | -0.98 |
| | -1.00 | 0.57 | -2.20 | 0.13 |
| | -1.00 | -3.33 | 4.92 | 0.47 |
| | [19.4] | [17.9] | [18.9] | [14.4] |
| Case 2 | -1.00 | -1.57 | 3.11 | -0.70 |
| | -1.00 | 1.52 | -4.51 | 0.45 |
| | -1.00 | -4.70 | 3.83 | 2.91 |
| | [19.1] | [17.7] | [19.0] | [14.3] |

Note: In panel B the degrees of freedom of $\chi^2$ statistic is the same as number of cointegrating vectors in each case. The critical value of $\chi^2_{(3)} = 6.25$, at the 10% level of significance.

# CHINA: RECENT POLICY PRIORITIES-- IMPLICATIONS FOR U.S INTERESTS AND POLICY GOALS[*]

*Robert Sutter*

## Introduction

Developments in China have posed serious challenges and opportunities for U.S. policy, especially since the Tiananmen crackdown of 1989 and the end of the Cold War. At various times, policy priorities chosen by China's leaders to deal with domestic and international developments have seemed at odds with U.S. interests and policy goals regarding promoting a functioning market system, political pluralism, non-use of force, nonproliferation of weapons of mass destruction and related technologies, and other concerns. At other times, Chinese leaders have appeared cooperative on such important U.S. interests as seeking stability in Korea, promoting international common ground on nuclear non-proliferation, Asian security, Asian financial stability, curbing international crime, terrorism and drug trafficking, and other issues.

. Sino-U.S. friction reached a high point during the Taiwan Strait crisis of 1995-1996, when U.S. naval forces were sent to the area to face Chinese military forces conducting provocative military exercises designed to intimidate Taiwan voters prior to important presidential elections. Since then, both the U.S. and Chinese administrations have endeavored to ease differences while seeking to broaden cooperation on a variety of economic, political, security, and other questions during a series of high-level meetings capped by Sino-U.S. summits held in Washington in October 1997 and in Beijing in June 1998.

Congress has remained keenly interested and actively involved in the evolution of U.S.-Chinese relations since the Tiananmen crackdown. Members have initiated hundreds of legislative actions, traveled to China, had repeated contacts with senior Chinese leaders, and watched carefully trends in Chinese development and their implications for the United States. This report is designed to help them to keep track of Chinese leaders' policy priorities and what they mean for U.S. policy concerns.

Chinese leaders have adopted recent policy priorities on a range of issues that they claim demonstrate greater common ground with the United States, though they frankly acknowledge that the policies reflect China's basic national interests. The Chinese leaders' recent policy priorities are detailed below, along with an assessment of how they relate to important U.S. policy concerns. This list and assessment are based in part on authoritative reviews of Chinese policy priorities appearing in official Chinese media since late 1997, and the author's consultations with over 100 U.S., Chinese, and other specialists during that time. For other CRS treatment of issues in U.S.-China relations see, *China: Pending Legislation in the 105th Congress*, by Kerry Dumbaugh, CRS Report 97-933F; *China-U.S. Relations in a Post-Cold War World*,

---

[*] Excerpted from *CRS Report for Congress*, 98-802F

CRS InfoPack IP 460; and *China-U.S. Trade, MFN Status, and Economic Relations*, CRS InfoPack IP 489.[1]

# Current Chinese Policy Priorities--The Primacy of Domestic Concerns

In the era following the death of Mao Zedong (d. 1976), Chinese Communist Party (CCP) leaders--directed for many years by senior leader Deng Xiaoping-- have focused on economic reform and development as the basis of their continued survival as the rulers of China. Support for economic liberalization and openness has waxed and waned, but the overall trend has emphasized greater market orientation and foreign economic interchange as critical in promoting economic advancement, to enhance the CCP leaders' political legitimacy and reinforce the continued CCP monopoly of political power. For a time, the leaders were less clear in their attitudes toward political liberalization and change, with some in the 1980s calling for substantial reform of the authoritarian communist system. Since the crackdown at Tiananmen in 1989, there has been a general consensus among the party elite to carefully control dissent and other political challenges, allowing for only slow and gradual political change that can be closely monitored by the authorities.[2]

In foreign affairs, post-Mao leaders retreated from the sometimes strident calls to change the international system, and worked pragmatically to establish relationships with important countries, especially the United States and Japan, but also China's neighbors in Southeast Asia and elsewhere, that would assist China's development and enhance Beijing's overall goal of developing national income and power.

The collapse of Soviet communism at the end of the Cold War posed a major ideological challenge to Chinese leaders and reduced Western interest in China as a counterweight to the USSR. But the opportunities resulting from rapid growth and modernization of China's economy soon attracted Western leaders once again, while the demise of the USSR gave China a freer hand to pursue its interests less encumbered by the long-term Soviet strategic threat.

Against this backdrop, Chinese leaders by 1997 were anxious to minimize problems with the United States and other countries in order to avoid complications in efforts to appear successful in completing three major tasks for the year:

- The July 1, 1997 transition of Hong Kong to Chinese rule;

---

[1] Among many other CRS products on China, see *China: Ballistic and Cruise Missiles*, by Shirley Kan and Robert Shuey, CRS Report 97-391F; *China's Military Owned Businesses*, by Shirley Kan, CRS Report 98-197F; and *China: Commission of Science, Technology, and Industry for National Defense*, by Shirley Kan, CRS Report 96-889F.

[2] For discussion of this background, see *China's Changing Conditions*, CRS Issue Brief 97049.

- The reconfiguration of the Chinese leadership and policy at the 15th CCP congress in September 1997, the first major party meeting since the death of senior leader Deng Xiaoping in February 1997;

- The Sino-U.S. summit of October 1997, which China hoped would show people in China and abroad that its leaders were now fully accepted as respectable world leaders following a period of protracted isolation after the 1989 Tiananmen crackdown.[3]

Generally pleased with the results of these three endeavors, Chinese leaders headed by President and Party chief Jiang Zemin began implementing policy priorities for the next few years. At the top of the list was an ambitious three-year effort, begun in full force after the National People's Congress (NPC) meeting in March 1998, to transform tens of thousands of China's money-losing state-owned-enterprises (SOEs) into more efficient businesses by reforming them (e.g. selling them to private concerns, forming large conglomerates, or other means).[4] Consequently, Beijing has embarked on major programs to promote economic and administrative efficiency and protect China's potentially vulnerable financial systems from negative fallout of the Asian economic crisis. Thus, at the NPC meeting in March 1998, it was announced that government rolls would be drastically cut in an effort to reduce inefficient government interference in day-to-day business management. And, China's new Premier, Zhu Rongji, initiated sweeping changes in China's banking and other financial systems designed to reduce or eliminate vulnerabilities seen elsewhere in Asia.

As a result of the September 1997 party congress and the March 1998 NPC meeting, a new party-government team was in place managing policy without the guidance and guidelines set by such great leaders of the past as Mao Zedong and Deng Xiaoping. There were problems reaching consensus on power-holding arrangements made at the Party and People's congresses, but on the whole top level leaders seemed to be working smoothly together pursuing Chinese policy interests. Although the economic reforms adversely affect the power and privileges of many party officials, there has been little sign of disagreement over the general policy emphasis on market-oriented economic reform.

The ambitious plans for economic reform, especially reform of the SOEs, are needed if China's economy is to become sufficiently efficient to sustain growth rates seen as needed to justify continued communist rule and to develop China's income and power. Shifting of economic decision making from directive party plans to a functioning market promises increased efficiency and growth. However, as the reforms also exacerbate social and economic uncertainties, the prospects of these tensions reinforce the regime's determination to maintain a firm grip on political

---

[3] See                                                              r memorandum for Congressional China Watchers, January 23, 1998 (Call 7-4257 for 7-765 1 to obtain a copy). See also, Joseph Fewsmith, "Jiang Zemin Takes Command," *Current History*, September 1998, p. 250-256.

[4] See also Barry Naughton, "China's Economy", *Current History*, September 1998, p. 273-278.

power and levers of social control.[5] By late 1998, instability caused by economic change and growing political dissent prompted the PRC leadership to initiate significant suppression of political dissidents and related activities. Observers judged that the repression would last at least though 1999 and possibly for the duration of the economic reform efforts.[6]

Against this background, foreign affairs generally remains an area of less urgent policy priority. Broad international trends, notably improved relations with the United States, support efforts by the Chinese authorities to pursue policies intended to minimize disruptions and to assist their domestic reform endeavors. The government remains wary of real or potential challenges posed by the recent Asian economic crisis, by Taiwan, by efforts by Japan and the United States to increase their international influence in ways seen contrary to Beijing's interests, by India's great power aspirations and nuclear capability, and other concerns.

## Domestic Reform

As money-losing SOEs are being consolidated, sold or streamlined, many workers are losing their jobs. While some find other jobs, many are unable to duplicate the mix of income and benefits they received from SOEs. In particular, the state enterprises are responsible for providing the "social safety net," i.e., housing, disability and old-age support, health care, and schooling, for the workers and their families. Meanwhile, the government streamlining plan announced at the NPC promises to remove around four million government employees from their positions, though many are expected to find jobs in related non-government agencies, institutes and enterprises.[7]

Not surprisingly, there has been an upsurge of unauthorized demonstrations, strikes, and some riots as a result of the layoffs. The authorities generally avoid Tiananmen-type tactics to deal with these events. If possible, they attempt to "buy off" or accommodate the demonstrators by providing funds to restore some jobs or benefits. Meanwhile, the People's Armed Police—much expanded and better trained since 1989—has proven to be much more adroit at crowd control. Of course, as the reforms of SOEs and other efficiency measures move into higher gear in later years, the authorities presumably will have less flexibility to reinstate jobs and benefits, and the scope of demonstrations may tax the abilities and discretion of the police. A critical assumption for maintaining employment and related social stability is to sustain high growth. With the recent Asian economic down turn, economic growth may have to come more from domestic investment than from foreign sources. Thus, the central

---

[5] See among others, Geremie Barme, "Spring Clamor and Autumnal Silence," *Current History*, September 1998, p. 257-262.

[6] Consultation with U.S. and PRC officials, Beijing, January 7-10, 1999.

[7] See *China's Economic Development: An Overview*, by Wayne Morrison, CRS Report 97-932; *China's Economic Future*, by John Hardt, CRS Report 97-246; *China's Economy: Findings of a Research Trip*, by Raymond Ahcarn; and *China's Response to the Asian Financial Crisis*, by Wayne Morrison, CRS Report 98-220.

government authorities took various steps in 1998 and 1999 to promote government financed domestic infrastructure projects and other means to keep overall economic growth high. The growth rate for 1998 was announced at 7.8%, though many analysts thought the actual rate was lower. The target for 1999 was around 7.5%.

The Asian economic crisis has diverted Chinese leadership attention from SOE and other reforms in several ways. Initially, Chinese leaders thought China would not be seriously affected by the crisis because its currency is not convertible, it holds over $130 billion in foreign exchange reserves, most of its foreign debt is medium and long term debt, and most investment in China comes from domestic savings (the rate of such savings in China is 40%).[8] As it deepened and spread, the crisis preoccupied Chinese leaders with such issues as:

- The need to support Hong Kong's economic stability;[9]

- How to deal with declines in Chinese exports to ailing Asian markets and growing competition in international markets from exports from Asian countries whose currencies have markedly depreciated;

- How to compensate for the loss of Asian investment in China, especially investment that was counted on to purchase some ailing SOEs, and Chinese investment losses in Asian countries;

- How to revise plans to join SOEs into Korean and Japanese-style conglomerates, which are now viewed with disfavor following the Asian crisis; and,

- How to speed reform of China's weak banking and finance systems to avoid a crisis similar to those elsewhere in the region.

As part of efforts to smooth foreign relations in order to focus on problems at home, Beijing has given more attention to expressing Chinese interest in human rights issues. Beijing has signed the UN Covenant on Economic and Social Rights and the UN Covenant on Political and Civil Rights; it has conducted numerous diplomatic dialogues with foreign groups, and released a few dissidents. Such actions have the effect of encouraging dissidents and others in China seeking faster political change to press their case, often during such events as major party or NPC meetings. Thus, former party chief Zhao Ziyang wrote a letter to the September 1997 party congress, and another just prior to President Clinton's visit to China in June 1998, calling for a reevaluation of the Tiananmen incident—a particularly divisive political issue. Others are arguing against the authoritarian controls of the present regime in articles and tracts published in China, or published abroad and sent back to China via fax and Internet.

---

[8] See, among others, *The Asian Financial Crisis*, CRS Info Pack IP245A.

[9] This is seen by many to depend on Hong Kong's ability to maintain the fixed value (the "peg") of its currency relative to the U.S. dollar.

The pressures for political reform and better human rights can be understood as coming from within the elite and from those outside the Chinese establishment. Many within the elite recognize that China will be unable to root out prevailing corruption—a major threat to the legitimacy of the CCP—without establishing mechanisms for a more accountable administration such as a freer press, more free elections, and greater rule of law. There is also the view that political reform and more accountable government are needed if China is to avoid the weaknesses of "crony-capitalism" that were so graphically illustrated elsewhere in the region during the Asian economic crisis. Those increasingly well-to-do Chinese entrepreneurs and intellectuals outside the state-controlled system often clamor for greater representation in government decision making. And it is widely held that regime legitimacy suffers so long as Beijing is unable to come to grips with the unjust verdicts on the Tiananmen incident. Meanwhile, outside the elite are dissidents seeking to take advantage of the Chinese government's human rights diplomacy and image building abroad to push for changes in the still coercive PRC regime. They sometimes strive to use the discontent of millions of unemployed and others who have suffered as a consequence of economic changes.[10]

The current Beijing leadership consensus clearly intends to resist such calls for change. Beginning in November 1998, authorities arrested and imprisoned numerous dissidents and curbed freedom of publications and some religious activities. The suppression was expected to last through 1999, and perhaps for the duration of the reforms. Meanwhile, ethnic dissidents, including some using violent means, also are pressing separatist cases; they are meeting stern repression, including frequent executions, by authorities in Xinjiang and Tibet.

## China's Ninth National People's Congress (NPC): Leadership and Policy Agenda--Results and Issues

Chinese leaders have been forthright in articulating their policy priorities in major party and government meetings. The most comprehensive recent review of their policy concerns came during deliberations at the 1998 Ninth National Peoples Congress. Held in Beijing March 5-19, 1998, the Congress established government leadership and policies that would guide Chinese developments for the next five years. Following broad policy guidelines and leadership selections made at the Chinese Communist Party's 15th Congress in September 1997, the NPC set an ambitious agenda giving priority to development issues involving broad economic reform and government streamlining.[11]

---

[10] This analysis comes from several Chinese specialists of U.S. affairs and U.S. specialists of Chinese affairs interviewed in 1998. It benefitted from the discussion of Carol Hamrin, David Shambaugh, and others at the conference, "Is China Unstable? Assessing the Factors," Sigur Center, George Washington University, Washington, D.C., June 19, 1998. See also *Current History*, September 1998, p. 268-272.

[11] This is taken in part from the review in "China's Ninth National People's Congress-- Results, Issues and U.S. Policy Concerns, " CRS memorandum for Congressional China Watchers, March 24, 1998 (call 7-7651 or 7-4257 for a copy); that assessment relied heavily on the insights of U.S.-China specialists Christopher Clarke, Carol Hamrin, and Lyman
(continued...)

*Leadership.* As expected, the Congress re-elected Party leader Jiang Zemin as President, while Li Peng, number two in the Party hierarchy, retired as Premier and became head of the NPC. Third-ranking party leader Zhu Rongji was elected Premier. Consistent with the Congress' emphasis on streamlining government, the number of vice premiers and state councillors was reduced.

Zhu was clearly the "star" of the Congress, especially during his masterful performance at a press conference at the end of the meeting, broadcast live by Chinese television, where, for an hour and a half, he handled with aplomb often tough and sensitive questions. (The press conference was broadcast live by Chinese television, something that Chinese leaders almost never allow.[12] For example, Chinese television carried no live coverage of Jiang Zemin's various activities in the United States in October-November 1997. There was always a time delay, presumably to allow for editing, if needed. Jiang's decision allowing for live coverage of his press conference with President Clinton in Beijing in June 1998 caused a media sensation among Chinese and Western journalists.)

Zhu has had overall responsibility for Chinese economic policies in recent years, and his focus has remained on economic reform. He presumably was a driving force behind the Congress' decisions to cut both the number and size of government ministries, reduce government interference in economic management, and reform ailing state-owned enterprises and the weak financial system.

Zhu's subordinates in running the economy include several officials close to him, notably newly appointed State Councillor and Secretary General of the State Council, Wang Zhongyu, and the head of the People's Bank of China, Dai Xianglong. The economic team also includes senior Vice Premier Li Lanqing and State Councillor and former foreign trade minister Wu Yi, who are not in Zhu's camp and have clashed with him on policy issues in the past.

Jiang Zemin appeared more successful than Zhu in seeing officials close to him rise to prominence at the Congress. All four vice premiers are closer to Jiang than Premier Zhu. The newly selected Vice President, party politburo standing committee member Hu Jintao, a former party leader in Tibet, was singled out by Jiang as a rising star of the next generation. In his mid-50s, Hu is about 15 years younger than Jiang and Zhu. Hu's selection for the vice presidency departed from past practice where the post was reserved as a sinecure for aging leaders. Among other things, Hu is expected to assist Jiang Zemin in meeting China's increasing requirements to travel abroad for negotiations and visits. Hu's initial trips as Vice President were to South Korea and Japan in April 1998.

---

[11](...continued)
Miller. This discussion also benefitted from a round table discussion of the Congress, Sigur Center, George Washington University, Washington, D.C., March 20, 1998.

[12] Zhu's press conference was carried by Chinese television on March 19, 1998. On recent leadership issues in China, see *Current History*, September 1998, p. 243-249.

Outgoing Premier and new NPC chairman Li Peng has few major allies in the new government line-up. Li is close to Luo Gan, a politburo member and State Councillor who is presiding over the party's political-legal commission--a leadership body that establishes policy for public security, judicial and legislative agencies. At the NPC, Li has had good relations with some newly appointed leaders, but the incumbent senior NPC vice chairman, Tian Jiyun, is a liberal leaning reformer long at odds with Li's more conservative orientation.

There was general continuity in leaders selected to direct defense and foreign policy. Jiang Zemin remained head of both the party and government military commissions, and the Vice Chairmen are Generals Zhang Wannian and Chi Haotian. Though having reached retirement age, Chi was retained as defense minister presumably because other leading candidates like General Staff Department head Fu Quanyou did not have the diplomatic skills to manage China's increasingly active military diplomacy. Zhang Wannian missed the NPC meetings and was reported to be ill. He had to postpone a visit to the United States in May, 1998.

Qian Qichen retired as foreign minister but remained a politburo member and Vice Premier. His successor, Tang Jiaxuan, was the vice foreign minister dealing with Asian affairs, especially Japan. Tang was a close associate of Qian, who retained strong influence in setting Chinese foreign policy.

*Policy Agenda.* Premier Zhu summarized China's policy agenda, focused on achieving more efficient economic development, as a "1-3-5" program.

*"One ensuring"*--Zhu said that current conditions in China and the regional economic crisis required China to grow by eight percent annually and to hold inflation to under three percent. He also stressed that China's currency would not be devalued in 1998 and that China would strongly support the Hong Kong currency's fixed value ("peg") relative to the U.S. dollar. To offset losses caused by the regional economic crisis, Zhu said China would rely on more spending on infrastructure, high technology, and housing.

*"Three putting in place"*--Zhu said this involved reforming the state-owned enterprises (SOEs), the ailing financial system, and the size and scope of government over the next three years. This highly ambitious program will focus on:

- revamping, privatizing, and consolidating the tens of thousands of money losing SOEs. Not only is this a major economic challenge, but it directly affects the welfare, housing, schooling, and pensions of millions of workers and their families.

- the Chinese banking and financial regulation system has many of the same weaknesses seen elsewhere in Asia, and is widely seen as insolvent. China is protected from immediate danger from the Asian economic crisis. But Zhu and other leaders have recognized that the current system has been a drag on development and a danger to future stability.

- government rolls at the central and provincial level generally are to be cut in half over the next three years as Beijing moves drastically to curb the government's role in the day-to-day management of enterprises and the economy while strengthening the government's ability to manage macro-economic levers. Heralding the sweeping reorganization and streamlining, leaders at the NPC decided to cut the previous 40 ministerial-level organs down to 29. Most of those eliminated were ministries and organizations involved in management of specific industries.

*"Five Reforms"*--This has involved making more efficient the management of China's grain reserve system, which has been bursting at the seams with surplus grain purchased with government subsidies; reducing administrative influence and allowing the market to determine investment choices; reforming the urban housing system--i.e., moving away from subsidized to free market housing; medical care reform; and greater reliance on income and other taxes rather than ad hoc fees to fund government activities.

**Issues.**

*Leadership.* The party and government line-up resulting from the 15th Party Congress in September 1997 and the NPC in 1998 have raised a number of questions and possible indicators regarding leadership power and policy:[13]

- How well will Zhu Rongji work with Vice Premiers and State Councillors, who are closer to Jiang Zemin, and some of whom have clashed with Zhu on policy issues in the past? Will Zhu continue to exert direct day-to-day oversight of the economy, or will he delegate that responsibility to senior Vice Premier Li Lanqing, who differs with Zhu on some issues?

- Will Zhu broaden his responsibilities to play a leading role in foreign policy, as did the previous Premier Li Peng? If so, how will he interact with Jiang Zemin and Vice Premier Qian Qichen, both of whom play central roles in Chinese party leading groups dealing with foreign affairs and policy toward Taiwan and Hong Kong?

- Will Li Peng, perhaps through his close association with Luo Gan, move to control policymaking dealing with public security, judiciary and legislative matters? If so, how will this affect Chinese policy dealing with dissent and other human rights issues?

- Defense policymaking has appeared well established, with Jiang Zemin, backed by Generals Zhang Wannian and Chi Haotian, in the lead. But leadership maneuvering could result from a protracted illness or death of Zhang Wannian.

*Policy Agenda.* U.S. and Chinese analysts have remained uncertain about the ambitious reform program laid out at the NPC. Sustaining high economic growth

---

[13] This section is taken from CRS Memorandum for China Watchers, March 24, 1998, *op. cit.* See also outgoing Premier Li Peng's work report and incoming Premier Zhu Rongji's press conference featured in Chinese media coverage replayed by the Foreign Broadcast Information Service (Internet version) during March, 1998.

likely will be difficult given lost markets in Asia for Chinese goods and lost Asian investment in China because of the Asian economic crisis. Eighty percent of outside investment in China came from Asia, according to Premier Zhu.

While few have doubted that there will be strenuous efforts to downsize the government, experienced analysts have pointed out that Zhu's plan is the fourth major government streamlining announced since the early 1980's; in each previous case government rolls have grown, not decreased. Most analysts consulted agreed that this time will be different, but adding millions of government employees to those seeking new jobs at a time of major state-owned-enterprise consolidation and reform seems likely to pose a formidable challenge to China's social stability.[14]

Meanwhile, plans to reform the SOEs and the ailing financial system have been considered for some time and appear reasonable, provided related reforms move in tandem. For example, provisions need to be made to support pensions for experienced workers from SOEs that are sold or otherwise go out of business. The authorities will need to consider how to allocate housing, medical care and other benefits for these workers and their families previously provided by the SOEs. Beijing has been working for years, thus far without major success, in coming up with viable social security, health care, retirement and other such systems. Meeting these challenges along with SOE and financial system reform in a three-year period represents a tall order.

Political reform received perfunctory treatment at the Congress. When asked at the March 19, 1998 press conference about a possible reversal of verdicts over the 1989 Tiananmen crackdown, Zhu Rongji adhered to the standard line. Popular dissatisfaction over official corruption has headed the list of reasons for greater government accountability and reform. Despite generally adhering to the party "line", Congress deputies voted negatively in large numbers on issues seen related to the authorities' handling of corruption and favoritism. Meanwhile, activists within and outside the party took advantage of the authorities' on-going efforts to improve China's human rights image abroad to press their case for greater government accountability, political freedom, and reconsideration of verdicts dealing with Tiananmen and the case of Zhao Ziyang, the party leader removed as a result of the 1989 crisis.

## Subsequent Complications of Reform

### Economic Complications.

Not suprisingly, the leadership's ambitious reform agenda has run into a range of problems, complications, and resistance. PRC officials have appeared likely to

---

[14] According to economists, numbers alone are not the full story; to have truly effective reform requires changing the role of the state bureaucracy from direct intervention in the economy, to a role of regulators of economic elements as is done in the West.

remain focused on dealing with these difficult domestic preoccupations for the next few years.[15]

The Chinese leaders remain unified behind top leadership choices and major policy initiatives made over the previous year. President Jiang Zemin remains the first among the senior party and government officials, and he and his colleagues are given credit for maintaining stability and improving China's international image. Jiang received positive publicity and support for his successful management of President Clinton's visit to China in June-July 1998.[16]

However, efforts to reduce and restructure government ministries and to purge an estimated four million cadre from government jobs are meeting strong resistance. According to media reports in mid-1998, Premier Zhu Rongji was unable to coerce compliance of the many ministries under his direct control. Only two thirds sent him required reports on how they would streamline operations, and most of those reports were returned because they didn't meet the established standards for cutting personnel. Meanwhile, some senior cadre who had been let go had moved to related private sector enterprises and had used their influence and connections to benefit themselves and their enterprises, often at the expense of the broader public good. The trend has added to widespread public cynicism about endemic corruption in government and related enterprises.

Housing reform has added to the public perception of corruption as some government offices have distributed apartments under their control to their cadre at very cheap prices. Other government offices have used their own funds to purchase apartments on the market, and then distributed them to their cadre as a fringe benefit. One report claimed that "flats are being given away according to seniority and special connections. Worse, large numbers of officials and their spouses are getting four or five apartments."[17]

The Chinese administration also has made little headway in dealing with the millions of laid-off workers from government ministries and state-owned enterprises. During a major leadership conference in May 1998 on unemployment, social security and retraining, the leadership proposed a "three-pronged strategy" with money for creating new jobs to come from central government coffers, local budgets and SOE funds. Unfortunately, the central government has few funds to spare and many of the SOEs are basically bankrupt. Sometimes, the central authorities propose that the unemployed consider unorthodox methods such as working on farms, starting businesses in interior provinces, or seeking jobs overseas. But the actual conditions of the period include large scale rural unemployment or underemployment, recession

---

[15] See among others CRS Issue Brief 97049. See also the discussion in "Sino-U.S. Summit Watch: Chinese Leaders' Policy Preoccupations and Flexibility on Summit Issues," CRS memorandum for Congressional China Watchers, May 28, 1998 (call 7-4257 or 7-7651 to get a copy). See also daily coverage of Chinese economic problems noted in *China Daily*.

[16] See Nancy Tucker, "A Precarious Balance: Clinton and China," *Current History*, September 1998, pg. 243-249.

[17] See among others *The South China Morning Post*, May 20, 1998.

in the interior provinces, and collapse of overseas job opportunities because of the Asian economic crisis.[18]

Sustaining the planned economic percent growth rate is critically important to allow Beijing to deal effectively with the wide range of problems associated with rising unemployment. And yet, by mid-1998, the growth rate was down to 7% annually, short of the target of 8%. Exports and foreign investment have continued to grow but at a slower pace in part because of the Asian economic crisis. Massive and prolonged mid-year floods in central China and in the northeast threatened to shave at least 1% off of China's projected growth for the year.[19] In response, the government resorted to bond issues and other sources of government spending on large infrastructure projects. This helped to boost the growth rate to 7.8% for 1998. The target for 1999 is about 7.5%

### Political Dissent and Pressures for Change.

Chinese leaders' worries over managing the complications of their ambitious government and economic reforms are mirrored in the mounting challenges posed by progressives and dissidents encouraging political reform.[20] Anniversaries in mid-1998 of such events as Deng Xiaoping's 1978 campaign to "emancipate thought" and "seek truth from facts," the 100th anniversary of the founding of Beijing University, the 1919 May 4th movement, and the 1989 Tiananmen incident prompted liberal intellectuals within the elite to press for greater changes. Some believed that Party leader Jiang Zemin has authorized a limited rehabilitation of liberal reformers who fell from power over the Tiananmen crackdown, as well as a more moderate attitude toward such student leaders at the time as Wang Dan. Wang was released on medical parole to the United States in early 1998.

More broadly, as a result of the party and state congresses over the previous year, development of "democratic politics" and "rule of law" has returned to the official agenda, after a nine-year hiatus. Immediate pursuit of political reform focuses on government downsizing and economic legislation. Top leaders have wanted to delay discussion of serious systemic political reform until much later, possibly 2010 or even 2020, when China attains a higher stage of development. There are no known major initiatives to protect human rights or promote democracy, but renewal of debates similar to those of the late 1980s over comprehensive reform of the Leninist system of party control of government, military, and social organizations began to appear.[21]

---

[18] For background, see discussion in CRS Issue Brief 97049.

[19] The floods were a central feature of western media coverage of China during July-August 1998.

[20] See Geremic Barme "Spring Clamor and Autumnal Silence," *Current History*, September 1998, p. 257-262; Margaret Pearson, "China's Emerging Business Class: Democracy's Harbinger", *Current History*, September, 1998, p. 268-272; and Tyrene White, "Village Elections," *Current History*, September 1998, p. 263-267.

[21] For background, see the discussion by Carol Hamrin, David Shambaugh and other

(continued...)

*Factors Favoring a Democratic Trend.*: Senior PRC leaders' talk about democracy is partly tactics aimed at improving China's international image, evading censure at the annual UN Human Rights Commission in Geneva, and improving the atmosphere for President Clinton's June 1998 visit, but it also reflects important new dynamics at work among the political elite:

- Popular dissatisfaction with official abuse and corruption is a driving force behind political reform. The NPC session in March 1998 stressed the theme of controlling corruption through rule of law. A significant minority of delegates rejected the reports by the outgoing Supreme Court and Procuratorate (prosecutors office), and opposed the new choice for Procurator-General because they did not adequately address problems. Subsequent government actions have signaled serious reforms in these institutions. Delegates reportedly demanded measures to prevent corrupt officials from taking advantage of impending economic and organizational reforms. Media commentary on "grass-roots democracy" programs, including village direct elections, has stressed their necessity for holding abusive officials accountable to the people.

- A growing middle class expands with government downsizing. Many state cadre move into the professions and business, and their interests shift from upholding bureaucratic privilege to holding officials accountable and creating a level playing field for non-bureaucratic actors. Many are quite knowledgeable about how to work the system and have a strong commitment to political reform.

- The Asian economic crisis has underscored for many in China the grave danger of unregulated "crony capitalism" and the practical necessity for democracy in Asia. That the "tigers" riding out the storm have the strongest legal system (Hong Kong) and/or democratic politics (Taiwan) has nudged PRC analysts to look more closely at these political-economic systems for potential application to the mainland. The demise of the authoritarian Suharto regime in Indonesia has underlined the point. The official argument that stability is a prerequisite for state enterprise reform now faces a counter-argument that only democratic reform can provide sufficient accountability to save China from political and economic crisis.

- The priority attached to achieving progress toward peaceful reunification with Taiwan and maintaining confidence in Hong Kong results in pressure to show movement toward democratization. It is clear to many in China that Taiwan independence will continue to gain support unless the island people are convinced the Mainland is making changes to its political system.

- Heightened global competition into the next century has produced a major new high-tech drive, spearheaded by President Jiang Zemin and Premier Zhu Rongji

---

[21](...continued)

prominent U.S. China experts at the conference, "Is China Unstable? Assessing the Factors," Sigur Center, George Washington University, Washington, D.C., June 19, 1998.

through a new Politburo leading group on science and education. Press reports on reform speak starkly of a "critical moment for China's destiny"--either join the "fast lane" in global development or slide into the "slow lane." Chinese media cite an outmoded political system as a major drag on competitiveness. This theme was reinforced, albeit implicitly, in a report by the Academy of Sciences warning that China must reverse a "severe brain drain problem" (e.g., more than a third of Beijing University graduates have left the country) if it was to catch up with the "recent rapid development of global information technology."[22]

- Improved prospects in U.S.-China relations have made it easier for reformers to experiment with "Western" concepts and pursue expanded exchanges in sensitive areas. Official legal cooperation, for example, allows legal reformers to push for change without being labeled "tools of containment."

*Factors Impeding a Democratic Trend.*: Political reform continues to be inhibited by:

- Different views of democracy and rule of law. China's leaders remain committed to "socialist democracy" as a variant of the Asian model of authoritarian government and market economics. They want only marginal, even glacial, changes to their highly-managed "consultative" feedback system. Jiang Zemin seems to define democracy as educated leadership. Progressives occupying mid-level bureaucratic or professional positions favor a much larger dose of elitist democracy for utilitarian reasons--accountable government would improve economic efficiency and help reverse the brain drain. Both groups are leery of a growing strain of populist democracy focused on the suffering of those marginalized by reform. Political dissidents who have no faith in top-down approaches work on grass-roots social organizing of a sort greatly feared by the government, especially as working class anger rises against managers and officials who profit from state enterprise reorganization. There is a split, however, between those who call for democratic revolution and those who pursue increasingly sophisticated tactics to pressure the government to abide by the constitution, law, and international covenants.

- Politics of Tiananmen. Just as in 1989 when the people blamed corrupt officials for profiteering that drove inflation, so NPC delegates and others have complained that "our workers are laid off for the good of enterprises while managers of the enterprises accept large bribes, leading to enterprise collapse." Leaders may be forced to consider further marginal revision of the verdict on Tiananmen. (They now speak vaguely of "political disturbance" rather than "counter-revolutionary turmoil.") Li Peng, still second-ranking party leader, probably will feel threatened by this, and the leadership certainly will split over bolder gestures to exonerate former Party chief Zhao Ziyang and provide amnesty for exiles, even though doing so would likely shore up regime legitimacy and help reverse the brain drain.

---

[22] See discussion of these issues in David Shambaugh (ed.), *Is China Unstable,*? Sigur Center, Washington, D.C., 1998.

A significant turning point came with the stepped up suppression of political dissidents, unauthorized publications, and related activities beginning in November 1998. Jiang Zemin, Li Peng, and others strongly endorsed the suppression. U.S. and Chinese observers thought that the firm emphasis on tighter political control would continue through 1999 and possibly longer because of:

- regime concern over growing unemployment and related social instability as a result of SOE and government bureaucracy streamlining;

- a perceived need to curb dissidents emboldened by Beijing's endorsement of UN human rights covenants and China's multifaceted dialogues with the United Nations, the United States and others in the West;

- regime concern that major decennial anniversaries in 1999 (e.g., the 80th anniversary of the 1919 May 4th movement, the 10th anniversary of the 1989 Tiananmen incident of June 4, 1989, and the 50th anniversary of the establishment of the PRC on October 1, 1949) could provide catalysts for disruptive behavior.[23]

## Trends in Military Affairs

There has been more continuity and less controversy over recent military policies and developments than policies and developments dealing with economic and political reforms and related social stability. China's announced 1998 defense budget of $11 billion increased official defense spending by about 13%--a real increase of some 8%. But this is only part of the story, with additional revenue coming from other ministerial allocations and from PLA commercial enterprises. In mid-1998, Jiang Zemin announced a major shift in policy, calling on the PLA to cut past ties with commercial enterprises. The cut was reported completed in December 1998, though many details regarding compensation, employee transfers and other issues remain to be worked out.

Estimates of the total resources available to the Chinese military range widely, with some putting the figure at more than Japan spends on defense (over $45 billion a year). But even the lower estimates contrast with cutbacks elsewhere in Asia as a result of the economic downturn. As China sustains its defense spending, it is expected to make relative gains. But it still finds it hard to keep up with constantly changing military technologies, and China is not expected to be able to match U.S. (or Japanese) armed forces for decades.[24]

*Changing Philosophy.* Lessons from allied operations in the Middle East and from the U.S. reaction to the Taiwan Strait crisis of 1996 prompted the PLA into reconsidering its strategy. The philosophy of a people's war of attrition has given way

---

[23] Consultations, Beijing, January 7-10, 1999.

[24] For a particularly useful overview of military developments in China, see Hans Binnendijk and Ronald Montaperto, eds., "Strategic Trends In China," U.S. National Defense University, 1998. See also CRS Reports 97-391, 98-197, and 96-889 cited in footnote one, as well as *China's Rising Military Power*, CRS Report 96-66F.

since the mid-80s to one of "active defense," for which the PLA aims to develop (albeit from a low base) a high-tech, rapid deployment capability with streamlined command structure, advanced information warfare (including better surveillance capability), and high-performance precision-guided munitions.

With no current threat to China's land borders, the PLA's priority is to build up its maritime force-projection and nuclear-capable, long-range and shorter-range missile capability to provide military options (e.g. to attack ports or other strategic sites) to successfully blockade (or invade) Taiwan should diplomacy fail; to reinforce sovereignty claims in the South China Sea; and to deter others, particularly the United States, from interfering in its maritime and other areas of interest.

*Restructuring.* The Army aims to reduce the standing force by 500,000 down to 1.6 million by 2000. While the force remains large in global terms, only a few divisions will be prepared for rapid deployment. The Navy has introduced four modern Russian kilo class conventional submarines and is planning to acquire two Sovremenny destroyers--complete with supersonic anti-ship missiles and helicopters after 2000. The Air Force is buying more long-range Russian SU-27 fighters and reportedly is interested in the more capable SU-30 multirole aircraft, as well as the latest air-to-air missiles.

Combined with plans for airborne surveillance, in-flight refueling, and both cruise and ballistic missile developments, these new capabilities would comprise a significant offshore deterrent capability to support China's interests in the region. And China aspires to have an aircraft carrier--though it would not be operational for at least a decade.

China faces significant problems in modernizing its military. The defense budget is stretched by the size of the force and will allow only incremental improvements. The PLA--hampered by low education levels, undeveloped tactics, and often primitive logistic support--is having difficulty assimilating high-tech equipment. Problems exist in indigenous design, development, manufacture and support for technologically sophisticated systems--indigenous weapon platforms and systems are often of poor quality and unreliable--and China remains reliant on Russia, Israel, and others for support.[25]

Critical aspects of modern maritime warfare that China has yet to master include joint war fighting doctrine, combined operations, anti-submarine warfare capabilities, ship-borne air-defense, and replenishment at sea. Lack of proficiency in these skills should work to China's disadvantage in any adversary engagement.

Looking to the future, China's push for a modern and effective fighting force, commensurate with its global standing, probably will yield results only slowly. And it is some way yet from possessing the capability to sustain a deployed force offshore--for example in Taiwan--though it likely will have, within a few years, a modest maritime capability to support its sovereignty claims. Even so, the PLA's modernization probably will generate concern, especially as regional countries

---

[25] See, notably, *Russian-Chinese Cooperation*, CRS Report 97-185F.

affected by the economic crisis apply the brakes to their own modernization plans. This in turn could highlight the importance of the U.S. security commitment to the Asia-Pacific.

Politics in the PLA have been managed relatively smoothly. PLA elders Liu Huaqing and Zhang Zhen retired at the 15th party congress and have been succeeded by Generals Chi Haotian and Zhang Wannian, though the latter do not have the senior party rank (Politburo Standing Committee member) enjoyed by Liu Huaqing.

On-going reform efforts saw the appointment of a respected technocratic civilian minister to direct the Commission for Science, Technology and Industry for National Defense (COSTIND).[26] The new director, Liu Jibin, was a vice minister of Finance and seems to have a mandate to curb abuses in the purchasing of military equipment and in entrepreneurial activities by the PLA. Jiang Zemin's subsequent injunction against PLA involvement with business underlined this reformist trend.[27]

# Foreign Policy Priorities

Against the background of a daunting domestic agenda, Chinese foreign policy, including relations with the United States, is less important. The Chinese leaders seek out opportunities where foreign relations assist Chinese development; and they seek to avoid entanglements and interactions abroad that would hamper effective growth. The Chinese authorities have priorities aside from economic development; they include protecting sovereignty and independence, and pursuing regional and global power and influence--but these have been tailored with a few exceptions (e.g., Taiwan), to be generally consistent with Chinese development goals.[28]

To secure China's periphery and relations with major world powers in order to deal with critical internal issues, Chinese leaders from President Jiang Zemin on down were unprecedentedly active in 1997 and 1998 in establishing often vague "partnerships" with a host of nations that emphasized the positive and endeavored to put off issues in dispute. Summits with the United States, Russia, Japan, France, Britain, the nine members of the Association of Southeast Asian Nations (ASEAN), the 16-member European Union (EU), and many others were replete with Chinese platitudes about the benefits of adopting "long term" and "strategic" policies that were assumed to promote a convergence among the relevant powers that would gradually see the many problems between China and its neighbors and other major powers diminish. Chinese officials and media made clear that China was not prepared to give much away in its long term efforts to promote China as a leading power in what Beijing sees as an emerging "multipolar" world after the Cold War. Indeed China's military modernization continues along past lines, though military leaders have gone out of their way to foster an unprecedentedly active diplomatic effort designed to

---

[26] For background, see CRS Report 96-889F, *op. cit.*.

[27] See, among others, *Washington Post*, July 23, 1998, p. 1.

[28] For background on Chinese foreign policy, see Samuel Kim (ed), *China and the World*, Westview 1998.

reduce international concerns over the China "threat." Beijing generally views recent international trends as supporting China's objectives, but there have been significant exceptions and causes of uncertainty and concern.[29]

For U.S. interests and policy, this priority of Chinese policy concerns has meant that China has a strong interest in cooperating with the United States, and little interest in confronting the United States, unless provoked. The United States is critically important in maintaining a stable balance of influence in East Asia and elsewhere around China's periphery conducive to Chinese goals of peace and development. United States-China trade and investment are of great importance for China. The United States is China's largest market; it is one of the largest outside investors in China. The United States-China relationship indirectly but in significant ways influences China's relations with other Western powers, Japan, and the international financial institutions that collectively provide billions of dollars of investment and loans for China annually. The summit meetings with President Clinton added greatly to the Chinese leadership's political legitimacy both at home and abroad.

For some time after the end of the Cold War, Chinese officials seemed to see their interests as well served by an emerging multipolar world. This implied that U.S. dominance would gradually decline, and that China and other power centers would enjoy more freedom of maneuver and other advantages as the United States confronted more and more difficulties at home and abroad. But in the latter part of the 1990s, especially in the context of improved U.S.-Chinese relations during the summit meetings of 1997 and 1998, Chinese officials began to adjust this view, notably pushing their goal of a multipolar world further into the future. In effect, they appear, for the time being, to see U.S. dominance of world affairs in somewhat less sinister terms than in the recent past. They tend to judge that greater Chinese cooperation with the United States would enhance U.S. power, not wear it down as was implied by past Chinese emphasis on creating a multipolar world. Nonetheless, the Chinese officials judge that China's power also will rise as it cooperates with the United States, and for the time being at least, that is what is most important. Developing a multipolar world order where U.S. power would decline relative to that of China and others remains a long-term Chinese objective.[30]

Beijing has continued to view U.S. policy toward China as one of "two hands"--a "soft" one of engagement and a "hard" one of containment. The improvement in U.S.-China relations in 1997 and 1998 is still seen as basically tactical, as the U.S. and China have continued to disagree on fundamental issues. Specifically, China perceives at least four U.S. positions working against core interests of the Chinese government,

---

[29] On recent Chinese foreign relations, see Denny Roy, *China's Foreign Relations*, Boulder, CO., Roman and Littlefield, 1998.

[30] See, among others, "Summit Watch: Beijing's Public Posture Emphasizes the Positive and Boosts President Jiang," CRS memorandum for Congressional China Watchers, June 25, 1998 (call 7-4257 or 7-7651 for a copy). See also Jiang Zemin's remarks at a major diplomatic conference in Beijing, reported in *China Daily*, August 29, 1998, p. 1. And see, Song Yimin, "The U.S. Security Strategy," Beijing *International Studies* 12-13, 1998, p. 1-16.

and the Chinese government apparently intends to resist them for the foreseeable future:

- The United States wants to remain the world's dominant power.
- The United States wants to remain the dominant power in East Asia.
- The United States intends to continue support for Taiwan.
- The United States continues to work gradually for a "peaceful evolution" in China that would over time bring the demise of the communist authoritarian regime.[31]

Nevertheless, there is increasing evidence that these and other differences are being called into question as a result of the continued upswing in U.S.-China relations and the concurrent ferment in Chinese intellectual and policy circles broadly questioning previous assumptions, including those about the United States. Thus, for example, one Chinese foreign policy specialist said on April 27, 1998 that the "containment" view of the United States was continuing to lose ground in China as more Chinese officials and specialists came to see the continued U.S. dominance in the world in more lasting and also more benign terms. Specifically, some specialists are now arguing privately that the U.S. world leadership is not a result of some sinister U.S. scheme to exert hegemony, which China must resist; it is said to reflect positive features of U.S. society and global systemic trends which have the support and encouragement of most countries in the world. A recent Chinese book "China Doesn't Want To Be Mr. No" argued that peaceful evolution toward democracy both globally and in China, backed by the U.S. and others, is a natural and positive process that works to the advantage of China's development.[32]

Meanwhile, Chinese media in the period before and after the June 1998 summit in Beijing generally eschewed criticism in dealing with issues of U.S. power politics or possible intrusiveness into Chinese affairs. Their discretion surpassed the efforts made to create a positive atmosphere prior to and following the October 1997 Washington summit. Thus, though Beijing media and PRC-controlled Hong Kong media occasionally took issue with specific U.S. actions, they pulled their punches on U.S. policies that in the past were featured regularly for criticisms including:

- U.S. policy toward Iraq
- NATO expansion
- U.S.-Japan alliance relations
- U.S.-Japan economic differences
- U.S. policy in the Middle East Peace Process

In addition, Chinese media played up positive statements by U.S. leaders, including President Clinton and National Security Adviser Berger, on the outlook for U.S.-China relations, while ignoring statements, such as those by Treasury Deputy

---

[31] See "The Chinese Defense White Paper," published by *Xinhua*, July 27, 1998 and replayed by FBIS.

[32] See, "Sino-U.S. Summit Watch: Clinton Administration and Chinese Officials' Motives, Expectations, and Outlook," CRS memorandum for Congressional China Watchers, May 11, 1998 (call 7-4257 or 7-7651).

Secretary Summers in late April 1998, that China's entry into the WTO would take a long time.[33]

Realpolitic analysis, not sentiment over U.S. visitors, lies behind Chinese leaders' calculus, according to U.S. and Chinese specialists consulted for this study.  Events in recent years, notably the Asian economic crisis and the nuclear testing crisis in South Asia, laid bare new realities of world power and what they mean for China.  As Chinese comment has assessed the impact of the economic crisis on Asia and the world economy, it has viewed the U.S. economy as supreme--"standing like a crane among chickens" as one Chinese commentator noted.  Of all international factors important for China's successfully coping with the crisis, close cooperation with the U.S. economic superpower is most important, according to this view.[34]

The rise of a new pole in the multipolar world--India, through its nuclear tests in May 1998--is viewed with alarm in China.  Beijing is well aware that India's motives focused in part on the Chinese "threat," especially China's nuclear arsenal and its reported support to reported Pakistani nuclear weapons programs and nuclear capable ballistic missile programs.  Unable to deal with the situation directly, China has taken on the role as an  active promoter of a strong U.S. policy in the region.  Beijing cooperates in unprecedented ways with the United States, involving presidential and foreign minister-level phone consultations, and a joint (U.S.-PRC) conducted meeting of the UN's Perm Five foreign ministers on the issue in Geneva on June 4, 1998.  Beijing has judged that with U.S. leadership, the great powers might be able to muster enough diplomatic, economic and other leverage on India and Pakistan to contain the crisis, avoid the creation of a threat to China's security, and avoid major entanglements and diversion of Chinese resources from the primary focus on nation building and development.[35]

Nonetheless, PRC officials remain wary of a possible U.S. compromise with India that would enhance New Delhi's international status as a nuclear power.  Such a U.S. move would trigger latent Chinese suspicions that the United States intends to use improved relations with India in order to balance China's rising influence in Asian and world affairs.  Meanwhile, Chinese officials have been privately critical of Russia's "soft" reaction to the Indian tests and continued Russian military and

---

[33] Based on coverage seen in U.S. Foreign Broadcast Information Service (Internet version) during this period. See also, Song Yimin, "The U.S. Security Strategy," Beijing *International Studies*, op. Cit; and Wang Haihan, "The Current Situation and Future prospects of Sino-U.S. Relations,"Beijing, *International Studies*, 12-13, 1998. P. 17-28.

[34] See, among others, *China's Response to the Asian Economic Crisis*, by Wayne Morrison, CRS Report 98-220; and "A Possible Chinese Decision To Devalue the Yuan " CRS memorandum for Congressional China Watchers, August 26, 1998 (call 7-4257 or 7-7651 for a copy).

[35] See, "South Asian Crisis: China's Assessment and Goals," CRS memorandum for Congressional China Watchers, June 11, 1998 (call 7-74257-7-7651) for a copy).

technology trade with New Delhi. They judge that Russia is using relations with India to balance China's rising influence in Asia.[36]

Elsewhere around its periphery, Beijing also has seen much to worry about and little ability to influence the situation, barring a cooperative stance with the United States. Beijing has made little headway in dealing with on-going high priority problems involving Taiwan, the U.S.-Japan alliance, and the unsteady situation in North Korea. Despite strenuous PRC efforts, Taiwan has remained openly determined to raise its political profile, especially among Southeast Asian nations seeking economic support from any quarter. Taiwan voters have seemed more inclined than ever to choose political leaders who will preserve Taiwan's separate status.[37] Since Taiwan represents such a sensitive issue of reunification and national security, and Taiwan leaders are among the few in the world openly defiant of China, Beijing gives a very high priority to dealing with the "Taiwan issue." Jiang Zemin and other senior leaders continue to press U.S. and others to curb contacts with Taiwan deemed offensive to Beijing.

Beijing has remained anxious over U.S.-Japanese efforts announced in 1996 to "revitalize" the alliance relationship. Chinese criticism has become more muted and focused on specific concerns regarding Taiwan, but Beijing continues to seek reassurances that the alliance does not target Chinese interests. Chinese officials were privately disappointed with Japan's refusal during Jiang Zemin's November 1998 visit to Japan to apologize more forthrightly regarding past Japanese aggression against China and to state its policy toward Taiwan along lines favored by Beijing. They are also concerned with Japanese efforts--in conjunction with the United States—to develop ballistic missile defenses against North Korea that have indirect but important implications for China's ballistic missile capability vis-a-vis Japan.[38]

Even though China provides the bulk of international food and energy aid to North Korea, Chinese officials are nervous about stability and a potential flow of refugees. Beijing has yet to establish a high-level dialogue with the reclusive Kim Jong Il.[39]

Other important foreign policy concerns along China's periphery involve the Asian economic crisis, Islamic fundamentalism, and suspicions of Chinese territorial ambitions in the South China Sea. Beijing has turned the financial crisis to its political benefit, garnering international kudos for its "responsible" stance in maintaining domestic economic growth and avoiding currency devaluation. But the fact remains that the crisis has complicated internal Chinese economic reforms, has a negative impact on Chinese growth, and has complicated Chinese expectations that

---

[36] Consultations, Beijing, January 7-10, 1999.

[37] See, CRS memorandum for Congressional China Watchers, May 28, 1998, *op. cit.*

[38] Consultations, Beijing. January 7-10, 1999.

[39] Chinese media coverage of Vice President Hu Jintao's visit to Seoul in April 1998 noted that while Beijing welcomed high-level contacts with the Kim Dae Jung government in South Korea, North Korea's leaders had not yet responded to Chinese requests for a summit. See also Jiang Zemin interview in Kyodo, February 24, 1998.

a model of economically open Asian authoritarianism would prevail in the region. On Islamic fundamentalism, Beijing has serious stability problems in Xinjiang and other parts of China caused, in part, by cross-border support of Islamic and pan-Turkic separatists. Though Southeast Asian governments and China are distracted by their serious economic problems, they remain vigilant in defense of their respective territorial claims to the disputed areas in the South China Sea. Reacting with extreme caution to fast-moving developments in Indonesia, Beijing generally has eschewed initiatives or comment that would exacerbate anti-Chinese violence or jeopardize fragile Chinese diplomatic relations with Jakarta. China's low posture also has avoided highlighting the image of student demonstrations working to bring down an authoritarian regime to people in China who still remember the Tiananmen incident.[40]

## Implications for U.S. Interests and Policy Goals

At one level of analysis, this state of affairs of considerable Chinese preoccupation and vulnerability should have argued for a strongly accommodating Chinese policy toward the United States in general and toward specific U.S. policy concerns in particular. It appeared that China very much needed to cultivate and promote good relations with the U.S. in order to help Chinese leaders deal with their many problems and concerns. In fact, the situation was quite different for a number of reasons.[41]

In particular, Chinese leaders' concern over the economic consequences of SOE reform and the Asian financial crisis has made the Chinese leadership more cautious in prompting economic openness and change along lines sought by the United States.[42] Under these circumstances:

- U.S. efforts to open Chinese markets to U.S. products have continued to meet with frustration.

- China has followed its own course--allowing for continued administrative protection and intervention in the economy--toward meeting conditions on entry into the World Trade Organization (WTO). These have not met requirements stated by the U.S. Trade Representative.

---

[40] See, CRS memorandum for Congressional China Watchers, May 28, 1998, op. cit. See also treatment in Denny Roy, *China's Foreign Relations*, op. cit.

[41] On issues in U.S.-China relations see *China-U.S. Relations*, Kerry Dumbaugh, CRS Issue Brief 98018.

[42] See, "China-U.S. Relations: Post Summit Stasis," CRS memorandum for Congressional China Watchers, July 24, 1998 (call 7-4257 or 7-7651 for a copy); "Chinese Priorities in 1998--Implications for U.S. Policy," CRS memorandum for Congressional China Watchers, January 23, 1998 (call 7-4257 or 7-7651 for a copy). See also, *China's Response to the Asian Financial Crisis*, Wayne Morrison, CRS Report 98-220.

- As China has continued to promote grain production in order to keep prices stable and consumer supplies high, the opportunities for U.S. grain exporters have been limited.

- Worried about declines in China's terms of trade with Asian countries, Beijing has focused all the more on exporting goods to the U.S. market, boosting the already very high U.S. trade deficit with China.

Meanwhile, the recent political trends and priorities in China have reinforced a tendency to go slow on significant change and to keep careful control of potentially disruptive situations. Pressures from disgruntled SOE workers, political dissidents, liberal reformers, ethnic separatists, and others have been growing. This has increased the opportunity for serious incidents or crackdowns complicating U.S.-China relations.

On specific PRC foreign policy issues of concern to the United States, Beijing's priorities pose mixed implications for U.S. interests and policy concerns.[43]

1. Human Rights: Beijing's willingness to sign or consider UN covenants and to engage in a flurry of diplomatic dialogues with Western and other countries in one sense represent steps forward for U.S. policy interests. But the positive results of these actions for conditions in China have been slow in coming. They have seemed designed most immediately to benefit China by hindering efforts of those in the United States and elsewhere who sought to criticize China or bring the Chinese case before the UN Human Rights Commission, (Beijing has given a very high priority to blocking this effort). Also by allowing leading dissidents to leave China on so-called medical parole, Beijing reduces their credibility and ability to promote political change inside China, according to many observers.

2. Weapons Proliferation: As part of agreements leading to the implementation of the U.S.-China Nuclear Cooperation accord in 1998, Beijing agreed to stop new nuclear cooperation with Iran. It had already offered safeguards regarding reported nuclear cooperation with Pakistan seen as assisting Pakistani efforts to develop nuclear weapons. The Clinton Administration hailed the change in Chinese behavior as a centerpiece of the October 1997 summit. China took further steps forward at the 1998 summit, notably agreeing to study membership in the Missile Technology Control Regime, and reaffirming a halt to ballistic missile cooperation with Pakistan. Skeptics alleged that Beijing made the compromise in part because China had already seen Pakistan develop a sufficiently sophisticated nuclear weapons and missile delivery program, and had become disillusioned with Iran's unwillingness to pay for Chinese support, and other reasons. They charged that China has continued actively to share missile and chemical weapons materials with Pakistan, Iran, Libya, and others in ways contrary to U.S. interests.

---

[43] Reviewed in China Watcher memos of July 24, 1998 and January 23, 1998. *op. cit.* See also Nancy Tucker, "A Precarious Balance: Clinton and China," *Current History,* September 1998, p. 243-249.

3. Taiwan: The so-called "Taiwan issue" is at the very top of Beijing's priorities in relations with the United States.[44] Reducing U.S. military and political support for the island leaders has remained a key element in China's broader effort in recent years to curb Taiwan's more assertive stance in world affairs and to pressure Taiwan over time to seek accommodation and reunification with the Mainland on terms agreeable to the PRC. Beijing has anticipated that giving high level attention to isolating Taiwan diplomatically while promoting cross Strait economic exchanges would dampen separatist feelings on the island and open the way to political talks on Beijing's terms. This calculus was at its height immediately after the U.S.-China summit of 1997 but later has been called into question by:

- the big victory by the pro-independence opposition party in island-wide local elections in late November 1997, and the victory in December 1998 elections by the ruling Nationalists under the leadership of Lee Teng-hui who strongly emphasized Taiwan's identity separate from mainland China;

- the impact of the Asian financial crisis on Taiwan's investment in the Mainland, with many in Taiwan holding back commitments until the situation in the region became more settled; and,

- the ability of Taiwan to conduct high-level diplomacy with Southeast Asian and other officials who shunned Taiwan contacts out of deference to Beijing but who now seek them out in order to obtain economic aid.

Beijing was pleased with President Clinton's affirmation on June 30, 1998 in Shanghai of the "three nos"—i.e., U.S. non-support for "one China-one Taiwan," Taiwan independence, and Taiwan representation in international organizations where statehood is a requirement; but the U.S. Administration subsequently reassured Taiwan by engaging in cabinet-level economic and defense contacts and by reportedly considering missile defense options for Taiwan.[45]

4. Hong Kong: U.S. officials support Hong Kong's continued autonomy while encouraging more political democracy.[46] Beijing is very careful to avoid a perception of meddling in Hong Kong affairs after the July 1997 changeover. Hong Kong leader C.H. Tung and his administration have been in the lead in managing several crises, notably the Asian financial situation, without anything but positive expressions of support from Beijing. U.S. critics aver that Beijing can afford a low key posture as Tung is following China's desired policies, including implementation of conditions, widely seen as non-democratic, for the May 1998 election of the new Hong Kong legislature.

5. East Asian Security: U.S. policy seeks to avoid conflict and support the peaceful resolution of differences in East Asia. Beijing has taken several steps in line

---

[44] For background see CRS Issue Brief 98034, *op cit.*

[45] For background see, *Taiwan*, CRS Issue Brief 98034 (updated regularly).

[46] For background see *Hong Kong: After the Return to China*, by Kerry Dumbaugh, CRS Issue Brief 95119.

with U.S. goals, though China's longer term aspirations appear designed to reduce U.S. power and influence.

Beijing has worked smoothly with the United States, South Korea and North Korea in the four party peace talks on Korea that began in December 1997. So long as its territorial claims are not strongly challenged, China has adopted a moderate position in handling territorial disputes with Japan and several Southeast Asian nations. China has shown increased interest in and cooperation with the ASEAN Regional Forum--using such multilateral consultations in part as a means to reduce regional support for the revitalized U.S.-Japan alliance, and thereby over time to isolate Tokyo and Washington.

To counter regional angst over China's rising defense spending and purchases of sophisticated Russian air and naval equipment that will substantially boost China's power projection abilities later on, Beijing has sent top uniformed officers on whirlwind tours and welcomed numerous foreign military delegations to China. Over 200 such exchanges took place in 1997, including with heretofore excluded states like Japan and South Korea, and an active pace has continued in 1998. The PLA high command, now among the most well traveled and internationally experienced in the world, has focused their sophistication on reducing international attention to arguments against a perceived "threat" from China, and discouraging some Asian powers, including Japan, from relying too heavily on the United States.[47] Beijing also released its first comprehensive defense white paper in 1998.

6. South Asia: India's nuclear tests in May 1998 and concurrent charges of a Chinese threat took Beijing by surprise. China condemned India's actions while expressing much milder regret over tests by Pakistan, China's longstanding ally in South Asia. Chinese leaders have hoped that their strong support for the United States and the UN security council's five permanent members in pressing the two sides in South Asia to halt further provocative action will ease dangers for Chinese security and international interests. They also have hoped to keep the critical U.S. policy spotlight on India, in the process avoiding U.S. and other international focus on China's longstanding reported involvement with Pakistani programs to acquire nuclear weapons and missile systems capable of delivering them. Leaders have appeared reluctant to get entangled in a protracted foreign policy dispute at a time of pressing domestic reform priorities. Thus, they are not prepared to join in economic or other sanctions by the United States.[48]

7. Russia, Central Asia, Middle East: Beijing has continued to support Russian efforts to counter the expansion of U.S. influence around Russia' periphery, notably through NATO enlargement. China has backed Russia's role in the former Soviet republics of central Asia and built up its own relations in the area in part as a hedge against what Beijing sees as expanding U.S. influence in the area. Beijing has acknowledged the U.S. leading role in the Middle East peace process and the strong U.S. military position in the Persian Gulf. It has gone along with the UN consensus

---

[47] This was discussed notably at a July 16, 1998 workshop sponsored by the Stimson Center, Washington, D.C.

[48] For background see CRS Memorandum for China Watchers, June 11, 1998, *op. cit.*

on sanctions against Iraq, but has been outspoken in supporting Russia's lead in endeavoring to end the sanctions as soon as possible and to crimp U.S. efforts to increase pressure on Saddam. It also has provided rhetorical support for France, Russia and others whose economic contacts with Iran have countered U.S. policy goals. Meanwhile, China has sought a more active role in the Middle East peace process, notably sending its highest level delegation ever to front line states in December 1997. China's pro-Arab stance complicates U.S.-led peace efforts, though Chinese officials aver they wish to cooperate with U.S. policy in the region.

## Short Term Outlook

Chinese leaders' strong preoccupation with domestic issues was mirrored in 1998 by Clinton Administration preoccupation with the fallout from the President's sexual wrongdoing, the report of Special Prosecutor Kenneth Starr, and congressional consideration of disciplinary actions against the President, up to and including impeachment. The Clinton Administration preoccupation deepened with the House Impeachment vote in December 1998 and the Senate trial in early 1999. Some Chinese officials privately expressed worry at the time that a decline in the President's influence would dampen momentum in U.S.-China relations and allow U.S. critics a freer hand to block and reverse some of the recent U.S. initiatives toward China. They were particularly concerned that pro-Taiwan forces in the United States would use the situation to launch legislation or other initiatives boosting U.S. military and political support for Taiwan leaders.[49]

There is little sign, thus far, that Beijing leaders have viewed the crisis in Washington as warranting substantial change in their own policy priorities. Chinese officials have expressed satisfaction with the results of the two summit meetings. They have appeared to believe that there is little likelihood of significant reversal in key areas of the U.S. relationship (e.g., access to the U.S. market for Chinese exports), and that, while debate continues in the United States over policy toward China, few Americans advocate a U.S. policy of confrontation with Beijing. Chinese observers recognize that further forward movement in U.S.-China relations will presumably require significant Chinese compromises on such sensitive issues as market opening, human rights, or weapons proliferation. For domestic Chinese reasons noted above, these compromises will be difficult for Chinese leaders. Also, given the politically weakened Clinton Administration, the ability of the United States to use substantial positive or negative incentives to encourage Chinese compromises may be more limited than in the past.

Meanwhile, Chinese officials recognize that complications in U.S.-China relations could arise in 1999 as a result of:

- U.S. dissatisfaction with China's crackdown on political dissent. Some believe that this could revive U.S. government interest in raising China's human rights record at the annual meeting of the UN Human Rights Commission in Geneva.

---

[49] Interviews, Washington, D.C., August 26-27, 1998; Beijing, January 7-10, 1999.

- U.S. pressure to open Chinese markets may increase, especially if there is no progress on China's entry into the WTO and the U.S. trade deficit with China continues to grow to record levels.

- The report completed by the House Select Committee on Technology Transfer to China. Reportedly quite critical of allegedly illicit Chinese efforts to acquire U.S. high technology, the report could negatively affect U.S. willingness to cooperate with China in these areas.

Nevertheless, these complications are not seen to require major shifts in China's current array of policy priorities, according to Chinese officials in Beijing.[50]

As a result, Chinese leaders appear prepared to carry on their relations with the United States without significant change. So long as there is no major retrogression on the U.S. side, they seem to see little need to alter policy priorities that give top billing to promoting economic and related government reforms while sustaining stable and generally cooperative relations in foreign affairs.

---

[50] Consultations, Beijing, 7-10 January, 1999.

# KOREAN SCIENCE AND TECHNOLOGY: A TRIP REPORT[*]

*John D. Moteff and Glenn J. McLoughlin*

## Introduction

This is a report on the findings of a research trip to the Republic of Korea (ROK, also referred to in this report as Korea). The purpose of the trip was to learn more about Korea's science and technology (S&T) structure, policies, and policymaking processes, the size and nature of its investments in research and development (R&D), and associated issues within Korea and between Korea and the United States. Information from this trip is being incorporated into a larger report written by the Science Policy Research Division at the request of the House Science Committee on the science and technology enterprises of other countries.

The trip consisted of interviews with representatives of leading science and technology institutions within the Korean government, private industry and academia. These interviews took place over a 14-day period in the cities of Seoul, Taejon, Ulsan, and Pohang. The institutions and organizations visited were, in chronological order: Science and Technology Policy Institute; Ministry of Science and Technology; Ministry of Trade, Industry and Energy; Ministry of Finance and the Economy; Korean Institute of Science and Technology; Ministry of Information and Communications; Ministry of National Defense; Lucky Gold Star Corporate Institute of Technology; Seoul National University; Samsung Advanced Institute of Technology; Korean Advanced Institute of Science and Technology; Electronics and Telecommunications Research Institute; Aerospace Research Institute; Research Institute of Industrial Science and Technology; Pohang University of Science and Technology; Pohang Steel Company; Hyundai Motor; and Hyundai Heavy Industries.

We would like to thank all of those who took the time to talk to us and for their candid responses and kind hospitality. We would also like to thank Science Counselor You-Hyun Moon from the Korean Embassy in Washington D.C. for his help in arranging the trip and those at the Ministry of Science and Technology who arranged our itinerary. Mr. Bruce Cho, Coordinator, Center for Science and Technology Cooperation was invaluable by accompanying us to meetings assisting us during our stay. Finally, we would like to thank the Korean Trust Fund at the Library of Congress for their financial support.

Rather than present a synopsis of each interview, this report highlights a few of the more interesting issues that cut across a number of interviews and which provided additional insight to our earlier research.

---

[*] Excerpted from *CRS Report for Congress*, 97-912STM

## Overview of Korean Science and Technology

In a relatively short period of time, the ROK has evolved from a rural agrarian society to a highly industrialized society. Korea is a country of about 45 million people. It now has the 11th largest national economy in the world (its 1995 GDP was $453.6 billion, US$). It is the world's leading manufacturer of dynamic random access memory chips (DRAMs), and a major producer of automobiles, steel, and electronic products. Hyundai has the single largest automobile production site in the world and Pohang Steel Company has the largest integrated steel mill facility in the world. In 1996, Korea was fully admitted into the Organization of Economic Cooperation and Development (OECD), and the country has set a goal of achieving a level of economic activity on par with the G-7 nations early in the 21st century.

To a large extent, this evolution has relied on the import of foreign technology. However, the country's capability for developing its own technology has grown as it has adapted and improved the technology it has imported and as it has engineered its own products through indigenous research and development. In 1995, the country as a whole spent $12.2 billion (US$) on research and development, or about 2.7% of its GDP..

## Policy Making Structure and Policies

A highly centralized government plays an important role in the country's science and technology enterprise, both as policymaker and performer of research and development. But it is private industry that is now the primary supporter and performer of research and development. Universities, to date, have played a minor role in research and development, although they do supply Korean institutions with adequate supply of scientists and engineers.

Since the 1960s Korea has pursued an explicit goal of industrialization. The strategies and policies employed to get there have been laid out in a series of 5-year economic plans. The need to develop the country's S&T capabilities to support its industrialization plans was recognized early. The Ministry of Science and Technology (MOST) was established in 1967, evolving from a group within the powerful Economic Planning Board. For nearly two decades MOST was the primary supporter of research and development in the country and a leading sponsor of many of the early institutions set up to develop the S&T infrastructure. It remains a very important player and has the primary responsibility of trying to coordinate the country's S&T efforts.

However, over time, as the private sector and other ministries have increased their support of research and development and pursued their own agendas, MOST's ability to coordinate activities has shrunk and become more difficult. In the past, coordination has been pursued in the National Science and Technology Council. The Council included 13 ministers and distinguished persons from the S&T community and was chaired by the Prime Minister. Although chaired by the Prime Minister, decisions were difficult to reach because no one had clear authority to make them. More recently, coordination has been pursued in a Ministerial Council for Science and

Technology, a similar group, but chaired by the Deputy Prime Minister who, as Minister of Finance and the Economy, exerts more influence on budgetary matters.

Korea's policies in S&T have been pursued with some continuity over many years. These include, among other policies:

- direct support for research and development at government and public research institutes;
- direct and indirect support for the training of scientists and engineers;
- the promotion of basic research;
- incentives to encourage private sector research and development;
- the promotion of international cooperation in S&T.

## Special Law for Scientific and Technological Innovation (STI)

In February 1997, the Korean National Assembly approved the Special Law for Scientific and Technological Innovation (STI). The law requires the government to develop a Five-Year Scientific and Technological Innovation Plan. This plan would lay out specific policy actions, programs, and investments government-wide in S&T for the years 1998 through 2002. The law specifies development or expansion of 10 general program areas. They are:

1. Promote national major R&D programs
2. Promote basic research nationwide
3. Promote research at universities and manpower training
4. Promote the engineering industry (e.g. firms that design and construct manufacturing plants)
5. Promote defense and dual-use technologies
6. Promote R&D activities in Small- and Medium-sized Enterprises (SMEs)
7. Promote S&T education (to include a major basic science facility)
8. Promote the diffusion of technical information
9. Promote the technology infrastructure in the public sector (including international S&T cooperation)
10. Promote the support of other S&T fields as needed.

A draft of the plan, providing specific information on policy goals and implementation, was just being circulated for comment at the time of our trip. A basic goal of the law is to increase government support for research and development to 5% of the federal budget and to 20% of the nation's total expenditure on research and development (from 2.2% and 19%, respectively, in 1995). Each of the ten areas are to have a detailed set of plans and budgets. The plan is to guide Korea's science and technology efforts into the 21$^{st}$ century and support its goal of achieving a level of economic activity on par with G-7 countries.

Opinions of this law were solicited in all of the interviews. Although the law does not seem to introduce any new major initiatives, everyone told us it represents the first time a truly integrated national S&T plan has been articulated. All government agencies, led my MOST, are participating in its drafting. By virtue of being called for by the Special Law, many government officials feel that the plan will carry more legal authority in subsequent budget battles and are optimistic that the plan's funding objectives can be met. The law and the plan is an attempt by the Korean government to transform Korea from a technology imitator to a technology innovator and to compete with more technologically advanced countries early in the 21$^{st}$ century.

But other Korean leaders appeared to be less confident regarding the impact this plan will have. First of all, even if the government does increase its funding for R&D, it would still represent a relatively small share of the nation's total investment. Private industry and its agenda will still set the overall direction. Also, those in private industry and at universities are not convinced that the government will be able to live up to its S&T funding objectives. There was also concern that an increase in funding for basic research will go to large science facilities and not to individual investigators. Some suggested that the Korean government wishes to compete for Nobel prizes or to emulate the large scientific research facilities of Japan and the United States as a matter of national prestige. Finally, not everyone believes that the country needs to do more basic research.

## Government Research and Development

The primary government supporters of research and development are the Ministry of Science and Technology (MOST), the Ministry of Trade, Industry, and Energy (MOTIE), the Ministry of Education (MOE), the Ministry of National Defense (MOND), and the Ministry of Information and Communications (MIC). About half of the government expenditure on research and development goes to government and public research institutes. Many of these institutes are governed by independent boards of directors, but are sponsored by and/or affiliated with one of the Ministries. MOST established the first government research institute (GRI), the Korean Institute of Science and Technology (KIST), in 1967. KIST pursues research and development in a broad range of areas. Many of the other institutes are more specialized. The primary mission of the GRIs is to support industry, performing the mid- to long-term research and development that industry is unlikely to pursue itself. There were 217 GRIs in 1994.

Beginning in 1982, the government began what it called a National Research and Development Program. The purpose of the program was to encourage joint research between private industry, government research institutes, and universities, both to increase the relevancy of public research and to allow everyone to leverage each others' investments. A great deal of consensus making by advisory panels from all sectors of the S&T community goes into selecting targeted areas for support. Research "teams" submit proposals which must compete with each other for funding. Public funds go to support the participation of government research institutes and universities in a given project. Private firms provide their own funds to support their participation in the team.

A number of ministries support their own National Research and Development Programs. MOST supports the Strategic Research and Development Program (supporting joint projects in biotechnology, computer software, aerospace, nuclear energy, and oceans research) and an International Cooperative Research and Development Program (which supports many of Korea's international cooperative research projects). MOTIE supports the Industrial Basic Technology Development Program. MIC supports the Telecommunications Technology Development Program.

In 1992, the government began an inter-ministerial national R&D program called the Highly Advanced National Program (HAN). This program supports two types of projects - product technology development and fundamental technology development. The first is more short-term oriented and supports projects aimed at developing new drugs and agrochemicals, integrated circuits for digital television and micro-machining and micro-machines. Fundamental technology development is longer-term in nature and supports projects in manufacturing superintegrated semiconductor devices, advanced electronic materials, and fuel cells. The areas supported by this program were selected after a vigorous analysis of where Korea might be able to achieve some comparative advantage, and it differs from the other national programs in that it is jointly supported and managed by a number of ministries.

The government places a lot of emphasis on national programs, yet we found that the private sector does not view them as particulary useful. Industry feels their needs are more immediate and that the national projects are not flexible enough to respond to rapidly changing markets. While the projects are suppose to be carried out "jointly", there apparently is little collaboration between team members. Each group pursues their research tasks separately. Private sector involvement in national programs is motivated by a sense of good citizenship and maintaining good relations with the government and government research institutes.

## Industry Research and Development.

Growth in private sector spending on R&D has outpaced growth in government spending on R&D. In 1982, the private sector accounted for 50% of the nation's R&D expenditures. In 1994 the private sector accounted for 84%. This dropped to 81% in 1995. Private sector research is focused in areas related to electronic components (e.g., DRAMs), electronic end-products (e.g., television) and transportation equipment (e.g., automobiles). Research and development in the private sector is also highly concentrated in a relatively few large conglomerates. According to the Korean Science and Technology Policy Institute (STEPI), 64% of private sector investment in R&D is concentrated among the top twenty manufacturing conglomerates. High-technology small- and medium-sized enterprises (SMEs), of which there are few, account for a small share of R&D expenditures.

Korea has about 50 conglomerates called *chaebols*. They are essentially privately owned and represent a form of vertical and horizontal integration not seen in the United States. The Korean *chaebol* (like their Japanese counterpart, the keiretsu) have extensive holdings in the supply of raw materials, the manufacture and production of intermediate- and end-products, and often the distribution (including import and export) of products. In addition, the larger *chaebols* have extensive real estate holdings, hotels and apartments, retail, and other services unrelated to their core businesses.

The four dominate *chaebols* in Korea are Daewoo, Samsung, Hyundai, and Lucky Gold Star (now called LG). Domestic competition in Korea is intense. Each of these firms compete with each other across a number of product lines. For example, there is intense rivalry between LG and Samsung in electronics. Hyundai is also prominent in the electronics business. Hyundai and Daewoo compete in automobiles. Samsung is now getting into automobile manufacturing. KIA, a third automobile manufacturer, is having financial difficulty. One of the people interviewed speculated that Samsung, which has no experience in automotive manufacturing, was entering the already tight market with the idea that it can force KIA out of business and then acquire its manufacturing facilities. Others did not dismiss this speculation. Whether this is true or not, it is an example not only of the intense rivalry between *chaebols*, but also the extent of the horizontal integration that has occurred.

Hyundai is a prime example of the strategic evolution of Korea's technological capabilities. Although Daewoo began manufacturing automobiles first, it did so in a jointly owned subsidiary with General Motors. Hyundai entered the market as an independent manufacturer. Still, it needed to import most of its technology (plant, design, parts, etc.) from Japan (Mitsubishi). As it grew, it continued to rely on imported technology, gradually developing the skills to develop its own technology while maintaining its independence. Hyundai began to design its own models and to build its own manufacturing equipment and has now designed, developed and is producing two of its own engines.

Most private sector R&D expenditures go to in-house research institutes or laboratories, of which there are thousands. Typically, each business unit within a large conglomerate has its own R&D center and each plant its own R&D capability. Most of the firms' R&D is done at these locations. Only within the last 10 years, and in some cases only more recently, have the chaebols formed corporate R&D units charged with developing more advanced technologies for next generation products, looking out 5 to 10 years. Industry leaders interviewed at Samsung, Hyundai, and LG all indicated that they view R&D as an investment, not as an expense (although those we talked to headed their firm's R&D activities). However, they also indicated that private industry does very little basic research and that the government must support that activity. Each of those firms support research at GRIs and universities, but not necessarily basic research. To one, support of basic research at universities was more like a charitable contribution.

## University Research and Development

Koreans are proud of the progress they have made in education. In 1953, 78% of its population was illiterate. Illiteracy was all but eliminated by 1980. Enrollment in terms of the percentage of eligible students in each age group who attend school has expanded at all levels (primary through university, including 2-year junior college). The number studying science or engineering has increased faster than total enrollment. In 1994, 43.5% of all university students were studying science or engineering. But, universities in Korea are traditionally education-oriented and have historically done little research, even in the sciences. Only 8% of the nation's R&D expenditures are spent at universities, even though universities hire the predominant share of scientists and engineers with PhDs.

There are 163 universities and colleges in Korea. Researchers from only three regularly publish in scientific and technological journals - Seoul National University, Korea Advanced Institute of Science and Technology, and Pohang University of

Science and Technology (POSTECH). Seoul National University is the most prestigious in the ROK, what some call the "Harvard of South Korea." It consistently draws the best and the brightest of Korean youth, and its graduates often attain high leadership positions in government, academia, and industry. It spends about $100 million a year on R&D. The Korean Advanced Science and Technology Institute (KAIST), established in 1971, is located in the Taedok Science Town in Taejon. While all other universities, private and public, fall under the jurisdiction of the Ministry of Education, KAIST was set up by the Ministry of Science and Technology to provide graduate education in science and engineering when few schools offered graduate programs. KAIST spends about $72 million per year on R&D. Pohang was established with a foundation grant from Pohang Steel Company (POSCO), a national enterprise. Pohang has risen to become one of Korea's premier research universities. In 1994, POSTECH attracted $30 million in R&D funding. It is modeled after schools like the Massachusetts Institute of Technology and California Institute of Technology in the United States. POSTECH, according to university officials, is the only Korean university that centrally manages its R&D funds. Other universities provide professors with R&D accounts which the professor manages.

A number of analysts, both inside and outside Korea, feel that the lack of university research will act as a barrier to Korea's aspirations in S&T and further economic development. These analysts believe that for Korea to compete with more industrialized nations in a more open and competitive market, they must be able to develop new technologies on their own. In turn, this will require greater investment in basic and longer term research than either private firms or government research institutes are willing to do. Over the years, the Korean government has sought to increase the amount of research performed at universities. In 1977, MOST set up the Korea Scientific and Engineering Foundation (KOSEF). In 1981, MOE set up the Korea Research Foundation. Both have as their primary mission to support university research. In 1989, MOST set up the Center of Excellence Program, establishing university-based Science Research Centers (SRCs) and Engineering Research Centers (ERCs) modeled after similar programs at the U.S. National Science Foundation. In 1995, there were 17 SRCs and 21 ERCs established at 15 universities. The Special Law again will emphasize the need to increase university research funding further.

A number of reasons have been given for the slow progress made in increasing university research. First, based on a Confucian tradition, universities are primarily educational institutions. According to several interviewees, research, but particularly technology development, even of a basic nature, is not highly valued in that tradition. Secondly, MOE bureaucrats are not typically scientists or engineers, so there is not a strong champion for research and development within the Ministry. And, finally, not everyone agrees that the country needs to do more basic research. We were told by some that basic research is still perceived as a luxury for a country with more immediate technological problems to solve.

Another concern expressed was that any additional funds going to university research will be diluted if the money is simply distributed evenly to all universities willing to set up research facilities. A number of interviewees admitted to a tendency in Korean culture related, perhaps, to the importance given to "saving face," that impels people and organizations to compete with each other across the board. If one university sets up a research facility, then every university wants to set one up. If one wants to start an aerospace department, then every university feels obliged to set one up.  Politically, it is too difficult to not treat everyone equally, making it hard to target investments.  It is only recently that Korea has set up a system by which universities must have their departments accredited by an outside body.  It has been proposed that increased funding for university research should be targeted to those demonstrating a high level of performance.

## Telecommunications

One of the best examples of the current tension between a national effort to increase basic research yet, at the same time, maintain technology development that will help improve the competitiveness of an industry in the near- to mid-term is telecommunications.  Government, industry, and academic leaders we met with expressed the virtually unanimous opinion that investments in high-technology fields such as telecommunications are vital for Korea's continued economic growth.  But who should benefit from the investments in telecommunications R&D, how to proceed with de-regulation of the market, and how to best encourage open competition among SMEs in the Korean telecommunications industry are still being debated.

There have been three major players in Korean telecommunications R&D - the Ministry of Information and Communications (MIC), Korean Telecommunications (KT), and the Electronics and Telecommunications Research Institute (ETRI).  Since the industrialization of Korea began, KT was the single national carrier with a monopoly over Korean communications services and technology.  MIC provided regulatory oversight of KT, ensuring that the Korean populations was being well served and helping to underwrite the cost of that service.  Both KT and MIC support R&D in information and telecommunication technologies at ETRI, a GRI under the auspices of MIC.  Founded in 1976, ETRI now has a budget of 300 billion won (about $350 million), two-thirds of which supports telecommunications R&D (25% supports computer software, 9% semiconductor R&D).  Most projects address near-term commercial needs.

The Korean telecommunications industry has been restructured three times over the last decade.  In 1990, the MIC introduced competition in the international telephone and mobile communications services.  In 1994, the government introduced more competition in the domestic market and in wireless services.  KT lost some of its privileged monopolistic control over markets it had owned for decades, but was restricted from entering other domestic communications markets. Telecommunications SMEs gained some limited benefits by providing local communications services..  Finally, beginning in 1995, MIC announced that it intended to completely open all facets of Korean communications services and technology.

These restructurings have had a decided impact on Korean telecommunications R&D.  In the past, ETRI was primarily funded by MIC and primarily served KT.  Now, SMEs are increasingly participating in ETRI's projects.  However, SMEs still only contribute about 17% of ETRI's budget.  KT contributes 33% and MIC contributes 50%.  KT is in the position of having to support R&D that its SME competitors can take advantage of.  According to several experts, KT may withdraw some or all of its support for ETRI in the near future unless this relationship changes. In addition, with deregulation has come increasing pressure to support more commercial and less basic and applied research, since the payoff of such research is not considered by many to be cost-effective.

## Defense Research and Development

The Ministry of National Defense is not a big R&D supporter. It does support some research through a couple of Agencies for Defense Development (ADDs). The Ministry also contracts out development work to private industry. Still, most of Korea's military hardware comes from the United States. Korea and the United States maintain a bilateral Defense Technology and Industrial Cooperation Agreement. Under the auspices of this agreement, the two countries have completed two cooperative R&D projects. One developed technologies to reduce the required safety area around ammunition storage sites, without reducing safety, security, and readiness. Another project is developing advances in after-launch guidance systems for surface-to-air missiles. Both sides view these projects as being successful and seek to negotiate others. Korea also co-produces under license a number of U.S. military systems, including the Korean Fighter (based on the F-16), the K-1 tank (based on the M-1), and the UH-60 Blackhawk helicopter.

Research undertaken by CRS analysts prior to the trip identified technology transfer associated with these co-production programs as being a sensitive issue between Korea and the United States, as is often the case with most countries engaged in co-production. The receiving country would like to get as much technology transfer as possible and to produce as many of the components of the system as possible. The trip revealed that third-party transfers are also a sensitive issue. Korea would like to sell some of the systems it co-produces to third countries. U.S. law prohibits them from doing so without a waiver. The United States has been reluctant to grant such waivers, in general, for many national security, proliferation, and commercial reasons. Some in Korea believe that the United States is being unreasonable, especially in regard to protecting U.S. commercial interest. These critics feel Korea should not be considered a competitor. They also feel that Korea has been a good ally and deserves to be granted waivers. They also suggested that such policies might work against the United States in future Korean procurement programs.

The tension associated with technology transfer and third-party transfers is part of the larger tension between North and South Korea. In the weeks preceding our trip, reports from North Korea focused attention on the desperate food shortages, the possibility of a massive famine, and possible civilian and military unrest in the North. One widely circulated report indicated that there were one million North Korean troops massed near the 38th parallel (only 50 kilometers from downtown Seoul). These reports appeared to heighten tensions in the ROK, which found their way into some of our interviews with Korean leaders. It is clear that most South Koreans view the United States as their most important and closest political and military ally. Any perceived slight in the US-ROK relationship, particularly when military and national defense is concerned, is considered very seriously in Seoul.

## International Cooperation

Globalization is a key element in Korea's overall S&T strategy. Because of its relatively small size, Korea will probably have to continue to rely, in part, on acquiring technology from wherever it can. And, it is expanding its global network to do so.

Japan has been the primary source of technology in the past, mainly for cultural and geographical reasons. But recently, the United States has become the dominant source of technology. Korea is now seeking to diversify and expand its network into other countries. In particular, it is expanding both public and private relationships with China, Russia, India, and both western and eastern European countries. It is also establishing networks in developing countries, especially those in Asia. A major initiative being pursued by the Korean government is to establish an S&T network within the Asia-Pacific Economic Cooperation (APEC). The initiative would allow scientists and engineers from APEC countries to do post-doctoral work in Korea.

The global network being established by Korea consists of many different types of relationships. Both public and private research institutes have set up facilities in other countries or have formed joint facilities with their counterparts in those countries. They enter into formal technology and information exchanges or in cooperative research projects and send researchers overseas to study. They will also contract research from foreign labs and universities. Korean R&D establishments, with support from the government, will also recruit foreign scientists and engineers to come and work in Korea.

The close ties between the United States and the Republic of Korea extend into the S&T arena. There are over twenty agency-to-agency bilateral S&T agreements between the two governments in areas such as fisheries, metrology, energy, environment, transportation, biomedical sciences, and nuclear safety. In 1995, a special Cooperative Program was created between the US National Science Foundation and the Korean Science and Engineering Foundation that created a summer institute in Korea for U.S. graduate students, the exchange of scientists and engineers, and the linking of research centers. In the private sector, the Korean government is active in trying to link Korean firms with U.S. firms in joint ventures, technology agreements, and personnel exchanges. While both sides look favorably on these efforts, the Koreans would like the relationship to evolve from technology transfer, where Korea basically licenses technology, to one where they are equal partners in new technology development.

## Conclusion

Korea is a highly industrialized country. It has shown in many areas that it can master the technology needed to be a world-class manufacturer of high-value-added products and can compete in world markets. However, even as the country improves on its technological capabilities, it still relies heavily on imported technology. While some we interviewed felt that Korea can continue to grow and compete by continuing to adapt and modify imported technology, many believe that Korea must be able to develop its own new technology for future products and production.

There is the opinion among many policy analysts that for Korea to develop its own new technology, the country must conduct more basic research. There is not, however, a consensus on this point. Some with whom we talked, both in academia and the private sector, felt that the country does enough basic research. If basic research were to increase, they say, it should not increase at the expense of applied research. While there is some debate about whether more basic research is needed, there was unanimous opinion that basic research had to be supported by government and performed by universities.

The ability of the government to increase basic research at universities was met with some skepticism by both academia and the private sector. Increasing government support for basic research at universities has not enjoyed much political support in the past. The new Special Law not withstanding, some still did not believe that it would enjoy enough political support in budget battles. A number of people expressed the opinion that the Ministry of Education exerts too much control over universities to allow them to manage basic research more effectively. Some people we interviewed felt universities themselves were to blame for not managing their research resources more effectively. Finally, some thought any increases in basic research would go to large science facilities in an effort to improve national prestige in the sciences.

While the country debates how to best develop the capability to develop its own technology, both the public and private sector in Korea are expanding their global network to acquire technology anywhere they can find it. This includes expanding ties with U.S. institutions and firms. The people we talked to were basically satisfied with U.S.-Korea S&T relations (except in the area of third-party transfers in military technology). There was some concern expressed about having been shut out of certain U.S. programs like SEMATECH (a U.S. semiconductor research consortium). Koreans, too, would like to be considered more as a partner than a licencee. The asymmetrical flow of technology from the United States to Korea is a politically sensitive issue on both sides. Although it does not seem to be as big an issue now, in the past, some in the United States have been critical of the United States (government and industry) "giving" technology away without getting much or anything in return. While in some cases Korea may not yet have its own technology to bring to the table, it does have money and skilled scientists and engineers in key areas (e.g., electronics). Korea promises only to become more of world player in technology, and U.S. policymakers may want to make sure that it takes advantage of what Korea has to offer.

# Beijing, Hong Kong and Taipei - Current Relations, Policy Priorities and Issues with the United States - Findings of a Study Mission[*]

*Robert Sutter*

Leaders in Beijing, Taipei, and Hong Kong are giving top priority to their respective pressing domestic concerns, and generally devote only secondary attention to issues and relations with one another within a framework that some (but not governments) call "greater China."[2] The findings of a study mission to Beijing, Taiwan, and Hong Kong in January 1999 indicate that economic cooperation and closer commercial relations among the three continue to develop, albeit at a somewhat slower pace than in the recent past, largely attributed to economic difficulties brought on by the Asian economic crisis. The findings of the mission are conveyed here for those in Congress with an interest in these topics. As noted below, the mission involved a variety of activities conducted by a CRS researcher in conjunction with various groups in the places visited.

## Beijing
### China's Suppression of Dissent and U.S.-China Relations

The Chinese government's ongoing suppression of political dissent, unauthorized publications, and related activities seen as challenging "stability" and the overall authority of the communist-ruled political system[3] is likely to last through 1999 and possibly longer, and have a dampening effect on U.S.-China relations, according to began in November 1998 and has included widespread arrests of political dissidents and prominent statements by President Jiang Zemin, National People's Congress Chairman Li Peng and others emphasizing the regime's determination to stop unauthorized political and other activities seen challenging to the prevailing social and political order.

---

[2] Some academics define "greater China" to include ethnically Chinese communities in Singapore, other southeast Asian countries, and elsewhere in the Pacific rim; some limit their concept of greater China to mainland China, also known as the People's Republic of China (PRC), Taiwan, and Hong Kong, formerly a British colony but since July 1, 1997 a special administrative region of the PRC. Others liken the term to greater Russia, greater Serbia, etc. See, among others, Harry Harding, "Taiwan and Greater China," in Robert Sutter and William Johnson, *Taiwan in World Affairs*, Boulder CO., Westview Press, 1994, pp. 235-276.

[3] For background on the suppression, see *China's Changing Conditions*, CRS Issue Brief 97049 (updated monthly).

---

[*] Excerpted from *CRS Report for Congress* RL30046

Beijing leaders are likely to continue through this year and possibly longer a firm emphasis on political control and stability for several reasons, according to Chinese and U.S. experts:

- The ongoing economic reforms involve streamlining state-owned-enterprises (SOEs) and sharp cuts in government employment, causing large-scale unemployment and related social instability. China's economic growth has slowed, raising more concerns about political and social stability. (The official 7.8% growth rate for 1998 was likely an exaggeration, according to observers in China.) The PRC leaders fear that dissidents' efforts to organize fellow discontented people could weaken and challenge the prevailing order.

- Political dissidents have been emboldened by the Chinese government's increasingly active human rights programs and diplomacy, which have included the signing of UN human rights covenants, and dialogues with the UN Human Rights Commissioner and with officials and non-government representatives from various western countries. Beijing leaders now judge that dissidents need to be restrained from exploiting the new Chinese government human rights activities for undesirable purposes.

- 1999 marks a number of major decennial anniversaries that are seen as providing catalysts for potentially disruptive dissident behavior. They include the 80th anniversary of the 1919 May Fourth Movement, the most celebrated outpouring of popular and intellectual demands for political and social change in 20th century China; the 10th anniversary of the June 4, 1989 Tiananmen crackdown; and the 50th anniversary of the October 1, 1949 founding of the PRC.

U.S. and Chinese experts agreed that the recent suppression of dissent would have negative consequences for U.S.-China relations:[4]

- Given PRC backsliding on human rights, the U.S. impetus for forward movement in sensitive areas of U.S.-China relations (e.g. disputes over trade, weapons proliferation, human rights, Taiwan, and Tibet) appears to have been reduced. (Reflecting a cooler public atmosphere in U.S.-Chinese relations, observers in Beijing noted that celebrations in Beijing and Washington marking the 20th anniversary of normalization of U.S.-PRC diplomatic relations on January 1, 1979 were notably low keyed.)

- Because of the continuing PRC crackdown on dissent, there may be more pressure in the United States, and especially in Congress, for a revived U.S. effort to bring the Chinese human rights record before the annual meeting of the UN Human Rights Commission in Geneva in February 1999. The Chinese leaders remain very sensitive to such an effort; they have devoted extraordinary

---

[4] For discussion of these issues, see, *China-U.S. Relations*, CRS Issue Brief 98018 (updated regularly), *Chinese Proliferation of Weapons of Mass Destruction: Current Policy Issues*, CRS Issue Brief 92056 (updated regularly) and *China-U.S. Trade Issues*, CRS Issue Brief 91121 (updated regularly).

efforts in recent years to curb U.S. and other western governments' support for such a UN review. They succeeded last year in persuading the United States and others not to push for a UN review of Chinese human rights practices.

- The suppression of political dissent was notably seen by some U.S. observers as reflecting a broader conservative trend that they claim has blocked U.S.-backed initiatives to promote dialogue between the Dalai Lama and Chinese officials. In particular, they claimed that strong U.S. efforts over the past year, including those by President Clinton during his summit meeting with Jiang Zemin in Beijing in June, tried to persuade Chinese leaders to show some flexibility and resume dialogue with the Tibetan leader. Though there was some U.S. hope after the summit that Jiang Zemin might move in this direction, he and other leaders reverted to a hard line by the end of the year, setting very difficult conditions for dialogue with the Dalai Lama. Jiang and other Chinese leaders reportedly were swayed by a prevailing conservative trend emphasizing stability which resulted most vividly in the widespread arrests of political dissidents at the end of 1998.

## Prospects for A WTO Agreement and Zhu Rongji's Visit to the United States

U.S. and Chinese specialists in Beijing in mid-January were generally pessimistic about the possibility of an agreement soon between the United States and PRC over China's entry into the World Trade Organization (WTO). [Clinton administration officials in late January 1999 disclosed that the U.S. and Chinese administrations were working on a plan to reach a WTO agreement in time for Chinese Premier Zhu Rongji's slated visit to Washington in spring 1999. One official gave the plan a 33% chance of working.[5]] Chinese officials were said to see no substantial early economic benefit from China's moving to meet U.S. requirements on China's WTO entry. PRC leaders were reportedly being influenced by Chinese officials representing sectors of the Chinese economy that would be negatively affected by market opening and other changes called for by the United States. PRC leaders appear particularly reluctant to make changes that would disrupt Chinese agriculture and financial services—both areas of keen interest to the United States. Meanwhile, PRC leaders expect to voice continued strong Chinese objections in order to block Taiwan's entry into the WTO prior to PRC entry.[6]

A U.S.-China agreement on China's entry into the WTO is thought to represent a possible centerpiece for Premier Zhu Rongji's visit to the United States. Some analysts in Beijing thought that Chinese and U.S. leaders might be able to reach compromises in order to achieve WTO accord in time for Zhu's visit. But others advised that U.S. compromises on sensitive trade issues could be difficult when it appears that Chinese authorities are backtracking on human rights, and when the U.S. trade deficit with China continues to grow to record levels. Meanwhile, Chinese and

---

[5] Interviews, New York City January 26, 1999, Washington, D.C., January 27, 1999.

[6] Beijing's position is reviewed in *Taiwan*, CRS Issue Brief 98034 (updated monthly).

U.S. observers also judged that as long as the Clinton Administration is preoccupied with the Senate trial of the President, it will be unwilling to make significant compromises on China policy that might antagonize Senators. The observers also judged that the PRC leaders' current emphasis on stability will make them less open to potentially disruptive economic changes needed for a WTO accord with the United States.

Against this background, several U.S. and Chinese experts speculated as to whether Zhu Rongji would postpone his visit to the United States. They acknowledged that there were many areas of U.S.-China cooperation following the summit meetings of 1997 and 1998 that could be emphasized as positive accomplishments during Zhu's visit. But they judged that media and official attention probably would focus on the possible absence of agreement on WTO, human rights and trade differences, and the implications of the classified report critical of China's efforts to acquire U.S. advanced technology that was released by a House special committee at the end of 1998. These developments would cast the visit in a negative light and subject Zhu to possible criticism at home and abroad. (They noted that Jiang Zemin's November 1998 visit to Japan had not met China's objectives and had resulted in some criticism of Jiang, and especially Foreign Minister Tian Jiaxuan, a Japan expert, for going ahead with the visit without assurances of its success.) One of the perceived disadvantages of postponing Zhu's visit is that it would signal a stalling in the forward movement in developing the "constructive strategic partnership" between the United States and China that was widely hailed by the two administrations during the summits in 1997 and 1998 but attacked by U.S. critics as misguided and unrealistic given continued serious human rights, trade and security differences between the United States and China.

## Current Policy Priorities

Chinese and U.S. experts were in agreement that PRC leaders will remain focused on domestic priorities for the rest of the year and perhaps for the rest of their terms in office (Jiang Zemin and other top leaders will retire from their party posts in the fall of 2002, and from their government posts in early 2003). Their priorities[7] include:

- Continued efforts to streamline and reform tens of thousands of money losing state-owned enterprises;

- Stepped up efforts to reform China's ailing banking and financial systems, with a view to avoiding the pitfalls faced by others during the continuing Asian economic crisis;

- Continued sharp reductions of central government and provincial government bureaucracies, especially those involved with managing specific sectors of the Chinese economy;

---

[7] For more detailed discussions, see *China: Recent Policy Priorities*, CRS Report 98-802, September 23, 1998. On economic issues, see *China's Economic Conditions*, by Wayne Morrison, CRS Issue Brief 98014 (updated regularly).

- Programs to privatize the heavily subsidized housing system in Chinese cities, and to establish social security and unemployment compensation systems for older and displaced workers;

- Efforts to remove the military from business enterprises and to stamp out smuggling and other malfeasance in the management of the Chinese economy;

- Heavy government spending on infrastructure and other projects designed to sustain a high enough economic growth rate (the goal is about 7 % for 1999) to absorb the many newly unemployed and displaced workers and thereby insure social and political stability; and

- Continued strong efforts against common criminals, dissidents, ethnic separatists and others seen threatening to the prevailing order.

Barring unexpected challenges from abroad, Chinese foreign policy is expected to receive lower priority. Beijing leaders are assumed to want to maintain the wide range of "partnerships" they have established with all major world powers and important neighboring countries around China's periphery. They are said to eschew initiatives that might complicate their very difficult agenda of domestic policy concerns.

Thus, as noted above, *relations with the United States* are expected to make some progress in areas of common ground noted in the 1997 and 1998 summits (e.g. environmental cooperation, cooperation on crime prevention, etc.), but forward movement on sensitive issues like human rights, WTO, Taiwan and Tibet is less likely as leaders in both capitals focus on pressing domestic concerns. Meanwhile, from Beijing's perspective, there has been some backsliding in U.S. policy toward Taiwan, as the Clinton Administration followed its repeated assurances on U.S. policy toward Taiwan during the 1997 and 1998 summits with cabinet level economic and military contacts with Taiwan counterparts and reported upgrading of U.S. weapons sales to Taiwan.

On the U.S. side, U.S. government dissatisfaction with Beijing's retreat on human rights is complemented by complaints among U.S. business representatives about difficulties in doing business in China and by U.S. military leaders about the failure of China to be more open in military exchanges with the United States. U.S. and Chinese experts were uncertain precisely what impact the completion of the report of the Select House Committee on alleged illicit U.S. technology transfer to China would have on U.S.-China relations, though it has already dampened enthusiasm for broader contacts and exchanges in these areas, according to many. The experts also anticipated some U.S. actions to respond to the record U.S. trade deficit with China, estimated at $57 billion in 1998.

*PRC policy toward Taiwan* has remained a mix of carrots (encouraging cross Strait trade and investment, and political dialogue), and sticks (Chinese military modernization, and strong PRC efforts to reduce Taiwan's diplomatic recognition abroad and its efforts to play a greater role in international organizations). Chinese officials have mixed feelings about the results of the December 1998 Taiwan elections. They recognize that the ruling Nationalist Party defeated the more pro-independence opposition party, suggesting that Taiwan voters favor a centrist position between the more radical extreme of Taiwan independence and reunification with the mainland. But this centrist position seems to be moving slowly and surely away from positions supportive of PRC approaches to Taiwan, and is seen to support President Lee Teng-hui's handling of cross Strait issues. In particular, some Chinese experts see Lee Teng-hui's continued efforts—supported widely in Taiwan—to carve out an identity for Taiwan people separate from the mainland—as antithetical to PRC efforts at eventual reunification.

There is little sign of change in *Beijing's continued "hands off" policy toward Hong Kong*, though Chinese leaders have stated that China would, if needed, support the Hong Kong dollar. Poor economic conditions in Hong Kong and the perceived difficulties the C.H. Tung administration has in winning popular confidence in Hong Kong are seen as problems for Chinese leaders, but not as warranting intervention, at least at this time. Oppositionists in Hong Kong led by the Democratic Party's Martin Lee are viewed by some U.S. and PRC experts as pushing harder for greater democracy in Hong Kong, with Lee notably hailing Taiwan's recent democratic elections as a salient model for Hong Kong. Some Beijing experts judge that given the suppression of political dissent elsewhere in China, one might expect efforts to curb Martin Lee and his cohorts, either through the initiative of the C.H. Tung administration or other means. Thus far, there is little sign of this.

*Japan* poses a significant foreign policy problem for Chinese leaders, according to U.S. and Chinese experts. Jiang Zemin's failure during his November 1998 visit to Japan to elicit a more forthcoming Japanese apology for past aggression against China and a more forthcoming Japanese statement supporting the PRC position on Taiwan was seen as a setback and a clear indication that Japan will not be easily moved to accommodate Chinese concerns over sensitive issues in the future. The Chinese reportedly are especially concerned about Japan's disregard of Chinese criticism and warnings to stop its efforts to revitalize the defense alliance with the United States, and to develop Theater Missile Defense efforts with the United States. The latter are seen to counter the PRC's ballistic missile advantage while the former is seen as implicitly covering Taiwan and strengthening Taipei's resolve to resist PRC pressure for reunification.

Chinese officials are watching closely the U.S. policy review over *North Korea*. They continue to counsel restraint and patience, arguing that recent U.S.-North Korea disputes have not reached a point where ongoing U.S. engagement with North Korea should be suspended. They strongly support the positive approach to the North by South Korea's President Kim Dae Jung.

Chinese experts showed keen sensitivity to *India*. They recognize that China has little ability to negotiate directly with India over the implications of India's May 1998 nuclear weapons tests because India has justified the tests on the basis of its view of a "threat" from China, and because Sino-Indian relations are also strained by long-standing differences over border delineation and Tibet. As a result, Chinese officials have been supportive of U.S.-led efforts to deal with the Indian nuclear problem in ways that would contain the threat of instability to Chinese interests. Chinese experts nonetheless remain wary that the United States might reach compromise agreements with New Delhi that would confirm India's status as a nuclear power, change the rules for entry into force of the Comprehensive Test Ban Treaty to accommodate India's concerns, or otherwise enhance India's power and prestige as a result of the May 1998 nuclear tests. The Chinese experts claim that if the United States were to follow such a course, it would revive Chinese fears that U.S. policy seeks to improve relations with India as a means to balance China's influence in Asian and world affairs, and thereby complicate smooth U.S.-China relations.

Chinese experts were privately very critical of Russia's policy toward New Delhi. This came despite continued Sino-Russian rhetoric of mutual cooperation and common opposition to U.S."power politics" in Iraq and elsewhere. Noting Russian arms sales and technology transfers to India, and Russia's "unsatisfactory" response to India's nuclear tests, the Chinese officials privately argued that Russia not only seeks to maintain its longstanding relations with New Delhi, but does so with an eye toward checking and balancing China's rising power in Asian and world affairs.

# Taipei

## Relations With the United States and the PRC

Taiwan government officials and non-government opinion leaders[8] appear cautiously optimistic about the short-term outlook for Taiwan in its ongoing competition with the PRC and its efforts to improve relations with the United States despite opposition from the PRC. Their reasons include:

1.  A perception that the upswing in U.S.-PRC relations seen during the summit meetings of 1997 and 1998 has run its course. Taiwan observers have seen this improvement coming at the expense of Taiwan interests and Taiwan-U.S. relations. Notably, they claim that President Clinton during his June 1998 visit to China publicly articulated the so-called "three no's" (no U.S. support for one China, one Taiwan; Taiwan independence; or Taiwan's participation in international organizations requiring statehood) because of PRC pressure. They also assert that the U.S. government curbed interaction with Taiwan in order to reassure the PRC of U.S. intentions during this period.[9] After the 1998 summit, it appears to Taiwan observers that both the United States and PRC administrations are preoccupied with domestic issues. The U.S. and PRC administrations also appear to face domestic opposition to making further compromises on economic issues (e.g. regarding China's entry into the WTO), Taiwan, human rights, or other sensitive subjects that would allow for further

---

[8] Consultations in Taipei centered on participation in a two-day conference sponsored by National Cheng Chi University on current trends and prospects for Taiwan in early January 1999. Conference activities involved formal presentations by 25 Taiwan and foreign specialists and in-depth discussion, along with meetings with senior government and intellectual leaders, including a one-hour discussion with President Lee Teng-hui and extensive interaction with Vice President Lien Chan, National Security Director Ding Mou-shih, and others

[9] See discussion in *Taiwan: The "Three No's," Congressional-Administration Differences, and U.S. Policy Issues*, CRS Report 98-837, October 1, 1998,

forward movement in the U.S.-PRC relationship. In particular, Beijing's recent economic policies appear to underline PRC unwillingness to make the kinds of economic policy reforms needed to meet U.S. requirements for China's entry into the WTO; and Beijing's recent suppression of political dissent has alienated the United States.

2.   The Clinton Administration has taken several steps to improve ties with Taiwan and thereby adjust the balance in U.S. policy toward the PRC and Taiwan after the Beijing summit. These have been done despite protests from the PRC. They include sending Energy Secretary Bill Richardson to Taiwan in November 1998 with a letter from President Clinton to President Lee Teng-hui, and an unofficial meeting in Washington in October 1998 between Defense Secretary William Cohen and the head of Taiwan's military chief of staff. There are also widespread reports that Taiwan and U.S. leaders are discussing ways to provide Taiwan with a means to defend against the growing ballistic missile threat from mainland China.[10]

3.   Taiwan's image as a political democracy and as a responsible actor in cross Strait relations assists its efforts to lobby for increased contacts, weapons sales and other interaction with the United States, despite PRC objections, according to Taiwan observers. Taiwan's December 5, 1998 elections[11] for the national legislature and for the Taipei and Kaohsiung municipalities clearly reflect Taiwan's "mature" and "responsible" democracy, according to Taiwan observers. The victory of the ruling Nationalist Party in the majority of the legislative races and in the closely watched Taipei's mayor's race has reassured many U.S. policy makers and opinion leaders that Taiwan voters do not favor more radical pro-independence candidates who might possibly provoke a PRC response that would increase tensions in the Taiwan Strait. Meanwhile, Taiwan's responsible image in the United States was enhanced when Taiwan and PRC cross Strait negotiators managed to improve the atmosphere during the trip of Taiwan's chief negotiator to the PRC in October 1998.[12]

4.   Taiwan's generally positive image in the United States was seen to stand in contrast to Being's recently poor image in the United States, especially as a result in particular of the suppression of political dissidents in the PRC. As a result, Taiwan observers speculate that U.S. officials may pay less heed to PRC complaints against improved U.S.-Taiwan relations and they will be less likely to pressure "democratic" Taiwan to compromise its interests in the cross Strait negotiations with the "authoritarian" regime in Beijing.

5.   Strong popular support for the Nationalist Party in the December 1998 elections has strengthened the position of Taiwan negotiators in cross Strait dialogue with

---

[10] Reviewed in *China and US. Missile Defense Proposals*, CRS Report RS 20031, January 28, 1999.

[11] See, *Taiwan's December 1998 Elections—Implications for U.S. Interests*, CRS Report 98-1018, December 30, 1998.

[12] See, *Taiwan-Mainland China Talks*, CRS Report 98-887, October 28, 1998.

the PRC, according to Taiwan observers. In particular, President Lee Teng-hui gained considerable credit for the Nationalist election victories, his leadership position in Taiwan remains strong, and his management of cross Strait issues enjoys wide support. These development are seen as undercutting perceived PRC strategies to criticize Lee as a "splitist," whose "extreme" views are out of touch with mainstream Taiwan opinion, and to seek Taiwan negotiating partners more accommodating to PRC concerns on cross Strait issues. As a result, it is expected that Taiwan negotiators will be better able to continue dialogue and seek small steps to settle some substantive economic and other issues but avoid accommodating PRC insistence for talks on political issues or PRC calls for Taiwan to open more widely to direct trade and communications with the mainland.

6.  Taipei does face a serious ongoing problem in maintaining formal diplomatic relations with its current 27 diplomatic allies (all small states) and in seeking a broader profile in international organizations and international affairs, in the face of strident PRC resistance. Nonetheless, Taiwan officials see PRC opposition as nothing new; it's a continuation of a longstanding PRC-Taiwan rivalry for international recognition. They also judge that Taiwan's positive international image as a thriving free market democracy, enhanced by the December 1998 elections and its continued good economic performance (5% growth in 1998) during the Asian economic crisis will assist Taiwan officials in their ongoing competition with the PRC.

## Current Policy Priorities

As relations with the United States appear more positive and cross Strait tensions appear to be under control for the time being, Taiwan voters are seen by Taiwan observers to be concerned mainly about improvements in domestic conditions that affect their everyday lives. Anxious to build public support prior to the next island wide elections, for the Taiwan Presidency in March 2000, Taiwan officials of both the Nationalist and opposition parties are focused on domestic programs that will appeal to the voters. In general, the priorities are:

- Maintaining effective economic policies to allow Taiwan's economy to continue to grow and become more competitive despite the Asian economic crisis.

- Broadening government efforts to provide more social welfare, including programs for the aged, needy, and unemployed, within the general constraints of a fiscally conservative government budget.

- Increased government spending on education programs to improve Taiwan economic competitiveness; on the environment, to remedy past abuses and provide better conditions for more sustainable long term economic development; on transportation to deal with persisting traffic problems in the densely populated island; and on law and order, to deal with widespread public concerns about crime and lax or corrupt government supervision.

Nationalist and opposition party leaders are focused notably on selecting candidates for the presidential race of March 2000. Despite his defeat in the Taipei Mayor's race in December 1998, Democratic Progressive Party leader Chen Shui-bian remains the front runner in seeking the party's nomination, according to Taiwan observers. Vice President Lien Chan is widely seen as the Nationalist Party leadership's front runner, but his candidacy faces several serious potential challenges. He is notably less popular than former Taiwan Provincial Governor James Soong, who is expected by many to challenge Lien for the party nomination, and perhaps to run as an independent if the party leadership rebuffs his challenge.[13]

# Hong Kong[14]

## Policy Priorities

The retreating economy is at the center of Hong Kong government policy concerns.[15] There was negative growth of 5% in 1998; the unemployment rate is 5.5%; and the economy is expected to decline 3% in 1999. Some big Hong Kong investors have complained that pressure from Martin Lee and other oppositionists for greater democracy in Hong Kong has eroded business confidence, though many dispute this. The banking system and the political structure of the government remain sound and are seen as sources for optimism about Hong Kong eventually recovering from the current serious downturn.

The administration of Chief Executive C.H. Tung is seeking to assist short term recovery and to chart plans for longer term growth, thus far without notable results. According to observers consulted during the study mission to Hong Kong, Tung and his associates are widely seen by Hong Kong observers as not politically astute, and not fully competent to deal with widespread popular discontent coming from the economic decline. Oppositionists led by Martin Lee continue to push for democratization more rapid than the pace called for under the Basic Law and other legal and administrative arrangements. But Tung's administration, strongly backed by the PRC, adheres to the current pace of democratization. Meanwhile, there are also ongoing problems in determining the power and influence of the civil service relative to the legislature (Legco), and of the civil service relative to C.H. Tung's personal staff.

---

[13] See, *Taiwan's December 1998 Elections*, CRS Report 98-1018, December 30, 1998.

[14] For discussion of Hong Kong, see *Hong Kong After the Return to China: Implications for U.S. Interests*, by Kerry Dumbaugh, CRS Issue Brief 95119 (updated regularly). See also *Hong Kong Update*, Center for Strategic and International Studies, Washington, D.C.

[15] Consultations in Hong Kong involved discussions over three days in mid-January 1999 with U.S., Chinese and other specialists in the Special Administrative Region (SAR) and in neighboring Guangdong Province. These included six small group discussions with foreign policy institutes and universities in Hong Kong and Guangzhou, the capital of Guangdong province, arranged by the U.S. Information Service.

Beijing continues to depend on Hong Kong for an estimated 60% of its outside investment, and is accordingly deeply concerned about the economic decline in the Special Administrative Region (SAR). (China also is the largest investor in Hong Kong.) Some observers in Hong Kong believe that PRC leaders are also concerned by Tung's less than favorable image for competence and political leadership. Nonetheless, Beijing is said to recognize that any sign of PRC unhappiness or meddling would lead to reactions in Hong Kong contrary to broad PRC goals of promoting prosperity and stability. They would also be seen by many as undermining Beijing's longer term goal to use the "success" of the one country, two systems model in Hong Kong to win support for PRC efforts to encourage Taiwan's reunification with the mainland.

Officials consulted in Beijing and Hong Kong also recognize Hong Kong's importance as a conduit for Taiwan's trade, investment and other interaction with the PRC. An estimated 20% of outside investment in the PRC comes from Taiwan, mainly through Hong Kong. It is cumulatively valued at $35 billion. Taiwan-mainland trade, mainly through Hong Kong, is valued at over $30 billion a year. In this context, Hong Kong officials give careful attention to facilitating Taiwan-mainland economic exchanges. They follow the example of their British predecessors in keeping Taiwan's unofficial political representatives in the SAR under fairly tight control, so as to avoid activities likely to provoke a negative reaction from Beijing.

Hong Kong observers see few difficult issues with the United States at present. While some in Congress press for faster democratization, the Clinton Administration avoids specific criticism in voicing general calls for greater democratization. The rule of law in the SAR meets with wide approval in the West, while episodes of market intervention during the past year have not eroded Hong Kong's free market image in the United States or elsewhere, according to Hong Kong observers. There are numerous textile, intellectual property rights, and other trade issues with Hong Kong, but in general trade tensions reportedly remain relatively low keyed.

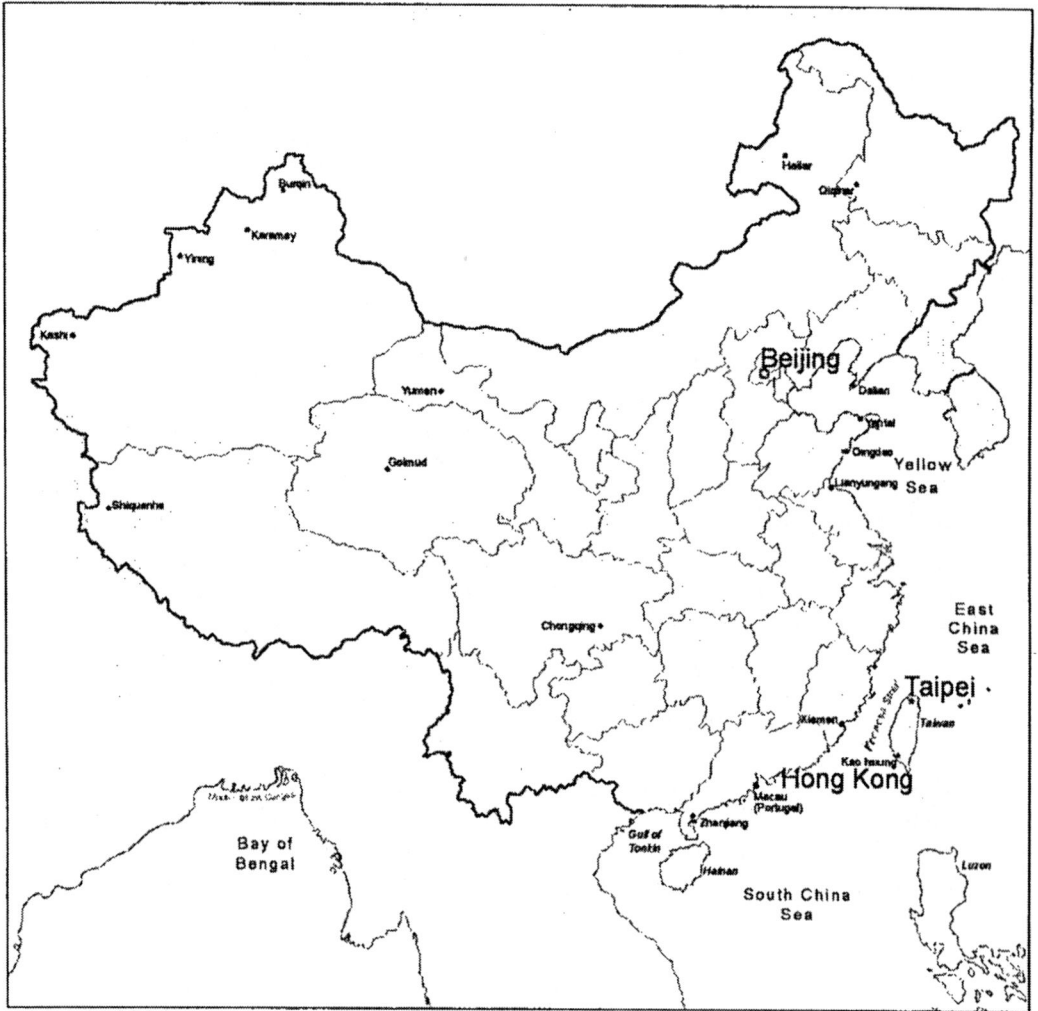

Adapted by CRS from Magellan Geographix.  Used with permission.

# SOUTH KOREA: "SUNSHINE POLICY" AND ITS POLITICAL CONTEXT[*]

*Rinn-Sup Shinn*

## U.S. Interest in South Korea's "Sunshine Policy"

U.S. interests in South Korea involve a range of security, economic, political, and North Korea policy issues. Of these, U.S. relations with the South Korean political leadership, especially over North Korea issues, are of continuing concern to the United States; the latter issues have strong implications for U.S. security interests.[1] For decades, the United States has supported South Korea's stable progress toward democratization. In this regard, the United States welcomed the inauguration in February 1998 of civilian President Kim Dae Jung's administration — the second since 1993 — as another significant milestone in South Korea's progress toward mature democracy.

U.S. concern for South Korea's policy toward North Korea, popularly known as the "sunshine policy," has drawn a renewed interest since 1998. President Kim Dae Jung's policy of engagement with the North represents a sharp break with the traditional emphasis on reciprocity. The reversal of direction from the right to the left has seemed to catch many in the South unprepared, leaving some confused and others conflicted.

This policy shift has been caught up in the partisan strife between President Kim's coalition government and the conservative opposition camp. The sunshine approach has endured thus far without a bipartisan show of consensus and support behind it. As a result, although the policy has been touted by the Kim administration as the only promising alternative to war, there has seemed some tenuousness with regard to the sustainability of the engagement policy as now constructed and played out—beyond President Kim's tenure in office ending in February 2003.

If President Kim has his way, the United States might find itself even more closely associated with the sunshine policy than it is now. Since late 1998, the Kim administration has urged the United States to adopt its own sunshine policy as the cornerstone of a new "comprehensive" U.S. policy toward the North.[2] Frustrated

---

[1] For coverage of broader issues, see CRS Issue Brief 98045. *Korea: U.S.-South Korean Relations—Issues for Congress*, by Robert G. Sutter. (Updated regularly).

[2] The new comprehensive policy will likely be based in part on a report to be prepared by William J. Perry, former defense secretary who was named in November 1998 by President Clinton to undertake a congressionally mandated interagency review of U.S. policy toward North Korea. See the provision on North Korea in Omnibus Fiscal 1999 Appropriations, H.R. 4328 (P.L., 105-277), *Congressional Record*, No. 149, October 19, 1998, H11098.

---

[*] Excerpted from *CRS Report for Congress* RL30188

with Pyongyang's recalcitrancy to its engagement policy, the Kim administration has pleaded for what amounts to a reinforcement from the United States.

From the U.S. perspective, the intent of the sunshine policy seems for the most part compatible with its overriding security interest in a denuclearized Korean peninsula. But there is a range of U.S. views about the appropriate means to use in order to achieve this desired end. Thus, many U.S. policy makers and other observers have mixed views on the efficacy of Kim's "sunshine policy" and its compatibility with U.S. policy on the Korean Peninsula.

## Quest for Political Stability

### Background

Kim Dae Jung, the dissident voice of a generation of crusaders for democracy, won the presidential election in December 1997 by a razor-thin margin.[3] He defeated Lee Hoi Chang of the center-right establishment that had dominated South Korean politics for nearly 50 years. Kim's success, on his fourth try, was a historic first for South Korea's perennial underdog—the opposition led by Kim.

Observers attribute this feat to several factors. The first was Kim Dae Jung's pre-election compact with conservative rival Kim Jong Pil, a former Prime Minister under the military-dominated regime of President Park Chung Hee, whereby he would have the constitution amended by the year 2000, if elected, in return for the latter's support for his candidacy. If amended, the constitution would allow for the establishment of a parliamentary cabinet system to replace the existing presidential system, presumably under the premiership of Kim Jong Pil (see Fragile Coalition) below. There is a consensus that this pact was crucial to President Kim as it was believed to have minimized a split in opposition votes.[4] The second factor was voters' anger and disgust with economic mismanagement and money scandals under the outgoing Kim Young Sam regime. The third was a split in votes for Lee Hoi Chang as a result of factional leader Rhee In-je's defection to seek the presidency for himself. The fourth was the alleged draft-dodging by two sons of Lee Hoi Chang. The fifth was a solid support for Kim Dae Jung from regional loyalists, "progressives," and labor union activists. Additionally, the absence of North Korean provocations in the run-up to the election (which always meant more votes for pro-government candidates in the past) is believed to have helped Kim Dae Jung. These factors seemed to have enabled him to surmount two disadvantages: his narrow political base in the less populous, poorer, and the negatively stereotyped Cholla region in the southwest

---

[3]In addition to information from printed sources in Korean, Japanese, and English, this report relies on interviews and consultations with nearly 40 South Koreans of varied backgrounds, conducted in Seoul, Korea, in September 1998; also useful were consultations since then with a number of specialists on Korean affairs in Washington.

[4]"NCNP-ULD Coalition Sets Sail for Dec. Election," *The Korea Times*, November 4, 1997, p.2. On the first anniversary of his victory in December 1998, President Kim is reported to have credited his triumph to the electoral coalition. [Editorial]: "Fate of Political Contract," *The Korea Herald* (Internet version), January 5, 1999.

and, as one source put it, "years of military propaganda that portrayed him, unfairly, as soft on the Communist North."[5]

The National Congress for New Politics (NCNP) is the political arm of President Kim, who rules in coalition with Prime Minister Kim Jong Pil and his conservative United Liberal Democrats (ULD). The two parties formed the cabinet, with the NCNP controlling more strategic portfolios. Prime Minister Kim is essentially second in command, but as a presidential appointee subject to the confirmation of the National Assembly, he has little or no power to initiate any policy on his own. In the current setting, President Kim's command and control seem to extend to the entire governmental system including the National Assembly (parliament) and even the independent judiciary.[6]

South Korea's political parties continue to be the virtual personal vehicles of their leaders. The weakest institutional link in the democratic process, they are organized to advance the interests of their leaders and regions. Principles and policies matter little as defining issues in partisan competition. A reflection of the personality-dominated and regionalized nature of partisanship, parties are formed and disbanded at will depending on their leaders' whims.[7] The current coalition parties are no exception. As Kim Dae Jung's NCNP and Kim Jong Pil's ULD are identified with the Cholla and Chungchong regions, respectively, so is the opposition Lee Hoi Chang's Grand National Party (GNP), with the Kyongsang region (see Map. South Korean Provincial Boundaries).

## Political Realignment

Political maneuvering for advantage and realignment consumed much of President Kim's first year in office.[8] Holding a minority with 120 parliamentary members between them in the 299-seat National Assembly, the coalition of NCNP and ULD wasted no time in trying to bolster their ranks at the expense of the opposition GNP that had a majority with 165 seats. This asymmetry was at the center of partisan strife since the inception of the coalition. However, realignment did not come easily, since South Korea's political culture allowed little leeway for conciliation or compromise. Another complication was the confusion coming from the suddenness of reversed political fortunes—an unprecedented opposition takeover of presidential power. Even as the ruling camp appealed for bipartisan collaboration, it seemed also to provoke the GNP by trying to undercut its majority status in the National Assembly.

---

[5][Editorial]: "Kim Dae Jung's Triumph . . .," *Washington Post*, December 21, 1997, C6.

[6][Editorial]: "Can the President Take Care of Everything?," *Dong-A Ilbo* (Internet version) *in Korean,* July 23, 1998; Paek Ki-ch'ol, "Cover Story - - DJP's Duel," *Hangyore 21 (Ch'ollian Database version) in Korean,* November 19, 1998.

[7][Stone Mirror]: "On Political Parties, Power, and Proportional Representation," by David I. Steinberg, *The Korea Times* (Internet version), March 1, 1999.

[8]"Politics Lags Far Behind Economy in Reform," *The Korea Herald,* December 25, 1998, p.2; "Kim Gets Low Marks for Political Reform," *The Korea Times,* December 31, 1998, p.2..

# South Korean Provincial Boundaries

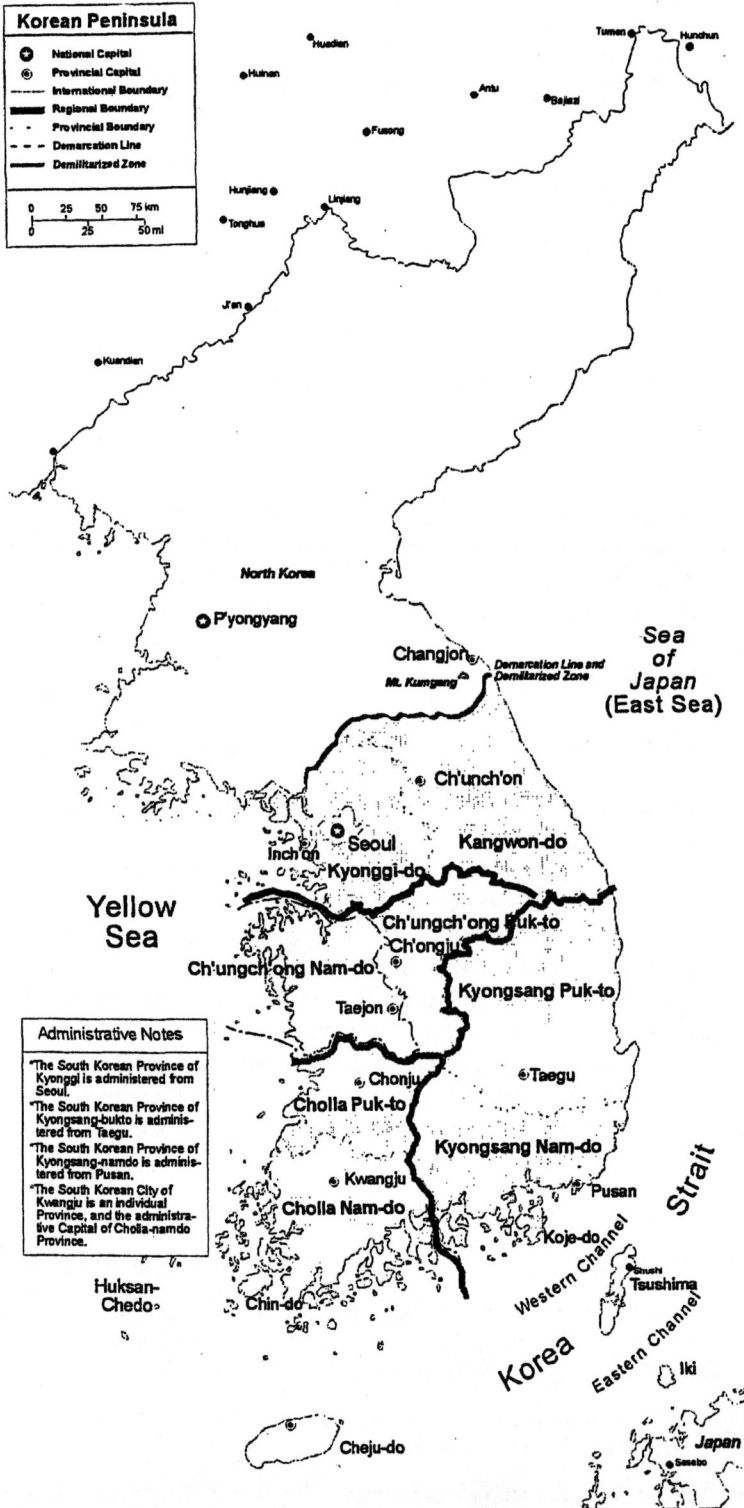

Adapted by CRS from Magellan Geographix. Used with permission.

For its part, finding its familiar world turned upside down, the GNP seemed unable to adjust to its new role as a loyal opposition. Indeed, within hours after Kim Dae Jung was sworn in, the GNP blocked approval of Kim Jong Pil as the presidential nominee for Prime Minister and went on to denounce the ruling camp for targeting GNP members for actual or threatened prosecution on charges of corruption.[9] As it turned out, the coalition eventually secured a majority by "welcoming" GNP defectors. By May 1999, the hard-pressed GNP seemed to face a crisis of identity.[10] If the ruling camp has its way in the coming months, more GNP members may break the ranks either to form a "new party"or to join the ruling camp. The GNP's possible fracture could lead to a major partisan realignment under a single dominant political machine controlled by the presidential complex called the Blue House.[11] Another possible fallout might well be the widening of the gulf between the Cholla-centered Kim Dae Jung administration and the largely Kyongsang-based GNP opposition.[12]

## Regional Favoritism

For decades, regionalism has been viewed as the most potent force in South Korean politics. Regional divisions defined partisan divisions and, more importantly, power alignment. From 1961 through 1997, positions of power and influence in politics, bureaucracy, the economy, and the military were disproportionately in the hands of those who hailed from the city of Taegu in the northern Kyongsang province—popularly dubbed "T-K mafia." The T-K group tended to form the backbone of the GNP (and its predecessors). In this period, the Cholla provinces suffered a benign neglect, if for no other reason than they happened to be the political stronghold of Kim Dae Jung, the vocal opponent of the military-dominated regimes under Park Chung Hee (1961-78), Chun Doo Hwan (1981-87), and Roh Tae Woo (1988-1992). It was no accident that under these generals-turned-presidents, who

---

[9]While rebuking the opposition for obstructing his plan for economic reforms by abusing its majority status, President Kim stated, "the prosecution's investigation is nothing more than judicial procedures for criminal offenders." *Yonhap* News Agency in English [Seoul], May 28, 1998. For his part, GNP leader Lee Hoi Chang offered a withering critique of the ruling camp that he claimed was undermining democracy by trying to dismantle the opposition, neutralize the legislature, tame the press, and use law enforcement authorities for inappropriate purposes. *The Korea Times* (Internet version), September 10, 1998.

[10]The crisis could be attributed to two possible factors: the GNP's failure to define a coherent policy agenda for partisan competition and a factional divide between the "mainstreamers" and "non-mainstreamers." "Rebirth of the GNP," *Chosun Ilbo* (Internet version), August 5, 1998.

[11]Such a scenario seems to fly in the face of President Kim's own wisdom; while in opposition, he once argued that political stability was possible only when the opposition was strong enough to check the ruling party from becoming 'arrogant,' as had been the case in the late 1980s. *The Korea Herald* [Seoul], February 2, 1996, p.2.

[12]Tension between the ruling and opposition camps reached a new height in May 1999, when GNP's Lee Hoi Chang announced an intention to launch a so-called "second pro-democracy campaign" against the Kim administration's alleged dictatorial pattern of governance. *Yonhap* in English, May 6, 1999; *The Korea Times* (Internet version), May 6, 1999.

were all from Taegu, the Cholla region was left behind as an economic backwater.[13] It has taken Kim Dae Jung's presidency to begin to redress the regional inequity—but not without an ironic twist.[14] Regional favoritism has continued to assert itself—now skewed to the Cholla and Chungchong regions under the control of Kim Dae Jung and Kim Jong Pil, respectively, at the expense of the T-K/GNP dominated power structure (see Map. South Korean Provincial Boundaries).[15]

## Inter-Regional Harmony?

Political stability is now believed to be a function of regional harmony. The two are believed to be crucial to President Kim's effort to extend the NCNP's narrow power base from the Cholla region into the GNP's stronghold in the Kyongsang region. On February 1,1999, for example, he vowed his intention to pursue stability through a harmonious inter-regional realignment.[16] If all goes as intended, this could go a long way toward forging what might be called a grand alliance between the Cholla and Kyongsang regions and, more importantly, to help the NCNP solidify its currently tenuous grip on power. To that end, the NCNP hinted at the possibility of enlisting support from the two major components of the opposition: the "T-K" group and former President Kim Young Sam's own group based in Pusan and the southern Kyongsang province.[17] If realized, the regrouping may lead to the establishment of a so-called "super-party" to set the stage for a new mandate at the general elections set for April 2000.

President Kim Dae Jung sounded hopeful that his NCNP could, by mid-2000, gain a broad national constituency under his initiative for electoral reform. He would like to replace the current single-member district constituency with a new format coupling district and proportional representation— in time for the general election next year.[18] But whether his initiative can pass a parliamentary test of bipartisanship

---

[13]As a result, a bulk of the Cholla work force had to migrate to the Seoul metropolitan region for employment, eventually to emerge as a major voting bloc for Kim Dae Jung outside of the Cholla region. (CRS interviews)

[14]"Kim Accused of Perpetuating Regionalism," *The Korea Herald*, March 31, 1998, p.2.

[15]For a case that regionalism reflects the personalization of power, see David I. Steinberg, *"Continuing Democratic Reform in the Republic of Korea: Issues and Challenges,"* a paper delivered before a Korea University conference, Seoul, June 19-20, 1996, p.14.

[16]*The Korea Times (Internet version)*, February 1, 1999.

[17]*Chosun Ilbo (Internet version)*, May 21, 1998; *Dong-A Ilbo (Internet version)*, January 27, 1999; *Hankyore* (Internet version), January 27, 1999; *Hanguk Ilbo*, February 2, 1999; and *JoongAngg* (Internet Service), January 28, 1999.

[18]At present, a voter will cast one ballot to elect a district representative; then, a party will announce a winner (or winners) from its list of ranked candidates for at-large proportional representation based on the total number of votes it received nationwide. Under the new initiative being debated, a voter would cast two ballots, one for a district representative and the other for a party of choice for proportional representation; the proportional winner would be decided from a party list of ranked candidates based on the aggregate number of votes the party won in one of the several electoral regions to be created. To minimize regional bias, the
(continued...)

is unclear at this time, since the opposition GNP is believed to oppose an electoral reform.[19] As of mid-May 1999, the prospect seemed dim for partisan reconciliation in the months ahead.

## "Progressive" Power Elite

Kim's presidency also marks a significant departure from the past by ushering in a new, post-Korean War generation of power elite—veterans of political activism against the military-dominated, authoritarian rule in the 1970s and 1980s.[20] Mostly in their forties, the new elite now occupies strategic positions of power and influence in government and in the broadcasting and print media as well.[21] Iconoclastic, nationalistic, and closely identified with President Kim's reformist stance, the new group is believed to embrace a so-called progressive vision of a new Korea, currently manifest in his ambitious agenda for a "Rebuilding Korea Movement."[22] The elite has been described as part of a liberal, left-of-center political subculture growing since the 1980s, more particularly since the early 1990s. Popular among intellectuals, academics, and center-left political activists, they appear to view a range of social, ideological, and political issues from a liberal or "progressive" perspective of the post-

---

[18](...continued)
names on the party list in an electoral region would be picked for the most part from among candidates of local origin.

[19]Absent bipartisan cooperation, President Kim's ruling coalition may pass an electoral reform bill through a simple majority. For an account of the coalition moving a record 130 bills through the National Assembly in less than 20 minutes—without the opposition being present, see Shim Jae Hoon, "Push to Shove: Democrat Kim Turns Parliament Into Rubber Stamp," *Far Eastern Economic Review* [Hong Kong], January 21, 1999, p.27.

[20]A significant milestone in that activism was a massive pro-democracy, civil uprising in 1980, in the southern Cholla provincial capital of Kwangju; a collateral consequence of the event was to mark the beginning of anti-American sentiments among South Korean students and youths because of their perception of the U.S. military complicity in the bloody South Korean military suppression of the uprisings. For an extensive report on alleged U.S. complicity, see *The U.S. Role in Korea in 1979 and 1980*, by Tim Shorrock: http://www.kimsoft.com/korea/kwangju3.htm.

[21]"History of Regionalism," *The Korea Times*, March 13, 1998, p.2; "Korea Undergoes 'Revolutionary' Changes with Reform Regime," *The Korea Herald*, December 22, 1998, p.2.

[22]Enunciated by President Kim in August 1998, this government-initiated grass-roots movement, with civic groups reportedly playing a leading role, seeks major changes in the political, economic, and social sectors (President Kim's "sunshine policy" toward North Korea is listed as part of the reforms envisaged in this movement). Facing opposition suspicions of ulterior motives behind the movement, President Kim, on February 3, 1999, was quoted as saying unequivocally that he had no intention of using the movement as a tool for gaining partisan advantage. *Chongwadae* [The Blue House] WWW in English (Internet version), February 3, 1999; Presidential Commission for Policy Planning. *Second Nation-Building: Direction of Grand Transformation and Reform* [in Korean]. Seoul: October 1998. 60 p.; "Kim Guarantee s Politics-Free 2nd Nation Building Reform," *The Korea Herald* (Internet version), September 28, 1998.

Cold War era.[23] Generally, these progressives tend to regard conservatives as obstacles to domestic reform or change.[24] Some also seem to scoff at conservatives at home and abroad, dubbed as "archaic security-mongers," as doing "more harm than good" in the Kim administration's quest for peace and stability.[25] Implicit in their thinking seems to be the notion that Seoul's effort to win the confidence of Pyongyang will be frustrated unless these hawks are persuaded otherwise or silenced.[26]

The progressive tendency is regarded as inevitable by many, since the post-Korean War generation—now accounting for some 70 percent of the South Korean electorate—are more attuned to pluralistic and democratic trends than the older generation. The potential political significance of this new demographic reality is not lost on the conservative ULD as well as the GNP. The latter, in particular, is reportedly contemplating a move away from its "deep-seated conservatism" in an intensified bid to address the socioeconomic concerns of the middle class and underprivileged.[27]

---

[23]On North Korea, for instance, South Korea's "young intellectuals" are said to be more concerned about how not to offend Pyongyang, apparently in the belief that "criticism of the North" is contrary to the spirit of progressivism. *Chosun Ilbo* (Internet version) in English, March 11, 1999.

[24]In September 1998, Professor Choi Jang-jip, then-Chairman of the Presidential Commission for Policy Planning, reportedly said at an NCNP forum that the party should break with the conservative ULD in favor of collaboration with the progressive wing of the "P-K" (for Pusan and the southern Kyongsang province) group under former President Kim Young Sam. *Chosun Ilbo*, September 16, 1998. For Choi's plea that South Koreans need to "adapt thinking to the transitional changes of the post-Cold War era," see *Chosun Ilbo* (Internet version) in English, January 18, 1999 (Choi resigned from his post reportedly under pressure from the Blue House, April 1, 1999). Of interest to the United States, prior to 1997, rarely did South Korean intellectuals publicly reveal themselves as "leftists"; this seems to be no longer the case today. The term "leftist" is taken to mean three broad categories, as one writer generalized: a doctrinaire Leninist-Marxist, a pro-North Korean "juche ideologue," and an "orthodox socialist" (a leftist in a Western socialist democracy). For a recent discussion on the leftwing phenomenon in South Korea, see Ho Yong-pom, "Leftists Have Declared Themselves," *Wolgan Chosun* [Seoul], December 1998, pp. 158-180, available on Internet in English translation by Foreign Broadcast Information Service (Document ID: FTS19981222000800).

[25][Editorial]: "Archaic Security-Mongers," *The Korea Times* (Internet version), April 11, 1999; this editorial asserted, "Defiance of hard core conservative political forces" to the sunshine policy will be counterproductive, "if not betrayal to the wishes of our forefathers for unification."; *Taehan Mail* (Internet version) in Korean, December 8, 1998. [Editorial]: "Kim Dae Jung Courts North Korea," *New York Times*, June 3, 1998, A28; Nicholas D. Kristof, "Seoul Leader Asks End to Sanctions on North Koreans," *New York Times*, June 2, 1998, A8; *Tokyo Shimbun* in Japanese, February 11, 1999, morning edition, p.3; *Chosun Ilbo* (Internet version) in Korean, March 8, 1999.

[26]*The Korea Times* (Internet version) in English, December 8, 1998.

[27]*The Korea Times* (Internet version) in English, April 14, 1999.

In any event, to this new generation, unresolved issues of the Cold War as they relate to inter-Korean relations appears to have much less real-life relevance. Observers suggest that the conventional assumptions about North Korea, the origins of the Korean War, and even the rationale for the current and future U.S. military presence in the South Korea can no longer be taken for granted. A case in point appears to be a sentiment among some South Korean progressives that Pyongyang's reported shift in its policy on U.S. military presence in the South can be construed as a "sign" of the North's positive response to the sunshine policy. The apparent policy shift was reportedly about redefining the status of U.S. forces to a peacekeeping role (see U.S. Troops as Peacekeepers?, below).[28] Increasingly, progressive thinkers seem to embrace the notion that South Koreans' conventional security assumptions should be reexamined to see whether their reliance on U.S. military deterrence enhances or hampers South Korea's chances for peaceful accommodation with North Korea.[29]

## Fragile Coalition

At present, perhaps the most worrisome situation in South Korean politics is the uncertainty President Kim faces over the future of his partnership with Prime Minister Kim Jong Pil.[30] At issue is the president's 1997 pre-election pledge that, if elected, he would push to accommodate the latter's demand for a constitutional amendment to make for a cabinet system accountable to the National Assembly.[31] Now Kim Jong Pil and his ULD are trying to nudge the President to honor his pledge so that the constitution can be revised no later than the end of 1999.[32] For years, Kim Jong Pil argued in favor of a cabinet system as a realistic solution to South Korea's two chronic political problems: 1) the deterioration of a presidential system into a virtual

---

[28][Editorial]: "Archaic Security-Mongers," *The Korea Times* (Internet version) in English, April 11, 1999.

[29]*The Korea Times* (Internet version) in English, November 21, 1998; *Yonhap*, December 9, 1998; "U.S. Remains Idle Despite Kim's Initiative," *The Korea Times* (Internet version) in English, December 10, 1998.

[30]Apart from the ongoing feud with the NCNP over the so-called "cabinet issue," the ULD voiced a dissenting view of President Kim's "sunshine policy" as unduly leaning toward "carrots" at the expense of "reciprocity"; it also takes issue with the ideological softness of some of President Kim's inner circle people. *The Korea Times* (Internet version), November 15, 1998; Hangyore 21 (Cauline Database version) in Korean, November 19, 1998; "NCNP, ULD Show Signs of Rift," *The Korea Times*, November 16, 1998, p.2; "ULD's Yi Tong-pok [Lee Dong-bok] Views ROK's DPRK Policy," *Wolgan Chosun* in Korean, January 1999, pp.62-73, in English translation by Foreign Broadcast Information Service (Document ID:FTS19990214000238). For a report that the two parties did not have a regular policy cooperation forum for the first six months of the coalition rule, see *The Korea Herald* (Internet version), September 14, 1998.

[31]This commitment as phrased in the pre-election coalition pact, November 3, 1997, is taken to mean "a public pledge before the nation." As cited in *Chosun Ilbo* (Internet version), January 19, 1999.

[32]An ULD lawmaker argued that, absent a joint ULD-NCNP effort to address the issue by the end of March 1999, ULD cabinet ministers will have no alternative but to withdraw from the coalition cabinet. *Hangyore (Internet version)* in Korean, March 3, 1999.

dictatorship; and 2) power alignment pivoting on the regional identity of a sitting President.[33] He maintains that a cabinet system based on an equitable regional power-sharing can remedy those problems. Kim Jong Pil may also hope a new cabinet system would boost his personal power.

Observers view the cabinet system issue as problematic for several reasons. First, were Kim Dae Jung to yield to Kim Jong Pil's pressure, he may have to share, from mid-2000, much of his power with the newly empowered cabinet (probably under Prime Minister Kim Jong Pil). Second, the GNP continues to support the existing presidential system, virtually ruling out a two-thirds majority needed for the constitutional amendment. Third, for now at least, President Kim's more pressing priority is to ride out the ongoing economic crisis, while keeping the refrain to honor his pledge at an opportune time.[34] Fourth, in the coming months, an equally pressing concern is likely to be on getting his electoral reform bill passed by the National Assembly—the centerpiece of his grand strategy for inter-regional harmony.[35] Fifth, political reconciliation with the opposition GNP looms as another presidential priority, given the need to pass political reform bills in time for the general election in 2000. Sixth, the NCNP is reportedly seeking, behind-the-scenes, either a merger with the ULD or a new "super-party" by absorbing dissident members of the GNP opposed to Lee Hoi Chang's leadership. And, lastly, the quest for dialogue with North Korea seems to be also a front-burner issue for President Kim.[36] Should North Korea respond in good faith to President Kim's engagement policy in the latter half of 1999, the NCNP may try to make a case for delaying the constitutional amendment to late 2002, claiming that dialogue with monolithic Pyongyang can be better handled under the existing presidential system.[37]

---

[33][News in Review]: "Imperial Presidency—Korean Tradition," *The Korea Times* (Internet version), April 21, 1999.

[34]President Kim reportedly revealed at a Blue House news conference on March 18, 1999 his intention to disclose his position on the cabinet system issue in "two to three months." *The Korea Times* (Internet version), March 19, 1999.

[35]Purported rationale behind the cabinet issue—a solution to distorted power alignment along regional lines—might be undercut if the grand "east-west" reconciliation is realized, as intended by President Kim's camp.

[36]"Seoul Preparing for S-N Summit: Kim," *The Korea Times* (Internet version), March 3, 1999. A GNP party memorandum submitted to the GNP leadership reportedly claimed —without offering proof—that the Kim administration's push for inter-Korean dialogue is designed, inter alia, to put to rest the notion of the constitutional amendment; the report also claims that the Kim administration's goal is to realize an inter-Korean summit meeting on August 15, 1999. *Chosun Ilbo* (Internet version) in Korean, February 19, 1999.

[37]Some observers opine that it will be a matter of *when, not whether*, President Kim will honor his pledge. In their opinion, the last thing President Kim will want is an historical legacy with an asterisk denoting that he betrayed a coalition partner (Author's interviews, in Seoul and Washington). A senior Blue House official, after meeting separately with the two Kims, is reported to have drawn an inference that there might be a "silent understanding" between them to defer the cabinet issue to the latter half of 1999. *Chosun Ilbo* (Internet version), March 4, 1999. It is reported that, in a face-to-face meeting on April 9, 1999, Kim Dae Jung and Kim Jong Pil agreed to refrain from broaching the amendment issue until after the end of August

(continued...)

# Sunshine Policy

## Overview

The policy of engagement with North Korea, popularly known as the "sunshine policy," was unveiled informally on December 19, 1997, the day after Kim Dae Jung won the presidency, suggesting that he came "prepared" to tackle the issue.[38] President Kim made it official in his inaugural address, on February 25, 1998. The policy has since been fleshed out to make it more receptive to skeptical Pyongyang and adjustable to situational needs.[39] In the closing months of 1998, expanding on this policy, the Kim administration began to advocate a more inclusive approach, one conditioned on reinforcement from the United states (see Coordination with the United States) below.[40]

The sunshine policy, South Korean observers judge, is the personification of Kim Dae Jung who is believed to be its architect as well as hands-on overseer.[41] It is

---

[37](...continued)
1999. *Hanguk Ilbo*, April 10, 1999, p.1; *Dong-A Ilbo* (Internet version), April 21, 1999. Nevertheless, the amendment might be skirted, as speculation goes, in light of President Kim's reported statement that the final decision would depend on factors such as public opinion and determination as to whether a cabinet system is really in national interest. *Hanguk Ilbo* (U.S. Edition) in Korean, April 16, 1999, p.1.

[38]"Kim DJ Espouses Sunshine Policy Toward North Korea: Clinton Asked to Arrange S-N Summit," *The Korea Times* (Internet version) in English, December 19, 1997.

[39]For the Kim administration's perspectives , see Hong Soon-young, "Thawing Korea's Cold War: The Path to Peace on the Korean Peninsula, *Foreign Affairs*, May/June 1999; *The Korea Herald* (Internet version) in English, March 18, 1998; Lim Dong-Won, "*'Sunshine Policy' and a New Era in Inter-Korean Relations*" (April 24, 1998, The Shilla Hotel), 5 p; "Major Points of Secretary Yim Tong-won's Address: 'Dismantling Cold War Structure in Korea to Lead to Virtual Reunification'," *Chosun Ilbo* (Internet version) in Korean, February 10, 1999; Yang Sung Chul, *Kim Dae Jung Government's Policy Toward North Korea: Theoretical Underpinnings and Policy Directions* (a paper prepared for the Conference on the United States and the Two Koreas at the Crossroads: Searching for a New Passage, Seoul, March 26-27, 1999, 12 p.; Park Sang-seek, *The Sunshine Policy: Why Should We Pursue It?* (a paper prepared for the Conference on the United States and the Two Koreas at the Crossroads: Searching for a New Passage, Seoul, March 26-27, 1999, 10 p.; Ch'oe Song, "'Government of the People': Principles and Direction of North Korea Engagement Policy," in *T'ong'il Kyongje* in Korean, August 1998, pp 10-24; National Security Policy Institute, *The Sunshine Policy: A Bridge Linking the North and South* in Korean, Seoul (no date), 48 p.; *North Korea/Unification Policy of the 'Government of the People'* in Korean, Issue Brief 148, May 14, 1998, by Lee Seung Hyun, Legislative Research and Analysis Service, National Assembly Library, Seoul, 11 p.

[40]*Taehan Maeil* (Internet version) in Korean, November 15, 1998.

[41][Editorial]: "Active Policy Toward Pyongyang," *The Korea Herald*, March 6, 1998, p.6; Emphasizing the need for scrupulous scrutiny of the Kim Administration's policy of "aggressive and even hasty rapprochement," this editorial argues: "Rightly or not ... [the] present inter-Korean policy matters are formulated and implemented following the dictation

(continued...)

rooted in Kim's belief that avoiding war is his overriding priority and that, figuratively, honey works better than vinegar in trying to entice the North to moderate and change. It seems also to reflect his conviction that South Korea must take the lead in trying to initiate steps for the settlement of inter-Korean issues.[42] The philosophical underpinning of the policy runs deep, as the sunshine policy is believed by many to be the culmination of an evolutionary process in the making since the early 1970s.[43]

The sunshine policy is in a stark contrast to the containment- and reciprocity-oriented policy pursued by the previous Kim Young Sam administration. Its objective, as one writer put it, is to use "sunshine" to enable North Korea to voluntarily remove its 'coat' of isolation and hostility and give up its vision of 'liberating' the South."[44] In setting the basic tone of his policy, President Kim vowed that while his administration would actively seek reconciliation and cooperation with the North, and also forswear any attempt to harm or absorb the North, it would not tolerate armed provocation of any kind by the North. To expedite the process of reconciliation, he also promised to encourage the South's private-sector to explore and capitalize on economic opportunities in the North without government intervention. However, major projects requiring public funding are to be subject to inter-government dialogue and reciprocity.

It seems that several assumptions underpin the sunshine policy. First is the Kim administration's overarching notion that there is an emergent need to help ease beleaguered Pyongyang's concerns about domestic and external uncertainties, which might cause the North to lash out in desperation, such as a major provocation or an invasion of the South. Second, in such a scenario, North Korea's formidable fire power positioned on the other side of the demilitarized zone (DMZ) could decimate the Seoul metropolitan region—home to 19 million people or 43 percent of the national total (1990 census), 46 percent (1994) of South Korea's gross regional domestic product, and the nation's major financial, educational, and cultural centers.[45]

---

[41](...continued)
of one man, the President."

[42]He is quoted as saying in June 1998, "for the first time in 50 years," the South took the initiative in implementing a policy toward the North." *The Korea Times*, June 25, 1998, p.2; "Kim Calls for Resumption of S-N Dialogue," *The Korea Times* (Internet version) in English, January 4, 1999.

[43]Choi Song, "'Government of the People': Principles and Direction of the Engagement Policy Toward North Korea," *T'ong'il Kyongje*, August 1996, p.13; he writes that the basic direction and specific contents of the current engagement policy were set forth in a University of London speech in August 1993.

[44]Yang Young-shik, "Kim Dae-jung Administration's North Korea Policy," *Korea Focus* in English, November-December 1998, p.51. The writer is the head of the government-funded think-tank, the Korean Institute of National Unification.

[45]"Hardline Posture of U.S. Congress on NK Worrisome," *The Korea Times* (Internet version), October 14, 1998; *The Korea Times* (Internet version), December 8, 1998; *The Korea Herald*, June 21, 1996. As of 1990, Seoul alone had nearly a quarter of the national
(continued...)

Third, peace and stability are essential to Seoul's effort to attract foreign investment and revive its economy. Fourth, a stable coexistence will enable the North to creatively adjust to the emerging situation without fear of being unraveled. Lastly, the Cold War-derived culture of confrontation will gradually dissipate to minimize the chances of renewed hostilities in Korea.

President Kim initially seemed hopeful that the two Koreas could achieve a significant breakthrough if they first revisited the historic inter-Korean Agreement on Reconciliation, Nonaggression and Exchanges and Cooperation that formally went into effect in February 1992 but since has remained on the shelf. He proposed an activation of the 1992 accord, an exchange of special envoys, a possible summit meeting,[46] reunion of separated families, and cultural and academic exchanges. His overtures also included an offer to provide a generous provision of food aid, assistance for agricultural reform, economic cooperation including investment in the Najin/Sonbong area, and continued cooperation in KEDO's [Korean Peninsula Energy Development Organization] lightwater nuclear rector project. In addition, he promised to address what he vaguely referred to as "other factors of imbalances between the two Koreas." Also underscored were two key points: one was that the process of engaging the North should be crafted to minimize the confrontational atmospherics of the past through a gentler and kinder approach.[47] The other was that this process should, in the near-term, aim for neighborly coexistence rather than the potentially convulsive end result of unification. At the same time, the President seemed realistic about the attendant difficulty in trying to mend the fences with North Korea, counseling patience and steadiness in dealing with wary Pyongyang and he was particularly emphatic about the critical importance of maintaining a robust deterrence against North Korean provocations.[48] Pyongyang would respond in time to his sunshine policy for a rational reason to ensure its survival, he judged.

Below are examined important developments and influences on South Korea's recent sunshine policy toward North Korea.

---

[45](...continued)
total of 43 million; the metropolitan region includes Inchon and the surrounding Kyonggi province. *Korea Yearbook*, 1995, p.547. For a "horribly destructive" scenario in a war on the Korean Peninsula, see Ashton B. Carter and William J. Perry, *Preventive Defense: A New Security Strategy for America*, Washington, D.C., Brookings Institution Press, 1999, p.218.

[46]Reportedly, President-elect Kim disclosed that he had earlier asked President Bill Clinton to help arrange an inter-Korean summit meeting. *The Korea Times* (Internet version) in English, December 19, 1997.

[47]Shim Jae Hoon, "Spring Thaw?," *Far Eastern Economic Review*, June 11, 1998, pp.30-31.

[48]*The Korea Times* (Internet version) in English (November 21, 1998) affirms the President's position by observing that the hawkish approach of the past to the North will no longer best serve Seoul's "security and other national interests"; it also observes that the formerly unpopular "dovish" strategy is "the proper approach" in the present circumstances.

## Reciprocity Test

The first critical test of the sunshine policy was reciprocity, which was set forth by the Kim administration as a guiding principle for inter-Korean cooperation. This came in April 1998, in Beijing, where North and South Korean governmental representatives met for the first time since June 1994. The meeting's outcome was not what the South might have anticipated. Seoul's apparent intention was to negotiate a reciprocal deal whereby it would send 200,000 tons of fertilizer to the North in return for the latter's agreeing to discuss the longstanding issue of reuniting separated families. But Pyongyang seemed interested only in procedural matters about the fertilizer delivery, disdaining Seoul's proposition that inter-government-level cooperation should be conditioned on the principle of reciprocity.[49] Seoul's position seemed politically necessary since, absent mutuality, South Koreans would be put off by Pyongyang's "arrogant" behavior as in the past. As it turned out, no deal was struck as Pyongyang mocked Seoul's "reciprocity" as a "logic" better suited for horse-trading than for collaboration between the two halves of the same nation. Pyongyang claimed that reciprocity was a norm applicable only in relations among sovereign nations but not between fellow countrymen. It then tried to take the moral high ground by chiding the Kim administration for treating an humanitarian issue as part of its mercantile pursuits.[50] For emphasis, Pyongyang reiterated, "We, being a sovereign country, cannot exchange our sovereignty for fertilizer. We can live without fertilizer but cannot live without sovereignty."[51]

Outwardly unfazed, a senior Blue House official stated: "Dialogue between the authorities will be based on reciprocity...'No forcing, no begging' and '*quid pro quo*' will be our policy."[52] By year-end, however, because of Pyongyang's disdain for mutuality, the Kim administration may have realized that reciprocity as originally intended might be unsustainable. Cabinet ministers began to publicly hint at the need for "flexible" reciprocity, with a renewed emphasis on the need for patience and an

---

[49]At the time of his state visit to Washington in June 1998, President Kim reportedly asked for U.S. help so that his administration's principle of reciprocity could be put into effect in North-South Korean relations. *The Political and Economic Significance of the Presidential Visit*), Special Issue Brief 153, June 18, 1998, Office of Legislative Research and Analysis, National Assembly Library, p.10.

[50]"S. Korean Authorities Responsible for Deadlocked Inter-Korean Talks," [North] Korean Central News Agency (*KCNA*) in English, April 24, 1998. To get a North Korean perspective on inter-Korean relations in general—and the sunshine policy in particular, it will be useful to note that North Korea defines the 1992 inter-Korean agreement on reconciliation, nonaggression, and exchanges and cooperation as an *intra-Korean* document and not an international treaty as maintained by President Kim Dae Jung. See [Commentator]: "Mutualism Cannot be Applied in North-South Relations," *Nodong Sinmun* [Pyongyang's Ruling Party daily organ], May 23, 1998, available in a translated text by Foreign Broadcast Information Service, Document ID: FTS19980525000044; for President-elect Kim's view, *Chosun Ilbo* (Internet version) in Korean, December 19, 1997.

[51]As cited in *Hankyore 21* (Ch'ollian Database version) in Korean, February 11, 1999.

[52]"*Sunshine Policy and a New Era in Inter-Korean Relations*," Remarks by Ambassador Lim Dong-Won, Senior Secretary to the President for Foreign Policy and National Security (April 24, 1998, The Shilla Hotel).

altruistic "demonstration of sincerity" in approaching the North. On December 26, 1998, for example, Foreign Minister Hong Soon-young was reported to have second-guessed "the mechanical application of the principle of reciprocity."[53]

Media commentators were quick to characterize the Kim administration's flexibility as a "retreat," if not "a desperate attempt" to draw Pyongyang into negotiations.[54] If true, the administration's purported offer, reported on January 14, 1999, to provide 500,000 tons (worth $100 million) of fertilizer to the North free of charge — conditioning it only on a "formal" request for fertilizer — seemed likely to reinforce such a characterization.[55] More to the point, the appearance of unilateral concessions without North Korean reciprocation may have fueled speculation that the Kim administration is bent on engagement at any cost and that Pyongyang might become even more "arrogant" toward the South, according to some South Korean observers. These observers viewed as unwise the Kim administration's reported shift to a flexible policy of aiding the North first—and waiting patiently for signs of favorable response from the North.[56] In a public lecture on April 28, 1999, Foreign Minister Hong seemed to confirm the shift, stating that the sunshine policy seeks to provide "political, economic, and social favors" to the North not in a "one-sided way" but to receive "rewards from the North sometime in the future." He hastened to add that, for now at least, there would be more emphasis on South Korea's "giving."[57]

In early 1999, the Kim administration was rebuffed again over reciprocity — in this instance, about an humanitarian issue. President Kim sought to exchange 17 ex-North Korean agents freed from prisons in the South for several hundred South Koreans believed to be in unacknowledged detention in North Korea. The South Korean Red Cross appealed for international cooperation in securing the release of these detainees, in addition to 231 South Korean prisoners of war believed to be in the North. The Kim administration, in April 1999, broached the issue at the 55th session of the UN Commission on Human Rights in Geneva. Pyongyang rejected the "exchange" proposal as "unjustifiable both from the humanitarian point of view and in light of international law,"claiming that if there were indeed such South Koreans

---

[53]*News Plus* (Internet version) in Korean, January 7, 1999; *Hankyore* (Internet version) in Korean, January 4, 1999.

[54][Editorial]: "Change in Mutualism Toward North Korea," *JoongAng Ilbo* (Internet version) in Korean, January 13, 1999; [Editorial]: "Modification of North Korea Policy," *The Korea Times* (Internet version) in English, January 11, 1999; *Chosun Ilbo* (Internet version) in Korean, January 5, 1999; and *The Korea Herald* (Internet version) in English, January 4, 1999; [Editorial]: "Hastiness Should Be Avoided in North Korea Policy," *Dong-a Ilbo* (Internet version) in Korean, February 18, 1999.

[55]The amount of fertilizer was the same as the North had requested in April 1998. Seoul's offer was viewed by one source as "a sharp setback in South Korean government's stand." See *Hankyore 21(Ch'ollian Database* version) in Korean, February 11, 1999; also *"Seoul To Provide 500,000 Tons of Fertilizer to North, Kang says,"* The Korea Herald (Internet version), January 15, 1999.

[56]*Dong-A Ilbo* (Internet version) in Korean, February 17, 1999; *Chosun Ilbo* (Internet version), February 17, 1999.

[57]*Yonhap* in English, April 28, 1999.

in the North, they came over to the North or joined the North Korean army on their own volition and that, if any case, they live "happily as [North Korean] citizens," with no desire to return to the South.[58]

## Consistency Test

The Kim administration has been tested in its ability to stay the "sunshine" course amidst provocations by North Korea. It claimed that the sunshine policy would be different from the previous government's policy which it criticized as "reactive and inconsistent." If the administration's reaction to the four instances of North Korean provocations between June and December 1998 is any clue, consistency may well remain an operative norm, short of a renewed North Korean invasion of the South.[59] Amid domestic criticism in June 1998, the Kim administration played down a reported North Korean submarine intrusion into the South Korean waters, possibly to minimize a hardline reaction that could derail the sunshine policy.[60] In July 1998, facing intensified public criticism in the wake of a new North Korean infiltration of spies into the South, President Kim was reported as saying that he would press the North "very hard" to obtain a promise not to repeat similar provocations. His administration also revealed its intention to put on hold some aid and economic cooperation programs, pending Pyongyang's apology, but then decided to forgo the intended step for the sake of consistency.[61]

Pyongyang denied the infiltration charges, blaming Seoul's "ultra-rightists" for staging the incident as part of a plot to embarrass the North. In the end, President Kim vowed his intention to stick to the engagement policy, not swayed by each and every instance of such North Korean provocation. This was affirmed on August 15, 1998, when President Kim extended an olive branch, proposing the establishment of "a standing dialogue mechanism" and expressing the readiness to send his envoy to Pyongyang to discuss a range of inter-Korean issues. He also stated that the Mt.

---

[58]*KCNA* in English, March 25, 1999; see also "Not a Single 'ROK Army Prisoner of War' Or 'Person Abducted by the North' Is In The Republic," *Nodong Sinmun* in Korean, April 2, 1999, p.5. *The Korea Herald*, October 12, 1998, p.3; [Editorial]: "Let the Captives Come Home," *The Korea Herald* (Internet version), March 15, 1999.

[59]For these and other instances of provocations, see *North Korea: Chronology of Provocations*, by Rinn S. Shinn [Washington] January 4, 1999. 13 p. CRS Report RL30004.

[60]The President reportedly stated,"If we change our position at the whims of the times and situation, we might face internal and external criticism and such a capricious change of mind will be of benefit only to the North. This way our policy is not confusing." "Policy on NK Not Wavering: Kim," *The Korea Times*, July 25, 1998, p.2.

[61]"Seoul Demands N.K. Apology, Curbs Aid, Economic Relations," *The Korea Herald*, July 16, 1998, p.1; "Inter-Korean Ties Face Tough Strain," *The Korea Times*, July 18, 1998, p.2; "ROK to Keep Peace Bid Despite NK Provocations," *The Korea Times*, September 28, 1998, p.2..

Kumgang tour project would proceed as planned (see Mt. Kumgang Tourism Project) below.[62]

Consistency seemed also to have weathered new uncertainties on the heels of two developments in August 1998: the discovery of a suspect underground nuclear complex 90 kilometers north of Pyongyang; and a Taepodong-I three-stage ballistic missile launch through Japanese airspace. In a speech before the UN General Assembly in September, South Korean Foreign Minister Hong stated that although his government "deplores these acts of provocation" as a serious threat to the South, the sunshine policy would remain so that the two Koreas could in time "enjoy the benefits of peaceful coexistence."[63] Critics argued, however, that the Kim administration seemed to make light of the security implications of the nuclear and missile issues, portending a potential policy coordination problem with the United States and Japan, both of whom viewed North Korean behavior with grave concern. The critics seemed perturbed particularly by the administration's alleged stance that the issues in question had more to do with the security interest of United States and Japan than with that of South Korea.[64]

In its defense of the sunshine policy, the Kim administration began to underline three major notions: 1) South Koreans and outsiders alike need to be patient and to think "long-term" in dealing with the North; 2) one should try to visualize, figuratively, the big picture of a "forest" (i.e., North-South Korean reconciliation) rather than be distracted by isolated "trees" (i.e., instances of provocative North Korean behavior) in relations between the two Koreas;[65] and 3) there is an urgent new need for a "comprehensive" policy to deal with "all pending problems" related to the North (see Coordination with the United States) below.

## Mt. Kumgang Tourism Project

Hyundai's Mt. Kumgang tour project is officially touted as the "first child" of President Kim's sunshine policy. Premised on the separation of civilian level

---

[62]"Kim Renews Sunshine Offer Despite Tension," *Reuters*. August 16, 1998; "'Sunshine Policy' Delivers Positive Results," *The Korea Herald*, August 15, 1998, p.19.

[63]"ROK to Keep Peace Bid Despite NK Provocations," *The Korea Times*, September 28, 1998, p.2; *Hankyore* (Internet version) in English, September 1, 1998..

[64]*Hankyore* (Internet version) in Korean, September 1, 1998. At National Assembly deliberations, opposition representatives reportedly argued that the Kim administration is trying to minimize the importance of Pyongyang's suspected underground nuclear facility in a bid to shield the sunshine policy from being called into question; *The Korea Times* (Internet version) in English, November 20, 1998. In this regard, possibly reacting to Seoul's stance on the underground nuclear facility, U.S. Defense Secretary William Cohen reportedly requested, on his visit to Seoul in mid-January 1999, a more proactive diplomatic effort by South Korea to persuade the North to open the underground facility to outside inspection. *Chosun Ilbo* (Internet version) in Korean, January 15, 1999.

[65][Editorial]: "DJ's Resolve to End Cold War," *Joongang Ilbo* (Internet version), February 12, 1999; the forest-tree metaphor is attributed to Lim Dong-Won, *The Korea Times*, February 25, 1999.

cooperation from that of inter-governmental cooperation, this project was supported despite North Korean provocations between June and August 1998. Approved by the leadership of both North and South Korea, it was launched in November 1998 by Hyundai business group as part of a 30-year plan to develop a tourist/resort complex at Mt. Kumgang on North Korea's east coast some 13 miles north of the DMZ (see Map. South Korean Provincial Boundaries).[66] In return for its "exclusive rights" to the tour project, Hyundai is obligated to pay $942 million to the North in monthly installments over a span of six years and three months, without any strings attached—a controversial arrangement because of its potential implications for South Korean and U.S. security interests.[67] Relatedly, Hyundai is reported to have discussed other possible projects with North Korean paramount leader Kim Jong Il. Among these projects are: offshore oil exploration, a 100,000 KW thermal power plant in Pyongyang, and an industrial complex on North Korea's west coast. As planned, the Hyundai group stands to earn reportedly as much as $3.7 billion from the Mt. Kumgang project alone on its initial investment of nearly $1 billion.[68] Not to be outdone, Hyundai's rivals — Daewoo and Samsung — sought to establish their own bases in the North but reportedly dropped the idea, for now at least, given Pyongyang's demand that they follow Hyundai's "precedent."

According to one analysis, the Mt. Kumgang tour project is potentially a "good business" investment in the long term, contingent on a substantially improved inter-Korean environment. For the near term, "many observers" are said to be "skeptical" about the rationality of the project since the project is "expected" to run a deficit of up to $127 million per year, unless a land route can be opened across the DMZ to the tour sites to save on the daily cost of ship leasing and crew wages amounting to $100,000.[69] Many seemed nonplused by the question over how Hyundai could continue the deficit tour project despite its ongoing "severe financial problems" since 1997.[70]

In any event, for the cash-starved and politically wary North, the Mt. Kumgang project seems to typify a risk-free way to "open up" to the outside world for earning

---

[66]*The Korea Times*, November 2, 1998, p.2. One potential complication is North Korea's unexplained refusal to comply with Hyundai's request for an agreement in writing.

[67]For details, see Ministry of Unification. *Kim Dae-jung's Policies on North Korea: Achievements and Future Goals.* Seoul: March 25, 1999, pp. 16-17; and *The People's Korea* [North Korea's publication in Tokyo] (Internet version) in English, February 3, 1999. Predictably, the cash deal drew strong criticism from opposition parliamentary members and other concerned commentators asserting that the money could be used for the North Korean development of nuclear and missile programs. For Rep. Lee Se-ki's critical remarks, see *The Record of Proceedings* in Korean, Committee on Unification, Foreign Affairs, and Trade, November 6, 1998. Secretariat of the National Assembly.

[68]*The Korea Herald* (Internet version), January 22, 1999.

[69]Kim Ki-Jung and Yoon Deok Ryong, *"Beyond Mt. Kumkang: Social and Economic Implications"* (a paper presented at the conference on "Kim Dae-jung's Sunshine Policy: Conceptual Promise and Challenges"), Georgetown University, Washington, D. C., May 17, 1999, pp.9-11.

[70]op. cit., p.10, 14-15.

hard currency—virtually at no cost to itself.[71] For one thing, it would potentially allow the North to extract benefits from the South essentially on its own terms.[72] For another, the North would be able to shield its local population from coming into contact with South Koreans under a stringent code of discipline. Visitors would not allowed to stray off tour routes or to talk to or fraternize with locals on pain of punishment by a fine. To ensure local isolation, the 6.2 mile-road from a makeshift dock at Changjon to the mountain tour sites is fenced with 8-feet high barbed wire.

## Pyongyang and The Sunshine Policy

Has Pyongyang's policy toward Seoul been any different under President Kim's sunshine policy? At first blush, it has seemed different because its February 3, 1999, overture for dialogue with the South contained a nuance of expression that can be construed as "a sign of change." Closely examined, this overture seemed to reflect a shift in style, not in substance. Thus far at least, there seems little to suggest that Pyongyang has lowered the bar in its attempt to use the South to its own advantage.

In a hint of change in February 1999, Pyongyang proposed a "reunification-oriented dialogue," repackaging its previous overture. Unlike a similar 1998 proposal, for instance, the proposal this time contained an explicit reference to a possible dialogue "between the authorities" of the two sides in the second half of 1999. Uncharacteristically, it also refrained from repeating Pyongyang's familiar demand for the dissolution of Seoul's counterintelligence unit—the Agency for National Security Planning, now renamed the National Intelligence Service (NIS). Initially, the Kim administration seemed to read the 1999 proposal as a welcome sign of change, courtesy of its sunshine policy.[73]

A close reading shows that the 1999 overture was essentially a reiteration of Pyongyang's past position. It argued that the dialogue should be guided solely by the principles and guidelines set forth by the "greater leaders" Kim Il Sung and Kim Jong Il.[74] Then, it urged the South to comply with its three preconditions before the dialogue could take place. Specifically, it demanded that the Kim administration should immediately: 1) cease cooperation and joint military exercises with "outside forces" [the United States]; 2) abrogate Seoul's national security law that is designed to control Pyongyang's covert operations in the South as well as pro-North Korean

---

[71]Pyongyang argued that the South Korean "rightwing reactionaries" opposing the Kumgang tour project are "a herd of traitors to the nation." *KCNA* in English, September 25, 1998.

[72]*KCNA* in English, April 27, 1999.

[73]*Hangyore* (Internet version) in Korean, February 4, 1999 [this newspaper was, before 1998, reputedly anti-establishment, anti-government, and anti-U.S. but now it is usually regarded as supportive of the Kim administration]. For ruling party lawmakers' upbeat statements on the possibility of Pyongyang's positive response "in the near future" see *The Korea Times* (Internet version), February 19, 1999. The Kim administration's so-called "affirmative" assessment of Pyongyang's proposal was acknowledged by the North, even while rejecting Seoul's objection to the preconditions laid down by the North. *KCNA* in English, February 8, 1999.

[74]*Radio Pyongyang in Korean to South Korea*, February 13, 1999.

activities among South Koreans; and 3) guarantee the freedom of activities for
"patriotic, pro-unification"[pro-North Korean] groups in South Korea.[75] North Korea
defined these conditions as the standards by which to judge whether the Kim
administration was "pro-unification" or pro-American.[76]

The Kim administration reacted with watchful prudence, aware that compromise
on those conditions would generate two equally unattractive consequences: adverse
domestic public opinion and probable complications for South Korea's security
alliance with the United States. Absent a unilateral—and unlikely—concession by
either side, relations between Pyongyang and Seoul are believed to remain frosty, with
or without the sunshine policy. Nevertheless, in Seoul, some with connections to the
South Korean government seemed to feel that, to break the inter-Korean deadlock,
the admittedly "superior" South should compromise first to make up for the
"economic and diplomatic weakness" of the "inferior North."[77]

It should be noted that, for years, these preconditions were among the
parameters of Pyongyang's attempt to turn the South into a permissive environment
for North Korean infiltration and covert operations.[78] To be sure, Pyongyang's
silence on the NIS, alleged to be the "notorious headquarters of anti-North fascist
plots," appeared to be revealing, but did not signify its willingness to condone the
NIS's existence. On the contrary, the North continues to press the South to
"dismantle" the NIS.[79] The silence was apparently calculated for effect because, in the
unlikely event that the National Security Law is abolished, the NIS will have no legal
standing on which to base its anti-spy operations. One may also note that the NIS
will be under the same legal constraints, should the Kim administration decide to
guarantee the freedom of pro-North Korean political activities in the South. A case

---

[75]"Broad-Ranged North-South Dialogue Should Be Brought To Realization," *Nodong
Sinmun*, March 5, 1999, p.5; *Hanguk Ilbo* (Internet version) in Korean, April 17, 1999;
[Unattributed talk]: "Providing Wide-Ranging Dialogue Is Development of the Fatherland's
Reunification," *Radio Pyongyang in Korean to South Korea*, February 13, 1999.

[76]*Korean Central Broadcasting Network* in Korean, February 24, 1999.

[77]["Taehan Plaza"]: "Path to Non-Absorption Peaceful Unification," *Taehan Mail* (Internet
version), February 13, 1999 [This daily newspaper is reportedly funded by the South Korean
government].

[78][Unattributed talk]: "The Anti-Reunification Criminal Act Should Be Stopped at Once,"
[North] *Korean Central Broadcasting Network* in Korean, March 17, 1999. For Pyongyang's
consistent line that South Koreans should collaborate with "Communists and with the North"
by rejecting reliance on the United States, see *Minju Choson* [North Korea's governmental
daily] in Korean, February 4, 1999, p.4. Pyongyang's standard, consistent line is that
"independence" [North Korea's code word for national liberation from the U.S. when applied
to inter-Korean issues] and self-reliant unification are possible only through an alliance with
the North; and that a pro-American line will perpetuate the South's dependency on
Washington and hence an indefinite national division. Yu Choon-taek, "Pro-American/Anti-
North Korean or Pro-North Korean/Anti-American?," *Ch'ongmaek* in Korean, March 1981,
p.17.

[79]["Open Statement" of the [North Korean] National Reunification Institute on the South
Korean National Intelligence Service, April 21, 1999] carried by [North] *Korean Central
Broadcasting Network* in Korean, April 30, 1999.

can be made, then, that the February 1999 overture was probably intended to gauge the efficacy of Pyongyang's reinvented, for lack of a better term, "dialogue card" that apparently has been designed to capitalize on the Kim administration's reputed craving for high-level talks with the North.

In the near term, Pyongyang seems certain to be ambivalent about the sunshine policy. The North has taken umbrage at that policy's alleged aim "to undress the North in all aspects of politics, economy, and military affairs."[80] And it has denounced the policy as reactionary and deceptive, a subterfuge aimed at the overthrow of the North.[81] Nonetheless, Pyongyang seems to have judged that this policy could be useful because of a possible "win-win" outcome in relations with the South, an outcome that would enable the North to have it both ways—extracting financial/economic benefits from South Korean firms such as Hyundai virtually risk-free without conceding anything to the South.

Some observers argue that Pyongyang is in a "no-lose" situation due to an apparent structural bias inherent in the sunshine policy. The popular notion in Seoul is that the fate of that policy will pivot on Pyongyang's action and that, therefore, the North may be able to affect the outcome of the policy either by going through the motions of a positive response to the South, or by withholding it from the South as a means of extracting further concessions.[82] Critics say that in its quest for "a positive response" from the North, the Kim administration could run the risk of playing into the waiting hands of the North.[83]

## South Korean Domestic Reaction

According to a USIA-sponsored, country-wide poll conducted in January 1999, "a majority of South Koreans" continue to support the sunshine policy; a similar majority was seen in a September 1998 poll.[84] Many observers offer the view,

---

[80]*KCNA* in English, March 11, 1999

[81]*Korean Central Broadcasting Network in Korean*, March 7, 1999; *KCNA* in English, March 11, 1999; *Minju Choson* in Korean, October 25, 1998, p.4.

[82]On the significance of Pyongyang's role, Lee Hong Koo, a former South Korean Prime Minister and also minister of unification, is quoted as remarking [prior to his current posting as Seoul's ambassador to Washington] that: "In North-South relations, 90 percent depends on North Korea...It does not depend so much on who is in Blue House." Nicholas D. Kristof, "South Korea's New President Appeals to North to End Decades of Division," *New York Times*, February 25, 1998, A8.

[83]A case in point is the concern expressed by the opposition Grand National Party that the North will capitalize on the Kim administration's "hasty approach" to Pyongyang. *The Korea Times* (Internet version), February 21, 1999.

[84]*USIA Briefing Paper*, U.S. Information Agency, Washington, D.C., February 12, 1999, p.1. A Media Research poll conducted for the Ministry of Unification in December 1998 [this poll was taken a couple of days prior to a firefight in which South Korean navy vessels sank a North Korean semi-submersible high-speed spy boat in South Korean waters] showed a 56% supporting the sunshine policy, but this was "a sharp decline" from the 72.6% approval rating

(continued...)

however, that the real measure of public support might be difficult to gauge for two reasons: one is the ephemeral nature of the public mood on the sunshine policy, and the other is the widely observed public tendency not to reveal their real opinions to strangers on what is believed to be "a sensitive" issue.

Under past authoritarian regimes, the South's policy toward the North was more often off-limits to the opposition, nor was it a subject to be addressed by free-lance journalists or academics. The policy was, in and of itself, a national security matter controlled exclusively by the Blue House and national security agencies. In 1993, however, when the democratically elected administration of the first civilian President Kim Young Sam took office, backed by pro-democracy activists, the North Korea policy veered to the left — briefly — for the first time since independence. Under pressure from conservatives and public opinion alike, the sometimes erratic policy could not be sustained. Even after a shift to the right, the Kim Young Sam administration (1993-1997) seemed hard pressed to maintain the delicate balancing act. When North Korea refused to acknowledge reciprocity or tried to force an issue, Kim Young Sam reacted, hardening his position to perceived slights from Pyongyang.[85]

The sunshine policy is intended to correct the failings of the previous administration.[86] But some South Koreans seem conflicted about this policy, which they see as having gone to the other extreme. As in the past, the current North Korea policy has been perceived by many essentially as a "Blue House" show, in this instance closely identified with President Kim's persona. That may yield apparent stability for the engagement policy during his tenure in office ending in February 2003, despite uncertainty about sustainability beyond. Respected for his expertise on unification and foreign policy issues, coupled with his reputedly forceful personality, President Kim has seemed to have a virtual free hand in directing the policy.[87]

President Kim is widely believed to have an advantage of being at the helm of an authoritarian, bureaucratized culture. In this milieu, past and present, people tend not only to defer to presidential authority but also try to be on the presidential side of a policy issue. It is not uncommon that a policy perceived to have a presidential imprimatur tends to go more often unquestioned in public. On the other hand, despite the predominant influence of the Blue House over the engagement policy, South Koreans do not seem as intimidated as they used to be when it comes to freedom of

---

[84](...continued)
registered in August 1998. As reported in *Chosun Ilbo* (Internet version) in English, December 21, 1998.

[85]This situation prompted Kim Dae Jung to remark, several days before the December 18, 1997 election, that Kim Young Sam's hardline policy on the North and lack of policy consistency caused "unnecessary conflict with the U.S. policy of soft-landing the North." "Kim Dae Jung to Take a More Flexible Approach to NK, If Elected," *The Korea Herald*, December 12, 1997, p.1.

[86]"Kim Dae-jung to Take More Flexible Approach Toward North Korea," *The Korea Herald*, December 12, 1997, p.1.

[87]*News Plus* (Ch'ollian Database version) in Korean, March 3, 1999.

expression or of the press. To be sure, it is an open secret in Seoul that the South Korean media continue to "self-censor" while reporting or editorializing on issues judged to be potentially offensive to the authorities. Nevertheless, critics and observers across the political spectrum have seemed able to make their case pro and con on the merits of the policy — albeit, in carefully measured expressions.

Domestic reaction also has been tempered by two key perspectives. First is an across-the-board consensus that war must be avoided. Second is a view of a majority that the engagement policy deserved the benefit of the doubt, a view augmented by the Kim administration's reasoning that the only way to find out whether the sunshine policy will work or not is to engage the North. There has seemed to be few public qualms about the rationale and structure of the policy, provided the South remained ever alert to Pyongyang's potential entrapment game or to the risk of falling prey to wishful thinking. Some observers opined that such thinking was reflected in the condescending notion that the sunshine policy reflects the confidence of a government that has the upper hand in overall national strength rather than "the submissive posture of a weak government."[88]

Among political circles, reaction to the policy differs along partisan as well as ideological divides. Political supporters of President Kim have seemed to follow the top-down line of reasoning premised on the notion that there are "signs"of a changing North Korea linked to "a pragmatic force" within the circles of the party, military, and government functionaries. The sunshine policy, the argument goes, has been not to "appease" the North but to help bolster this pragmatic group as a way to induce the North to "open up and reform" in the long run. This line of reasoning also underscores that the engagement policy is aimed at ending the Cold War on the Korean Peninsula.[89] South Koreans have been asked to be patient and not to expect a quick return on the long-term engagement policy.

Dissenting views have come mainly from the opposition GNP, insurgent members of the ruling coalition partner ULD, a dwindling number of concerned journalists, and foreign and inter-Korean affairs specialists on the center-right. Despite their reservations about the sunshine policy, though, they have appeared to agree generally with the rationale for the policy in broad terms.[90] Critics have tended to argue that even as the policy may help allay — eventually — Pyongyang's concerns about its survival, it still might not be able to cajole the North to lower its guard on the touchy question of openness and reform. In this reasoning, the critics have taken a skeptical view of the Kim administration's "haste" in trying to stretch the notion of reciprocity to an indefinite future. From Pyongyang's perspective, non-transparency and isolation are believed to be critical to its survival, used to keep the adversaries at

---

[88]Yang Young-shik, "Kim Dae-jung Administration's North Korea Policy," *op.cit.*, p.52; *Taehan Mail* (Internet version) in Korean, February 13, 1999..

[89]Park Sang-seek, "Why Should We Pursue Sunshine Policy?," *The Korea Herald* (Internet version), March 26, 1999.

[90]For example, GNP leader Lee Hoi Chang is reported to have once said that "the GNP does not denounce the engagement policy altogether." *The Korea Times* (Internet version) in English, March 16, 1999; also "GNP Head Lee Raps 'Sunshine Policy'," *The Korea Times*, July 17, 1998, p.2.

bay and guessing on the "unpredictability" of its intentions and actions.[91] It might be wishful thinking, critics have opined, to anticipate a desired change in the North in the foreseeable future. Having exploited, for lack of a better term, a "reverse-sunshine-card" to ensure its survivability, a self-centered Kim Jong Il regime might decide to keep its Stalinist ways more or less unchanged; and worse still, buttressed by large conventional military forces coupled with a reasonable suspicion of nuclear capability, it might even try to bully the South to accede to its terms for coexistence or unification.[92]

### U.S. Troops as "Peacekeepers"?

The preceding line of reasoning has suggested that an isolated and insecure Pyongyang may refuse to make concessions unless it can gain guarantees of absolute regime survival. To Pyongyang, an eventual U.S. military withdrawal from the South has appeared most important in this regard. Barring that, some analysts say that, Pyongyang might acquiesce in continued U.S. presence, albeit, in a neutral "peacekeeping" role.[93] If Pyongyang's reported "shift" in policy is true, the implication seems to be that the United States might be pressed to relinquish its defense obligations to the South as part of a new role as "peacekeepers" in Korea. To the consternation of critics in Seoul, the Kim administration reportedly tried to take Pyongyang's so-called "policy shift"as a sign of Pyongyang's positive response to the sunshine policy.[94] Later, blaming "media competition and misunderstanding," the Kim administration clarified that the structure and disposition of "all forces on the Korean Peninsula" can be addressed only after substantial progress is achieved on establishing a peace regime on the peninsula.[95]  President Kim is known to favor continued U.S. military presence even beyond Korean unification—but without explaining in what capacity.

---

[91]For typical North Korean style of negotiation, see Chuck Downs, *Over the Line: North Korea's Negotiating Strategy.* Washington, D. C.: The AEI Press, 1999.

[92]A similar concern was voiced in 1994 by Defense Secretary William Perry as a likely scenario with the North commanding "an unchecked nuclear capability" and large conventional forces. William Perry, *"U.S. Security Policy in Korea"*: Address to the Asia Society, Washington, DC, May 3, 1994, in *U.S. Department of State Dispatch*, May 9, 1994, p.227.

[93]For this "shift in policy" and a view that the South Korean-U.S. military alliance should be redefined "in a future-oriented way," see Yi Ch'ol-ki, "We Should Again Think About the Status of the US Troops," *Hangyore* (Internet version) in Korean, April 20, 1999.

[94][Editorial]: "Unwarranted NK Policy Shift," *The Korea Times* (Internet version) in English, April 7, 1999.

[95]*Hankyore* (Internet version) in Korean, April 7, April 11, 1999; [Editorial]: "The Status of USFK [U.S. Forces in Korea]," *Chosun Ilbo* (Internet version) in English, April 7, 1999; "Why Confusion Over USFK?," *Hanguk Ilbo* (U.S. Edition), April 8, 1999; *Taehan Mail* (Internet version) in Korean, April 8, 1999..

## Coordination with the United States

By mid-1998, President Kim seemed to have become convinced of an emergent need to craft a new approach within his overall sunshine policy. This may have reflected his disappointment at a lack of a positive response from Pyongyang to his overture for dialogue and because of his concern that Seoul and Washington could end up working at cross-purposes, to Pyongyang's advantage. Apparently, it was unsettling for the Kim administration to realize that Seoul and Washington might have a divergent focus in dealing with the North—Seoul being absorbed in the narrower issues germane to the two Koreas, as opposed to Washington's global concerns about nuclear and missile proliferation.[96] The Kim administration also seemed troubled by a perceived lack of a clear road map in Washington's North Korea policy.[97] It was against this backdrop that President Kim seemed to sense the need to integrate the South Korean and U.S. policies into a more coherent and coordinated framework.

In June 1998, in an interview with the *New York Times* several days prior to his state visit to Washington, President Kim called for the United States to change its North Korea policy by increasing economic and political engagement with the North. As part of a more future-oriented and flexible approach, he suggested that the United States end its economic sanctions against the North, without setting conditions.[98] In addition, he urged the United States to normalize its relations with the North to help the North end its isolation and "open up" to the outside world.

His notion of a new U.S. approach seemed to take shape rapidly, having gained a new urgency precipitated by two security-related developments in August 1998. One was the public disclosure of the existence of a possible underground nuclear facility in the North; the other was Pyongyang's launch of a three-stage Taepodong-I ballistic missile through Japanese airspace. President Kim seemed worried by the disquieting prospect that his sunshine policy could be derailed by a U.S. congressional reaction to these developments. Particularly at issue was the Omnibus Appropriations Act for FY 1999 specifying that no new funds could be allocated for KEDO after March 1, 1999, without the presidential certification that North Korea is in compliance with all provisions of the U.S.-North Korea Agreed Framework of October 1994. Another key issue was the congressionally mandated presidential certification by June 1, 1999, that the United States is making "significant progress

[96]Pak Che-kyun, "A Chasm in the ROK-US-Japan Coordination System," *News Plus* (Ch'ollian Database version) in Korean, March 3, 1999.

[97]The concern over the "road map" issue seemed to have been fueled since late 1998, in the wake of Washington's perceived "hawkish" reaction to Pyongyang's nuclear and missile issues; the Kim administration apparently judged that such a hard-line, case-by-case reaction to every single instance of North Korean behavior would not only be futile but also adversely influence the sunshine policy. The Kim administration seemed to argue that the United States needed to put the North Korean issues in a broad perspective and thus its plea for "a comprehensive" U.S. approach. *JoongAng Ilbo*, February 9, 1999; *JoongAng* (Internet Version) in English, February 12, 1999; *The Korea Times*, (Internet version), December 10, 1998; *Yonhap* in English, April 8, 1999.

[98]Nicholas D. Kristof, "Seoul Leader Asks End to Sanctions on North Koreans," *New York Times*, June 2, 1998, A1.

in negotiations with North Korea on reducing and eliminating the North Korean ballistic missile threat." President Kim seemed to fear that a hardline reaction from Washington might put North Korean hardliners into a bellicose mood.

Crystallized by year-end in the form of a "package deal," Kim Dae Jung's new approach, or a "comprehensive engagement policy," can be seen as an extension — on a grander and more inclusive scale — of his sunshine policy. Vague as it was, it became the centerpiece of the Kim administration's diplomatic agenda tailored to gain unqualified support from the United States (especially from congressional Republicans), Japan, China, and Russia. Specifically, following up on his earlier June 1998 suggestions, President Kim proposed that the United States improve its economic and diplomatic ties with the North, provide economic assistance, and guarantee Pyongyang's national security—conditioned on for the latter's reciprocal commitment to end its nuclear and missile programs and to refrain from military provocations against the South.[99] He further suggested that U.S.-Japanese normalization of relations with the North no longer be predicated on parallel progress in inter-Korean relations.[100] A major departure from the policy of his predecessor, the shift seemed to signal the Kim administration's concerted effort to reinvent the inter-Korean environment to make it more hospitable to a wary Pyongyang, one which still appeared to be operating on the basis of a distorted vision of reality.[101] Part of that effort included Seoul's resolve, as a senior Blue House official stated, "to leave no stone unturned to persuade them ["hawkish" U.S. Republicans and other U.S. skeptics] into accepting our practical proposal."

The Kim administration has hoped that the comprehensive engagement policy is adopted by the Clinton administration's North Korea policy coordinator William Perry as the centerpiece of the so-called "Perry report." Appearing on a CNN program, on May 4, 1999, President Kim expressed his wish that the report would incorporate what he called the "five tasks" of the South Korean-U.S. engagement policy. The tasks included: 1) pursuit of reconciliation and cooperation between the two Koreas based on the 1992 inter-Korean basic agreement; 2) an early normalization of relations between the United States and Japan, on one side, and North Korea, on the other; 3) fostering of an international environment conducive to

---

[99]*Ch'ongwadae* WWW in Korean, December 8, 1998; *The Korea Herald* (Internet version) in English, December 9, 1998; *The Korea Times* (Internet version) in English, December 8, 1998.

[100]This seemed to depart from President Kim's own position as of December 30, 1997, when, even as he urged Japan and the United States to promote economic relations with North Korea, he stressed that they should not allow the North to seek dialogue with Tokyo and Washington to the exclusion of South Korea. President Kim made the point to then-Japanese Foreign Minister Keizo Obuchi on his to Seoul at that time. *The Korea Herald* (Internet version) in English, December 31, 1997; earlier in the same month, then-candidate Kim Dae Jung was reported to have also said, "... any improvement in the North's relations with the United States and Japan should be made in harmony with progress in inter-Korean relations." *The Korea Herald,* December 12, 1997, p.3.

[101]The previous administrations' position was that improvement in the U.S.-North Korean relations should be conditioned on similar progress in North-South Korean relations. Kim Jae-il, *Sisa Journal*, December 25, 1997, p.51.

Pyongyang's fulfilling its role as a legitimate member of the world community; 4) arms control coupled with the removal of weapons of mass destruction from the Korean Peninsula; and 5) the creation of an inter-Korean peace system by replacing the current armistice system in effect since 1953.[102]

## Conclusions

President Kim Dae Jung's leadership marked a significant milestone in South Korean evolution towards mature democracy. That came as an unprecedented transfer of power from the center-right establishment to a center-left minority in opposition, accompanied by an equally historic shift in the regionally defined center of power. These changes arguably reflected the advent of a new generation of power elite steeped in the politics of liberalism, not to mention the politics of fragile coalition rule between two regionally-based, ideologically disparate parties. The thrust of these developments has tended to harden the personality-dominated partisan divide along regional and ideological lines, making bipartisan accommodation even more difficult — especially as regards President Kim's reputedly dovish "sunshine policy." Political stability has seemed elusive, punctuated by false starts and failed expectations of bipartisanship. The tenuousness of coalition rule raises the specter of continued uncertainty in the months ahead — with President Kim reportedly eyeing a new political alignment to include politicians from the rival region now identified with the opposition camp.

The ongoing partisan standoff provides a volatile political background influencing President Kim's sunshine policy—and by extension, critical U.S. security interests as well. Thus far, this engagement policy has endured and may well stay the course through December 2002, when South Koreans must elect a new President (by law President Kim is required to step down in February 2003). The prospect of new leadership raises the question of whether the sunshine policy as now constructed and played out can be sustained beyond 2002. The prospects are unclear, given the lack of a bipartisan show of support for the policy, coupled with a potential fault-line within the ruling coalition. Also contributing to this uncertainty seems to be a "wait-and-see" attitude among the center-right political leaders and others in the elite who are friendly to the pre-1998 foreign affairs establishment. The dividing line of pros and cons, however, does not appear to be as hardened as it may seem. Criticism of the sunshine policy is not about the grand design and structure of the policy but about its potential negative results for some South Korean interests.[103]

---

[102]*The Korea Times* (Internet version) in English, May 5, May 6, 1999;

[103]On May 24, 1999, President Kim named Lim Dong-won, his senior aide for national security and foreign affairs, as new Minister of Unification. The President's principal point man on the sunshine policy, Lim replaced Kang In-dok, one of the reputed hardliners on North Korea and the frequent target of North Korean criticism that Kang's ministerial role would not bode well for the future of inter-Korean dialogue and reconciliation. *Yonhap* in English, May 24, 1999; *The Korea Herald* (Internet version) in English, May 25, 1999; *The Korea Times* (Internet version) in English, May 24, 1999. On May 26, 1999, a North Korean commentator gloated over Kang's departure, noting that Kang had "disrupted" the North-South dialogue by "waving the so-called reciprocity card." [North] *Korean Central*

(continued...)

Critics' concerns have focused on the mechanics of implementation. To achieve a credible consensus on the engagement policy, a case can be made that the Kim administration should make its decision-making process more transparent so that the sunshine policy can be popularly embraced as a truly national, rather than "a Blue House," policy; many South Korean analysts seem troubled by the perception that key decisions on the policy continue to be made by a few in the privacy of the Blue House.

Another concern is over the Kim administration's perceived "retreat" on the principle of reciprocity, now stretched to mean a policy of "aiding-the-North-first" in vague hopes of Pyongyang returning the favor sometime in the future. Critics maintain that such a "wait-and-see" attitude will more likely embolden the North to try to exact more concessions from the South in a high-priority bid to maintain its "military-first" policy at the expense of other sectors of society. The Kim administration's attitude toward reciprocity, or lack of balance between carrots and sticks, as the argument goes, will more likely run the risk of compromising South Korea's national security.

The perceived urgency of the Kim administration's efforts to reach out to the North seems to belie the administration's own counsel to both domestic and foreign audiences to be patient. Many critics suggest that the administration should be more cool-headed in trying to read signs of Pyongyang's so-called "positive response" to the sunshine policy.

President Kim urges the United States and Japan to normalize their relations with North Korea, not minding the absence of parallel progress in inter-Korean relations. Critics tend to argue that, if realized, this might leave South Korea with minimal leverage needed to keep inter-Korean relations on an even keel, making it difficult to steer the North toward a desired end if only because a self-centered North Korean regime will be less likely to be accommodating.

Observers note that Washington seems concerned about a perception that the Kim administration and the United States have different perspectives on dealing with Pyongyang's nuclear and missiles issues. Absent an agreement on policy priorities, this could pose a problem in policy coordination. Moreover, analysts have argued that there is a need for South Korea, together with the United States and Japan, to clarify when to stand up to Pyongyang to counter its "unacceptable behavior."[104]

---

[103](...continued)
*Broadcasting Network* in Korean, May 26, 1999.

[104]Richard L. Armitage, "A Comprehensive Approach to North Korea," in *Strategic Forum*, National Defense University, No. 159, March 1999.

Defenders of the sunshine policy seem convinced that this policy deserves to be tried out. The new paradigm may not yield the desired outcomes in the short term, but President Kim's engagement policy is an improvement over the North Korea policies of the previous South Korean administrations, policies they said were reactive, inconsistent, and, above all, unproductive. Reciprocity, they argue, need not be the determinant of engagement; South Korea has the strength and enough resolve to be able to pursue a policy of "aid-first-and-rewards-later." In their view, what South Koreans need is an act of faith in the inevitability of reconciliation and cooperation between the two Koreas.

# JAPAN'S "ECONOMIC MIRACLE": WHAT HAPPENED?*

*William H. Cooper*

What happened to the Japanese "economic miracle?" Since the beginning of the 1990s, Japan has been experiencing slow economic growth and recession along with high unemployment and other problems. These trends in the 1990s compare starkly with the 1970s and 1980s, when Japan's rapid economic growth and development drew admiration from much of the world, including many in the United States, and thrust Japan into the elite club of major industrialized countries. Japan even became established in the minds of some as a model for economic growth and development for other economies to follow. But Japan's difficulties have cast a cloud over its economic prospects and tarnished, perhaps unnecessarily so, its image as a leading economic power in Asia and the world.

Japan's economic problems and the prospects for the Japanese economy have broad implications for the United States and the world as a whole. The problems have emerged and grown as economic crises hit economies in East Asia, Russia, and Latin America and, to some extent, have exacerbated those crises. Japan's economic difficulties have reignited tensions with the United States as the U.S. trade deficit has soared and have raised concerns in the United States and elsewhere about the likely brake they would have on economic growth in this country and the world as a whole.

The economic crisis in Japan was the subject of legislation in the 105th Congress in the form of Congressional resolutions extorting the U.S. Administration to press Japan toward taking measures to restructure its economy and stimulate economic growth. It is likely to remain of interest to the 106th Congress as the U.S. trade deficit with Japan grows and as some sectors, particularly steel, are adversely affected.

This report examines recent economic trends in Japan that paint a picture of a very difficult economic and financial situation and reviews the main factors that have contributed to it. It examines the impact of the crisis on the U.S. economy and on U.S.-Japan economic ties and presents the options available to U.S. policymakers to protect U.S. interests. Events in Japan are evolving. This report will be updated as warranted.

---

* Excerpted from *CRS Report for Congress* RL30176

# Trends in the Japanese Economy:
# Examining the Indicators

The image of the Japanese economy in the United States, around the world, and within Japan has changed many times in the post-war period. From the 1950s to the 1960s, Japan was viewed as a poor but advancing economy relying on the production of labor-intensive goods to drive its reindustrialization. In the 1970s and especially in the 1980s, Japan developed into the world's second largest, and a fully industrialized, economy, on track to overtake United States as the leading economy in the world. Its success in the production of autos, computers, and other sophisticated goods, its high growth rates, and the rapidly increasing Japanese standard of living helped form this image. Some observers even viewed Japanese economic policies and structure as the "model" to be emulated (and it often was) by other East Asian economies.

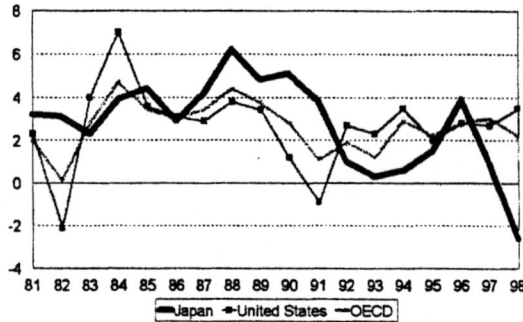

**Figure 1. GDP Real Growth Rates, 1981-98**

Source:OECD

Japan ▬ United States ◆ OECD ━

But that popular image of Japan has changed almost 180 degrees in the 1990s, as Japan has undergone various difficulties highlighted by slow, and at times negative, economic growth rates. As with many popular images, both the positive and negative ones of Japan have been somewhat exaggerated. Japan was never an invincible economic juggernaut as some writers viewed it in the 1980s, nor is it now a collapsed economy. Nevertheless, most experts would argue that Japan faces both near and long- term challenges that call for bold policies.

## Japan's GDP Growth Rates

Japan experienced impressive, though declining, economic growth rates in the post-war era. From 1960-1970, Japan averaged an annual real (adjusted for inflation) GDP growth rate of 11.0%; from 1970-1980— 5.4%; and 1980-1990— 4.1%. Most economists argue that declining average economic growth rates are commensurate with a maturing economy.[1] Despite the declining trend, Japan's economic growth rates remained on average above those of the United States and the

---

[1] CRS calculations based on data in OECD *Economic Outlook 64* December 1998. p.191. As economies develop they are able to import technology from more advanced countries. Investment in these technologies allow less advanced economies to develop and grow rapidly. But as they become more mature, the stock of available technology diminishes as countries must innovate, a longer and more expensive process.

other industrialized countries of the Organization for Economic Cooperation and Development (OECD).[2]

Economic growth trends for Japan in the 1990s have declined markedly raising concerns both in and outside Japan. From 1990-98, Japan's real GDP grew on average 1.6%, substantially below previous trends, and as the graph in figure 1 indicates, even below U.S. and OECD trends, especially after 1992.

The decline in Japan's GDP growth has been very pronounced in the last two years as indicated in figure 2. That graph indicates that over that period, Japan experienced negative growth in the last quarter of 1997 and all four quarters of 1998, the markings of a major recession. Over time, slow or negative growth undermines business and consumer confidence in the economy and diminishes residents'

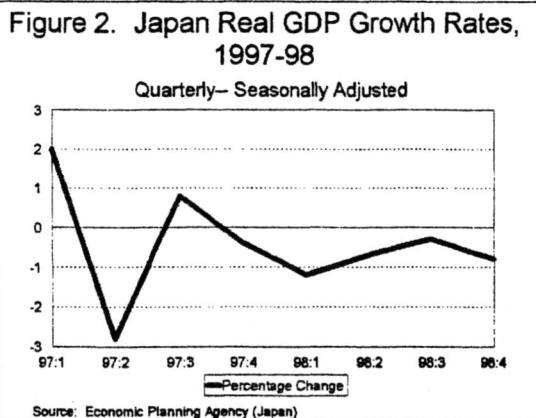

Figure 2. Japan Real GDP Growth Rates, 1997-98

Quarterly– Seasonally Adjusted

Source: Economic Planning Agency (Japan)

standard of living. Poor economic growth can eventually undermine confidence in political leadership.

## Unemployment

Japan's anemic economy has led to growing unemployment, a relatively new problem in recent Japanese history. Recently Japan's unemployment rate has exceeded that of the United States, although it has remained below those of most West European countries and the OECD average. From 1981-1990, Japan had an annual average unemployment rate of 2.5% compared to 7.1% for the United States.[3] But Japan's unemployment rate has increased steadily in the 1990s. By the end of February 1999 it had reached 4.6%.[4]

## Standard of Living

Japan has incurred low inflation rates, much lower than rates in the United States and OECD countries as a whole. In 1998, Japan has at times experienced deflation— negative rates of change in price levels. Extended periods of deflation can be a

---

[2] The OECD is a group of the 29 most industrialized economies, including the United States and Japan.

[3] OECD. p. 212.

[4] Economic Planning Agency (Japan). *Essentials of Monthly Economic Report and Main Economic Indicators*. April 1999. p. 10.

problem for an economy because declining asset prices discourage investment. Figure 3 depicts Japanese inflation rates compared with the United States and the OECD countries as a whole from 1988 to 1997.

**Figure 3. Inflation Rates: Japan, U.S. and OECD**
Changes in Consumer Prices, 1988-97

Source: OECD

Despite its economic problems, Japan remains one of the wealthiest countries in the world whose citizens enjoy one of the highest standards of living. Japanese citizens enjoy one of the world's highest per capita/GDP rates. In 1996, it was nominally $36,509, compared with $27,821 for the United States. Measured using purchasing power parity (PPP)— which takes into account exchange rate and cost of living differences— Japan's per capita GDP was below that of the United States — $23,235 compared to $27, 821— but still above that of many other industrialized economies.[5] Japanese citizens pay much higher

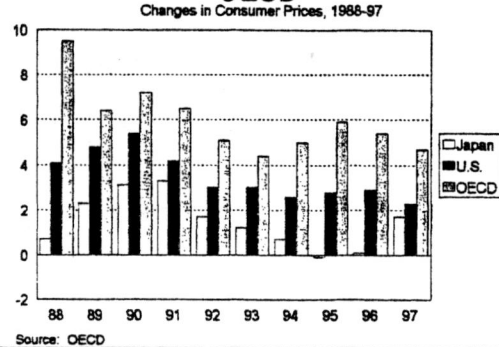

**Figure 4. Japan's Current Account Balances**
1986-98

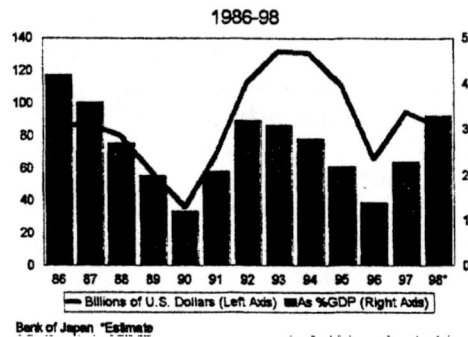

— Billions of U.S. Dollars (Left Axis)  ■As %GDP (Right Axis)
Bank of Japan  *Estimate

prices for housing, fuel, food and other staples than do U.S. citizens, thus decreasing their standard of living somewhat. Japan's citizens enjoy the highest average life span (80 years) in the world (compared with the United States— 77 years.)[6]

## Foreign Trade Balances

Japan has continually run surpluses in its current account (balances on merchandise trade, investment income, and unilateral transfers) primarily due to large surpluses in its merchandise trade but increasingly as a result of rising income from investments abroad. (Figure 4.) The current account surpluses are reflective of a high domestic household savings rate in Japan, around 15% of disposable income. At times the trade surpluses have presented a political problem for Japan as countries, such as the United States, that continually run bilateral trade deficits with Japan, have considered the deficits reflective of unfairness in Japan's trade policies and practices and have encouraged Japan to reduce its surpluses. The trends have become more pronounced recently and have generated public concern from political leaders in the United States and other nations. On the other hand, Japan's large savings provide a

---

[5] Source: OECD. OECD Economic Surveys: New Zealand. 1998. Paris. p. 190.

[6] Source: World Bank. *World Development Indicators— 1998* . Washington. P. 105, 106.

pool of financial capital to the United States and other low- savings countries that need to borrow capital for investment. Japanese capital, for example, helps to finance the U.S. national debt.

## Impact of Japan's Economic Problems

Japanese poor economic conditions have implications for Japan, the United States, and beyond. For Japan itself, continued slow growth or recession eventually could seriously damage the standard of living of the average Japanese citizen. Falls in national income would mean a decline in tax revenues that would worsen Japan's already difficult fiscal situation. Continued slow growth could affect business confidence and consumer confidence causing them to delay or reduce investment and spending, further exacerbating the gloomy economic trends. Furthermore, pronounced and extended poor economic performance can undermine popular confidence in political leaders and create political instability. Prime Minister Hashimoto was forced to resign his position after his party, the Liberal Democratic party (LDP), performed poorly in the July 12, 1998, upper-house parliamentary elections. The Hashimoto's government's ineffective response to the economic problems were largely blamed for the voters' rejection of the LDP, especially in the urban areas.

# Factors Contributing to the Economic Problems

The causes of Japan's economic problems are varied and complex. They are rooted in some immediate factors: the burst of the assets bubble in the early 1990s and Japanese government macroeconomic policies that immediately precipitated the crisis. But they are also rooted in the fundamental structure of the Japanese economy—the complex web of government regulations and business conglomerates.

## "Burst of the Bubble"

The trigger of the crisis was the burst in the assets "bubble" in the early 1990s. The assets "bubble" refers to the run up of prices on land, stocks, and other assets in the mid-1980s to unsustainable levels. The bubble resulted from loose monetary policies intended to dampen the effects of an appreciating yen on exports in the mid-1980s and from liberalization of capital controls that unleashed funds seeking higher yields. In addition, banks were searching for new customers as firms, their biggest borrowers, turned from banks to equity markets for their financing. Banks turned to real estate and real estate-based loans as their targets. The sudden inflow of capital drove up asset prices.

The phenomenon fed on itself perpetuating inflated asset values. Investors used the inflated assets to collateralize loans which they used to buy more assets. The inflated asset values created a "wealth effect" making consumers and businesses feel flush with cash, leading them to spend and invest accordingly. Business investment and consumer spending soared. Stock prices skyrocketed as the Nikkei index jumped from 10,000 to 40,000 between 1984 and 1989. Real estate prices increased so rapidly as to make homes in Japan's biggest cities unaffordable without extra long-term mortgages. Japanese investments in U.S. real estate and businesses triggered fears of an "invasion" of U.S. industry. These trends contributed to high economic growth in Japan in the mid-1980s: Japan's real GDP grew an average of 3.9% per year; it peaked at 5.8% in 1988.

But beginning in 1989 and into the early 1990s, the Japanese monetary authorities determined that the low interest rates and the highly expansive money supply were not sustainable and threatened the economy with inflation. Japan's central bank, the Bank of Japan, raised its official discount rate from 2.5% in May 1989 to 6% by August 1990. The money supply growth was slowed dramatically and contracted in absolute terms in 1992.

Tightened credit and money supply brought a halt to asset buying, and the speculative bubble "burst" by the end of 1990. Stock prices plummeted. By the end of 1992, the Nikkei average had bottomed out at 60% below its 1989 peak and has remained virtually at that level.

The economy was especially hard hit by the sharp drop in land and property prices which spawned a wave of defaulting loans, much like the U.S. savings and loan crisis of the 1980s. In Japan as a whole, land values declined an average 22% from 1991 to 1997. In the six largest Japanese cities where land values had jumped more than 200% from 1985 to 1991, they declined 56% from 1991 to 1997. Commercial real estate in these areas declined 72%.[7] Business investment in plant and equipment declined 20% in real terms from 1991, its peak, to 1996, increased 7.1% in 1997 but fell 11.4% in 1998.[8] The sharp downturn in asset values along with the tightened monetary policy precipitated a decline in economic growth in 1991 that began the continuing period (except for a blip in 1996) of economic stagnation in Japan that has worsened.

## The Financial Sector "Crisis"

The asset bubble exposed deep-seated structural problems in Japan's financial sector which contributed to Japan's anemic economic performance. The collapse of the real estate market and the stock market left many Japanese banks with a huge volume of loans which were not likely to be repaid. The financial crisis was due in part to the use of stocks and real estate as collateral; the number and size of the loans ballooned with the rise in asset values and actually fed the bubble and collapsed when the bubble burst.

The crisis has been caused also by government practices, particularly those of the Ministry of Finance, that oversees the banking sector. The practices included the so-called convoy policy, that of promoting growth throughout the banking sector with the stronger banks assisting the weaker ones, rather than allowing weaker ones to go bankrupt or merge with stronger ones. The collapse of the market also exposed

---

[7] Source: Management and Coordination Agency. Statistics Bureau. (Japan) *Japan Statistical Yearbook 1998*. Tokyo. p. 562.

[8] Ibid. p. 139 and Economic Planning Agency. (Japan).*Essential of Monthly Economic Report and Main Economic Indicators*. March 1999. p. 3.

questionable accounting practices that allowed banks to hide non-performing loans rather than having to write them-off.

On June 6, 1995, the Director-General of the Banking Bureau of Japan's Ministry of Finance testified before the Diet that Japan's banks and cooperative based financial institutions held 40 billion yen (or about $400 billion) in non-performing loans, or about 9% of Japan's GDP at that time.[9] Many analysts assumed that the Japanese government had under-reported the extent of the non-performing loan problem. The officially reported value of those kept increasing to around $550 billion by July 1998, but outside analysts and non-Japanese officials have placed the value at closer to $1 trillion, or about 1/4 Japan's GDP.[10]

The strain of the banking crisis and tighter capital/asset requirements from the Bank for International Settlements (BIS) challenged long-held government banking oversight policies and banking practices. The small institutions, including the *jusen*, or housing loan institutions, were the first hit with bankruptcy and closure. Between 1993-1996, all seven jusen closed as did several credit cooperatives, and a small regional bank. In 1997, a mid-sized life insurance company— Nissan Life Insurance and Sanyo Securities Co, both collapsed. More importantly in 1997 Yamaichi Securities and Hokkaido Takushoku Bank, Ltd. were allowed to fail, the first time in post-war Japanese history that major financial institutions were allowed to go under.[11] In 1998, the government nationalized the Long-Term Credit Bank (LTCB) and Nippon Credit Bank under a banking rescue program passed by the Diet in October 1998.

The burst of the bubble marked the beginning of Japan's economic crisis. The impact that the burst bubble has had on the financial sector has helped prolong and deepen the economic stagnation. A strong, stable financial sector is vital to the health of an economy. It is the sector that channels capital, the life-blood of a market economy, from those who have it (savers) to those who need it (investors). If that life-blood is slowed or cut off, the economy suffers.

## Recent Fiscal and Monetary Policies

Some analysts have also pointed to Japanese government fiscal and monetary policies as contributing to the economic malaise. Japan's fiscal situation deteriorated severely in the 1990s. From 1990 to 1995, the Japanese general government fiscal balance went from a surplus equivalent to 2.9% of GDP to a deficit equivalent to 3.7% of GDP. Gross debt increased from 65.1% GDP in 1990 to 80.6% GDP in 1995. Net debt (essentially gross debt minus social security contributions) increased

---

[9] U.S. Library of Congress. Congressional Research Service. *Japan's Banking Crisis: Causes and Probable Effects*. CRS Report 95-1034 E, by Dick K. Nanto. October 6, 1995. p. 6.

[10] Sanger, David. E. Japan's Bad Debt is Now Estimated $1 Trillion. *New York Times* . July 31, 1998. p. A1,A8.

[11] Lincoln, Ed. Japan's Economic Mess. *JEI Report*. May 8, 1998. no. 18A. p. 10.

to 11% GDP in 1995, and it is expected to grow as the aging Japanese population contributes less to government revenues and takes more in social security payments.[12] The deteriorating public finances resulted from the slowdown in economic activity in the early 1990s in Japan, due in part to the burst of the bubble, plus the additional costs of a series of stimulus packages.[13]

In anticipation of the fiscal problems Japan would face, the powerful Ministry of Finance strongly promoted more austere tax and expenditure policies. One of the major pillars of the austerity program was the passage of the Fiscal Structural Reform Act in 1997. Among other things, the act required that by Japanese fiscal year 2003, the government would no longer be able to issue bonds to finance budget deficits, and the general government deficit would have to decrease to 3% of GDP.[14]

The government began to take other measures to reduce its budget deficits. In April 1997, it increased the consumption tax from 3% to 5% and reversed a temporary tax reduction that had been imposed earlier to stimulate demand.[15] The government had timed the fiscal austerity measures in anticipation of a long-awaited recovery in Japan's economic growth. Indeed in 1996, real Japanese GDP increased 3.9% after lackluster growth the previous years of the decade.[16] The general government deficit decreased to 2.8% in 1997 indicating a tighter fiscal policy. But the fiscal contraction, while financially prudent, contributed to the return of economic stagnation in 1997 and thereafter. Japan's recent monetary policy has been loose.

One school of thought on Japanese economic policy argues that Japan's macroeconomic policies have played the key role in Japan's economic stagnation. Economist Adam Posen, a member of this school, argues that the burst of the bubble was caused by the inappropriate contractionary fiscal and monetary policies in the early 1990s.[17] He further argues that when the government introduced fiscal stimulus to boost demand, it was too little too late. The one exception was in 1995, when the government implemented a large fiscal stimulus package, and it resulted in the boom in economic activity in 1996. He argues that the Japanese economy still has room to grow through fiscal stimulus (potential growth) without triggering inflation nor would the extra fiscal debt overly burden the Japanese economy.

MIT economist Paul Krugman is another member of this school but focuses on the role of monetary policy. He argues that the Japanese economy has entered into a "liquidity trap:" At very low interest rates individuals will willingly hold (not spend)

---

[12] OECD. *OECD Economic Surveys: Japan— 1996-1997.* Paris. p. 54-55.

[13] Ibid. p. 59.

[14] Aghevli, Bijan B., Tamim Bayoumi, Guy Meredith. *Structural Change in Japan: Macroeconomic Impact and Policy Challenges.* International Monetary Fund. Washington. 1998. p. 174.

[15] OECD. *OECD Economic Surveys: Japan— 1996-1997.* Paris. p. 61.

[16] Ibid.

[17] Posen. Adam S. *Restoring Japan's Economic Growth.* Institute for International Economics. Washington. August 1998. 186 p. Ibid.

all additions to the supply of money, thus making monetary policy ineffective through interest rate changes.[18]

## Structural Economic Problems

Another group of analysts argues that macroeconomic factors (fiscal and monetary policies) are not as important as structural rigidities within the Japanese economy, in addition to those in the financial sector that led to the financial assets bubble. Such rigidities, they argue, have not only led to Japan's economic problems but will prevent Japan from realizing its full growth potential unless they are removed.

One such economist, Richard Katz, argues that Japanese economic problems are rooted in what he calls its "dual economy."[19] The Japanese economy is really a two-segmented economy, he argues. One segment is highly efficient and consists of sectors that have proved competitive in the world economy and are highly productive. This segment would include industries producing cars, electronic products, computers, semiconductors, and capital machinery. The second segment are those sectors that are very inefficient with low productivity. They survive through protective government regulations and private business practices. This segment includes industries that produce glass, cement, paper, petroleum products and petrochemicals, processed foods, and basic steel. It also includes many elements of the service sector, such as financial and retail services.

According to Katz, and others, the Japanese economy had been able not only to survive but thrive until recently because the competitive part of the dual economy was so efficient that it was able to prop up the noncompetitive part. They did so by having to depend on those sectors for their inputs. For example, the car manufacturers would buy flat glass, basic steel, and other components from domestic manufacturers but at higher prices than they might have had to pay if they bought from more efficient foreign suppliers. They sold their products through designated retailers. They also had to pay high prices for energy.

This arrangement could continue as long as the export sectors remained sufficiently competitive to absorb the costs of the less efficient sectors. But Katz argues that in the mid-1980s, with the sharp appreciation of the yen, Japanese exporting firms could no longer absorb the costs without sacrificing their ability to compete globally. Many of the industries, particularly the car manufacturers and electronics manufacturers, were forced to relocate operations abroad.

With demand for Japanese exports cut and producers moving abroad, Japan made up for the loss of demand by pouring more of its financial resources into investment driven by a loose monetary policy. This strategy allowed Japan to boost growth rates in the 1980s. Yet, Katz points out, those investments were inefficient, yielding lower returns than investments made in other industrialized countries. The

---

[18] Krugman. Paul. *Japan's Trap.* MIT. May 1998. (http://web.mit.edu/krugman/www./japtrap.html)

[19] Katz, Richard. *Japan— the System that Soured: The Rise and Fall of the Japanese Miracle.* M.E. Sharpe. Armonk, NY. 1998. 463 p.

continual pouring of funds into assets created the bubble and sowed the seeds of the economy's destruction. When the bubble burst in the early 1990s, it signified the end of the "last hurrah of a faltering system trying to pump itself up."

Along with Japan's "dual economy, Katz points to a second, related problem with the Japanese economy— a chronic inability to consume all that it produces. The Japanese economy saves too much largely because of the lack of an adequate social safety net and social security (retirement) program. If that savings cannot be exported it is "consumed" through investments which have become increasingly inefficient, or pumping up of the economy through government public works programs.[20]

## The East Asian Financial Crisis

The currency crisis that hit several large East Asian economies —Thailand, Indonesia, Malaysia, and South Korea — from mid-1997 contributed to prolonging Japan's economic problems.[21] Japan had become more reliant on East Asia as an export market and the growth in Japanese off-shore production in East Asia created customers for exports of Japanese technology. In 1996, Asia accounted for 44% of Japanese exports. In 1997, after the onset of the Asian crisis, the share declined to 42% and by the end of 1998, to 35%. In 1998, Japanese exports to those countries most sharply hit by the financial crisis declined dramatically: South Korea— 36.4%; Thailand— 30.7%; Malaysia— 30.7%; and Indonesia— 54.5%. Furthermore, in 1998, imports from the countries hardest hit by the financial crisis declined very sharply: South Korea— 69.3%; Thailand— 74.6%; and Malaysia— 78.2% The decline in imports made it more difficult for these countries to export their way out of the crisis. (Japanese imports from Indonesia actually increased 58.8%.)[22]

In addition, Japanese banks had been heavily exposed in those countries. At the end of 1996, before the Asian crisis hit, 62.3% of international lending by Japanese banks was to eight East Asian economies: Indonesia, South Korea, Thailand, Malaysia, the Philippines, Taiwan, Hong Kong and Singapore.[23] Japanese banks faced the possibility of their loans there going bad which added to the banking sector's already enormous problems.

---

[20] Ibid. p. 8.

[21] For information on the Asian financial crisis see CRS Report RL30012. *Global Turmoil: Contagion, Effects, and Policy Responses.* by Dick K .Nanto.

[22] Ministry     of     Finance     (Japan).     Obtained     from     website: http://www.mof.go.jp/english/trade-st/199828ce.htm>.

[23] U.S. Library of Congress. Congressional Research Service. *The Asian Financial Crisis, the IMF, and Japan: Economic Issues*. CRS Report 98-434E, by Dick K. Nanto. p.26-27.

# Japan's Response to the Economic Problems

The examination above of Japan's economic problems demonstrates that a number of factors have contributed to them: the burst of the asset bubble; the crisis in the financial sector; macroeconomic policies; structural problems in the economy; and the East Asian currency crisis. Successive Japanese governments in the 1990s have responded with piecemeal initiatives on these various fronts with little in the way of near-term success, judging by Japan's continuing poor economic outlook.

## Macroeconomic Measures

Macroeconomic policies are defined as a government's policies on spending and taxation (fiscal policy) and on currency and credit emissions and interest rates (monetary policy). These economic policy tools can be very powerful, but their use is constrained by the financial resources available to a government and also by the need to maintain price stability.

**Fiscal Measures.** Since 1992, the successive Japanese governments have passed and implemented seven "economic stimulus packages," combinations of tax cuts and spending increases, to try to boost the limping economy. But they have had to do so against the backdrop of an aging population that will, in time, demand more in terms of pensions and contribute less in taxes putting additional demands on the government budget.

In the last two years, the Hashimoto government followed by the Obuchi government introduced the two largest spending packages in Japan's post-war history reflecting the dismal shape of the Japanese economy. On April 24, 1998, the Hashimoto government announced a ¥16 trillion (roughly $125 billion) fiscal stimulus package. The package included tax rebates, tax cuts, and new public works spending. The package was criticized by fiscal conservatives for putting Japan further in debt. But others criticized it for not going far enough.[24]

Significantly, as part of the stimulus package, the government backtracked on prior commitments to reduce the fiscal debt burden under the 1997 Fiscal Structural Reform Act: It rolled back the deadline from March 31, 2004 to March 31, 2006 for reducing the government deficit/GDP ratio to 3%; extended by two years the date for prohibiting new issues of general revenue (deficit-financing) bonds from after FY2003 to after FY2005; and added contingencies for skirting the ban once it is in effect to take into account poor economic growth. The stimulus package likely provided a temporary prop to the economy, but it was not enough to turn things around. The economy continued to decline in the third quarter and into the fourth quarter of 1998.

Pressure on the Japanese government to do more grew from inside Japan and from foreigners, including Clinton Administration officials and members of the U.S. Congress. In the meantime, Prime Minister Hashimoto resigned in July 1998 in the

---

[24] Choy, John. Japan's Fiscal Stimulus Plan Plays to Mixed Reviews. *JEI Report*, May 1, 1998. p.4.

wake of the poor showing of the LDP in upper-house parliamentary elections, itself a product of economic problems.[25]

The Obuchi government took office, facing more pressure as Japan's economy continued in recession. On November 16, 1998, it approved the second stimulus package of the year valued at ¥23.9 trillion (roughly $176 billion), the largest package ever. The plan included more spending on social infrastructure and loans to small and medium-sized firms who were unable to get funds because of the post-bubble credit crunch. It also contained a controversial program to distribute coupons redeemable for consumer goods and worth about $160 each to the elderly and to families with children.

In a major policy change, the government made previously temporary cuts in income taxes and corporate taxes permanent. Furthermore, the government claimed that the package contained ¥15 trillion in *ma-mizu* (real water), a term applied to net new spending.[26]

The extra spending is a political gamble for Japanese political leaders. If the stimulus packages prove effective, the Japanese economy could return to sustained economic growth. However, if the economy does not grow, or does not grow sufficiently to boost business and consumer confidence, then Japan is faced with a very high debt burden which would become harder to pay off if the economy is not generating increasing income. Japan already has the highest deficit/GDP ratio among industrialized countries. (See figure 5.)

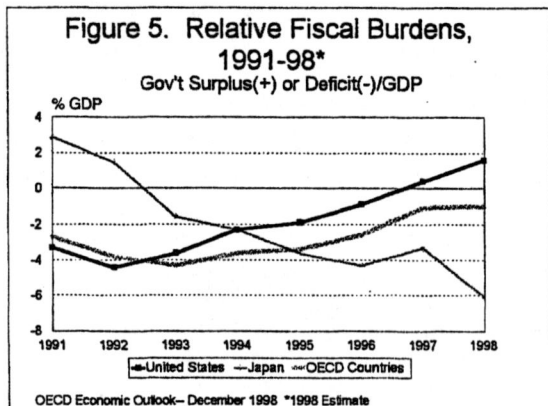

Figure 5. Relative Fiscal Burdens, 1991-98*
Gov't Surplus(+) or Deficit(-)/GDP

OECD Economic Outlook– December 1998  *1998 Estimate

**Monetary Policy.** The Japanese authorities have maintained a loose monetary policy since September 8, 1995, a policy commensurate with a slow growing or recessionary economy. The Bank of Japan has maintained its official discount rate (the rate at which it lends funds to other banks) at a nominal (not adjusted for inflation) 0.5% since that time. The BOJ had dropped the interest rate in stages from 6.0% in August 1990. Short-term and long-term commercial rates have also been low in nominal terms. It is important to note that Japanese monetary policy has not been as loose as it might first

---

[25] Choy, John. *Tokyo's Latest Stimulus Package Gets Cool Reception. JEI Report.* November 20, 1998. p. 2.

[26] Some critics of Japanese fiscal policies have argued that stimulus packages have been ineffective because they have largely consisted of "old water," that is, funding that has already been committed but is front-loaded. In doing so, these critics argue, the Japanese government makes the value of the packages appear larger than they actually are.

appear. Inflation rates in Japan have been very low, far below those of most industrialized countries. Therefore, real (adjust for inflation) interest rates in Japan, which are the effective rates, are higher in many countries. In addition, even though nominal interest rates have been low, the growing problems in the banking sector have stifled credit expansion.[27]

## Banking Reform and Other Structural Changes

Many Japanese policymakers and other observers long recognized that Japan's financial sector was highly inefficient and subject to corruption. Heavy government regulations prevented the sector (including banks, trust banks, securities companies, insurance, and other credit institutions) from adequately responding to the competitive demands of a global economy. These problems became especially apparent when the financial bubble burst and banks were left holding bad loans. The proliferation of troubled banks challenged the long-held government policy of trying to keep all institutions afloat, the "convoy system." Government regulations made it difficult for banks and other lenders to offer new financial services that were tailored to new markets. Troubled domestic financial institutions could not merge with foreign institutions to shore up their capital base and the financial sector was isolated from foreign competition.

In November 1996 the Hashimoto government announced a sweeping program of financial reforms, popularly called the "big bang." Among other things, the program is designed to break down barriers among the various types of financial institutions to increase competition among them. The main provisions of the big bang include:[28]

- imposing higher penalties on financial institutions for illegal acts;
- loosening government restrictions on management of investment trusts, pension funds, and other assets;
- allowing individuals and companies to make foreign currency transactions without prior government approval;
- making the Bank of Japan independent of the Ministry of Finance;
- opening the Japan Financial Inspection Agency;
- eliminating licensing requirements for securities brokerages;
- eliminating restrictions on commissions on securities trades; and
- removing barriers to banks, insurance companies; trust banks, and securities companies from operating in one another's sectors;

In addition to the "big bang," Japan signed the World Trade Organization's (WTO) financial services agreement in December 1997 which requires signatory governments to allow foreign firms to participate in domestic financial markets. Furthermore, in April 1998, the Bank of Japan began to enforce tighter capital/asset ratios as required by the Bank of International Settlements (BIS). Enforcing these standards may have curtailed the ability of Japanese banks to lend. Japan and the

---

[27] IMF, *World Economic Outlook*, October 1998. p. 113.

[28] Taken from CRS Report 98-475E *,Japan's "Big Bang"and Other Financial Deregulation. by Dick K. Nanto.*

United States also engaged in bilateral negotiations and agreements aimed toward opening Japan's markets for insurance and other financial services to foreign competition.

The "big bang" is designed to be implemented over time and will affect the economy gradually. But Japan faces the immediate crisis of a banking sector in deep trouble, which has led to the loss of depositors' confidence and to a "credit crunch" (insufficient credit available to viable lenders). In October 1998, the Japanese parliament approved a program initiated by the government of Prime Minister Obuchi. The program includes over $500 billion in funding, to deal with nonperforming loans and weak banks. It also includes the establishment of new government agencies to manage and otherwise dispense with nonperforming loans and failed banks.[29]

Financial reform is very important but only a part of the economic restructuring efforts that the Japanese government has taken in the 1990s. Japan has grappled with economic restructuring for many years. In 1986, a report released by an advisory commission led by former Bank of Japan chairman Haruo Maekawa asserted that Japan needed to take measures to stimulate domestic demand by relying less on exports to stimulate economic growth in the face of growing trade surpluses and political pressure from trading partners, including the United States. These measures were to include economic deregulation. But the Japanese government did little in response.

Faced with continued economic stagnation in the 1990s, the Japanese government seems to have taken economic reform more seriously. Also the government's poor response to the crisis, including the loss of many lives, that hit the Kobe region after the 1995 earthquake there manifested the corruption that existed in some government ministries, the lack of effective inter-ministerial coordination, and arcane and inefficient government regulations.

The Japanese government has embarked on deregulation and restructuring on a number of fronts. In March 1995, the government initiated a Deregulation Action Program (DAP), a three-year program (FY1995-FY1997) designed to make regulations the exception rather than the rule in the Japanese economy. The initial program targeted about 1,100 measures to be taken but was revised and increased to 2,800 by March 1997. Among other things, the program focused on strengthening the enforcement of the Anti-Monopoly Act, Japan's main authority for anti-trust activity, in order to improve efficiency and increase competitiveness in Japanese industries. In addition, the DAP would reduce barriers to entry of new firms to industries, review regulations that inflate prices of electricity and other utilities, cut consumer protection regulations and environmental regulations to "minimum required," and reduce regulations that bar entry of foreign entities into the Japanese economy. The program focused on regulations in the following areas: housing and land; information and telecommunications; distribution; standards, certification and import procedures; financial services including securities and insurance; energy; labor; and others.

---

[29] Choy, John. Bank-Rescue Legislation, Recapitalization Plan Move Quickly through Diet. *JEI Report*. October 16, 1998. 39B p. 1-3.

In 1996, the Hashimoto government raised the priority of economic restructuring. It did so by introducing a multifaceted economic reform program that included reform in administration (the government ministries and other agencies responsible for economic matters); fiscal structure (discussed above); financial system (discussed above); and education.

To date Japan has made small but noticeable progress in deregulation. More large retail stores have established a presence in Tokyo and other cities giving Japanese consumers wider choices at reduced prices. The telecommunications sector is under reorganization with the privatization and eventual breakup of Nippon Telegraph and Telephone (NTT); removal of barriers between the domestic and long-distance markets; and easing of barriers to permit more rapid introduction of new services such as cell phones. In the energy sector, price controls on gasoline and restrictions on establishing self-service stations have been lifted and the deregulation of the electricity sector is being considered.[30]

Transportation costs for freight and passengers are much higher in Japan than in other industrialized countries. Japan has heavily regulated the entry of new firms ostensibly to prevent supply capacity from getting too large. To reduce costs and improve efficiency the government has liberalized restrictions on the number of airlines and flights to introduce more competition in the industry and barriers in shipping and passage transport (trains, buses, and taxis) are being loosened. The government is taking steps to improve efficiency of land use by revising regulations on land use and housing.[31]

Legislation was passed to reorganize the government in order to reduce the number of ministries and streamline their operations, cutting costs and bureaucratic red tape. Importantly, the government has boosted resources at the Fair Trade Commission to improve enforcement of anti-competition laws and has increased penalties for violations.[32]

Although the Hashimoto and Obuchi governments have taken major steps to reform the Japanese economy (and these steps have had results), critics point out that Japan's path to economic restructuring and reform remains a long one. The OECD argues that Japan needs to accelerate the pace of reform implementation or else see popular confidence in the program erode. It also needs, according to the OECD, to expand efforts in banking, telecommunications, energy, land-use reform, taxation policy, and other areas for economic restructuring to be effective.[33] Economist Richard Katz argues that Japanese efforts to date have only skimmed the surface of what needs to be done, and that Japan needs to undertake more fundamental changes that eliminates the "dual economy," primarily by more radically reducing the

---

[30] OECD. *OECD Economic Surveys: Japan 1998*. Paris. 1998. p. 124-128..

[31] Ibid. p. 129-130.

[32] Ibid. p. 138-140.

[33] Ibid. p. 12-14.

government's role in economic decisionmaking.[34]  Economist Edward Lincoln remains skeptical that Japan can address the financial practices that got the economy in trouble in the first place.[35]

## Impact of Crisis on the U.S. Economy and the U.S. Response

As the second largest economy in the world, Japan makes an impact.  And when changes, positive or negative, occur in the Japanese economy, they can have significant effects on the rest of the world, especially smaller countries that are highly dependent on trade and foreign capital.  The United States is the largest economy in the world— twice the size of Japan— and, therefore, not as vulnerable to external economic changes as are smaller countries.   Nevertheless, Japan's economic stagnation has affected the U.S. economy, especially in foreign trade balances and investment flows.

One result of Japan's economic stagnation has been the rise in financial capital outflows from Japan.  For many years, Japan has been a net "exporter" of financial capital, a product of a high savings rate that exceeds its rate of domestic investment.  But during the recent periods of recession in Japan, the capital outflows have surged as the savings rate has remained high while the rate of growth in domestic investment has at times been negative. The United States has, for many years, been a net "importer" of financial capital, a product of a very low savings rate that is exceeded by its rate of investment.  The United States has been a major recipient of capital from Japan, especially in the last two years.  It has, therefore, experienced increasing surpluses in its bilateral capital account with Japan, much of which has been in the form of deposits by Japanese investors in U.S. banks.[36] The inflows of capital from Japan help to augment the pool of capital available to investors in the United States, putting downward pressure on U.S. interest rates.

The mirror image of the capital account in the U.S. balance of payments is the current account.  If the United States runs up surpluses on capital account, it must then run up deficits on current account.  The U.S. current account deficit with Japan soared to $64.1 billion in 1997 and probably exceeded that amount in 1998 based on preliminary data.[37]

The closely watched merchandise trade balance is a major portion of the U.S. current account balance with Japan.  U.S. merchandise trade balances with Japan have steadily deteriorated (except in 1996)  since Japan's asset bubble burst at the

---

[34] Katz, p. 13-21.

[35] Lincoln. Edward J. Japan's Financial Mess. *Foreign Affairs*. Vol. 77. no. 3.  p. 63-64.

[36] U.S. Department of Commerce.  Bureau of Economic Affairs.  *Survey of Current Business*.  January 1999.  p. 37.

[37] Ibid.

beginning of the 1990s. The U.S. merchandise trade deficit with Japan soared over 50% between 1991 and 1994, from $43.4 billion to a record $65.7 billion. From 1994 to 1996 the trade deficit with Japan declined as U.S. exports jumped 26%. But since 1996, U.S. exports to Japan have declined while U.S. imports have increased causing the deficit to increase. By the end of 1998 the deficit reached $64.1 billion.

### Table 1. U.S. Merchandise Trade with Japan, 1991-1998
($ billions)

| Year | Exports | Imports | Balances |
|------|---------|---------|----------|
| 1991 | 48.1 | 91.5 | -43.4 |
| 1992 | 47.8 | 97.4 | -49.6 |
| 1993 | 47.9 | 107.2 | -59.4 |
| 1994 | 53.5 | 119.2 | -65.7 |
| 1995 | 64.3 | 123.6 | -59.3 |
| 1996 | 67.5 | 115.2 | -47.6 |
| 1997 | 65.5 | 121.7 | -56.1 |
| 1998 | 57.9 | 122.0 | -64.1 |

Source: U.S. Department of Commerce. Bureau of the Census. Exports are total exports valued on a f.a.s. basis. Imports are general imports valued on a customs basis.

Since 1997, Japan dropped from being the second most important U.S. export market, after Canada, to the third most important (with Mexico moving up). It has remained the second most important source of imports to the United States. U.S. exporters of computers and computer components, agricultural products (such as corn and soybeans), and lumber and wood products saw their markets in Japan shrink substantially, especially in 1997 and 1998. U.S.-based car manufacturers, who were just beginning to make inroads in the Japanese market saw their exports to Japan shrink as well, albeit from a small base. Some exporters, such as producers of aircraft and parts, and integrated circuits, actually increased their business in Japan in 1997 and 1998. U.S. import levels from Japan largely remained flat in the last two years, but U.S. imports of iron and steel products from Japan increased more than 100% during the last two years.[38]

The direct impact of Japan's economic problems on the U.S. economy is at the margin at most. Indeed, while Japan has been enduring unprecedented economic stagnation during the 1990s, the United States has been experiencing robust economic growth which has also led to unexpectedly low unemployment levels with modest inflation. It can be argued that U.S. economic growth might have been somewhat

---

[38] U.S. Department of Commerce. Bureau of the Census. Data obtained from World Trade Atlas data base (CD-ROM version.)

larger if Japan had been enjoying the high growth rates of the 1980s and before; but even at that, the contribution to overall U.S. GDP would likely have been small.[39]

Nevertheless, as the second largest economy, a strong Japan makes a significant contribution to world economic growth, and its stability is critical to ensuring the stability of world financial markets and the world economy as a whole. As the world's largest creditor, Japan is the source of large volumes of financial capital to the United States and other countries, sudden withdrawals of which could have strong, adverse effects on U.S. and world financial markets. Japan is also a dominant force in the International Monetary Fund, the World Trade Organization, and other multilateral and regional economic organizations.

The United States also has a strong interest in the economic and financial stability in East Asia. The negative effects of Japan's economic problems on those countries thus indirectly affects the United States. Some observers have argued that Japan's failure to increase imports from East Asia have forced those countries to sell more in the U.S. market thus increasing U.S. trade deficits with those countries. There is not much foundation to this argument since the growth in U.S. trade deficits with those countries was primarily the result of decreased U.S. exports rather than increased U.S. imports.

Japan's poor economic performance has tended to dominate U.S.-Japan relations in the 1990s. U.S. policymakers, the business community, and the agricultural sector have been eyeing economic developments in Japan as U.S. export markets have been shrinking with the rest of the Japanese economy. They are also concerned that Japan would strive to "export" its way to recovery by maintaining a weak exchange rate to boost the price competitiveness of Japanese exports in the U.S. market. In that regard, U.S. policymakers in the executive branch, including the President, and in the Congress, have been pressing Japan to stimulate domestic demand by increasing public spending and cutting taxes and to proceed with reforming its banking sector and restructuring the rest of its economy.[40]

For many years, the United States has made restructuring and economic deregulation directly or implicitly elements of trade negotiations with Japan. U.S.

---

[39] While increasingly important trade in goods and services is still only a small part of the U.S. economy. In 1997, U.S. exports of goods and services and imports of goods and services accounted for 12% and 13% of U.S. GDP, respectively. U.S. trade with Japan in goods and services accounted for 11% and 13% of total U.S. exports and imports, respectively. CRS calculations based on data in U.S. Department of Commerce. Bureau of Economic Analysis. *Survey of Current Business.* January 1999. p. 10.

[40] For example, in a February 26, 1999 speech before the National Press Club in Tokyo, Deputy Treasury Secretary Lawrence Summers said that Japan's economic challenge is to create domestic-led economic growth by fully implementing the stimulus packages and to conduct a monetary policy that does not undermine the stimulus while also avoiding deflation. In addition he noted the importance of Japan stabilizing its banking sector, and restructuring and deregulating other parts of its economy. U.S. Department of Treasury. Office of Public Affairs. *Japan and the Global Economy: Deputy Treasury Secretary Lawrence H. Summers National Press Club Tokyo, Japan.* p. 2-4. February 26, 1999. Press Release RR-2983.

negotiators and industry representatives have long argued that government policies and regulations, by effect if not by design, protect inefficient domestic producers from foreign competition and provide Japanese exporters with an unfair advantage over competitors in the United States and other countries. Furthermore, the structure of Japanese business, especially the dominance of cross-ownership conglomerates *(keiretsu)*, their business practices, and their tolerance by the Japanese government have prevented U.S. firms from competing in Japanese markets to a degree, these firms believe, that is commensurate with their competitiveness in other markets. Deregulation, competition policy, and economic restructuring underlie many of the current bilateral sector specific trade disputes with the United States: flat glass, autos and auto parts, photographic film, and insurance.

The Reagan Administration engaged Japan in the Market-Oriented Sector-Selected (MOSS) negotiations that targeted Japanese government regulations and other impediments to imports from the United States in selected sectors. The Bush Administration negotiated with Japan under the Structural Impediments Initiative (SII), which targeted government policies and regulations and private business practices across sectors. The Clinton Administration combined the two types of negotiations under the U.S.-Japan Framework for a New Economic Partnership.

In June 1997, the United States and Japan agreed to give top priority to bilateral discussions on deregulation under another new framework, the "Enhanced Initiative on Deregulation and Competition Policy" that targets such issues in both economies. The two sides meet regularly and report annually on progress made in addressing the issues. The United States has used the "Enhanced Initiative" to defend its interests as Japan pursues deregulation and economic restructuring. U.S. negotiators want to make sure that Japan deregulates sectors of special importance to U.S. exporters and investors, such as telecommunications, housing, medical devices and pharmaceuticals, retail distribution, and legal services. The United States also has targeted reform of Japan's administrative guidance procedures (make them more transparent) and enforcement of laws against anti-competitive practices.[41]

In the latest round of negotiations, disagreements have emerged over the issue of NTT charges for interconnecting rights, that is, for access to NTT transmission lines for outside telecommunications services. The United States claims that high fees help to keep competing firms out of the market.

The Congress has had a long-standing interest in economic developments in Japan both regarding the impact of Japan on the United States and U.S. interests, and as conditions in Japan affect the regions and sectors that individual Members represent. The Congress has conveyed these interests in hearings as part of its oversight responsibilities and at times through legislation. During the 105th Congress the House passed H.Res. 392 (391-2) on July 20, 1998, and the Senate passed S. Res. 216( passed as S. Amdt. 3280 to S.2260) on July 23, 1998, demanding the U.S. Administration to press Japan toward taking measures to restructure its economy and stimulate economic growth.

---

[41] "Administrative guidance" is the practice of Japanese government ministries of advising industries they regulate on production and investment decisions.

Many members of the 106th Congress have raised concerns about the sharp increases in steel imports from Japan and other countries. On March 20, 1999, the House passed H.R. 975 that would require the President to take measures to cut imports of steel to a level that existed prior to July 1997. Similar legislation has been introduced in the Senate.

## The Outlook for the Japanese Economy

Few would deny that Japan has been and remains in a very serious economic situation. The unprecedented (for post-war Japan) poor economic growth rates, rising record unemployment rates, and the lack of business and consumer confidence paint a rather dismal picture for an economy that was the "economic miracle"for many decades. The build-up of the assets bubble in the 1980s (and its burst at the beginning of the 1990s) triggered Japan's economic problems. The sudden drop in the values of real estate, stocks, and other assets sharply cut into the wealth of Japanese and set the banking sector, suddenly holding billions of dollars in bad loans, reeling. The crisis has adversely affected the sense of well-being of the average Japanese citizen.

The near-term outlook for the Japanese economy is not promising, according to the major economic forecasters. The Japanese government's own Economic Planning Agency forecasts growth of only 0.5% GDP in Japan Fiscal Year (JFY)1999 (April 1999-March 2000).[42] The Industrial Bank of Japan (IBJ) projects a 0.6% decline during JFY 1999. [43] Sumitomo Trust forecasts a 0.9% contraction for that period.[44] In December 1998, the OECD projected a calendar year 1999 growth rate of 0.2% for Japan but revised its projection in April 1999 downward to -1.4%. The World Bank has projected a 0.9% decline for calendar year 1999.[45]

If many observers agree that Japan's economic situation remains serious they disagree on the fundamental causes, and therefore on the solution. The debate pits those who argue that fiscal stimulus and/or monetary stimulus will unleash economic growth against those who argue that such macroeconomic measures will provide a short-term spurt at best unless Japan undertakes fundamental structural changes.

Determining which school of thought is correct is a task beyond the scope of this report. Nevertheless, based on Japan's experience in the 1990s, one can conclude that Japan's road to recovery depends on a proper balance between macroeconomic policies and economic restructuring. The rise in the asset bubble and its burst resulted from structural problems within the banking sector. Confidence within that sector will have to be rebuilt if it is to exercise its important role as a financial intermediary in the Japanese economy. Japan can also realize important productivity gains which would contribute to economic growth if it pursues deregulation and restructuring in other

---

[42] Economic Planning Agency. Coordination Bureau. *The Japanese Economy: Recent Trends and Outlook— 1999*. Tokyo. February 1999. p. 15.

[43] *The Daily Japan Digest*. April 9, 1999. p. 1.

[44] *The Daily Japan Digest*. April 13, 1999.

[45] *The Daily Japan Digest*. April 8, 1999.

important sectors. At the same time, as Japan's experience in 1996-97 proved (when economic recovery was truncated by a premature tightening of monetary policy and increase in taxes), if the government does not conduct the correct fiscal and monetary policies, economic growth can be prematurely aborted.

In pursuing macroeconomic stimulus, the Japanese government is constrained by the limitations of its revenues and of its ability and willingness to borrow to finance deficits. It is constrained in pursuing deregulation and restructuring by the ability and willingness of policymakers to confront the various interest groups within the bureaucracy and elsewhere that have had a vested stake in the status quo.

Japan's efforts in the last few years indicate that, at least on the surface, Japanese policymakers are convinced that they have attained the political will to overcome obstacles to reform of the Japanese economy. Prime Minister Obuchi affirmed such an understanding in a recent statement:

> The systems and processes that made us so successful in the past no longer work. They have become heavy shackles that hold us down. It is not easy to abandon the formula for previous successes. Yet we realize that unless we adopt a more flexible economy driven by the market, Japan is doomed to economic and technological decline.[46]

Skeptics might argue that the world has heard these or similar words from previous Japanese leaders who later failed to put them into practice. Optimists might cite the poor economic situation that Japan finds itself in and conclude that it will force to Japan to act.

## Implications and Policy Options for the United States

U.S. economic policy toward Japan has reflected a broad range of U.S. national interests and pressures, and U.S. policy will have to continue to reflect those interests if it is to be effective. These interests include those in the American business community and agriculture that are looking for unfettered access to markets and strong Japanese demand for their exports and investments as well as those who are wary of competition from Japanese production. Beyond the specific interests of individual sectors are the overall interests of the United States in a robust and stable Japanese economy.

Japan is the largest economy in East Asia where it accounts for roughly 2/3 of GDP of the region. Japan serves as a model for economies in transition, such as China and Vietnam, and is critical as an engine of economic growth in the region, especially as a number of the economies are trying to emerge from the currency crisis.

In the foreign policy and national security area, Japan is an important world partner and chief ally in Asia. The two countries face the mutual threat of an unstable

---

[46] Obuchi, Keizo. Japan's Quiet Reforms. *The New York Times*. April 29, 1999. p. A29

North Korea and also the challenge of how to manage relations with a rapidly emerging China. A strong and robust Japan is vital to fulfilling its role as a partner of the United States in meeting these foreign policy challenges.

But as important as Japan's economy is to the United States, the direct policy influence the United States can have on the Japanese economy is limited at best. The United States could promote economic growth in Japan by selling yen for dollars or by boosting U.S. interest rates to drive down the value of the yen. A more expensive dollar/cheaper yen would make Japanese exports cheaper and would increase Japanese exports to the United States, all other factors remaining the same. But such a policy option would present other problems for the United States: Increased imports from Japan would increase the U.S. trade deficit, which could prove politically sensitive especially with those sectors of the U.S. economy feeling the increased competition from Japanese imports. Furthermore, higher interest rates would slow down U.S. economic growth.

National sovereignty restricts the influence the United States can exert in shaping Japanese economic policy, although outside pressure has often raised the consciousness in Japan with respect to a problem and can speed up decisionmaking. Decisions on macroeconomic policy and economic reform are within the purview of the Japanese government, and policymakers will undertake them within the context of what they perceive to be Japan's national interests.

But those limitations have not prevented the United States from defending its interests and pressuring Japan to move forward with deregulation and economic stimulation. The United States will likely continue to do so in bilateral negotiations on sector specific issues and on the broader issues of foreign investment and deregulation. The United States also will likely continue to work with Japan on such issues in multilateral fora, such as the World Trade Organization (WTO), and the Organization for Economic Cooperation and Development (OECD). An effective U.S. approach in these negotiations would underscore the mutual benefits to both countries of Japan following U.S. suggestions.

In the long term, if successful, Japan's efforts to overcome its economic difficulties might present the United States with significant opportunities. Many of the structural problems that some experts have cited have also been impediments to U.S. exports and investments in Japan and the source of much friction between the two countries. If Japan can successfully address these structural problems, it would likely improve market access in Japan and help alleviate the bilateral trade and investment friction. In the nearer term, the best U.S. defense against continued economic stagnation in Japan will be maintaining U.S. economic strength.

# JAPAN'S CHANGING SECURITY OUTLOOK[*]

*Richard P. Cronin*

## Introduction

Changes in Japan's security environment during the late 1990s have prompted a perceptible shift in the outlook of Japanese officials, legislators, the media, and the general public regarding defense issues. The main sources of concern are North Korea's ballistic missile programs, China's rising military power and regional influence, and the spread of nuclear weapons. Thus far, the Japanese response has been cautious and limited, with continuing deference to the anti-military provisions of the post-World War II "peace" constitution and in close cooperation with the United States. Within the past two years, however, movement towards a more assertive security posture appears to have gained momentum. For the time being these shifts appear likely to enhance rather than detract from U.S.-Japan defense cooperation, but certain aspects of these indicators of new thinking about security issues could have significant negative consequences for U.S. regional security interests if not handled adroitly both in Washington and Tokyo.

## Congressional Interest and Role

U.S.-Japan security relations are of concern mainly to Members and Committees with responsibilities or interests related to North Korean nuclear and missile proliferation issues, China's potential emergence as a military adversary, and/or U.S. military readiness. U.S.-Japan security issues normally generate little legislative impact, but Congress periodically holds hearings and occasionally expresses its views on U.S.-Japan issues in the form of resolutions and committee report language. Members of Congress regularly interact with Diet Members in legislative exchanges. In the course of these discussions Members have been exposed to subtle, but nonetheless significant, changes in Japan's security outlook since the end of the Cold War. The U.S. public and even some U.S. legislators and Executive branch officials may be formulating their views on the basis of assumptions that are of decreasing validity in the new regional security environment in the Asia-Pacific region.

Congressional concerns about U.S. military readiness arising out of the NATO air campaign in the former Yugoslavia, as well as concerns about the leakage of sensitive nuclear and other information and technology to China as a result of that country's apparent espionage activities in the United States, would appear to raise the level of importance of the multifaceted alliance between the world's two largest and most technologically advanced economies, and the first and, arguably, the second

[*] Excerpted from *CRS Report for Congress* RL30256

most potent military powers in the western Pacific. This report explains and analyzes the reasons for Japan's changing security outlook, its response to date to new threat concerns, and the implications for U.S. regional security interests.

# Sources of Japan's Growing Sense of Insecurity

The end of the Cold War has not brought the benefits for Japan's security environment that its leaders and many analysts anticipated. On the contrary, the sharp decline in the threat previously posed by the ballistic missiles and naval and air forces of the former Soviet Union has been replaced by a number of new and more complex security challenges. Although these threats are perhaps of a lower magnitude than the previous risk of becoming the object of Soviet aggression or a target in a U.S.-Soviet nuclear exchange, in some ways they appear to have a higher probability of actually materializing. Moreover, the new sources of potential threat have emerged at a time when Japan's national self-confidence has been shaken as a result nearly a decade of economic stagnation, a highly fluid political situation, and an inadequate institutional structure for crisis management and strategy formulation.

## Regional Sources of Security Concern

The primary sources of Japanese concern include the emergence of a North Korean nuclear and ballistic missile threat, the rise of China's economic and military power and related concerns that Beijing may have hegemonic designs, and the persistence of long-standing territorial disputes with China, South Korea, and Russia. The Asian financial crisis that began in July 1997 also has created rising anxieties about regional stability. The political turmoil in Indonesia and other Southeast Asian countries directly and indirectly threatens a number of Japanese economic, political, and financial interests. These include a serious increase in piracy in principal shipping routes such

**Figure 1. Japan and East Asia**

Adapted by CRS from Magellan Geographix. Used with permission.

as the Straits of Malacca and in the South China Sea. The Asian financial crisis has also seriously weakened the Association of Southeast Asian Nations (ASEAN), an important regional dialogue partner.[1]

**Growing Concern About North Korea.** Concern about an emerging missile threat from North Korea arguably has had more impact on in Japan's changing security outlook than any other factor. Pyongyang's launch of a three-stage version of its medium-range (4-6,000 km) *Taepodong-2* missile (English transliteration varies) at the end of August 1999, which passed over the main Japanese island of Honshu, created consternation within the government and deeply affected Japanese public opinion. The intrusion into Japanese territorial waters of two specially equipped North Korean spy ships in March 1999, caused further deep concern in Japan and affected the overall level of public support for beefing up Japanese security.[2] In early and mid-July 1999, the government of Prime Minister Keizo Obuchi issued several stern warnings to North Korea about the political and economic consequences should it launch another *Taepodong-2* missile.

**Concerns About a Rising China.** Japan has long had a complex relationship of cooperation and rivalry with China. Beginning about the mid-1990s, as China's economy continued to generate strong growth and its military modernization program proceeded, China began increasingly to appear to present potential hazzards to Japanese interests. Japanese officials, analysts, and legislators readily admit in private their worries that China aspires to future regional hegemony. Meanwhile, the benefits of Japanese business investment in China and official loans and grants averaging about $1 billion a year, have not been realized as fully as had been expected. Significantly, while Japan continues to cultivate good relations and economic cooperation, it gives every indication of intent to resist China's bid for regional dominance, should it occur. Thus while Japan supports China's desire to play a larger international role and welcomes its participation in Asian regional organizations, Japanese officials do not shrink from criticizing China or resisting diplomatic pressures on issues such as U.S.-Japan security cooperation or Taiwan. (See section on "The Burden of History",

---

[1] In addition to the sources cited below, this report incorporates the findings of three separate research trips to Japan since November 1996, including a visit to Okinawa in August-September 1998, and numerous other exchanges with Japanese officials, political leaders, and academic analysts in Washington. The author most recently conducted interviews in Tokyo with U.S. and Japanese officials, Diet (parliament) Members, and academic defense and foreign policy analysts in late March 1999. The analysis below reflects a gradual, but clearly perceptible, evolution of Japan's security outlook in the direction of greater security consciousness and activism.

[2] From December 1995 to March 1999, according to a poll conducted for the U.S. Information Service, public identification of North Korea as a potential threat to regional peace and Japan's security rose from 23 percent to 44 percent. Moreover, this shift was not just a reaction to recent developments, but rather a steady upward trend throughout eight polling samples. Concern about China as a threat to peace dropped from 19 percent to 9 percent during the same period, but varied widely over the eight samples. Also, respondents were split about 38-36 on the question of whether China was a peaceful power or an expansionist one, with 36 percent choosing the former description and 38 percent the latter. USIA *Opinion Analysis*, Office of Research and Media Reaction (M-77-99), April 30, 1999.

below.)  This represents a significant change from Japan's position in the 1980s and
early 1990s.

During a July 1999 visit to Beijing, Prime Minister Obuchi attempted, reportedly
with less than complete success, to put Sino-Japanese relations on a more even keel.
Although the countries reached a bilateral accord on the terms for China's entry into
the World Trade Organization (WTO), making Japan the first major country to do so,
the official Chinese media continued to criticize the revised U.S.-Japan defense
cooperation guidelines and sought to put Japan on the defensive over the U.S.
bombing of China's embassy in Belgrade.

**Territorial Disputes.**  Regional tensions have been kept alive by the existence
of direct conflicts of national interest, such as rival claims to island groups in the Sea
of Japan on the part of Japan and China, Taiwan, South Korea, and Russia.  During
the past several years Japan's  maritime safety agency and self-defense forces have
engaged in symbolic deployments to defend claims in the Sea of Japan against China
in regard to the small island groups known respectively by Japan as the Senkakus and
by China as the Diaoyous,  and vis-a-vis South Korea in regard to the islands known
respectively as the Takshima and Tokdo group.[3]  These conflicting claims have
important implications for fishing and underseas resources access.  Incidents arising
out of the disputes have contributed to the rise of  nationalistic sentiment among the
Japanese public.

Efforts to resolve these disputes have not succeeded, but neither have the
concerned governments shown any desire to escalate them.   The Japanese and South
Korean governments reached an agreement on fishing rights prior to the October
1998 visit to Tokyo by President Kim Dae Jung, but the negotiators put off any effort
to resolve the larger issue of sovereignty.  No progress has been made on the dispute
with China, which also involves overlapping claims by Taiwan.  Japanese efforts to
achieve a breakthrough with Russia on the competing claims to what Japan calls its
"Northern Territories" — four small islands in the Kuriles group that Japan acquired
by treaty from pre-revolutionary Russia in the late 19th century but were seized by the
former USSR in the closing days of World War II — also have failed thus far.

**The Burden of History.**   These concrete sources of friction have been
exacerbated by the legacy of Japan's past aggression against its Asian neighbors.  The
Japanese public has responded with increasing irritation at what is seen as excessive
harping on Japan's wartime role by China, both Koreas, and, occasionally, other Asian
neighbors.  Successive governments have tried to put the issue to rest, but it has been
kept alive by the provocative remarks of a small, but highly vocal group of ultra-
nationalist politicians who periodically inflame relations with China and other Asian
countries by denying even the most basic historical facts of Japan's wartime
depredations, such as atrocities against civilians committed by the Japanese army in

---

[3] For background see Senkaku (Diaoyu) Islands dispute: the U.S. legal relationship and
obligations. CRS Report No. 96-798, Sept. 30, 1995 [by Larry A. Niksch.]

Nanking, China, at the start of the Sino-Japanese war in 1937, widely known as the "Rape of Nanking".[4]

In general, the Japanese public tends to regard the ultra-nationalists with disdain, but not so much as to make them unelectable. Over the years a number of senior LDP figures have had to resign cabinet posts for denying the historical record and seeking to justify Japanese imperialism as a legitimate action to "liberate" Asian countries from western colonial rule. These recalcitrant ultra-nationalists are a source of continuing embarrassment to the Japanese government, if not to the LDP.

Partly because details of Japan's wartime role largely remain tabu subjects in schools and the media, younger Japanese especially find it hard to understand why their neighbors continue to belabor matters that are half a century old. They also suspect, not without some grounds, that some of these criticisms by Asian neighbors, especially China and North Korea, are designed put Japan on the defensive in order to extract benefits such as development loans, in the case of China, or reparations, in the case of North Korea, or to deter the expansion of Japan's regional security role.

In late 1998 the issue of Japan's past aggression on the Korean Peninsula was put to rest, at least at the official level, between Japan and South Korea, but if anything it has become a larger factor in Sino-Japanese relations. In the case of South Korea, part of Japan's empire between 1910 and 1945, the willingness of President Kim Dae Jung to shelve the issue during an October 1998 visit to Tokyo was reciprocated by the Liberal Democratic Party (LDP)government of Prime Minister Keizo Obuchi. In the joint communique Obuchi gave the first ever written apology for Japan's past treatment of Korea.[5] A subsequent November 1998 visit to Japan by Chinese President Jiang Zemin went badly, however, due to the Japanese government's refusal to accommodate China's demand that it provide the same written apology in the wording of the joint Obuchi-Jiang declaration and publicly support the Chinese formulation on the Taiwan issue. The Japanese government refused to go beyond past expressions of "remorse" and, unlike President Clinton's statement in Shanghai in June 1998, Prime Minister Obuchi also declined to declare formally Japan's opposition to Taiwan's membership in the United Nations and other bodies for which statehood was a prerequisite. Jiang, in return, spent a good part of his visit venting harsh criticism of Japan for being insufficiently contrite about the war and taking an anti-Chinese position on the Taiwan issue.[6]

---

[4] This incident has been well documented in photographic and written records, including pictures of Japanese imperial troops bayoneting and beheading civilians. One of the most noteworthy recent books is The Rape of Nanking: the Forgotten Holocaust of World War II, by Iris Chang. New York, NY : Basic Books, 1997.

[5] In the past various leaders, the Diet (parliament) and even the Emperor have made various oral and written expressions of "regret" for what Japan inflicted on its neighbors, but until Obuchi's statement they had steadfastly avoided the word "apology" (or its Japanese equivalent).

[6] Peter Landers with Susan V. Lawrence, Sorry, No Apology. *Far Eastern Economic Review* (FEER), Dec. 10, 1998: 21. For background on the controversy over President Clinton's Shanghai remarks, see CRS Report 98-837 F (Oct. 1, 1998), Taiwan and the "Three

(continued...)

## Doubts About Japan's Place in U.S. Asian Strategy

In the eyes of some Japanese policymakers, non-official analysts, and media commentators, adverse trends in Japan's immediate security environment have been matched by concerns that U.S. regional interests are either shifting or weakening. Notwithstanding an April 1996 joint affirmation of intent to revitalize the U.S.-Japan alliance to meet the needs of the 21st Century, during the visit to Washington of then-Prime Minister Ryutaro Hashimoto, some Japanese analysts and policymakers appear concerned that at some point in the future the U.S.-Japan alliance may no longer suffice to protect Japanese security.

**Double-Edged Concerns About U.S. Policy Toward China.** Concerns about U.S. policy toward China have been a particular cause of Japanese uneasiness. These concerns are double-edged; Japan worries when Washington appears to give paramountcy to U.S. relations with China, and also when U.S.-China relations deteriorate to the point of complicating Tokyo's own relations with Beijing. Before the downward spiral in U.S.-China ties that began in late 1998, and intensified with the May 1999 accidental bombing of China's embassy in Belgrade, some Japanese leaders and analysts had criticized what they saw as an increasing U.S. tendency towards "passing" Japan in the interest of consolidating a new strategic relationship with China. Concern that China aspires to regional hegemony reportedly even had prompted some Japanese foreign ministry officials to hope that Chinese President Zhu Rongji's April 1999 visit to the United States would not go well. The *Asahi Shimbun*, a major national daily with a tendency to criticize the government, reported in early April 1999 that "a number of Ministry of Foreign Affairs (MOFA) officials welcome China's current troubles in its foreign policy toward the U.S." The article explained that these hopes were driven by "a sense of antagonism toward China, which is growing into a major power, and a feeling of antipathy toward a country [China] that continues to give 'advice' to Japan on historical views and the like."[7]

In the near term, Japan's concerns both about U.S. steadfastness regarding alliance issues and a "tilt" towards China would appear to have lessened as a result of Prime Minister Obuchi's May 1999 state visit to Washington, and the ongoing fallout from the accidental bombing of China's embassy in Belgrade, later the same month. The latter incident, however, has created a new set of diplomatic problems for Japan, that of balancing two different but important relationships. Japan and China reached agreement on terms for Beijing's admission into the WTO during a visit by Prime Minister Obuchi in early July, 1999, potentially creating another complication in U.S.-Japan-China relations, since Tokyo's conditions are less stringent than those being sought by the United States.

At the end of the day, no matter how Japanese policymakers may finesse the search for balance, they still face the reality of an increasingly powerful and assertive neighbor, and heavy dependance on a security partner with global interests and

---

[6](...continued)
No's," Congressional-Administration Differences, and U.S. Policy Issues. [by Robert Sutter.]

[7] *Asahi Shimbun* (Tokyo), April 10, 1999: 2.

distractions. How to deal with this situation remains a matter of great controversy. Some call for drawing closer to the United States while also hedging against a possible future weakening of US. support by developing a parallel, autonomous, military capability. Others who support the alliance, but downplay the threats posed by North Korea and China, have called for the reduction or elimination of U.S. bases and the significant reduction or phasing out of the 43,000 or so U.S. military personnel stationed in Japan.[8]

**Impatience with U.S. Trade Demands and Unsolicited Economic Advice.** On a more narrow plane, the Japanese public and Japanese political leaders have shown increasing impatience over trade policy criticism from the United States. Japanese analysts, officials, and commentators, as well as some American specialists, see the customary U.S. tendency to pressure Japan on trade issues while taking its support for granted on international political and security issues, as more pronounced under the Clinton Administration. The U.S. criticism rankles all the more because of the apparent failure of Japanese-style government-led economic management to adjust adequately to economic globalization, and the reality that many sectors of the Japanese economy would be uncompetitive without various forms of direct and indirect protection from global market forces. Japan's trade surpluses have continued to mount in recent years, but mainly because of a fall in imports, not an expansion of exports. Japan also is continuing to struggle with the consequences of a massive overhang of corporate debt as a result of the collapse of its late 1980's economic "bubble."

Resistance to unwanted advice and pressure on trade and economic issues has grown stronger as Japan's ability to take decisive actions has been undercut by the realities of coalition politics, and its pride has been wounded by the failure to regain a growth path after nearly ten years of economic stagnation. Unsolicited advice from Clinton Administration policymakers on how Japan should boost its economy has been particularly resented, even by some who agree that the advice itself is sound.[9]

**Resentment of Perceived American Unilateralist Tendencies.** Even on issues in which the United States and Japan share similar goals, as in the case of U.S. policy towards North Korea, Japanese analysts, commentators, and policymakers also

---

[8] See, for instance, former coalition prime minister Morihiro Hosokawa's article "Are U.S. Troops in Japan Needed?", in *Foreign Affairs*, July/August 1998: 2-5. Hosokawa supports a gradual cutback in U.S. forces based in Japan and their eventual withdrawal, but continued dependance on the U.S. nuclear umbrella. The leader of the opposition Democratic Party, Naoto Kan, has taken a similar position, as has Koichi Kato, a mainstream LDP leader currently a rival of Prime Minister Obuchi for the presidency of the party and, hence, the prime ministership.

[9] A late 1998 poll commissioned by the U.S. Information Agency found that 54 percent of the respondents agreed with the statement "while the U.S. economic advice may be good, its tone is high-handed and irritating." Only 23 percent agreed that "the U.S. talks to Japan as a friend and equal when it provides economic advice." Slightly over half of the respondents (51 percent) also agreed with the statement "the U.S. is pressuring Japan only because it benefits America to have a weak Japan," and only 27 percent disagreed. USIA, Office of Research and Media Reaction, *Briefing Paper* (B-121-98), Nov. 16, 1998, p. 1.

are troubled by what they perceive as an American tendency to act unilaterally on regional issues without sufficient regard for Japanese perspectives and concerns, or that undercut Japan's own policies. For instance, despite claims to the contrary by U.S. officials, Japanese policymakers often complain that the Administration has not adequately consulted them about its policies towards North Korea, even as it expects Japan to shoulder about $1 billion of the cost of constructing two light water reactors for Pyongyang under the U.S.-DPRK Agreed Framework of October 1994. Intellectually, Japanese officials may understand why, for instance, Japan has been excluded from the so-called "Four Party" talks involving the United States, the two Koreas, and China. Viscerally, they nonetheless still resent being left out, especially since this seems, in their view, to play into North Korean regime's strategy of making engagement with the United States the main pillar of its survival.[10]

Among recent concerns, Japanese officials have complained privately that they regarded the U.S. reaction to North Korea's August 31, 1999, missile launch as disconcertingly mild. Japanese officials reportedly were angered by learning, just ten days after Pyongyang's provocative missile launch over Japanese territory — an event that created a major media and political tempest — that the Clinton Administration would supply North Korea with 300,000 tons of food grain, ostensibly as a humanitarian action unrelated to other issues. The U.S. announcement followed the successful conclusion of U.S. negotiations with North Korea to get that country to agree to resume the "canning" of spent nuclear fuel, as provided for under the October 1994 U.S.-North Korea Agreed Framework. Although the Administration defended its action as a humanitarian response to a UN appeal whose timing was dictated by the desire to obligate funds before the end of the fiscal year on September 30, the Japanese Government and other critics saw the announcement as sending the wrong signal to Pyongyang. [11]

This and other U.S. actions reportedly have caused Japanese officials to worry that the United States might negotiate an agreement with North Korea concerning its missile program that addresses only its *exports* of missiles, and not the development and testing of missiles capable of hitting Japan.[12] As a reflection of its concerns that the United States gives inadequate attention to Japanese positions on Korean Peninsula issues, the Japanese government has proposed expanding the current Four Party talks to include both Japan and Russia.

U.S. military involvement in the former Yugoslavia also has reinforced Japanese concerns about a perceived American tendency towards unilateralism. While the

---

[10] This assessment is based on numerous conversations with relevant Japanese and U.S. officials both in Washington and Tokyo beginning in late 1996 and continuing as recently as May 1999, and is also validated by frequent Japanese press commentary along these lines. Generally, U.S. officials reject the validity of the complaint, asserting that they maintain close and frequent consultation and take Japanese views and interests into consideration, and argue that including Japan is not possible due to strong North Korean objections.

[11] David E. Sanger, U.S. to Send North Korea Food Despite Missile Launching. *New York Times*, Sept. 10, 1998: A3.

[12] Japan to Ask US for clear Policy on DPRK Missiles. *Tokyo Kyodo News Service* in English, Jan. 22, 1999.

Japanese government has expressed "understanding"of the reasons for the U.S./NATO policy towards Belgrade, and has committed Japan to aiding the region's postwar rebuilding, it also has expressed concern about what is viewed as a lack of an adequate basis for military involvement under international law such as a UN resolution. Perhaps more to the point, Japanese officials were "dismayed" by the bombing of the Chinese embassy in Belgrade by U.S./NATO aircraft, despite American insistence that it was accidental, and regarded the growing strains in U.S. China relations as "undesirable for the security of Japan."[13]

### Challenges to Japan's Standing in Asia

Concerns about being taken for granted by the United States have been reinforced by the reality that in its own "backyard" — Southeast Asia — Japan's standing and ability to influence events have deteriorated as a result of the Asian financial crisis and its aftermath. Japan has earned some credit from its neighbors for its efforts to ameliorate the regional economic and financial crisis by granting aid and massive export credits. As of early 1999 announcements of aid to the crisis countries totaled $80 billion, according to the Ministry of Foreign Affairs, including a $30 billion package for Southeast Asia. Both Japan and its neighbors understand, however, that these governmental measures do not begin to compensate for the drag imposed by Japan's economic weakness and the withdrawal of capital by hard pressed Japanese banks. Moreover, a significant proportion of the loans and export credits benefits Japanese joint venture manufacturing firms in Southeast Asia, either directly or indirectly. Thus, instead of engaging with the United States and Europe as the "core economy" and de facto leader of the East Asian region, as it aspired to do in the early 1990's, Japan now faces American and European pressure to stimulate its economy and calls from Asian countries to increase its imports of their products.

# Changing Japanese Attitudes Towards Security Issues and the U.S.-Japan Security Alliance

Taken together, concern about regional threats to Japan's security, worries about Japan's place in U.S. strategy, and anxiousness about recent blows to its regional standing, have generated mixed reaction in Japan, including a small and gradual shift towards more assertive nationalism. At present, the trend has cross-cutting, but generally favorable implications for U.S. security interests. The United States is always overwhelmingly named the "most friendly" country in public opinion polls, and about three-fourths of the Japanese people express support for the U.S.-Japan security alliance and expect it to continue for at least the next five to ten years. At the same time, the Japanese people, and to a certain extent Japanese officialdom, appear to believe that the United States is less friendly to Japan than in the past. [14]

---

[13] *Yomiuri Shimbun* (Tokyo) report quoted by the *Japan Digest*, May 11, 1999: 1.

[14] USIA, Japan Public's Views on the U.S. Economy, U.S. Relations. *Briefing Paper* (B-30-99), April 8, 1999.

## Initiatives to Strengthen U.S.-Japan Security Cooperation

Japan's first response to its new security environment was to draw closer to the United States. A series of incidents, beginning with the 1994 confrontation over North Korea's nuclear program, underscored to both Japanese and American planners and policymakers that the U.S. forward military presence in Asia remained crucial to the region's stability, and that the U.S.-Japan alliance was critical to that role. Beginning about mid-1994 U.S. and Japanese officials began to take a closer look at the practical realities with regard to U.S. logistical capabilities and Japan's ability to make up for capacity that has been lost in the post-Cold War draw-down of American forces and the competition for resources vis-a-vis other competing priorities.

**Revised U.S.-Japan Defense Cooperation Guidelines.** The centerpiece of recent efforts to enhance U.S.-Japan defense cooperation is a September 24, 1997, agreement that revises a more limited set of defense cooperation guidelines that had been agreed to in 1978. The previous guidelines had been drawn up at a time when the main consideration was increasing the effectiveness of the combined military forces to defend the Japanese islands, the U.S. bases located thereon, and air and sea approaches to Japan from a Soviet attack. The commitment of both governments to revise the guidelines — as affirmed during an April 1996 summit meeting between President Clinton and then-Prime Minister Ryutaro Hashimoto — served to symbolize the changed security situation in Asia after the end of the Cold War.

The new defense cooperation guidelines cover three situations:

**(1) "Cooperation under normal circumstances,"** including expanded information sharing, policy consultations, cooperation in multilateral security dialogues and regional defense exchanges, and cooperation in support of U.N. peacekeeping activities and humanitarian relief;

**(2) "Actions in response to an armed attack against Japan,"** including a series of steps to respond when an attack on Japan is imminent, and when an armed attack takes place; and;

**(3) "Cooperation in situations in areas surrounding Japan that will have an important influence on Japan's peace and security (situations in areas surrounding Japan)."**

The third situation, the most significant and most controversial change to the existing defense cooperation guidelines, would — if the necessary enabling legislation was adopted by the Japanese Diet — provide for cooperation to meet a range of possible regional contingency situations. Although Japanese forces would still be prevented from participating in combat operations in support of U.S. forces engaged in a regional conflict, the new guidelines greatly expanded the types of non-lethal supplies and logistical support that the Japanese military could provide to U.S. forces in the event of a regional conflict. As drafted by Japanese and American officials, Japanese forces could conduct search and rescue operations in areas surrounding Japan, the Japanese government could allow U.S. forces to use Japanese military and civilian airfields, and Japanese forces could resupply U.S. vessels at sea (except for weapons and ammunition) and conduct operations to clear mines from high seas shipping routes (but not from other countries' territorial waters.)

***Japanese Government Motivations.*** Among other troubling factors motivating the bureaucrats of the Ministry of Foreign Affairs (MOFA), was the realization that had the mid-1994 confrontation with North Korea led to a war, the Japanese SDF, Defense Agency, and relevant civil ministries would have lacked the clear legal authority to provide vital logistical support to U.S. forces. Japanese officials were particularly mindful of the political fallout that resulted from Japan's inability to materially support allied forces in the 1990 Operation Desert Storm war against Iraq. In that conflict, the Japanese government came under strong criticism from Congress and the American public for rebuffing — on constitutional grounds — U.S. requests for material assistance.[15] Japan's contribution of $13 billion to support the U.S.-led effort to drive Iraqi forces out of Kuwait was not viewed in the United States as fully compensating for the failure to put people — even civilian aid workers — on the ground, or to carry out medical and refugee airlift assignments.

Although the U.S.-North Korea confrontation was eased by the October 1994 U.S.-DPRK Agreed Framework, both the relevant American and Japanese officials felt an urgent the need to address the issue before any new crisis arose. This concern caused MOFA to initiate a broad review of the legal and bureaucratic obstacles to providing a timely and effective response to a Korean Peninsula contingency. MOFA officials were particularly concerned that the failure of Japan to provide direct assistance when Americans troops were spilling blood in Korea would shatter the alliance — and with it — the main pillar of Japanese security policy. [16]

Other motivations appear to have included the desire of the Defense Agency and the military hierarchy to gain greater operational latitude and enhance their status in a society that still holds strongly anti-military feelings stemming from the memory of pre-World War II and wartime militarism. Many Japanese officials, nationalist-minded politicians, and commentators, also began to argue that the emerging post-Cold War security environment required an upgrading of the government's ability for crisis management. The governmental structure developed during the Occupation era gives great power to the individual ministries and their civil service bureaucrats, and little coordinating or crisis response authority to the Prime Minister and Cabinet. The latter concern was driven home by the Kobe earthquake of January 1995, when a lack of coordination kept the ground self-defense forces from providing timely assistance to the civil authorities.

---

[15] Although some Japanese political leaders, most prominently Ichiro Ozawa, urged the government to respond to a U.S. request that Japan send minesweepers and other material assistance, the Government of Prime Minister Kiichi Miyazawa concluded that the constitutional ban on collective security prevented even the sending of military aircraft for refugee evacuation.

[16] This assessment is partly based on interviews with U.S. Embassy and Japanese Ministry of Foreign Affairs officials during the author's visit to Tokyo in December 1996.

## Continuing Opposition To U.S. Bases

At least until the emergence of major public concerns about the security threat from North Korea, nationalistic feelings also seemed to lie behind hardening attitudes regarding U.S. bases in Japan. Although the Japanese public supports the U.S.-Japan alliance by a large margin, a substantial part of the public has suspicions about the purposes of U.S. bases and only a bare majority supports the U.S. military presence. A survey of 3,000 Japanese voters conducted by the *Asahi Shimbun* in mid-March 1999, and parallel polling by the Gallup organization in the United States, showed, among other findings, that only 31 percent of the Japanese public believe that the purpose of U.S. troops in Japan is to defend Japan, while 38 percent think the troops are there to support U.S. global strategy and 19 percent think their purpose is to prevent Japan from turning into a military power.[17] The same *Asahi Shimbun* poll found that only 28 percent of the Japanese respondents thought the current scale of the U.S. military presence was "good" while 63 percent thought that the U.S. presence should be scaled down.

Considered from the baseline of a peak in anti-bases sentiment after the September 1995 abduction and rape of a 13 year-old schoolgirl by three U.S. servicemen, an incident that outraged the Japanese public, the strength of the opposition to the U.S. military presence actually appears to have declined somewhat. An *Asahi* poll conducted in October 1995 found 73 percent favoring reductions in the U.S. base structure, whereas a Spring 1996 survey found that 67 percent favored reductions in the U.S. military presence. [18] The decline from the September 1995 peak seems unlikely to represent a favorable long-term trend, however, but rather a partial recovery of public support as the impact of the rape incident has dissipated with the passage of time. U.S. and Japanese defense and foreign policy officials readily acknowledge their fear for the political consequences of a major air accident or high profile criminal incident involving U.S. military personnel or dependents.[19]

Perhaps more significant, the number of mainstream politicians who call for the reduction and eventual phasing out of U.S. bases has grown in recent years. Political leaders from all parties except the Communists now support the alliance, but the Democratic Party (DP), the second largest after the LDP, calls for a reduction or phasing out of the U.S. military presence, as do a number of other members, including some in the ruling LDP. Moreover, because of the DP's tepid stance on this issue and its low standing in the polls, the party may be tempted to seek to build its popularity and position itself as the organizing center of a non-LDP coalition on the basis of a strong platform emphasizing the need to reduce the U.S. military presence in Japan.

---

[17] Extracts from the *Asahi Shimbun*, April 13, 1999. P. 14.

[18] *The Japan Digest*, May 16, 1996: 2.

[19] This assessment is based on interviews with U.S. and Japanese officials, and pro-bases civilians, in Okinawa and Tokyo during late August and early September, 1998, and similar interviews in Tokyo in March 1999.

**Figure 2.  Principal U.S. Forces and Bases in Japan (Except Okinawa)**
(Data Source: Defense of Japan, 1997)
*Note: Since this chart was prepared the USS Independence CVBG
has been replaced by the USS Kitty Hawk.*

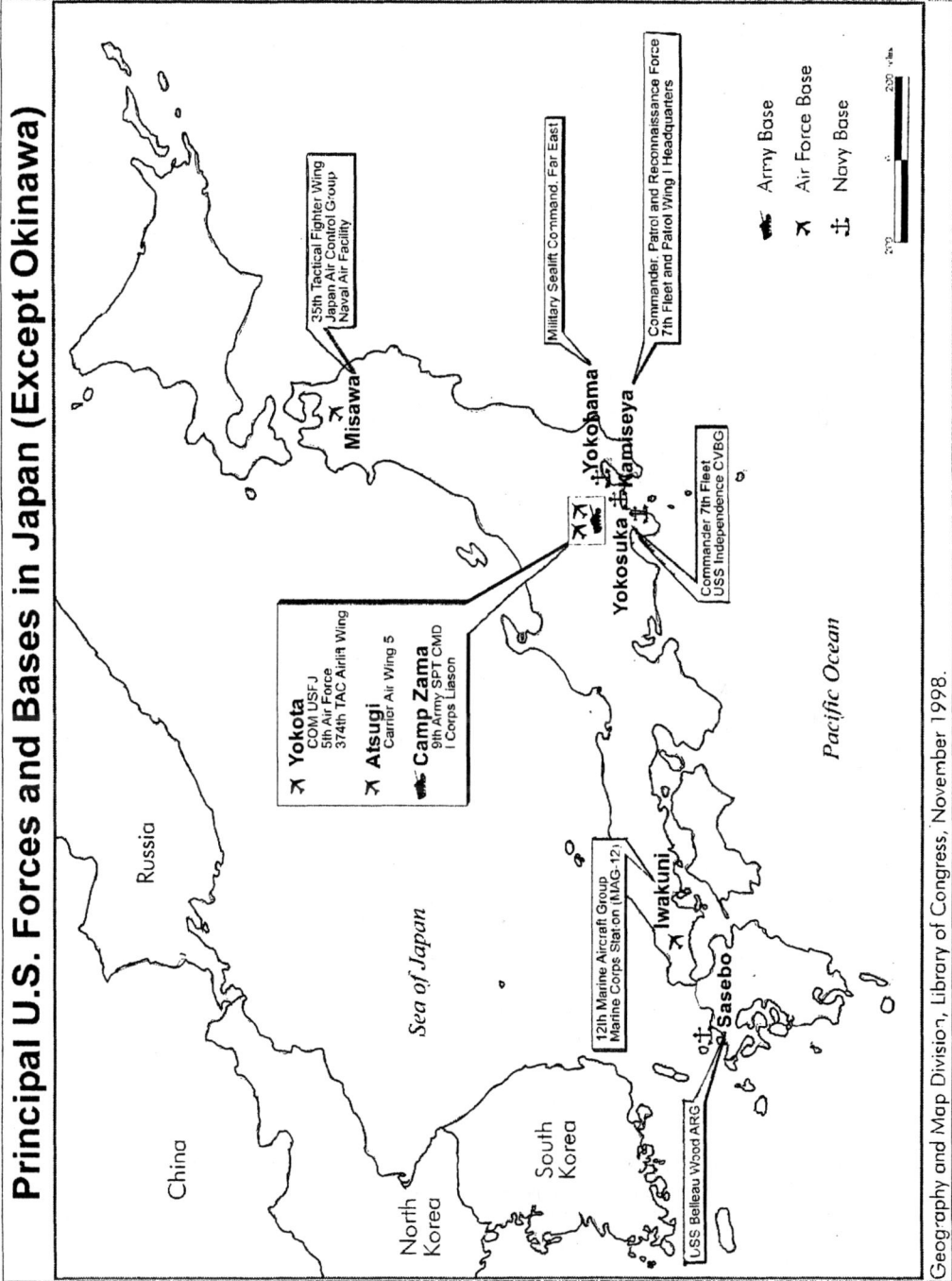

**The Okinawa Problem.** The strongest and most vocal opposition to the U.S. military presence in Japan traditionally has come from the people of Okinawa. This small island is located about halfway between Kyushu, the southernmost "big" island in the Japanese archipelago, and Taiwan. Although U.S. bases make an important contribution to the local economy, Okinawans have long resented the fact that although the island contains less than one-percent of Japan's total land area, it hosts more than half of the U.S. forces and 75 percent of the bases, training sites, and other installations in the whole of Japan, as measured by land area.

Some of the most important U.S. bases in the western Pacific are located in Okinawa. These include Kadena Airbase, which supports strategic airlift operations to East Asia and even the Middle East, two-thirds of a division-size Marine Expeditionary Force, and Futenma Marine Air Station (MAS), which has runways and parking aprons of sufficient size to accommodate the large cargo planes that would deliver helicopters from the United States in an emergency. U.S. Marine Corps sources point out that apart from bases on the main Japanese islands, Okinawa is the only location in the western Pacific that is within the flying range of the Korean peninsula by the workhorse CH-53 helicopters. The northern part of the island also hosts large training areas that the U.S. military officials describe as providing unique opportunities to maintain the readiness of U.S. forces in the region. For instance, Okinawa hosts the only ranges outside the U.S. mainland at which American forces in the Pacific can conduct live firing exercises. These same attributes, however, also give rise to complaints from Okinawans as sources of noise, traffic disruption, and threats to their safety.

The Okinawa problem is complicated by factors beyond U.S. control. Okinawans are proud of their ethnic identity and culture as the former kingdom of the Ryukyus, and they continue to resent their forceful incorporation into the Japanese empire in the late 19th century. The prefecture continues to have the highest unemployment and lowest per capita income in Japan. Okinawans also remain keenly aware that the current U.S. military presence in Okinawa was the consequence of the decision by Japan's World War II high command to "sacrifice" the island to delay an American invasion of the "home" islands. The island was taken by U.S. forces after the last and bloodiest land battle of the Pacific campaign, with the loss of one hundred thousand or more Okinawan civilian lives in addition to nearly 200,000 Japanese and American combatants. The United States returned Okinawa to Japanese sovereignty in 1972 but retained most of its military facilities.

Anti-base feeling in Okinawa intensified considerably following the September 1995 rape incident. In response, the U.S. and Japanese governments formed a Special Action Committee on Okinawa (SACO) charged with finding ways to reduce the impact of U.S. military operations and training on the quality of life in Okinawa without unacceptably degrading military operations and training. In April 1996, during a visit to Washington by then Japanese Prime Minister Ryutaro Hashimoto, the two governments announced their acceptance of a preliminary report of the SACO that provided for the return during the next 5-7 years of 11 areas, provided that suitable other locations could be found, either in Okinawa, or in other parts of Japan. As finalized in December 1996, the plan would return some 20 percent of the area currently used by the U.S. military, almost all of it used by the U.S. Marine Corps. Among the more important proposals, were plans to relocate the Futenma Airbase, (see **Figure 3**) which lies in the middle of a densely populated area, and Naha Port, (see **Figure 3**), in the prefectural capital, which Okinawans think could be better used to promote the development of a free trade zone. [20]

**Figure 3**: **U.S. Bases in Okinawa**
Source: Japan Defense Agency: Defense of Japan, 1998

Reference 15. Deployment of U.S. Forces, Japan, in Okinawa

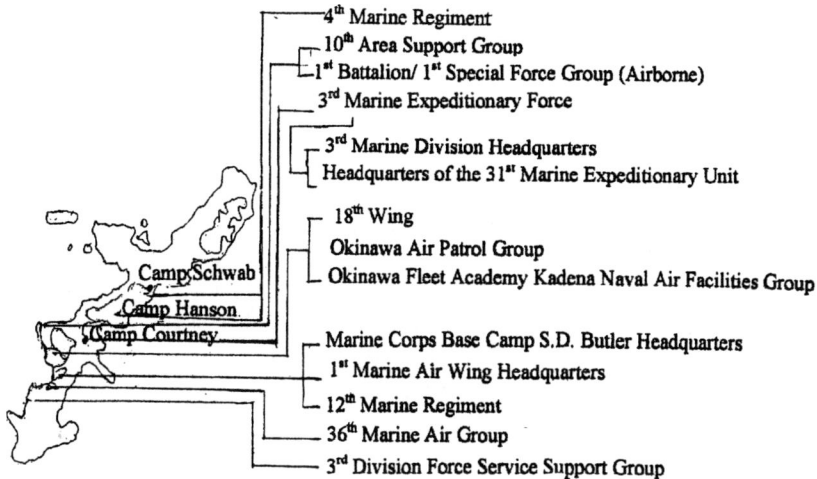

4th Marine Regiment
10th Area Support Group
1st Battalion/ 1st Special Force Group (Airborne)
3rd Marine Expeditionary Force

3rd Marine Division Headquarters
Headquarters of the 31st Marine Expeditionary Unit

18th Wing
Okinawa Air Patrol Group
Okinawa Fleet Academy Kadena Naval Air Facilities Group

Camp Schwab
Camp Hanson
Camp Courtney

Marine Corps Base Camp S.D. Butler Headquarters
1st Marine Air Wing Headquarters
12th Marine Regiment
36th Marine Air Group
3rd Division Force Service Support Group

For several years action on these relocation plans was blocked by the governor of Okinawa prefecture, Masahide Ota, whose dominance of the political scene since the early 1990s was facilitated by support from Socialist-leaning local government employees and teachers unions. A proposal by the government of then-Prime Minister Ryutaro Hashimoto to build an offshore heliport, as a partial replacement of the Futenma MAS, drew opposition from a variety of groups, including the community likely to be closest to the base, environmentalists and fishermen, and the traditional anti-bases groups.

**Developments Concerning U.S. Bases in Okinawa.** The prospects for retaining the U.S. bases on Okinawa increased in late 1998, when the voters elected a new prefectural governor with ties to the business community, Keiichi Inamine. During the campaign and afterward, Inamine expressed interest in finding ways to accommodate U.S. bases while gaining support from Tokyo for improving the island's long-neglected economic and transport infrastructure. Among other ideas, the new governor, has expressed willingness to consider ways to relocate the Futenma MAS and Naha Port via the construction of joint-use civil-military facilities. Subsequently, a number of towns and cities which formerly rejected the idea of hosting new U.S. bases, have come forward to seek participation in base relocation projects that might

---

[20] For further background, see CRS Report 96-646 F, July 1996, Okinawa Bases and Other Issues in U.S.-Japan Security Relations [by Richard P. Cronin].

contribute to their infrastructure and economic development.[21]    U.S. military authorities in Okinawa say that, in principle, joint use facilities are acceptable.[22] Unless untoward incidents spoil the current atmosphere, the political situation now appears more favorable than in many years for the continued use of this strategically located island by U.S. air, naval, and ground forces.

## Source of Japan's Seeming Inconsistency: Rising, Omnidirectional Nationalism

One reason for the seemingly inconsistent views of the Japanese public on the issue of how best to protect Japan's security in the post-Cold War era is that nationalism is rising, though it lacks evident militaristic overtones, and its effects tend to be omnidirectional.  Japan's neighbors as well as the United States, in the future, may feel the effects of stronger Japanese assertiveness in the form of greater resistance to being pressured on trade and other issues.  Japan also appears embarked on a slow but deliberate and steady development of defense capabilities that do not just compliment those of U.S. forces, but also provide limited self-sufficiency.

Among other manifestations, growing Japanese nationalism was evident in the media and political response to the flare-up of long-standing territorial disputes with China and South Korea in 1995 and 1996.  A series of incidents in 1995 involving China, in fact, was provoked in the first instance by the actions of Japanese ultra-nationalists.[23]    A 1996 war of words with South Korea and a series of action-reaction naval deployments arose out of a more substantive fishing dispute in the area around the Takeshima group.

One of Japan's most prominent ultra-nationalists and a leader of the Senkakus campaign, Ichiro Ishihara, recently was elected governor of the Tokyo Metropolitan Area against a lackluster field of candidates.  Ishihara ran on a campaign of both denying Japanese wartime depredations against China *and* calling for the return of Yokota Air Base, in the western Tokyo suburbs, which is headquarters for U.S. Forces, Japan (USFJ), and a significant logistical facility in its own right.  Most analysis suggests that the voters elected Ishihara on the basis of his promises to shake

---

[21] Four Okinawa Towns, Hungry for Subsidies, Offer to Host U.S. Facilities. *Japan Digest*, March 31, 1999: 1.  As part of its $5 billion in annual host nation support (HNS) of U.S. forces, the Japanese government provides subsidies to communities that accommodate U.S. bases.

[22] Conversations with U.S. military officials in Okinawa during August 1998.

[23] The confrontation in the Senkakus began after the Japanese Maritime Safety Agency (coast-guard) failed to interfere in the construction of a makeshift "lighthouse" on the largest island by Japanese ultra-nationalists, provoking Chinese complaints.  At one point a flotilla of more than 60 MSA craft turned back some twenty or more fishing boats containing protesters from Hong Kong and Taiwan, with the accidental loss of one life. Reportedly, in August 1995 Japanese fighters also scrambled to ward off an intruding Chinese Su-17 fighter. Rocks of Contention, *Far Eastern Economic Review (FEER)*, Sept. 19, 1996: 14-15.

up the metropolitan administration, but his views clearly were not seen as disqualifying by a significant portion of the electorate.[24]

Japanese nationalism at the official level was apparent in the stiff rebuff to Jiang Zemin during his November 1998 visit to Japan (see discussion above) over demands that Japan give a written apology for its past aggression against China. Public hostility towards North Korea, which has grown since the August 1998 launch of North Korea's *Taepodong-2* missile, has strongly influenced the government's stance regarding food and other assistance, and terms for normalization of relations. Following the missile launch the Japanese Government indicated that it would withdraw its commitment to provide about $ 1 billion towards the construction of the two light water nuclear power plants in North Korea as called for under the Clinton Administration's October 1994 "Agreed Framework" with North Korea. Japan pulled out of an October 1998 meeting that was to finalize the cost sharing agreement for the project, which is being carried out under a multilateral Korean Peninsula Energy Development Organization (KEDO), and reportedly only signed the agreement in early November after intense U.S. pressure.

A U.S. Information Agency (USIA) poll taken in Japan during the fall of 1998 sheds some light on Japanese threat perceptions and response preferences. Following North Korea's August 31, 1998, missile launch, some 76 percent of Japanese respondents viewed North Korea as threatening in various degrees to Japanese security, a slightly higher number than during the mid-1994 confrontation over North Korea's nuclear program. Longer term data from the *Jiji Press*, a news service, concerning countries that are "disliked"'show a steady rise in public disfavor of North Korea from about 25 percent in 1970 to nearly 70 percent in the first quarter of 1999.[25]

Increasing nationalism may also be seen in pending legislation that would officially recognize the wartime-era "Rising Sun" flag, the *Hinomaru*, and national anthem. The latter two symbols have long been points of contention between the right and the left in Japanese politics. Some Japanese, especially members of left-wing parties and teachers unions, have long associated the symbols with wartime militarism

---

[24] The LDP-endorsed candidate, an uncharismatic former diplomat, came in with 12.7 percent of the vote. Ishihara, best known for co-authoring a 1989 best-seller, *A Japan That Can Say No* [to America], made provocative, anti-PRC remarks during the campaign, and also called for the return of Yokota Air Base, in a suburban area in western Tokyo, the headquarters of U.S. Forces, Japan (USFJ). Most Japanese and western press analysis suggests that the electorate mainly voted for Ishihara on the basis of his promise to shake up the metropolitan area administration and as a rebuff to the LDP, but it would appear that the 30 percent of the voters who supported him did not find his ultra-nationalist views disqualifying.

[25] USIA, Office of Research and Media Reaction, Opinion Analysis, Japanese Public's Views of China (M-77-99). Although the poll analysis mainly concerned China, it included data compiled by the *Jiji Press* on North Korea and the USSR/Russia as well. Concern about Russia has fallen sharply since the mid-1990's, but remains significantly higher (about 35 percent) than China, whose "disliked" status is about 15 percent, and holding relatively steady after the spike caused by the 1989 Tiananmen Square massacre.

and, in the case of the anthem, Emperor worship.[26] The legislation appeared likely to pass during the current Diet session until the New *Komeito* ("Clean Government Party"), a well-disciplined opposition party associated with the *Soka Gakkai* ("Value Creation Society"), a lay organization of the *Nichiren Shoshu* Buddhist sect, whose support the Obuchi government needs to insure upper house passage, withdrew its support.[27] Nonetheless, the very fact that the legislation was introduced and still has a fair chance of passage, indicates the extent to which Japan appears to be shaking off its phobia against anything associated with the war.

# Continuing Legal and Political Restraints on Japan's Freedom of Action

Even though Japanese policymakers and the public increasingly accept that Japan's security is threatened by a recalcitrant North Korea armed with ballistic missiles that can strike Japan, and that the country may face a future threat from China, resistance to a drastic change in the country's security posture remains strong. Significant segments of the public retain deep reservations about or outright opposition to measures that would expand the role of the Japanese military. This group can be expected to fight a vigorous political battle against proposals that they perceive as violating the constitution, and also to oppose overt constitutional revision. On balance, support for reinterpreting or revising Article 9 of the constitution is probably at an all-time high — more than 50 percent, depending on how the question is posed — but this still implies a very cautious attitude towards loosening the constraints on the SDF.

## Flexible Interpretation of the "Peace" Constitution

Within the "bedrock" constitutional limits, Japan in recent years has taken a number of steps to lower the bar in regard to limitations on the role of the SDF Initially, Japan's post-Cold War initiatives responded to concerns that related more to international politics and alliance relations with the United States, than direct security concerns. Eventually, however, these political objectives gradually gave way to anxieties about Japan's physical security and potential threats to its significant economic interests in the East Asian region.

**Authority to Participate in UN Peacekeeping Activities.** In 1992, in the wake of sharp criticism by the United States and allies of Japan's failure to provide even medical teams or evacuation aircraft during Operation Desert Storm against Iraq, the Japanese parliament (Diet) approved the International Peace Cooperation Law (short title.) The new authority allows non-combat participation in UN peacekeeping operations and humanitarian disaster relief. Starting with the UN peacekeeping mission in Cambodia, Japanese Self-Defense Forces and national police personnel have participated in a number of peacekeeping operations in Asia, Africa, and the Middle East, including Rwanda, Mozambique, and the UN Observer Force

---

[26] *Tokyo Shimbun*, May 17, 1999: 2; and *The Japan Digest*, May 19, 1999: 2.

[27] *Japan Digest*, May 21, 1999: 1.

(UNOF) on the Golan Heights, but only in cases in which conflict has ceased and the country in question has agreed to welcome UN peacekeepers.

**Participation in Military-to-Military Relationships and High Level Defense Coordination with Regional States.** Beginning with its advocacy and support of the multinational ASEAN Regional Forum (ARF) in the early 1990s, a 20 country "talk shop" based on the Association of Southeast Asian Nations (ASEAN) and its neighboring and developed country "dialogue partners," Japan has increased its profile in regional military relationships. Japan has hosted and taken part in numerous military-to-military exchanges and dialogues with neighboring countries, and conducted high level dialogues. The Japanese Defense Agency also publishes annually a highly detailed report entitled Defense of Japan that seeks to provide transparency and reassurance about its military posture, budget, and weapons system acquisitions.[28]

All of the foregoing have been carried out in the interest of reassuring neighboring countries that its military programs do not amount to a return to militarism, and also to set an example to other countries — most notably China — as to how to provide more transparency concerning defense programs. Recently, beginning with President Kim Dae Jung's October 1998 visit to Japan, the Japanese government has also raised the level of its consultation and cooperation with South Korea. This action responds partly to growing concerns about North Korea's missile program and other disturbing actions, but also, it appears, with the intention of gaining more leverage in respect to the U.S.-North Korea-South Korea relationship.

## Constitutional Limitations on the Exercise of Self-Defense

Article 9, the "No War" clause of Japan's postwar, U.S.-imposed "Peace Constitution," constitutes the main legal impediment to what a leading conservative politician, Ichiro Ozawa of the Liberal Party (*Jiyuto*), has called "normal country" status. Recent developments notwithstanding, Japan remains an "abnormal country" in that the constitution renounces war as a sovereign right as well as the threat or use of force to settle disputes, and also states that "land, sea, and air forces, as well as other war potential will never be maintained." Over time, and often in response to U.S. pressure, the Japanese government gradually has abandoned a strict interpretation of those provisions while continuing to give deference to the "spirit" of the law. A gradual shift towards rearmament began during the time of the Korean War (1950-1953), in which Japan played an indispensable role as a base for U.S. air operations, a rear area for ground troops and naval forces, and a source of non-lethal war material. In response to pressure from the U.S. Occupation Authorities, Japan reestablished its military forces under the rubric "Self-Defense Forces"(SDF) and asserted that the right of self-defense against a direct attack on Japanese territory was an inherent right and therefore constitutionally permissible[29].

---

[28] These exchanges are enumerated and described in the annual *Defense of Japan* publication.

[29] *Japan: A Country Study.* Federal Research Division, Library of Congress, 1992: 312; Japan Defense Agency, *Defense of Japan*, 1998 (English version): 68.

Gradually, Japan developed ground, air, and maritime forces whose equipment and capabilities dove-tailed with those of the United States. For instance, during the height of the Cold War, Japan accepted responsibility to protect the sea lines of communication leading to Japan out to a distance of 1,000 nautical miles in the direction of Southeast Asia. Toward this end, Japan built more than 50 anti-submarine navy destroyers and some 100 Lockheed-Martin P3-C maritime patrol aircraft, which it built under license from the U.S. manufacturer. Japan also undertook to build up a force of nearly 200 F-15 air superiority fighters, most of which were also constructed in Japan under license.[30]

As a consequence of these initiatives, Japan acquired the most technologically advanced and, arguably, the most powerful air and naval forces in East Asia, but the SDF remains dependent on the United States to cover critical gaps in its defenses. Also, the limited defense build-up still leaves the Japanese military almost devoid of a power projection capability — a fact of considerable importance to a number of Japan's neighbors.

## Continuing Ban on Participation in Collective Security Activities

Notwithstanding the progressive erosion of constitutional restraints, over time, several important limitations on Japan's military posture remain. These include (1) a long-standing legal determination that self-defense can only be exercised at the lowest possible level, (2) a ban on the possession of weapons that are characterized as offensive, and (3) a ban on participation in collective security arrangements.

Perhaps the most important limitation remains a determination by the cabinet two decades ago that the requirement for minimal self-defense precludes the right to engage in collective security aimed at protecting any other country. Under this interpretation, Japan can cooperate with U.S. forces in the defense of Japan itself, but cannot provide active military assistance to the United States in a conflict involving the United States and a third country, nor can it join any regional defense pact or participate militarily in United Nations peacemaking or peacekeeping operations.[31]

# The Politics of National Security in Post-Cold War Japan

Unlike the Cold War era, during which most security policy decisions were made in the context of a political system characterized by single party dominance, and the reality of total dependence on the U.S. conventional and nuclear defense umbrella, the collapse of the LDP's former hegemony and the emergence of a more complex security environment have made defense policymaking an intensely political process. The politics of the issue cut across a number of traditional relationships. During the Cold War era, important defense policy decisions normally were initiated by the MOFA with a secondary role on the part of the JDA, cleared with the Ministry of

---

[30] Types and Quantities are from Japan Defense Agency, The Defense of Japan, 1998: 428-431.

[31] Japanese Defense Agency, *The Defense of Japan*, 1998: 68.

Finance (MOF) as regards budgetary considerations, and considered in the LDP Policy Affairs Research Council (PARC), where interest groups might exercise influence.[32] Once approved by the LDP leadership, initiatives normally received perfunctory consideration in the Cabinet, if at all, and at most encountered ineffective, symbolic opposition in the Diet on the part of the Japan Socialist Party (JSP). Until the mid-1990s, when it entered into an alliance of convenience with the LDP, the JSP (now the Japan Social Democratic Party) maintained a policy of adamant opposition to the U.S.-Japan security alliance. Normally, the LDP took care respect the sensitivities of the JSP, lest it employ delaying tactics.

Following the collapse of the LDP's single-party dominance in mid-1993, and the onset of rule by diverse coalitions, foreign, defense, and domestic policy could no longer be made through informal negotiations among the PARC and the relevant bureaucrats. Nor could the bureaucrats themselves reach decisions that crossed ministerial lines. As a consequence, a number of important national policy issues, including how to deal with Japan's banking system crisis, the formulation of economic stimulus packages, and, most recently, negotiating a viable compromise on the legislation that facilitates the September 1997 U.S.-Japan Defense Guidelines Agreement, fell to the senior leaders of the political parties themselves. The outcome of these negotiations revealed much about Japan's changing security outlook and the post-Cold War role of the U.S.-Japan security alliance.

## A Case Study in Japanese Security Policymaking: The U.S.-Japan Defense Cooperation Guidelines of September 1997

The progress towards gaining legislative sanction to the revised U.S.-Japan defense cooperation guidelines that were agreed to by both governments in September 1997 presents a revealing case study in the limitations of Japanese decisionmaking on security issues. Both because of a preoccupation with legislation dealing with urgent but controversial financial and fiscal legislation, the Hashimoto government's draft legislation languished in the Diet for more than a year before being taken up in earnest. Eventual passage of the legislation, with some modifications, only was achieved as a result of strenuous efforts by the LDP leaders to find common ground with enough other parties to produce a working margin to pass the legislation in the 252-seat upper house, where the LDP, was 22 seats short of a majority.

**Defense-Driven Political Realignment.** As testimony to the importance of the issue to the LDP government and the foreign and defense bureaucracy, the ruling party's leaders in January 1999 reached a controversial bargain to form a coalition with the small Liberal Party, headed by Ichiro Ozawa, a mercurial figure who had made numerous enemies in the ruling party when he defected to form an anti-LDP coalition in mid-1993. The LDP's need to be assured of Ozawa's support caused its leaders to negotiate with him to join the government, despite the antipathy of many of his former party colleagues. Likewise, the LDP found it necessary to negotiate

---

[32] A 1993 article by the Research Committee of the LDP's Policy Affairs Research Council noted "In a way, we may say that the PARC is the sole organ for undertaking the work of 'prior review' of bills and for sending them to the Diet." Tokyo *Kankai* (in Japanese), Jul.-Aug. 1993, p. 112-117.

with the New *Komeito*, with 24 seats in the upper house, to gain its support from outside the cabinet.

Because of strong opposition to certain parts of the legislation by the dovish Democratic Party (DP), or *Minshuto*, the largest opposition party, the LDP leaders decided to concentrate on the normally anti-military but otherwise rightist New *Komeito*. The well-funded New Komeito has often played a swing role in Japanese politics. Its decision to work with the LDP on the guidelines legislation appears largely to have been a function of its aspirations to share power, rather than any change in its pacifist-minded but otherwise anti-leftist ideology. The DP all but ceased to be a factor in the final days before the legislation was taken to the floor of the lower house, because its demands for changes were too large to be accommodated. As a result, the LDP found itself in a centrist position between its smaller coalition partner, the more hawkish Liberals, led by Ozawa, and the more dovish New Komeito

**The North Korea Factor.** The perception of a growing threat from North Korea played an important psychological role in influencing the debate. In addition to existing concern about North Korea's possible effort to continue covertly its nuclear weapons program and its August 31, 1998, Taepo Dong-2 missile launch, North Korea committed a new provocation even as amendments to the defense guidelines legislation were being negotiated. In an unprecedented action on May 23, 1999, the MSDF — i.e., the Japanese navy — came to the assistance of the lightly equipped Maritime Safety Agency (MSA) vessels in chasing high speed North Korean boats, presumed to be spy ships, that had intruded into Japanese waters and lingered for several days. The naval vessels fired warning shots — a first in the postwar era — but the chase was called off by Tokyo when the North Korean vessels reached international waters.

This incident created a national political uproar and demands from defense-minded legislators that the government craft new, less restrictive, rules of engagement for the MSDF. The Obuchi briefly gave consideration to revising the law governing the SDF to allow operations within Japanese territorial waters against armed intruders — a task previously restricted to the Maritime Safety Agency (MSA) and national police. As of early June 1999, however, the Japanese government reportedly decided not to press for giving the SDF territorial authority "because there were cautious arguments within the government and the LDP about a simplistic increase of SDF powers.[33] However, the MSA and the MSDF were told to take a number of measures to increase their cooperation and coordination. Other governmental responses imply a national commitment to increased self-sufficiency in military hardware and intelligence capabilities.

Using language that is unusually assertive for Japan, the Obuchi government has characterized its policy towards North Korea as "dialogue and deterrence." During consultations with the U.S. Korean policy coordinator, William Perry, before his May 28, 1999, trip to Pyongyang, Japan reportedly emphasized strongly the need to address Japan's concerns about North Korea's missiles and the abductions of a number of Japanese nationals by North Korean agents in the 1970s and 1980s..

---

[33] *Mainichi Shimbun*, June 4, 1999: 2.

Based on Perry's conversations with North Korean leaders, it appears that Japanese concerns regarding the kidnappings and other humanitarian issues are not likely to be addressed in the near future. After debriefing the U.S. envoy during his return visit to Tokyo, a Japanese Ministry of Foreign Affairs (MOFA) spokesman reportedly observed that "There was a sense that the North's response was more severe toward Japan than to any other country," and that Pyongyang continued to maintain an unbending policy on the abduction issue.[34]

## Outcome of the Diet Debate

After extensive negotiations on particular controversial provisions, the lower house of the Diet (House of Representatives) finally passed three related bills on April 27, 1999, just before Prime Minister Obuchi's departure for the United States and his state visit to Washington, that gave effect to the guidelines. One extended an existing U.S.-Japan Acquisition and Cross-Serving Agreement (ACSA) to apply to crisis situations. Another gave the navy (MSDF) authority to rescue Japanese nationals abroad in the event of a threat to their lives, a power already held by the air force (ASDF). The third and most important bill provided the government with the legal authority it needed to carry out the most critical parts of the new defense guidelines.

The upper house (House of Councilors) passed the bills on May 24. As enacted, the legislation generally followed the provisions drafted by the Ministry of Foreign Affairs and the Defense Agency, but also incorporated a number of changes and deletions. As passed, the guidelines legislation allows for a number of important enhancements to the support that could be provided to U.S. forces in a variety of regional crisis or conflict situations. The legislation gives the Japanese military the authority, for the first time, to carry out detailed joint planning with U.S. forces for meeting a range of contingencies, with the knowledge that the Japanese government has the necessary legal authority to fulfill its obligations under the resultant plans. From the perspective of many U.S. observers, the new arrangements may still appear highly constrained, but in the Japanese context the new powers given to the Japanese government and the military services represent a significant step towards more equal burden sharing in the event of regional crises or conflicts.

The negotiations on the final wording of the bills reveals much about the state of the body politic on the issue of how to respond to a new security environment. The modifications to the draft bill appear to provide some marginal gains and losses for U.S. interests. The main points of contention and their outcome are the following:

(1) *Definition of "situations in areas surrounding Japan."* The Liberal Party leader Ichiro Ozawa failed to get the LDP to add a clarification of the area covered by the most controversial phrase in the draft guidelines bill, especially the question of whether it included Taiwan (Ozawa maintained it did, as did some of the more nationalistic LDP leaders). However, in the description of the types of situations covered by the phrase, the LDP and New *Komeito* agreed to add another example situation, *viz.* "a situation that may lead to a direct armed attack against Japan if left

---

[34] *Sankei Shimbun*, June 1, 1999: 2.

unattended." This would appear to be a subtle advance towards a broader conception of self-defense, although this interpretation was explicitly rejected (see below.)

(2) *The limits of "self-defense."* The addition of the change cited above reportedly was adopted as an alternative to Ozawa's desire to introduce the concept of "quasi-emergencies," i.e., situations that did not involve direct attacks on Japan, but ones for which a military response would be appropriate. However, because of the sensitivity of the ban on collective defense arrangements, the government and the LDP stated that the phrase adopted above referred to situations in which Japan would provide rear-area support to U.S. forces, and did not mean the exercise of "self-defense" — i.e., did not allow for an armed military response.[35]

(3) *The definition of "rear areas."* The legislation allows the mobilization of military forces to provide non-combat rear area support of U.S. forces, including the air and sea rescue operations in rear areas. The parties apparently reached a consensus that rear areas meant Japanese territory and adjacent high seas and the air space above, where there was "no possibility of a battle act."[36]

(4) *Ship inspections on the high seas in the event of an embargo situation.* The three parties failed to reach agreement on this issue and it was put off to be dealt with in future legislation or as an amendment during upper house consideration. Reportedly, the New *Komeito* was adamant that inspections of foreign vessels could only be allowed in the case of a UN-sanctioned embargo. The Liberal Party leader Ozawa, on the other hand, perhaps thinking of a Korean contingency in which a Security Council resolution might be blocked by China or other permanent members, reportedly was adamant against restricting this activity to one involving UN sanctions.[37] As of early June 1999, Japanese press coverage suggests that the LDP and other parties are a long way from reaching agreement on a compromise that could gain passage.

(5) *Cooperation of Ministries, Local Governments, and the Private Sector.* The incorporation into the legislation of authority for the Japanese government to "request" ministries and local governments to make facilities available to U.S. forces also proved controversial. This part of the legislation, which is said to be very vague, apparently was not changed from the draft bill but remains highly contentious, especially with local government officials and the private sector. Reportedly, Japanese air carriers already have complained that any levy to transport U.S. troops or equipment was "pie in the sky."[38] Some local officials reportedly have also stated that they would refuse to cooperate with a government request for assistance, but others have simply called on the government to provide clarification on what would be required via written regulations or plans.

---

[35] *Nihon Keizai*, April. 27, 1999: 3.

[36] *Ibid.*

[37] *Ibid.*

[38] *Tokyo Shimbun*, April 28, 1999: 27.

(6) *Requirements for Diet Notification.* The New *Komeito*, as did the non-participating Democratic Party, wanted prior notification of the Diet before support could be provided to U.S. forces in a situation in the area surrounding Japan. The LP leader, Ichiro Ozawa, insisted that prior notification was impractical, and would undermine the effectiveness of the new commitment. Ultimately, the negotiators agreed that the Diet would be notified beforehand "in principle," but that in an "emergency" the government could act first and notify the Diet later. Practically speaking, most situations requiring the invocation of the authorities in the legislation are likely to be emergencies of some degree, hence commentators have noted that the provision would not appear to undercut the purposes of the new guidelines.

## Implications of the Guidelines Legislation and Japan's Changing Security Outlook for Tokyo's Future Regional Security Role

Despite the seeming "hair splitting" aspect of the amendments to the guidelines legislation adopted prior to formal Diet consideration, the outcome generally has been welcomed by Clinton Administration officials and deemed highly significant by Japanese observers. Although the guidelines legislation represents the most significant manifestation of Japan's changing security outlook, the attitudes and concerns that influenced the internal debate both before and during the legislative phase would appear to have wider implications. The foregoing analysis suggests the following key findings:

(1) Because the Japanese military now has, for the first time, the authority to plan with the U.S. military to meet various contingencies, and the government has legal authority to call upon the civil sector, American planners and policymakers can have more assurance, albeit not absolute certainty, that SDF rear area support and Japan's civil airfields, ports and other transportation infrastructure will be available in a crisis. Access to Japan's civil sector, in particular, has become increasingly important due to post-Cold War reductions in U.S. airlift capacity. U.S. military planners maintain that access to civil airports, transport, and fuel supplies would shorten significantly the time required to reinforce U.S. troops in South Korea and achieve a military victory in the event of a North Korean attack.[39] This assessment seems even more significant in view of the current the large commitment of U.S. combat and transport assets to operations in the former Yugoslavia.

(2) The failure of legislation to address the ship inspection issue leaves an important gap in the defense cooperation guidelines agreement. The issue would appear to be more important in an economic embargo situation than in a military conflict, although an embargo could be part of a conflict situation. In any event, the MSDF presently lacks the authority to use force to carry out such a mission.

---

[39] This assessment was provided by U.S. military briefers during a visit to Hdq., USFJ, in August 1998.

(3) The importance that Japan attached to passing the legislation attested to Japan's continuing commitment to the U.S.-Japan alliance, but the debate also suggests that center of gravity of Japanese opinion has shifted significantly in the direction of a more assertive and more autonomous — but not independent — self-defense posture. In light of Japan's new security outlook, constitutional issues are no longer off limits to discussion among Japanese leaders and the public. The broad debate on the constitution or its reinterpretation, that many in Japan have called for, could come sooner rather than later as a consequence of this legislation and the evolving regional security situation, as perceived in Japan.

(4) Pacifism and anti-militarism retain a considerable hold on the Japanese population, but in general the country increasingly appears to be prepared psychologically to defend its territorial waters and airspace and its regional interests within the context of the bilateral alliance, and appears to have edged closer towards contemplating participation in collective security activities. This assessment has been underscored by the recent increase in Japanese diplomatic and security consultations with the government of South Korea, and a tightening of U.S.-Japan-South Korea trilateral consultation.

(5) In general, public support for an increased defense capability is strongest for actions that boost Japan's own capabilities rather than actions that increase reliance on or cooperation with U.S. forces. For instance, on the question of how Japan should respond to perceived increasing threats to Japanese security emanating from North Korea's missile program, respondents in the above-cited USIA poll published in November 1998 indicated a higher preference for measures *other than* close defense cooperation with the United States. Presented with options, the respondents ranked their preferences in the following order:

- About 70 percent favored increased security cooperation with both South Korea and China;

- 54 percent favored developing an independent Japanese satellite reconnaissance capability;

- A bare majority — 51 percent — favored "early" passage by the Japanese parliament of the then-pending legislation to implement new defense cooperation guidelines, which had provoked public debate as to whether they applied to situations involving Taiwan, and;

- Only 43 percent supported cooperating in the development of a ballistic missile defense system, while 32 percent opposed such cooperation.[40]

(6) As a consequence of the furor over the North Korean spy boats, Japan appears also to be moving towards a more robust defense of its territorial waters. Although movement on this issue appears stalled as a result of considerable domestic opposition to giving the SDF the authority to operate within Japanese territory and

---

[40] USIA, Office of Research and Media Reaction, Briefing Paper: Japanese Public Opinion on Economic Issues, North Korea. Nov. 16, 1998, p. 2.

territorial waters, the government and the ruling parties (LDP and Liberal Party) have begun broad discussions on means to beef up Japan's territorial defense.[41] For the time being, the Obuchi government apparently has decided that the issue could be addressed adequately by strengthening the MSA with more ships and better armament, and increasing its cooperation and coordination with the NSDF, but any new incidents are likely to reopen the question.

## Broader Implications for U.S.-Japan Security Relations

The combination of rising security-mindedness and continuing vestiges of anti-military sentiment now prevailing suggests a future U.S.-Japan security relationship that is potentially stronger but also is likely to be more complex and difficult to manage. The passage of the defense guidelines legislation by the Diet in late May 1999 underscores the continuing importance that Japan attaches to the U.S. connection, but also signals a substantial shift of the of the parameters of the debate in the direction of a more active defense posture. For instance, while the opposition Democratic Party voted against the bill dealing with support to U.S. forces in regional contingencies, it did support the bills relating to the ACSA agreement and legalizing the participation of the Maritime Self-Defense Force (MSDF) in the evacuation of civilians in crisis situations. Only the Social Democrats and the Communists opposed all three bills.

Given the zero-sum perceptions of Japan and China regarding each other's relations with the United States, Japan's changing security perspectives provide both opportunities for the United States to reinforce regional stability, as well as certain hazzards. The established U.S. goal of maintaining and enhancing defense cooperation with Japan while avoiding a counterproductive reaction on the part China and perhaps other countries, will likely require deft diplomacy.

Additionally, Japan's agreement to the new guidelines does not guarantee its response in any particular crisis, nor continuing support of U.S. policy. Security-minded nationalists like Ichiro Ozawa seek an all-around enhancement of Japan's ability to play a regional security role, not just dutiful support of U.S. policy. Many other Japanese leaders feel similarly. Consequently, the achievement of a new level of U.S.-Japan defense cooperation, coupled with a rising desire for a more independent regional policy, suggests that it remains highly important to take Japanese views and interests into consideration in the formulation of U.S. policy.

Finally, a number of straws in the wind suggest that in the longer term, Japan is likely to seek to reduce its current near total dependence on U.S. military power for its security. On the one hand, the United States and Japan are likely to remain each other's most natural Asia-Pacific allies for the foreseeable future, and Japanese officials continue to assert that the U.S.-Japan alliance will remain the bedrock of Japanese security policy. On the other hand, political leaders and opinion makers from various points on the ideological spectrum continue to speak wistfully about finding other ways of insuring the country's security, such as through multilateral cooperation and confidence-building.

---

[41] *Sankei Shimbun*, May 26, 1999: 3.

The most likely course for Japan will be to incrementally but steadily increase its own defense capabilities while also seeking to promote the development of regional institutions for confidence-building and cooperation. Such changes would also imply a reduction in the U.S. military presence as it is currently constituted. At present, most analysts judge that the Northeast Asia region offers bleak prospects for forming anything akin to NATO or the Organization for Security and Cooperation in Europe (OSCE), but a number of political leaders from both the left and the right have indicated a willingness to consider constitutional revisions that would legitimatize Japan's participation in collective defense arrangements or multilateral security institutions.

These aspirations may not be realistic, but they appear to be symptomatic of a broadly based desire to reduce Japan's dependance on the United States, if possible. Should the Korean Peninsula become stabilized in the future, pressure for the withdrawal of the U.S. Marines from Okinawa seems almost certain to intensify. Japan's response to the perceived longer term threat from China would appear to depend greatly on the future shape of the triangular U.S.-China-Japan relationship.

**Alternative U.S. Responses.** Since the end of the Cold War, a number of American and Japanese analysts have projected alternative ways for the United States to maximize the benefits of U.S.-Japan security cooperation while minimizing the dangers of a breakdown in security ties. Some emphasize the desirability of increased Japanese burden sharing coupled with more sharing of decisionmaking on the part of the United States. This approach, it is argued, will best protect the long term U.S. interest in continued access to "strategic" Japanese bases while reducing the relative U.S. defense burden and making the alliance more compatible with the Japanese public's desire to be rid of the U.S. military bases that are most disruptive of day-to-day life.[42] Other analysts have proposed changes in the alliance that would "harness" Japan's strengths more closely to U.S. policy objectives, including the creation of a "comprehensive security" pact, including a revised mutual security treaty and a common market agreement, that would mesh both the economies and the defense establishments in a relationship involving more Japanese reciprocity.[43]

These proposals may be useful as a means of conceptualizing alternative U.S. policy approaches, but the record of nearly five decades of close security cooperation

---

[42] See for instance Mike Mochizuki and Michael O'Hanlon, A Liberal Vision for the US-Japan Alliance. *Survival*, v. 40, no. 2, Summer 1998:127-134; Mochizuki and O'Hanlon, The Marines Should Come Home: Adapting the U.S.-Japan Alliance to a New Security Era. *Brookings Review*, v. 14, spring 1996: 10-13; Mochizuki (ed.), *Toward a True Alliance: Restructuring U.S.-Japan Security Relations.* Washington, Brookings Institution Press, 1997; and Chalmers Johnson and E. B. Keebn, East Asia Security: the Pentagon's Ossified Strategy.*Foreign affairs*, v. 74, July-Aug. 1995: 103-114.

[43] This approach is developed most explicitly in David L. Asher, A U.S.-Japan Alliance for the Next Century. *Orbis*, vol. 41, no. 3, Summer 1997: 343-374. See also Joseph Nye et al, Harnessing Japan: A U.S. Strategy for Managing Japan's Rise as a Global Power. *Washington Quarterly*, Spring 1993: 29-42, and James E. Auer, The Imperative U.S.-Japanese Bond. *Orbis*, v. 39, Winter 1995: 37-53.

suggests that both Japanese and U.S. policymakers are more likely simply to seek to adopt incremental responses to changing circumstances. Moreover, Japan's own longer term "vision," to the extent that one exists, may not be identical or even compatible with that of the United States.

For the near term, the main challenge for U.S. policymakers is likely to be that of keeping the bilateral alliance central to Japanese security policy and factoring Japanese perspectives into U.S. policymaking. Except in the case of a radical change in the East Asian security environment, a Japanese shift towards a more multilateral security posture, such as one based on a mechanism for regional confidence-building and cooperation, or participation in some form of collective defense system involving the United States and other friendly countries, would appear likely to create increased political pressure to reduce or eliminate U.S. military bases in Japan. Already, as noted above, both ends of the political spectrum as well as those who could be characterized loosely as belonging to the center-left, call for reducing and eventually eliminating the U.S. military presence in Japan. Some would reduce it gradually, others more quickly.

In the longer term, even an alliance that still appeared indispensable to Japanese planners and policymakers could, as a practical matter, loose its political support unless it adjusts in ways that the public believes make it a continued necessity. This would seem to require, in particular, demonstrating that the security relationship supports concrete Japanese interests and policy goals, and not just those of the United States, or vaguely defined mutual interests. Although this may seem axiomatic, it is not necessarily the Japanese perception that U.S. and Japanese objectives are identical or even compatible. Given Tokyo's still limited capability for strategic decisionmaking and crisis management, how Washington deals with issues affecting Japan's interests, and the quality of interaction and consultation, appear likely to be crucial factors in determining Japan's future defense posture and degree of security cooperation with the United States.

**North Korean Challenge for U.S.-Japan Policy Coordination?** The most likely near-term test of U.S. responsiveness to Japan's security perspectives could come in the American response to a new test by North Korea of its Taepo Dong-2 missile. The Japanese government has clearly staked out a position that seems to all but guarantee the withdrawal of Japanese financial support for KEDO's light-water reactor project in North Korea should Pyongyang ignore Tokyo's warnings against a new test. On July 1, shortly after the upper house of the Diet approved a contribution of $1 billion to KEDO, Foreign Minister Masahiko Komura reportedly declared that while Japan supported KEDO as "the most realistic framework for preventing North Korea from developing nuclear arms," Japan's aid would not be delivered to KEDO later in July, as scheduled, if Pyongyang conducts a new medium-range missile launch. Komura noted pointedly that "whether or not there is prior notice, and whether or not it has a satellite on the tip makes no great difference from the viewpoint of security for Japan and Northeast Asia."[44]

---

[44] *Nihon Keizai Shimbun* ("Japan Economic News) report cited by the *Japan Digest*, July 2, 1999: 1.

suggests that both Japanese and U.S. policymakers are more likely simply to seek to adopt incremental responses to changing circumstances. Moreover, Japan's own longer term "vision," to the extent that one exists, may not be identical or even compatible with that of the United States.

For the near term, the main challenge for U.S. policymakers is likely to be that of keeping the bilateral alliance central to Japanese security policy and factoring Japanese perspectives into U.S. policymaking. Except in the case of a radical change in the East Asian security environment, a Japanese shift towards a more multilateral security posture, such as one based on a mechanism for regional confidence-building and cooperation, or participation in some form of collective defense system involving the United States and other friendly countries, would appear likely to create increased political pressure to reduce or eliminate U.S. military bases in Japan. Already, as noted above, both ends of the political spectrum as well as those who could be characterized loosely as belonging to the center-left, call for reducing and eventually eliminating the U.S. military presence in Japan. Some would reduce it gradually, others more quickly.

In the longer term, even an alliance that still appeared indispensable to Japanese planners and policymakers could, as a practical matter, loose its political support unless it adjusts in ways that the public believes make it a continued necessity. This would seem to require, in particular, demonstrating that the security relationship supports concrete Japanese interests and policy goals, and not just those of the United States, or vaguely defined mutual interests. Although this may seem axiomatic, it is not necessarily the Japanese perception that U.S. and Japanese objectives are identical or even compatible. Given Tokyo's still limited capability for strategic decisionmaking and crisis management, how Washington deals with issues affecting Japan's interests, and the quality of interaction and consultation, appear likely to be crucial factors in determining Japan's future defense posture and degree of security cooperation with the United States.

**North Korean Challenge for U.S.-Japan Policy Coordination?** The most likely near-term test of U.S. responsiveness to Japan's security perspectives could come in the American response to a new test by North Korea of its Taepo Dong-2 missile. The Japanese government has clearly staked out a position that seems to all but guarantee the withdrawal of Japanese financial support for KEDO's light-water reactor project in North Korea should Pyongyang ignore Tokyo's warnings against a new test. On July 1, shortly after the upper house of the Diet approved a contribution of $ 1 billion to KEDO, Foreign Minister Masahiko Komura reportedly declared that while Japan supported KEDO as "the most realistic framework for preventing North Korea from developing nuclear arms," Japan's aid would not be delivered to KEDO later in July, as scheduled, if Pyongyang conducts a new medium-range missile launch. Komura noted pointedly that "whether or not there is prior notice, and whether or not it has a satellite on the tip makes no great difference from the viewpoint of security for Japan and Northeast Asia."[44]

---

[44] *Nihon Keizai Shimbun* ("Japan Economic News) report cited by the *Japan Digest*, July 2, 1999: 1.

A senior U.S. Defense Department official confirmed on June 30, 1999, that U.S. intelligence had detected evidence of possible preparations for a test, and warned that such an event would have serious consequences.[45] In view of the depth of Japanese concerns and the political sensitivity of the issue, a new North Korean *Taepo Dong*-2 test, if it occurs, may also constitute a crucial test for U.S.-Japan security coordination and a bell-wether of future alliance cooperation.

---

[45] David E. Sanger and Eric Schmitt, U.S. Warns that Arms Race May Begin Between Koreas. *New York Times*, July 1, 1999: A3. The article noted in addition that the Defense Department was concerned not only about a North Korean test, but also that South Korea might feel compelled to violate a long-standing agreement with the United States not to build missiles with a range greater than 180 kilometers (108 miles).

# INDEX